FREE BOOKS

www.forgottenbooks.org

You can read literally <u>thousands</u> of books
for free at www.forgottenbooks.org

(please support us by visiting our web site)

Forgotten Books takes the uppermost care to preserve the entire content of the original book. However, this book has been generated from a scan of the original, and as such we cannot guarantee that it is free from errors or contains the full content of the original.

OLD SCOTTISH CLOCKMAKERS

ENTRANCE DOOR OF MAGDALEN CHAPEL, COWGATE, EDINBURGH.

OLD SCOTTISH CLOCKMAKERS

From 1453 to 1850

COMPILED FROM ORIGINAL SOURCES
WITH NOTES

BY JOHN SMITH

AUTHOR OF "THE HAMMERMEN OF EDINBURGH AND THEIR ALTAR"
"MONUMENTAL INSCRIPTIONS IN ST CUTHBERT'S CHURCHYARD,
EDINBURGH" (SCOTTISH RECORD SOCIETY SERIES); ETC.

SECOND EDITION—REVISED AND ENLARGED

WITH ILLUSTRATIONS

EDINBURGH
OLIVER AND BOYD, TWEEDDALE COURT
LONDON: 33 PATERNOSTER ROW

FOREWORD

THE abundance and variety of Clocks and Watches everywhere needs no comment here. They are part of our daily life, and it is safe to say that no other article of domestic or public utility has so many enduring associations.

Perhaps these latter are more emphasised in what are commonly termed "Grandfather Clocks," a name which at once suggests honoured ancestors long since departed. Throughout the length and breadth of Scotland they are to be seen, and they are treasured by their possessors amongst the most valued of heirlooms. Although many owners could readily tell to whom their clocks belonged originally, yet how few could give any information about the craftsmen who made and left so many fine specimens of their skill behind them. It is only but fair that the names of these patient and clever men should be held in remembrance. For that purpose this compilation has been undertaken.

In 1903 a first edition of this volume was published, and its instant success made clear that its contents were acceptable to a very large number of people. The names, data, and notes there given were reproduced in numerous papers and magazines all over the country, so much so that the intense interest aroused stimulated me to make further inquiries which are embodied in this volume. It may be mentioned that the occurrence of the Great War prevented its appearance sooner.

The subject is one of some difficulty, as most of the men pursued their daily labours in obscure villages and country districts, and never had an opportunity of being chronicled in written or printed records. The fortunate practice of affixing their names on their handiwork is the only clue available.

A careful search into likely sources has unearthed a mass of information which is surprising. The printed and documentary notes quoted are in a large number of instances almost the words of the men themselves, and we thereby get a peep into the thoughts and trade customs of the period in which they lived. In addition, several cognate matters, such as parentage, marriage, and other personal details about some of the craftsmen have been inserted, making this issue practically a new and fresh contribution to our knowledge of the rise and progress of one of the most important arts in Scotland. The present volume does not claim to give the name and date of every clock and watchmaker working in Scotland during the period reviewed. In a field of such an unknown and wide range, allowance must be made for omissions and errors. Our aim, primarily, was to rescue and preserve the memory of men who in their day and generation made themselves equal in capabilities to their English contemporaries who lived and worked in more favourable surroundings.

My sincere thanks are due to a number of noblemen and gentlemen who freely granted permission to view and reproduce some of the clocks, etc., in their possession.

A selection of North of England, Irish, and Isle of Man clock and watch makers is given in the Appendix. These are culled from a variety of sources for the purpose of increasing the scope of this work.

JOHN SMITH.

25 ST JAMES' SQUARE,
EDINBURGH, 1921.

LIST OF ILLUSTRATIONS

ix

INTRODUCTION

THE extent to which the use of clocks and watches prevailed throughout Scotland during the fifteenth and sixteenth centuries cannot now be definitely ascertained. That there were a number of public clocks in various parts of the country so widely situated as Peebles, Stirling, Dundee, etc., as early as the middle of the fifteenth century, has now been satisfactorily proved, and gives rise to the surmise that Scotland could compare favourably with England, and even with the Continent, as far as numbers are considered at so early a period.

All the evidence available as to the time of their introduction into Scotland shows that the citizens of the larger towns were not only acquainted with such timekeepers, but appeared to be quite familiar with their convenience as compared with sundials. Along with this the provision made sometimes for their purchase, and, in all cases, for their upkeep and repair, shows that they were costly articles to buy, and that their maintenance was a severe tax on the owners. Probably introduced under the auspices of the Church, naturally the attention needed, after their erection, was under the care or supervision of a priest. In a number of the old records of such places as Peebles, Stirling, and Dundee (q.v.), it will be observed how careful the citizens themselves were, both in the purchase of, and attention to, their public clocks.

Possibly if more of these old Burgh Records were looked into, and we can only mention here that a very large number throughout Scotland have not been investigated, surprising evidence would be found bearing on the early use of "knoks." The priestly supervision proves that they were of foreign manufacture, and although the natives at that time were ignorant of their mechanism, this state of matters did not continue long, for towards the end of the fifteenth and the opening years of the sixteenth century native artisans arose who soon became quite competent to manufacture and repair these clocks. Certainly they were not a large number, and what there were appear to have had their hands pretty full. We only mention two—William Purves and David Kaye, and in the extracts given from the Burgh Records of Aberdeen, Dundee, Stirling and Edinburgh, it will be observed that the services of these men were in great demand. Probably there were more, but their names have not been preserved. All through the sixteenth century the numbers were limited, and not until the beginning of the seventeenth century do they appear to have increased; and strange to say, the large towns seem to have had the fewer. This is made very clear in the notes on the Magdalen Chapel, Edinburgh, where, in language sometimes quaint and even pathetic, the struggle which the Hammermen of Edinburgh had in settling on a maker, and the trouble and expense incurred, are described. By 1650 clockmakers increased in number and came to be recognised as a branch of the locksmith trade, and as this made them members of the various Hammermen Incorporations, the minutes of their transactions record the progress and encouragement given to the art of Clockmaking.

These Incorporations were of old foundation—Edinburgh dating from 1483—and there is scarcely a town or district in Scotland which has not had a Hammermen's Incorporation, some, of course, being of later creation. Each had its independent jurisdiction, and all of them did not at the same period allow clock and watch makers to become members. Among the first to do so was Edinburgh in 1646, Glasgow, 1649, Haddington, 1753, and Aberdeen, by some oversight not till 1800.

It is interesting to notice that by the middle of the eighteenth century clockmakers reached a high state of excellence in the making of the ordinary movements of a timekeeper; but instead of endeavouring to simplify parts or make new improvements, a large number of capable men devoted their time and ingenuity to constructing clocks with curious movements. It may here be stated that there is no account to be found of any Scotsman registering a patent in connection with clock-making during the whole of the eighteenth century. These clocks appear to have been regarded as the " Hall Mark " of a craftsman's ability, and culminated in the productions of John Smith of Pittenweem, details of which are fully given in the notes on clocks of that maker on p. 353.

As the nineteenth century rolled on this class of work fell into abeyance, and out of it arose the manufacture of astronomical clocks, which not only required great ingenuity in their construction, but very accurate calculations for their performance. Fortunately Scotland had men equal to the task of making such clocks, and we need only mention Thomas Reid and Robert Bryson, whose productions in that class of · work bear testimony to the great skill and excellence our native craftsmen arrived at.

The period when watches began to be used and made in Scotland, is one of which no authentic information can be given. During the sixteenth century watches in Scotland were undoubtedly of foreign make, and probably regarded as curiosities. Limited in number, they are credited as being mainly in the possession of royal personages. Except David Ramsay (q.v.), who was regarded as being the first Scotsman to manufacture a watch, there is none other who could be named as a contemporary at this period in Scotland. The Edinburgh Hammermen's records are silent as to watches and watchmakers in the sixteenth century, and it is not until the close of the seventeenth century that we find any mention of them. The arrival of the Roumieus, 1677 to 1717, gives us authentic data to go upon, and from this period onwards, the manufacture of watches in Scotland reached a high state of excellence that has not been equalled by any other country.

The adoption of Free Trade and other factors had a direct influence on these old trade incorporations. The consequence was a failure of direct supervision of the workmen and apprentices. This, combined with the importation of the cheap American clocks, helped to extinguish an industry and a class of craftsmen who had been as necessary in every village and town as the doctor or minister. The cheapness of these imported movements made it impossible for our own craftsmen to compete with them, and a wave of mistaken prejudice having arisen against the preservation of these long case clocks, large numbers were destroyed for no other reason than that they were thought to be old-fashioned.

About 1880, the artistic education of all classes brought about a different state of opinion. The desire of lovers of the quaint and useful to acquire a genuine specimen of these old craftsmen's art soon created a demand which has quite outgrown the supply. In connection with this demand there has arisen a practice that deserves the severest condemnation—large numbers of clock cases being spoiled by the introduction of inlays quite foreign to the period when the clock was made. It is perhaps unnecessary to mention these absurdities as they are easily seen on a case that is overdone, the old maker using only lines or banding of the wood, with perhaps a shell or two in the door and base, making a fitness of the whole that appeals at once to the beholder. Of course we do not allude to marquetry, which is a different treatment, but considerable care should be exercised in buying a clock with the case largely and often vulgarly decorated. The same warning applies to cases that are carved, plain oak cases being nearly always selected for this maltreatment. It is not unusual to see a case, beautiful in proportion, of the orthodox Chippendale design, completely disfigured with what appears to be Old Scotch or Jacobean carving, a treatment that belongs to a period long before Chippendale lived, and, to complete the absurdity, with a date added which the maker's name on the dial proves to be a gross fabrication.

This warning was given in the former edition of this work, and it is encouraging to see that it has borne fruit, for the practice has fallen greatly into abeyance. The information in this volume as to when these makers lived makes it a difficult matter to hoodwink those who pay any attention to the subject, and who can at once detect the work of the fabricator.

During the past ten years or so, large numbers of queries

have been received from possessors of old clocks, asking if the maker is considered a good one. Many of these queries have been sent from America, Australia, and other parts of the world. The same answer applies to all, if after a period of one hundred or more years the clock still performs its useful duty well, no better reply can be made than the clock itself gives as to the merits and capabilities of its maker.

                                                    J. S.

CLOCKMAKERS' LAND, BOW, EDINBURGH. Now demolished.

House and Workshop on fourth floor of Paul Roumieu, the first watchmaker established in Edinburgh, 1677-94. Drawn by T. H. Walker, Esq., from the measured drawing by the late Thomas Hamilton, 1830. (See p. 323.)

OLD SCOTTISH CLOCKMAKERS

ABERCROMBIE, JAMES. Aberdeen, 1730.

ABERDEEN. Notices regarding the Common Clocks of the Burgh of, from the year 1453 to the year 1692.

22nd May 1453.—"The same day has granted the said Aldermen and Council to Johne Crukshanks the service of keeping of the orlage for this year and to have for his fee for the service of it, xls., and has sworn the great oath to do his delligent business to the keeping of it."

22nd November 1493.—"The said day the Aldermen and divers of the Council and community present for the time, for the bigin, reformation and upholding of the common knok in the tolbooth, granted to David Theman, goldsmith, forty shillings of the three booths under the tolbooth—for the quhilkis [which] the said David and his assigns shall duly big, reform, and uphold the said knok, by sight of the town as efferis."

4th April 1533.—"The said day the provest, bailies and council, conduct and feit William Wallace to rule, set, guide and keep their knok of the tolbooth, for the quhilkis they promised him yearly during their will four merkis (Scottis), for the payment of the quhilkis they assigned the mails [rents] of the booths under the tolbooth—that is to say, ilk booth ane merk—and ordained the master of wark to pay him yearly another merk in complete payment of the said four merks. And the said William obliged himself to mend the said knok and make her sufficient and as sufficient as ony man in Scotland can make her, for the quhilkis the town shall pay him xxs., that is to say,

1   A

xs. now in hand, and the other ten when the knok is sufficiently mended and strikes as she suld do."

10*th January* 1535.—"The said day the council present for the time commanded and ordained their provest Andro Cullane to send their Tolbooth knok to Flanders, and cause mend the same, and gif it can nocht be mendit to buy them an new knok on the town's expence."

12*th January* 1536.—"The said day the provest and council present for the time, ordained Andro Cullane to write for the man that makis the touns knokis and cause him to come home with the same and set her up at the town's expence, and what expence he makes thereon he shall be thankfully paid of the same again."

23*rd July* 1537.—"The said day the provest and council present for the time thought expedient and ordained that their own knok, which was reformed and mended by Friar Alexander Lyndsay, should be set and input again in the most convenient place of their tolbooth where she might be securely kept, and that to be done immediately by the advice of the correkar of the same at the tounis expensis."

13*th October* 1537. — "The said day the council devised and ordained that there should be five merkis given to Friar Alexander Lyndsay for the completing of their knok, quhilk they ordain to be taken up of the readiest of their mails [rents] of Don."

4*th October* 1538.—"The said day the council assigns five merks to be given to David Bruce yearly by the dean of guild for his good service to be done in keeping and temporing of their knok within the Tolbooth for his fee."

27*th June* 1539.—"The said day the council ordained Mr Andrew Tulidaf, dean of guild, to pay William Purves five merks (Scottis) for the mending of their knok in the tolbooth, the quhilk he delivered to him at command of the provest this day and was discharged thereof (on the quhilk he took note)."

This William Purves is undoubtedly the same clockmaker who was a burgess of Edinburgh in 1540; see notes also on the clocks of Dundee and Stirling Burghs.

4th July 1539.—"The bailies ordained Mr Andrew Tulidaf, dean of guild, to pay Robert Vyschert xs. for the painting of the tolbooth horologe within viij days."

22nd May 1548.—"The said day Robert Hovesoun, valcar, is convicted by the sworn assize for the spoiling of the tounis knok of their tolbooth, and the said Hovesoun is ordered to reform and mend the said knok by the aid of craftsmen as far as he hath skaythit [spoiled or damaged] her in any way, and for the offence done the assize ordered him to come on Sunday come eight days and gang sark alane, bare feet and bare leg, afore the procession with an candle of wax of ane pound weight in his hands, and there after to ask the provest and bailies forgiveness on his knees in the town's name—and if he commit ony sick lik faut in time to comeing to be burnt on the cheek and banished the town during the tounis willis."

7th April 1560.—"The said day the bailies ordered Johnne Lowsoun, treasurer, to pay and deliver to David Elleis xxxiijs. iiijd. for the keeping of the knok of the tolbooth, from the decease of William Barclay quhill the feast of Whitsunday next to come."

5th December 1582.—"The said day the haill council being warned to this day, ratified and approved the contract made between the council and Jon Kay Lorymer, anent the mending of the town's three knoks and buying from him of the new knok, for payment to the said Jon of two hundred merks conform to the said contract and consenting to the lifting and raising of the said sum of the haill burgess of guild and craftsmen of the said burgh, and to be taxed every one according to their power and possession."

17th December 1595.—"The said day the provest and council considering that the two common knokis of the burgh, to wit, the kirk knok and the tolbooth knok, since Martinmas last has been evil handled and ruled and hes nocht gane during the said time, therefore feit Thomas Gordone, gunmaker, to rule the said two knokis and to cause them gang and strike the hours rightly both day and night quhilk the said Thomas promised faithfully to do, for the quhilk the council ordained him to have for his pains in ruling both the said knokis weekly six schillings aucht pennies."

25th January 1597.—"The quhilk day the provest, bailies, being conveened upon the supplication presented to them by David Andersone, younger, bearing that he had devised an instrument of his own ingenuity to draw and make dials or sun horologes, and that he was willing to make one on the fore wall of the said burgh which should show hours very justly by the sun with every month of the year the langest, shortest, and equi-noctiall dayis and when the same should be perfect and ended he would refer his recompence for his pains to the guid discretion of the provest, bailies and council at their pleasure; the which supplication being thought reasonable they allow David to upput one dial or sun horologe on the tolbooth on sic pairt thairoff as sall be thocht meit and expedient."

30th September 1618.—"The said day in respect the town's common knokis to wit, the kirk knok, tolbooth knok, and college knok, are out of all frame and order and are not sufficient and able to serve the town pairtlie because they are auld and worne, and pairtlie for want of skilful men to attend them, therefore, it is thought meet that the magistrates write south with all diligence and try quhair the best knock-macker may be had and cause bring him upon the town's charges to this burgh and visit the knokis thairof, that such of them as may be mended be accord-ingly done and sic as will not mend be made new as soon as the same can be conveniently gotten done."

1st December 1630. — "The council grants forty pounds of fee yearly to Robert Mailing for his pains in rewling of the town's three clocks, to wit, the Kirk clock, Greyfriars Kirk clock, and Tolbooth clock, and ordains the town's treasurer to answer him of twenty merks and the master of kirk work of forty merks yearly, in complete payment of the said sums during his service at the two usual terms in the year Whitsunday to

Martinmas in winter by equal proportions beginning the first term's payment at Martinmas last, and so forth, thereafter aye quhill (until) he be discharged by the council."

19*th September* 1632.—"The provest, bailies and council nominates and appoints Alexander Willox, wricht to be keeper and rewlar of the town's common clockis, to wit, the tolbooth clock, the clock of the high kirk, and college kirk, as likewise to ring the town's common bell in the tolbooth steeple at five hours in the morning and nine hours at even and ilk Wednesday to the Council at aucht hours in the morning for the space of an year next after the date hereof, and grants to the said Alexander for his service and fee during the said space the sum of one hundred merks (Scottis) to be paid to him quarterly by the master of kirk wark. Likewise the said Alexander being personally present accepted the said charge in and upon him and promised to do honest duty therein."

11*th June* 1645.—"The quilk day anent the supplication given in to the provest, bailies and council by Robert Melvill, son to umquhill David Melvill, stationer burgess of this burgh, making mention that quhair his said umquhill father being but an cautioner for Edward Raban, printer of this burgh, for payment to the master of mortified moneys of this burgh of the principal sum of five hundred merks (Scots), yet by his own consent before his death allowed that such a number of books should be given to their honours of the council for satisfaction of the said sum ; likewise it pleased their worships of the council to give the credit of the selling thereof ay and until they were sold without any definite time, because the supplicant could not take upon him to be comptable (accountable) for the money and prices thereof, but according as the occasion should serve that the books were bought by several persons who were pleased to buy, which might postpone the full payment many years and that not through any fault in the supplicant, because he never bargained other ways but to give payment as he should receive it, beseeching therefore the council to take to their consideration how more certainly and shortly their worships might be satisfied if it would please them to consider the supplicant's good offer, which was that he might be employed for ruling of the clocks and bells within this burgh ay and quhill the time that the payment which is termerlie for such a work may exhaust the full sum of the books which as yet are to the fore, and would be a most sure and certain payment to the town and that within a definite time. Quilk being read and considered by the Council, the said Provost, Bailies and Council nominates and appoints the said Robert to enter presently with the keeping and ruling of the town's common clocks, to wit, the tolbooth clock, the clock of the kirk, and college kirk—and ordain the fee due to him therefore to be allowed in payment of the two hundred and seventy-eight pounds fifteen shillings and fourpence restand by the said Robert to the said master of mortified money conform to the desire of the said Robert's supplication, and if he shall be found deficient to be removed upon his first fault.—Likewise the said Robert being personally present accepted the said charge and promised to do honest duty therein, and instantly received from Alexander Willox, late ruler of the said clocks and bells, the key of the baras and steeple of the Grayfriars kirk, quhilk opens also the door of the clock, and the key that opens the Grayfriars door. Item, the key of the kirk door of Saint Nicolas kirk with ane key for ye doors of the laich and high tolbooth."

3rd September 1651. — "The said day Patrick Wanhagan and Wm. Cook was received and admitted by the Provost, Bailies and Council for ruling of the kirk and tolbooth clocks and to the ringing of the council bell weekly on Wednesdays and the said tolbooth bell and kirk bell on preaching and lector days and to the ringing of the five hour bell in the morning and the nine hour bell at evening, and to use all other duties belonging to the said office as freely in all respects as umquhill Robert did use the same at any time heretofore for payment of such sums of money and fees as the said umquhill Robert received for his service in the said office ; to wit, four score merks of money yearly from the treasurer, aucht pounds money yearly from the dean of guild, and forty merks money yearly from the master of kirk wark, during the will and pleasure of the provest, bailies and council allanerlie."

16th April 1672.—" The said day anent the supplication given in to the council by Patrick Kilgour, knockmaker in the said town, mentioning that quhair he being desired by some of their number to come to this burgh for going about his employment therein, he held it his duty to obey their desires and that if they should be pleased to accept of his service and to admit him freeman of his calling and grant him freedom of public burdens for his lifetime for what might concern his employment and give him assurance thereanent he should endeavour to carry and behave himself dutifully as becomes ; and withal in further testimony of his respects for the credit and good of this burgh he should oblige himself to make and deliver unto them before Lammas next ane knock of brass about the bigness of ane house knock, which should be ane pendulum of the best form which should go for aucht days at one winding up and should strike the hours punctually, and should have a good bell with the motion of the day of the month, and should have an pais, and should stand no higher from the floor than the height of an man and he should oblige himself that the knock should be as sufficient and handsome as any knock made elsewhere and that he should uphold the same good and sufficient during his abode in this burgh as in the said application was contained, which the Council having heard and considered they agree and condescend that the petitioner shall have free liberty for going about his calling and employment within the said burgh and that he shall be free of any taxation or impositions within the same, in so far as may concern his calling during his lifetime he always giving assurance for performance of what is above mentioned to be done by him betwixt and the time above expressed in manner above set down and no other ways. Likewise Patrick Moir, bailie, Alexander Gordon, master of Kirk wark, John Andersone, William Thomsone and Robert Clerk, persons of the Council dissanented that the said Patrick Kilgour should be free from taxation with the said burgh for his calling for any time coming."

9th November 1692.—"The said day William Soupar, master of kirk wark, having presented to the provest, bailies and council his condescendence and agreement with Patrick Kilgour, watchmaker in the said burgh, anent the ruling of the kirk clock and ordering the better ringing of the bells—which is as follows: That the said Patrick shall bind himself by contract to translate the said clock into ane pendulum work conform to the newest fashion and invention done at London for regulating the motion of the said clock and causing her to go just.

"*Item*, to make some new stangs and nuts for the movement of the four hands for the making of them go all equal alike;

"*Item*, to rectify the motion of the globe with a new screw wheel of iron for turning the said globe about;

"*Item*, to make an engine to cause the pendulum and the four hands be in constant motion as well in the time that the paces are a drawing up as at other time, so that the clock shall not at any time stop her motion;

"*Item*, to cause the said clock strike the hours swifter that the people may not weary in telling of them;

"*Item*, to bush the privat holes which are worn in the said clock to the effect the wheels may run the easier and not stop, and to help the stopping of the half hours and cause them ring at their due time;

"*Item*, to raise the great bell in the said steeple and to cast and found two new cods of bell metal for the said bell to hang and ring in them, and to renew the two gudgeons of the said bell and to do all and sundry other things necessary for the causing the said bell and other bells in the said steeple ring more easily.

"For which he is to have two hundred merks after finishing of the same.—And likewise represented to them that he had agreed with the said Patrick Kilgour to maintain and uphold the said clock of Saint Nicolas Kirk well going and in good order, as also the motions of the globe and movement of the four hands, and also to furnish oil for the said clock and three bells in the said steeple on his own proper charges during his lifetime and residence within this burgh, and to have therefore forty merks yearly.—The present bailies and Council grant warrant to the said William Soupar—to enter in contract in the terms above written."
—*Aberdeen Council Register and Burgh Record.*

ABERNETHY, Scott. 96 Kirkgate, Leith, 1836-50.

ADAIR, James. Charlotte Street, Stranraer, 1820.

ADAIR, Stair. Castle Street, Stranraer, 1820.

ADAM, John. 11 Smith Hills, Paisley, 1820-38.

ADAM, John. Candle Street, Alloa, 1837.

ADAM, John. High Street, Lanark, 1835.

ADAM, Joseph. Clock Dial Maker, Glasgow, 1837.

ADAMSON, Charles. High Street, Montrose, 1820-37.

ADAMSON, John. Crossgate, Cupar-Fife, 1837.

ADAMSON, ——. Anstruther, 1818.

"WATCH LOST.—There was lost in the neighbourhood of Colinsburgh about ten days ago a Silver watch, maker's name, T. Birness, London, No. 4006. Whoever has found and will return it to Mr Adamson, Watchmaker, Anstruther, will receive one guinea of reward."—*Edinburgh Advertiser,* 20th March 1818.

ADAMSON, ——. Kilmarnock, 1850.

AITCHISON, Alexander. Edinburgh, 1765.

"One of the boys educated in George Heriot's Hospital was bound apprentice to James Cowan, 29th January 1765."—*E. H. Records.*

AITCHISON, John. 27 South Bridge, Edinburgh, 1850.

AITCHISON, ROBERT.   Edinburgh, 1756-90.

"One of the boys of George Watson's Hospital, booked apprentice to James Cowan, Edinburgh, 24th July 1756."

He appears to have been the first apprentice this celebrated maker indentured.

"Discharged of his indentures by James Cowan 23rd July 1763. Presented a bill craving an essay and essay masters to be appointed in order to his being admitted a freeman Clock and Watch maker in Edinburgh Hammermen, 7th May 1768. Admitted on 12th November 1768, his essay being a horizontal watch movement, begun, made and finished in his own shop in presence of Alex. Farquharson, William Downie and James Sibbald, essay masters, and James Cowan, landlord."--*E. H. Records.*

Was in partnership with William Turnbull (q.v.) at this date, the firm being known as Turnbull & Aitchison.

"A WATCH LOST.—That about four weeks ago or thereby a Metal Watch was lost in the neighbourhood of Edinburgh, having a tortoise-shell case stained on the outside of a lightish coloured ground, with a variety of figures painted thereon, in particular the figure of a butterfly, maker's name, Woods, Shrewsbury. There was a steel chain at the watch and a pebble seal having thereon a lion rampant. Motto, Courage, and J. C. under it. Whoever has found the said watch will please restore it to Robert Aitchison, watchmaker, opposite the City Guard, Edinburgh, who will give a handsome reward therefor, or in case the said watch may have been sold to or pledged with any person, it is requested that they will immediately restore it to the above R. A., who besides paying what may have been given or advanced upon the watch will give a guinea of reward and no questions asked."—*Caledonian Mercury,* 23rd January 1783.

"A GOLD WATCH CASE LOST.—Yesterday, the 26th current, there was lost betwixt the hours of one and three afternoon a plain gold watch case between Edinburgh and the Botanic Gardens. Whoever finds the same and will return it to Mr Robt. Aitchison, watchmaker, back of the City Guard, shall be handsomely rewarded. It is entreated that goldsmiths and others to whom it may be offered for sale will please retain it and give information as above."—*Ibid.*, 26th May 1783.

"A WATCH LOST.—There was lost on Sunday last at Leith, or in passing over some ships to go by boat, a remarkably neat silver watch, maker's name, Robt. Aitchison, No. 503. If any person has found the same and will return it to Mr Aitchison, watchmaker, High Street, Edinburgh, they will receive a reward of two guineas and it is entreated that if the watch is offered for sale she may be stopt and information given to Mr Aitchison."—*Ibid.*, 15th September 1788.

Sale of the Stock of Watches, etc., and utensils which belonged to the deceased Robert Aitchison, watchmaker in Edinburgh, advertised in *Caledonian Mercury*, 31st December 1790.

"Alexander Aitchison, medical student, Edinburgh, served Heir General to his cousin, Robert Aitchison, watchmaker there, dated 22nd June 1790. Recorded 29th June 1790."—*Services of Heirs.*

AITCHISON, WILLIAM. 91 South Bridge, Edinburgh, 1807.

AIKEN OR AITKEN, DAVID, sen. Carnwath, 1790-1845.
"David Aitken, watchmaker at Carnwath, served Heir General to his father, John Aiken, Tailor there, dated 4th March 1803. Recorded 9th March 1803."— *Services of Heirs.*

AIKEN OR AITKEN, DAVID, jun. Carnwath, 1840-75.

AITKEN, ALEXANDER. 98 Queen Street, Glasgow, 1836.

AITKEN, GEORGE. Parliament Square, Edinburgh, 1781-85.
"Compeared on 3rd November 1781 and presented his essay, being a clock timepiece with dead seconds, begun, made and finished in the shop of Samuel Brown, in presence of Samuel Brown, landlord, David Murray, Robert Clidsdale and Thomas Sibbald, essay masters, as they declared."—*E. H. Records.*

"WATCH AND CLOCK MAKING.—George Aitken, Parliament Square, returns his grateful thanks to the public and his customers in particular, at the same time takes the liberty to inform them that he has on hand at present for sale a good assortment of watches and clocks at very reasonable prices. Such as please to favour him with their orders may depend on having their commissions punctually attended to.

"*N.B.*—Repeating watches and all other kinds of watches properly repaired."—*Edinburgh Evening Courant*, 14th November 1785.

AITKEN, JAMES.   Markinch, 1837.

AITKEN, JAMES.   64 Broomielaw, Glasgow, 1841.

AITKEN, JOHN.   Edinburgh, 1750-1779.

"Son of John Aitken, wright in Canongate, booked apprentice to John Steil, Edinburgh, 28th July 1750. Transferred to James Cowan and discharged of his indentures by him on 24th July 1756. Presented a bill to be admitted a freeman clock and watch maker in Edinburgh Hammermen, 6th May 1758. Compeared on 3rd February 1759 and presented his essay, being a watch movement made and finished in his own shop, as James Cowan, his landlord, Daniel Binny, and George Aitken, his essay masters declared, which was found a well wrought, etc., and the said John Aitken was admitted a freeman clock and watch maker of this Incorporation."—*E. H. Records.*

"HOUSES AND GROUND IN CANONGATE TO BE SOLD.—All and whole that tenement of land lying in the Canongate and on the north side thereof, a little above the Tolbooth, consisting of three stories, a cellar, a garret, a bowling green, summer house and garden, which belonged to John Aitken, late watchmaker in Edinburgh, and paid of rent yearly preceding Whitsunday last £27, 10s. stg.

"Creditors of the said John Aitken are requested to meet in John's Coffee House upon Monday, the 25th January at 12 o'clock midday."—*Caledonian Mercury*, 4th January 1779.

Admitted a member of Lodge St David, Edinburgh, 14th June 1758.

AITKEN, JOHN.   New Street, Dalry, Ayrshire, 1850.

AITKEN, PETER.   96 Argyll Street, Glasgow, 1841.

AITKEN, ROBERT. Island, Galashiels, 1836.

AITKEN, WILLIAM. Haddington, 1805-37.

ALCORNE, JAMES. Edinburgh, 1733-60 (see below).

ALCORNE, RICHARD. Edinburgh, 1694-1738.

"Son to Mr Henry Alcorne, essay master of his Majesty's Mint, Edinburgh, booked apprentice to Andrew Brown, Edinburgh, 10th November 1694. Compeared 25th September 1703, and presented his essay, viz., a pendulum clock with alarum and short swing, a lock to the door with a key, which was found a well wrought essay, etc. His essay masters were Andrew Brown and Murdoch Grant; his essay was made in Richard Mill's shop. He paid the boxmaster [or treasurer] fifty-three pounds six shillings and eight pennies (Scots) as the half of his upset [or entry money] and the other half was paid to William Herring."

3rd February 1740.—" A motion being made to score Mrs Alcorne out of the quarterly pension roll in respect of her litigious humour, and refusing the composition offered to her by the Earl of Home. The house ordains her to be informed of this motion, and if she accept not of the offer made her by the said Earl they will next quarter day score her off."—*E. H. Records.*

" James Alcorne, son of Richard Alcorne, clockmaker, Edinburgh, served Heir General to his grandfather, Henry Alcorne, Essay Master to the Mint in Scotland, recorded 15th March 1733."—*Services of Heirs.*

" James Alcorne, Watchmaker, Edinburgh, served Heir General to his father, Richard Alcorne, watchmaker, dated 3rd November 1735. Recorded 19th January 1738."—*Ibid.*

" James Alcorne, son of Richard Alcorne, watchmaker, served Heir General to his grandmother, Margaret Henderson, wife of Henry Alcorne, 1st July 1760."—*Ibid.*

ALEXANDER, ALEXANDER. Elgin, 1845.

ALEXANDER, JAMES. Turriff; born 1796; died 1838; succeeded by his son George.

ALEXANDER, GEORGE. Turriff, 1838-50, son of above.

ALEXANDER, David Crichton.   Kilmarnock, 1837.

ALEXANDER, George.   27 Timber Bush and 62 Shore,
    Leith, 1813-25.   *See* Robert Alexander, Leith.

> "Patent granted unto George Alexander, watch-
> maker in Leith for his improved mode of suspending
> the card of mariner's compass, being on a principle
> entirely new."—*Specification of British Patents.*

ALEXANDER, James.   Elgin, 1820-45.

> "James Alexander, watchmaker in Elgin, served
> Heir General to his father, James Alexander, merchant
> there, dated 10th November 1845.   Recorded 14th
> November 1845."—*Services of Heirs.*

ALEXANDER, James.   Kincardine O'Neil, 1846.

ALEXANDER, John.   Edinburgh, 1667-1707.

> *The 7th day of December* 1667.—"The quilk day
> Jon Alexander, sone lawfull to Alexander Alexander,
> indweller in the Canongate, is booked apprentice to
> Robert Smith, clockmaker."
>
> *The 17th day of August* 1671.—"The quilk day in
> presence of the Deakone, compeired personallie Jon
> Alexander, sometime prentice and servand to Robert
> Smith, clockmaker, burgess of Edinburgh, and presented
> his essay to wit, ane kist lock with ane key, ane sprent
> band, ane clok, ane munter, ane sun dyell, qlk was
> found ane weill wrought essay, able to serve his
> Majesties lieges.   And thairfore they have admitted the
> said Jon Alexander to be ane ordinary freeman in the
> airt and trade of clockmaker's trade, etc."—*E. H. Records.*

ALEXANDER, John.   Canongate, Edinburgh, 1790.

ALEXANDER, Mary.   Turriff, 1837.

ALEXANDER, Robert.   Edinburgh, 1708-18.

> Son to the deceased above John Alexander,
> clockmaker, burgess of Edinburgh, compeared on
> 11th December 1708, and presented his essay (viz.):
> "Ane eight day pendulum clock, and a lock to the door
> with a key, which was found a well wrought essay, etc."
>
> The rest of the formula is the same as given in the
> minute dealing with the father's admission, it also

applying to every freeman, clock and watch maker, on his admission to the Incorporation of Hammermen of Edinburgh.

"His essay masters were William Brown, elder, and Richard Alcorne, his essay was made in his mother's shop. He payed the boxmaster 110 merks for his upset, 20 merks for the Maiden Hospital,[1] and the said Robert Alexander in token that he consents and approves of the Incorporation's Act anent the Maiden Hospital, had subscribed the double of this act in the Scroll Book."—*E. H. Records.*

Little is known about this maker, but the fact of his name appearing regularly till the year 1718 in these records makes it apparent he was at that date located in Edinburgh.

ALEXANDER, ROBERT. Tolbooth Wynd and Shore, Leith, 1751-1825.

There were apparently three generations of this name, but authentic proof is awanting to connect these Leith makers with the above. All evidence available makes it almost certain that they belong to the same family. Unfortunately, it is not until the year 1751 that we have documentary proof of this firm's location. In that year Robert Alexander entered into a law plea with the Incorporation of Hammermen of Edinburgh, about a servitude over a wall that divided their respective properties in the Cowgate, Edinburgh. Then in the *Edinburgh Evening Courant* of the 25th July 1764, there appears the following advertisement: "Lost on Thursday last between Leith and Restalrig, a silver watch with a shambo string, the maker's name, T. Bennett, London, No. 5640. Whoever has found and shall be pleased to return the same to Robert Alexander, watchmaker in Leith, shall have a suitable reward, and if offered for sale it is hoped will be stop'd."

In 1773 his son's name appears as being established in Tolbooth Wynd, and nearer the end of the century, as

[1] This refers to the Trades' Maiden Hospital which had been founded a year or two before this date, an institution that is still carried on.

being at Middle of the Shore, emerging in the beginning of the next as No. 62 Shore. This last shop was carried on under the same name, till the year 1826 when all record of it disappears. Of course, it could not have been in the hands of one individual for so long a period, and in tracing this family we find that there died at Rose Bank, Broughton Road, Edinburgh, on 24th March 1830, Mr Robert Alexander, late watch and compass maker, Leith, aged 84 years. As this person is designated as having been at 62 Shore, thus we have the unique record of father, son, and grandson, all bearing the same name, continuing a business for the long period of nearly eighty years.

ALEXANDER, ROBERT. Bathgate, 1761.
   See note on Linlithgow Town Clock.

ALEXANDER, ROBERT. Wigton, 1770.

ALEXANDER, WILLIAM. 28 Arcade, Glasgow, 1841.

ALEXANDER, WILLIAM. 11 Nelson Street, Trongate, Glasgow, 1836.

ALEXANDER, WILLIAM PATERSON. Balfron, 1836.

ALEXANDER, W. A. 9 Nelson Street, Trongate, Glasgow, 1836.

ALISON, JOHN. High Street, Montrose, 1798-1822.

ALISON, JOHN. Foot of Broad Wynd, Leith, 1796.

ALISONE, JAMES. Edinburgh, 1641-47.
   The Incorporation of Hammermen, Edinburgh, as is well known, had their meeting-place in the Magdalen Chapel, Cowgate, an old religious foundation which had been left to them in trust in 1547. They piously carried out the wishes of the foundress, Janet Rhynd, so far as the charitable side of the trust lay.
   The Reformation in 1560, however, abolished the religious supervision for which the foundress stipulated in her deed. The wooden belfry having been found unsuitable, they, in 1618 agreed to build a steeple. This quaint and modest spire was finished in 1627 and

still stands. It contains a large bell, which they were at the expense of bringing from Flanders, but it was not till 1641 that there is mention of a "Knok." The introduction of this clock was the means of James Alisone's name appearing in their records. Always cautious before incurring expense, they sent for this maker from Cupar in Fife to enquire as to cost, etc. He carried out the contract, and in the notes on the clock and bell of the Magdalen Chapel will be found all that is to be gleaned about this man, who evidently was not resident here after 1647. *See also* note on Dundee Town Clocks.

ALLAN, JAMES. Cheapside, Kilmarnock, 1820-37.

ALLAN, JAMES. Wellington Place, Aberdeen, 1836.

ALLAN, JAMES. Holburn Street, Aberdeen, 1846.

ALLAN, JAMES. Kilmarnock, 1807.

ALLAN, JOHN. Canongate, Edinburgh, 1800.

ALLAN, WILLIAM. Kilwinning, 1837-50.

ALLAN, WILLIAM. Aberdeen, 1703.

ALLAN, WILLIAM. Aberdeen, 1807.

"Margaret M'Kenzie or Allan, wife of George M'Kenzie, merchant, Aberdeen, served Heir General to her father, William Allan, watchmaker there, dated 18th April 1807. Recorded 25th May 1807."—*Services of Heirs*.

ALSTON, JOHN. Tolbooth Wynd, Leith, 1794.

ALSTON, JOHN. 77 Princes Street, Edinburgh, 1811.

ALSTON, JOHN. 32 Nicolson Street, Edinburgh, 1806.

"A GOLD WATCH LOST.—There was lost on the forenoon of Wednesday, the 16th November, somewhere near the Head of the Pleasance, a Gold Watch, with a metal chain. It is requested that the person who may have found it will return it to Mr John Alston, watchmaker, No. 32 Nicolson Street, and he will be handsomely rewarded."—*Edinburgh Evening Courant*, 17th November 1808.

B

ANCRUM, THOMAS.   Edinburgh, 1703.

"Son to William Ancrum, wright in Edinburgh, is booked apprentice to Andrew Brown, Edinburgh, 13th May 1703."—*E. H. Records.*

ANDERSON, ANDREW.   Dundas Street, Comrie, 1837.

ANDERSON, CHARLES.   Aberdeen, 1699.

ANDERSON, GEORGE.   36 Green, Aberdeen, 1837.

ANDERSON, GEORGE.   South Street, St Andrews, 1860-92.

Son of William Anderson (see below), died 9th May 1892, aged 77 years.   Business continued to present day.

ANDERSON, HENRY.   Tulliallan, 1820.

ANDERSON, HERCULES.   Bervie, 1837.

ANDERSON, JOHN.   Dunse, 1776-1802.

"John Anderson, clockmaker in Dunse, served Heir General to his father, Alexander Anderson, Portioner of Redpath, dated 14th April 1802.   Recorded 16th April 1802."—*Services of Heirs.*

ANDERSON, WILLIAM.   South Street, St Andrews, 1832-67.

Died 4th July 1867, aged 76 years.

ANDERSONE, DAVID.   Aberdeen, 1597.

See note on Aberdeen Town Clocks, page 1.

ANDREW, ALEXANDER.   Portsoy, 1830.

ANDREW, WILLIAM.   Huntly, 1837.

ANDREW, WILLIAM.   Perth, 1791-95.

Apprenticed to Patrick, Gardener, Perth, 1791; admitted freeman of Perth Hammermen Incorporation, 1795.

ANGUS, George.   72 Broad Street, Aberdeen, 1790-1830.

"NOTICE TO WATCHMAKERS.—A box containing fourteen silver watches for George Angus, Aberdeen, Watchmaker, under address to Mackie & Mackenzie, merchants there, was forwarded the 19th of August from the Mail Coach Office, Edinburgh, on its way from London, and has never since been heard of.   The delay is supposed to have taken place south of Dundee. G. Angus subjoins the numbers of the watches and requests that if any of them be offered to sale, they may be stopped. Any person who has found the box will receive a handsome reward by applying to him or to any of the mail coach proprietors upon the road. Numbers, etc., of the 14 watches : Two, George Angus, Aberdeen, No. 218-219, pinions of seven leaves ; twelve, T. Berress, London, No. 1194, 1200, 1198, 1199, 2001, 2002, 2003, 2004, 2005, 2007, 2008, 2009. A fitler frame, and dial, 2 gross chain hooks, four files."—*Edinburgh Evening Courant*, 27th August 1799.

"John Angus, Advocate in Aberdeen, served Heir General to his father, George Angus, watchmaker there, dated 13th February 1830. Recorded 23rd February 1830."—*Services of Heirs.*

"His son John Angus, M.A., was Town Clerk of Aberdeen for 35 years, 1840-1875. A younger son James, also M.A., a distinguished student, attended the Mathematical Faculty, University of Louvain, 1826-7. He died in Aberdeen, 5th February 1828, in the 21st year of his age."—*Aberdeen Weekly Free Press*, 21st November 1914.

ARBUCKLE, JOSEPH. German Clock Maker, 4 Broomlands, Paisley, 1836.

ARCHDEACON, THOMAS. 8 William Street, Greenock, 1837.

ARGO, ——. Peterhead, 1784.

ARGYLE, DUKE OF. Whim, Peeblesshire, 1730.

"Whim, a small property in Peeblesshire, was purchased in 1730 by the Duke of Argyle. His Grace was a clever artist and mechanic. It is reported of him that he made a clock to perform for thirty years with only once winding up, and for a case put it into the skeleton of a favourite horse. An old woman came into his workshop with a pot to mend, and as the workmen happened to be out, she took his Grace for the blacksmith, and asked him to put a foot on her pot. The Duke fell to work, finished the pot, and would take no payment, telling her to come back again when it went wrong. She gave him many thanks, and, as a recompense, promised to knit a pair of stockings for him, but what was her surprise when a servant in rich livery entered and unbonneted before the blacksmith. The poor woman, when she knew it was the great Argyle, shook and trembled, and although assured he was not angry with her went home with a quaking heart."—*Edinburgh Evening Courant*, 6th June 1839.

ARMOUR, JOHN.   Kilmaurs, 1780-1808.

ARNOT, THOMAS.   Edinburgh, 1723.

"Son to the deceast George Arnot, Balgerthly; booked apprentice to Thomas Gordon, Edinburgh, 23rd March 1723."—*E. H. Records.*

ASHENHEIM, JACOB.   61 New Buildings, North Bridge, Edinburgh, 1818-38.

AULD, WILLIAM.   Edinburgh, 1795-1823.

"Was discharged of his indentures by Thomas Reid, 4th May 1799.   Compeared on 3rd May 1806, and presented his essay, the detached escapement of a clock begun, made, and finished in the shop of Thomas Reid, landlord, in presence of Robert Green, Laurence Dalgleish, and Thomas Sibbald, essay masters, as they declared, and was accordingly admitted a member of the Hammermen."—*E. H. Records.*

Assumed as partner with his master, Thomas Reid, in 1806, the business being then carried on in Parliament Close.   They removed in 1809 to 33 Princes Street, carrying it on till 1823; being at this latter date in No. 66, when both partners retired from active business.

For a fuller account of the class of work which this well-known firm executed, the reader is referred to the notes on Thomas Reid.   There it will be seen that it was of the most intricate character, and it is safe to say that both partners must have had complete satisfaction in their art, seeing it was so congenial to both of them.   Possibly there are few business partnerships where two partners have shown such devotion to each other as Thomas Reid and William Auld.   Closely related by marriage ties during life, in death they were not divided.   Both sleep their last

sleep in the one tomb, which is situated in the Old
Calton Burying Ground, Waterloo Place, Edinburgh,
and it records in a remarkable manner the close
connection that existed between these two men. The
tomb is situated on the south wall of the burying
ground, and is enclosed with high walls and iron gate;
the southmost end being entirely occupied by the
memorial stone, which is divided into three compart-
ments, two of smaller size, one on each side; leaving the
centre compartment a great deal larger. The pediment
on top bears that it is the burying-ground of William
Auld. The inscription on left-hand compartment is
as follows:—

"To the memory of John Auld, Merchant, St
Andrews, died 1751, and was buried in the Cathedral
Church Yard.

"William Auld, Printer, Edinburgh, died 1777,
and was buried in the Grey Friars Church Yard.

"Malcolm Ogilvie, merchant, Edinburgh, died 1792,
and was buried in the Grey Friars Church Yard.

"Alexandria Ogilvie, widow of William Auld, printer,
afterwards wife of Thomas Reid, watch maker, Edinburgh, and was buried in Grey Friars Church Yard."

On right hand compartment :—

"To the memory of William Auld, Clock and
Watch Maker, Edinburgh. Born 11th November 17—
(stone illegible), died 6th October 1846; and of Isabella
Scott or Auld, his spouse. Born 18th May 1779, died
10th October 1850. Also Catherine Scott, her sister,
born 20th September 1780, died 10th October 1863."

These inscriptions occupy a modest space in the
memorial stone, the larger part being taken up with the
epitaph of Thomas Reid, the account of which will
be found in the notes on that maker, where it is given in
full, as signs are not awanting that in a few years it will
be a matter of some difficulty to decipher the lettering,
owing to decay in the stone, unless steps are taken
to recut them. Seeing that the whole tomb has been
erected by William Auld, it indicates in a remarkable
manner, the esteem that he held for his partner
and relation, Thomas Reid. That the esteem was

reciprocated is shown by Thomas Reid, dedicating his famous treatise on clock-making to William Auld, remarking in the introduction that his practical knowledge is a sufficient testimony for so doing. These examples go to show the harmony that existed between these two men, which Auld as long as he lived never forgot, and, as will be noticed further on, was remembered by him in a manner that even to this day preserves the honoured name of the firm of Reid & Auld.

Although retired from active business in 1823 his interest in his art was not allowed to lie dormant, for at a meeting of the Royal Scottish Society of Arts held on 31st May 1841 the following donation was made :—

"A timepiece of Parisian manufacture, which belonged to the late Mr James Cowan, watchmaker, Edinburgh, made for him while he resided in Paris in 1749, and which on his death in 1781 became the property of Mr Thomas Reid, watchmaker, Edinburgh, his successor. Presented by Mr William Auld, 69 Great King Street, Edinburgh."

Again, at a meeting of the same society held on 24th November 1845, the following donations were laid on the table :—

"1. An engraved print with letterpress description of a beautiful bronze clock, supposed to be of the best Florentine period, the original works by Romilly of Geneva, now the property of Mr B. L. Vulliamy, clockmaker to the Queen, London. Presented through William Auld, Esq., by Vulliamy.

"2. Engraved portraits of the following Horologists: (1) Julien le Roy, Horologer du Roi ancien Directeur de la Societa des Arts; (2) Abraham Louis Breguet, Member de l'Institut Royal de France; (3) Mons. Vaucher, Horologer; (4) Mons. Loque, Bijoutier. Presented by William Auld, Esq., 67 Great King Street, Edinburgh, who was thanked by the meeting for these donations."

It may be here noted that Mr Vulliamy was after this elected an honorary associate of the Royal Scottish Society of Arts, and he later donated some valuable records in connection with the new clock which was about to be made for the Houses of Parliament, London.

However slight these gifts may now appear, yet it was only a foretaste of his deep interest in Horology, which culminated in his founding through this Royal Scottish Society of Arts what became to be known as the " Reid and Auld Bequest."

Intimation of this Bequest was made public at a meeting held on Monday, 10th November 1851.

" The President intimated to the meeting that the finances of the Society had been increased by the legacy of £200 bequeathed by the late William Auld, under the title of the Reid and Auld Bequest, and which had now been paid to the Society.   The terms of the bequest are : ' That the annual interest is to be given in one, two, or three prizes to Master or Journeymen clock and watch makers for the best model of anything new in that art or line of business, and if no model is invented in the course of any year, or one so trifling as to be unworthy of attention, then the produce of the bequest for that year to be paid by the Society in charity to such of the poor of the trade residing in and within ten miles of Edinburgh as the treasurer of the Society in his discretion shall select."

Accordingly, the bequest took its place in the prize-list of the Society and the earliest mention of it which we have been able to find occurs in the published *Transactions* for the year 1854-55, where it is entitled " The Reid and Auld prizes."

" For the first, second, and third best models of anything new in the Art of Clock or Watch making by journeymen or master watch or clock makers, if these should be considered worthy of prizes, a sum of Ten Guineas, divided amongst them in such proportion as the Prize Committee shall fix according to merit."

This formula continues to be the only way of announcing the bequest down to present day, the only alteration being the amount of money proposed to be given each year, which, generally speaking, was either seven or eight guineas. As far as we have been able to find, this Reid and Auld Bequest is the only one of its kind in Scotland left exclusively for the encouragement of the Science of Horology, and we now give a list of the prize-winners who satisfied the examining committees from time to time as being considered worthy of the prize :—

"To Mr Henry Kerr, 10 South Saint James Street, Edinburgh, for the superior workmanship displayed in the execution of an Electric Clock Pendulum, exhibited by him on 13th April 1857.

"*Note.*—This prize is awarded by the Committee not for the pendulum, but for the superior workmanship shown in it. The Reid and Auld prize fund being for rewarding superior workmanship exhibited in anything new in the Art of Clock or Watch Making by journeymen or master. — The Reid and Auld prize, value three sovereigns.

"To Mr Frederick James Ritchie, Clock and Watch maker, Edinburgh, for his working model and description of the Clock Drop for the Time Ball on Nelson's Monument, Edinburgh. Exhibited and read 25th April 1859. —The Reid and Auld Prize, value nine sovereigns.

"To Frederick J. Ritchie, Edinburgh, for his communication on the means adopted for securing extreme accuracy in the Time Gun signal, read and illustrated by a working model and experiments, 22nd July 1861.— The Reid and Auld Prize, value seven sovereigns.

"To Henry Kerr, Clock and Watch Maker, Dundee, for the ingenuity displayed in the two new Gravity Escapements invented by him and exhibited to the Society, 13th April 1863.—A grant of five sovereigns out of the Reid and Auld Bequest.

"To Victor Kullberg, Chronometer and Watch Manufacturer, 12 Cloudesly Terrace, Islington, for his description of improvements on the Chronometer Balance, read and illustrated by a model and drawings, 11th April 1864.—The Reid and Auld Prize, value seven guineas.

"To Frederick James Ritchie, Clock and Watch Maker, Edinburgh, for his paper on Electro-Sympathetic Clocks and Time Signals (No. 4297); read and illustrated by drawings and models, 28th April 1873.—The Reid and Auld Prize, value ten sovereigns.

"To George H. Slight, C.E., Workshop Superintendent, Trinity Wharf, London, for his description of an improved Centrifugal Governor for regulating the Revolving Machinery of Light Vessels and Lighthouses, read 11th January 1875, No. 4332.—The Reid and Auld Prize, value five sovereigns.

"To Frederick James Ritchie, for his paper on a Method of Correcting Clocks by Hourly Currents of Electricity; read and illustrated by drawings and instruments on 11th March 1878.—The Reid and Auld Prize, value ten sovereigns.

"To George W. Warren, Watchmaker, London, for the description of his instrument for Registering and Printing the Fares on Omnibus, Tramcar, and other Tickets, and simultaneously issuing the same, read and illustrated by the instrument and drawings, 22nd March 1880.—The Reid and Auld Prize, value ten sovereigns.

"To John S. Matheson, Chronometer Maker, Leith, for his contrivance for winding up Chronometers without reversing their suspension, described and illustrated by an example read on 22nd November 1880.—The Reid and Auld Prize, value three sovereigns.

"To Peter Stevenson, Philosophical Instrument Maker, Edinburgh, for his description of Meteorological Apparatus constructed for the late Lord George, 8th Marquess of Tweeddale (No. 4497); illustrated by drawings and instruments and by some of the volumes of Records continued for ten years. Read on 25th February 1884—A Reid and Auld Prize, value ten sovereigns.

"To William Sturrock, Jeweller and Watchmaker, 12 St Andrew Square, Edinburgh, for his paper on Sturrock & Meek's Automatic 24 hours' Dial for Clocks and Watches (No. 4514); read on 27th April 1885 and illustrated by a large Model Dial.—A Reid and Auld Prize, value five sovereigns.

"To Walter Macdowall Hardie, Printer, Edinburgh, for his Fluid Prisms of novel construction, exhibited and described on 12th April 1886 (No. 4537).—A Reid and Auld Prize, value ten sovereigns.

"To William Sturrock, Watchmaker, 12 St Andrew Square, Edinburgh, for his paper on an Electric Illuminated Time Indicator; read and illustrated by the instrument in action on 23rd January 1888 (No. 4570).—A Reid and Auld Prize, value three sovereigns.

"To William Sturrock, for his paper on a Magnetic Electric Time Indicator (No. 4643), read on 11th January 1892.—A Reid and Auld Prize, value three sovereigns.

"To John Davidson, Watchmaker, Wick, for his paper on an Automatic Memorandum Clock (No. 4662), read on 28th November 1892.—A Reid and Auld Prize, value ten sovereigns.

"To W. B. Blaikie, Edinburgh, for his paper on the Cosmosphere (No. 4716), read on the 25th March 1895.—A Reid and Auld Prize, value twenty sovereigns.

"To William Shaw, for his paper on an Electric System of Mechanical Ventilation (No. 4767), read on the 11th April 1898.—A Reid and Auld Complimentary Silver Medal."

This last date, 1898, represents nearly a period of fifty years that the fund has been in existence, and it would be invidious to continue it down to date, but our purpose is to call attention to this unique and little known bequest and to show how it has been taken advantage of during that long period. No doubt surprise will be exhibited in reading over these awards for it is difficult in some cases to see where the terms of the bequest come in, but it will be noticed that the trend of the inventions submitted are more or less in connection with electricity, showing the fascination this subject has with a large number of inventors. It must be a matter of congratulation to Scotland that the first to enter the field of the application of Electricity to Horology was our countryman Alexander Bain (q.v.).

Of course it is well known that it is now a matter of some difficulty to invent anything new in Horology, but it is easy to see that something more practical will have to be tried to render the bequest of any use. This view of the matter has apparently dawned on the Society itself, for as late as 1894 a strong appeal was made in their own published *Transactions*, calling attention to this and other bequests in their hands, and inviting applications from the public, but evidently without much success. Seeing the prize has only been awarded some eighteen times in half a century, one would naturally suppose that the latter part of the bequest, namely, the relief of poor clockmakers would have been regularly attended to, but, strange to say, it is not till about 1876 that the first mention of a donation for a charitable purpose appears. In that year a sum of five guineas was allowed to poor clockmakers, and from that date up to 1897 sums varying from £2 up to £12 in one year were applied to charity. This latter sum was only given once, and the average works out at something like £4 annually spent in relief of poor clockmakers.

This again brings out the curious fact that either clockmakers in necessitous circumstances are practically non-existent or else the terms of the bequest are unknown.[1] Want of funds cannot be blamed for this state of affairs, for the sum of the bequest stood in 1874 at £576, 7s. 3d., consisting of capital £322, 15s. 8d. and revenue unexpended amounting to £253, 11s. 7d., the whole producing for that year a revenue of £28, 5s. 10d. and in 1896-97 the fund stood at £809, 5s., producing an income of £61, 2s. 5d.

This splendid result speaks volumes for the careful manner with which the original sum has been invested and watched over by the Royal Scottish Society of Arts, but surely something could be done to make this Reid and Auld Bequest of more use and benefit to the trade in Scotland. It might be presumptuous to say how this could be done, but the hint can only be thrown out that if steps were taken to apply the funds, or even a part of them, to the prize list of the technical schools or colleges in Edinburgh or wherever the science and art of Horology is taught, an impetus would be given to an industry that at the present moment is almost entirely overlooked and starved for want of such a special fund as the Reid and Auld Bequest, which is, as we have shown, now lying practically useless.

[1] A special circular was issued by the Royal Scottish Society of Arts in 1907 drawing attention to this matter.

AUSTEN, JOHN.   Dundee, 1836.

AYR OR EYR, BENJAMIN.   Edinburgh, 1765-70.

"Booked apprentice to James Duff, Edinburgh, 12th February 1765. Was by the consent of parties allowed to serve out the remainder of his time with James Cowan in place of James Duff, his present master, on 23rd March 1770."—*E. H. Records.*

BAIN, ALEXANDER.   Hanover Street, Edinburgh, 1838-77.

"Mr Bain's name will always be honourably associated with the progress of electric science, more especially with the adaptation of electricity to the purposes of daily life. His special department was what may be called electro-horology, and to him the public are indebted for originating one form of electric clock which, with certain modifications, has been found of immense service as an exact means of measuring time.[1] As it turned out, however, the sanguine inventor was found to have reckoned without his host. The soil not unfrequently became too dry to set up the necessary galvanic action and, of course, the alternative of having a chemical battery as an adjunct to the clock proved a formidable drawback to the general utility of the invention. It was found, moreover, that a pendulum moved by electricity, owing to unsteadiness in the supply of the motive power, did not keep the most exact time, and the more recent attempts at electric clockmaking have aimed at the removal of such irregularity by applying the current in a different way.

"At the same time Bain's invention has been turned to good account in a modified form, which he himself does not seem to have originally contemplated. It was Wheatstone, who, on the first introduction of the electrically-moved pendulum, suggested the idea of an electrically-controlled pendulum, which was taken up

An account of Mr Bain's clock is given on p. 35. In that description it will be noted that the pendulum was employed to move the clock, and had this expectation been realised there can be little doubt that electric clocks would soon have come to be in general request, seeing that most people would gladly be saved the trouble of daily or even weekly winding up the domestic time-keeper.

and successfully worked out by Mr Jones of Chester. Under this arrangement a standard clock is enabled by means of an electric current to regulate the pendulum motion of any number of other clocks, and so make the latter keep time with perfect precision. It is thus that the clock which fires the time gun on the Castlehill, as well as several other clocks in Edinburgh, are controlled by a standard clock at the City Observatory, and indeed, the method is now in use all over the country for the purpose of keeping public clocks up to Greenwich time.

"But Mr Bain's versatile inventive faculty was not confined to this particular department. His attention was early directed to the improvement of the apparatus in use in telegraphy, and after various experiments, in which his knowledge of chemistry came to his aid, he produced the electro-chemical printing telegraph which bears his name, and which, although temporarily discarded for the Morse or American system, seems yet destined under the hands of subsequent inventors to ultimately supersede all others.

"At a time when the attention of electricians was being directed to fast-speed automatic telegraphy, it was only natural that Bain's chemical system should be taken up. Wheatstone employed it as an improved recorder for his well-known self-acting system, but it was left to an American, Mr Edison, to utilise it to the greatest extent, and show what it is capable of accomplishing. By the employment of several wires and an automatic transmitter the almost incredible speed of upwards of 1000 words a minute has been obtained. 'This being done,' remarked Sir Wm. Thomson at the British Association meeting at Glasgow, 'by the long neglected electro-chemical method of Bain, long ago condemned in England to the helot work of recording from a relay and then turned adrift as needlessly delicate for that.'

"To this extent has Mr Bain's original invention been already perfected, and with it his name is probably destined to be best known. Enough has been said to show that Mr Bain was well entitled to be regarded as a public benefactor. It would appear, however, that he himself did not reap much permanent benefit from the efforts of his inventive genius. At one time he is understood to have realised a considerable fortune, but this he subsequently lost, mainly, it is believed, through the over-sanguine prosecution of the undertakings which absorbed his attention. For one thing, he is said to have invested heavily in a stock of electric clocks from which he found it impossible to realise anything like the return he had expected.

"On leaving Edinburgh he betook himself to London, but it does not appear that he there succeeded in retrieving his position, and latterly his friends found it necessary to take steps for affording him pecuniary assistance. A representation of his case to the Royal Society secured from that body a donation of £150. An application was likewise made to the Government to have his name put on the Civil List, and in the beginning of December 1873, a letter was received from Mr Gladstone intimating that he had been granted a pension of £80 per annum. Meanwhile, poor Bain had quitted London for the North, leaving the matter in charge of a friend to receive any communication which might be directed to him from Downing Street.

"When the welcome announcement of his pension came, the beneficiary could nowhere be heard of. The circumstances were communicated to us, but a considerable interval elapsed before personal inquiries and advertising led to his discovery. This well-bestowed recognition of his labours, however, Mr Bain did not long enjoy. He was recently stricken by paralysis, and completely lost the power of his lower limbs. He was received at the New Home for Incurables at Broomhall, Kirkintilloch, where he died last week, and was interred in the burying-ground in the neighbourhood known as the Old Aisle Cemetery.

"Mr Bain, who was a widower, was about sixty-six years of age, and a native, we believe, of Thurso. Photographs of him were recently presented to the Society of Telegraph Engineers in London, and the American

Society of Telegraphers at Philadelphia. As already stated, Mr Bain's valuable discoveries brought him but little fame or reward during his lifetime; his memory is therefore the more entitled to the grateful remembrance of all who take an interest in the advancement of science."—*Scotsman*, 10th January 1877.

This kindly-worded memoir was evidently written by one who had known him well, and may be taken as authoritative. The *Dictionary of National Biography* gives a short account of him, and supplements the foregoing information that he served his apprenticeship with a watchmaker in Wick, and also that he received as much as seven thousand pounds for his electric telegraph patent. This large sum of money was principally lost in litigation, a fact fully brought out after his death, for we notice in contemporary newspapers that even then claims were put forward by some taking full credit for the invention, implying that the claimants had at least a good share with the success or otherwise of the same.[1] Be that as it may, the opinion held at the present time is that Alexander Bain, if not the first in the field, was the first Scotsman to enter the then unknown science of Electricity as applied to Horology. Subjoined is a list of his patents and dates compiled from the *Specifications of British Patents*, as published by the Patent Office, No. 9, old series—

1st Patent, dated 11th January 1841, No. 8783, granted to Alexander Bain and John Barwise.

2nd Patent, dated 27th May, 1843, No. 9745, granted to Alexander Bain.

3rd Patent, for electric telegraph, dated 25th September 1845, No. 10,838, granted to Alexander Bain.

4th Patent, for clocks, dated 19th February 1847, No. 11,584, granted to Alexander Bain.

5th Patent, for clocks, dated 29th May 1852, No. 14,146, granted to Alexander Bain.

[1] A book entitled *An Account of some Remarkable Applications of Electric Fluid to the Useful Arts, with a Vindication of Mr Alexander Bain's Claim to be the First Inventor of the Electro-Magnetic Clock*, published in London, 1843, by John Finlaison.

The following non-technical accounts of his inventions and robbery of his premises are deserving of preservation, as the sources from which they are taken are difficult to get together, but they give scant justice to the talents of one, who, unfortunately in these days, is wellnigh forgotten.

"Society of Arts Meeting held on 14th April 1845.— In the absence of Mr Alexander Bain, the patentee, Mr Bryson, V.P., exhibited and described Mr Bain's Electro-Magnetic Clock. The clock was exhibited in action by means of a current obtained from the earth.

"Mr Bain obtains the electricity by which his clocks are moved from the earth. He buries a quantity of coke in the ground and at the distance of a few feet or more he buries one or more plates of zinc. These two elements with the intervening soil form a galvanic battery from which a uniform current of electricity of very low tension is obtained. It is the constancy of this current which renders it available as a motive power for time-keepers. The current is led from the coke and the zinc by means of copper wires, the two ends of which terminate in the upper part of the clock. To obtain motion from this current, Mr Bain forms a pendulum of fir rod, and instead of the ordinary bob he employs a coil or bobbin of copper wire, the wire being covered with cotton thread. In the centre of this bobbin is a hole, upwards of an inch in diameter, through which is passed a case containing two sets of bar magnets, having their similar poles placed opposite each other with a small interval between them. The coil has freedom of motion along the case containing the magnets, and when the pendulum is at rest the coil stands over the adjacent similar poles of the magnets. From the coil proceed two wires up the back of the pendulum rod. One of these is attached to the steel spring by which the pendulum is suspended, and that is in metallic connection with the copper wire proceeding from one of the elements of the battery (say,

ELECTRO-MAGNETIC CLOCK.

By Alexander Bain, Edinburgh ; patented 1845. Shown at the Glasgow Historical Exhibition, 1911. The property of William B. Smith, Glasgow. (See p. 32.)

the zinc). The other wire from the coil terminates in a metallic disc near the point of suspension of the pendulum, while the wire proceeding from the other element of the battery (say, the coke) terminates in a screw on one side of the disc above mentioned.

"This disc is like a small inverted pendulum capable of falling to the right and left alternately when its centre of gravity becomes changed by the alternate motion of the pendulum. When the disc falls to the one side the current flows through the wire, but when it falls to the other side upon a detent the current is broken. On the return of the pendulum the disc again falls on the screw attached to the wire and renews the connection betwixt the positive and negative sides of the battery. By this contact a stream of electricity passes through the wire and coil, and as this takes place when the pendulum is at its extreme point of deviation, at each alternative beat, the coil has at that moment one of the sets of bar magnets nearly in its centre.

"Previous discovery had shown that, when a coil of copper wire is thus situated with respect to a bar magnet, it will immediately, on a stream of electricity being passed through it, and provided it has freedom of motion, be impelled towards one or other of the poles of the magnet according to the direction of the current of electricity.

"It is this fact of which Mr Bain has availed himself to give motion to the pendulum of his clock, and, accordingly, whenever the pendulum is at its extreme point of deviation from the perpendicular on one side, as already described, it receives an impulse in aid of its gravitation from the action of attraction and repulsion of their different poles exerted by the bar magnets on the electrified coil of wire forming the bob of the pendulum. When the pendulum moves to the other side the disc falls to the opposite side, and the current of electricity being thus broken the pendulum returns by the action of gravity alone. In this manner, Mr Bain maintains the oscillations of the pendulum, which thus

C

becomes the prime mover of the clock, and by simple mechanical adaptations is made to drive the three index wheels. Mr Bain's invention, however, does not end here, for by a very ingenious contrivance he can make the principal pendulum clock keep in motion as many as twenty or thirty other clocks which will keep exact time with itself.

"Mr Bain has contrived several methods of connecting the pendulum with the wheels of the clock, and one in particular, where the connection is maintained without contact and consequently without friction. These were explained to the meeting as was also the plan which Mr Bain has in view for making the electric clocks strike the hours.

"The great advantage which these clocks present over those of ordinary construction is that they never require to be wound up. Their accuracy as time-keepers will depend on two points—the uniformity of the electric current obtained from the ground and the perfect compensation of the pendulum for temperature and moisture, an element of importance in the construction of all clocks. So far as experience goes, report speaks favourably of the performance and uniformity of the electric current, and if this point is established Mr Bain's invention must be regarded as completely successful, and his clocks will be introduced into general use.

"It was mentioned that Sir Thomas Brisbane, whose eminence as an astronomical observer is well known, has ordered one of these clocks from Mr Bain in order to institute a series of observations upon its qualities as a time-keeper. This, however, has chiefly in view its fitness for nice or astronomical purposes, as from the trials already made for six or eight months past, it would appear that the Electric Clock keeps as accurate time as our house clocks on the common construction, and is stated to be no more expensive.

"Thanks were voted to Mr Bain for exhibiting the Clock and to Mr Bryson for describing it."

" Society of Arts Meeting held on 12th May 1845—Mr Alexander Bain, the patentee, exhibited and described his Electro-Magnetic Telegraph.

" One of the varieties of this telegraph was exhibited in action. This was stated to be by far the simplest of the electro telegraphs which have been invented. It acts by means of a single wire, and can be laid down at the rate of about £50 per mile, besides the telegraph apparatus which will cost about £12 for each station. When any signal is given it is known at all the stations instantaneously, and by a simple contrivance it is known to which or from which the message has been sent. One of these telegraphs is to be shortly laid down on the railway from Edinburgh to Glasgow. Mr Bain also explained the way in which he made the discovery leading to the simplification of the electric telegraph."

" The public is aware of Mr Bain's invention of the electric clock which derives its motive power from currents of electricity in the earth. Mr Bain has invented and patented another kind of electric clock, which was exhibited here on Wednesday by the inventor to a few scientific gentlemen, the clock being in Glasgow and the pendulum in Edinburgh. By means of the electric telegraph constructed along the railway by Mr Bain, he intimated his wish that the pendulum at the other end of the line should be put in motion. The answer was given with the rapidity of thought, for the machinery in the clock instantly began to move, though the two were forty-six miles apart. They were joined by means of the wire of the telegraph in such a manner that by a current of electricity the machinery in the clock at Glasgow was made to move correctly according to the vibration of the electrical pendulum in Edinburgh.

" The same result could at one and the same time have been produced in a clock at the Linlithgow and another at the Falkirk stations as well as at the Glasgow terminus; that is to say, the Edinburgh pendulum could have equally regulated all the three which would thus have moved together like one machine. In like manner, Mr Bain informed us, were the telegraphic wires extended over the whole of Scotland, and every railway station or town on the line had its own electric clock, the pendulum at Edinburgh would propel and regulate them all. And still further, were England and Scotland united in one grand chronometrical alliance, a single electric pendulum of this description placed in the Observatory at Greenwich would give the astronomical time correctly throughout the whole country."—*Edinburgh Evening Courant*, 4th May 1846.

"About nine o'clock on Friday night, Mr Bain, patentee for electric clocks, and who lately erected one in Hanover Street, had occasion to leave his workshop, which is situated in an upper flat in Hanover Street, to go to the Post Office for a few minutes. On his return he found the door on the pass key in the same manner in which he left, and on entering was amazed to find that the premises had been robbed of several gold and silver watches, also a splendid chronometer enclosed in a mahogany case, valued at £50. It is not known by what access the thieves got to the premises. It is supposed that they entered by a skylight window from the roof which was open, as Mr Bain had not observed it open during the day. Information was given to the police, who are on an active outlook for the depredators. The loss sustained is thought to be upwards of £130."—*Edinburgh Evening Courant*, 10th April 1845.

BAIN, GEORGE. Upper Wynd, Brechin, 1837.

BAIN, JOHN. Stirling, 1786.

"A WATCH LOST.—On Saturday there was lost within the town of Stirling, a silver watch with the proprietor's name printed within the case, having a steel chain and cut ciphered seal, maker's name, Beaunett, London, No. 6593. Any person who has the same is desired to return it to John Bain, watchmaker in Stirling, who will see the person properly rewarded. It is entreated that watchmakers and others will keep the marks above mentioned in their eye and stop it if offered to sale."—*Caledonian Mercury*, 6th September 1786.

BAIRD, WALTER. Argyll Street, Glasgow, 1848.

BAIRNSFATHER, ALEXANDER. Edinburgh, 1780-87.

Booked apprentice to James Howden 22nd March 1780. Discharged of his indentures 27th March 1787.

BALLANTINE, WILLIAM. Edinburgh, 1798.

"Booked apprentice to George Skelton 12th June 1798. Discharged of his indentures 4th August 1804."— *E. H. Records.*

BALLANTYNE, JAMES. Edinburgh, 1756.

"Booked apprentice to Thomas Hall, Canongate, 14th October 1756."—*C. H. Records.*

BALLANTYNE, ——. High Street, Paisley, 1846.

BALLANTYNE, WILLIAM. Edinburgh, 1778-1806.

"Lost, a silver watch, maker's name, Gibson, Alnwick, No. 146. It was dropped between Corstorphine and Edinburgh on the 8th curt. Any person who has found the same will please return it to William Ballantyne, clock and watch maker, Head of Canongate, who will reward them handsomely."—*Edinburgh Evening Courant*, 15th February 1798.

"To be sold by public roup on Thursday the 27th January 1778, the first story and south garret of a tenement in the west side of the Pleasance, a little above the Cowgate Port, and nearly opposite to Mr Macfarlane's stable. The first story of this tenement is possessed by Mr Ballantyne, watchmaker, who pays £7, 4s. of rent."—*Caledonian Mercury*, 26th November 1777.

BALSILLIE, ANDREW. Crossgate, Cupar-Fife, 1835.

BANFF—Notices regarding the Kirk Clock of the Burgh of, from 1626 to 1886.

25*th March* 1626.—"William Williamson, on his admission as freeman and burgess, binds himself to rule and hold the knok in temper sufficiently daily in time coming during his health and abiding in the town on payment to him of 20 merkis yearly, and gif the knok happen to be ane quarter ane hour out of temper the said William discharges ane quarter's payment of his ordinary fee."

1628.—"Payments occur in Treasurer's accounts for handling of the knok of the sums of £9 Scots and 100 merks, this last being paid to the schoolmaster."

17th June 1721.—"Orders the Provest and Bailie Sym to speak to John Reid, clockmaker, to notice the kirk clock and report what will be needful to cause her right."

18th May 1724.—"Paid to John Reid, watchmaker, £80, 10s. Scots for the kirk clock."

1761.—"The steeple of the church is reported in a ruinous state. The magistrates appoint the bells to to be taken down and likewise the clock."

23rd April 1762.—"Lord Findlater agrees to give 120 guineas for an entry on all lands and heritages belonging to his son Lord Deskford holding of the town, and offers to give 40 guineas more in a present to furnish a clock for the new steeple, or to finish the steeple if the voluntary contributions fall short."

12th December 1766.—"John Marr, mason, cleared [finished] anent his work at the steeple. The west dial of the steeple clock has hour and minute hands, two others have only hour hand. A thirty-hour clock has been preferred to an eight-day one. A bell of 30 inches diameter to be put up in the steeple for striking the hours and to be made in London."

5th December 1767.—"The town's funds are greatly exhausted this year by repairs on the harbour and other public works and purchasing a clock and bell, which, with the expenses of the dial plates and putting up, cost above £160 Sterling."

1786.—"Keeping the clock in repairs, £60."

1830.—"Valued this year at £15."

1886.—"Salary of keeper of clock, £3, 3s."

From the *Annals of Banff*, New Spalding Club Series.

BANNERMAN, GILBERT. Banff, 1821.

"Marjory Bannerman or Gardiner, wife of William Gardiner at Battle, served Heir General to her father, Gilbert Bannerman, watchmaker, Banff, dated 28th February 1821. Recorded 5th March 1821.—*Services of Heirs.*

BARCLAY, DAVID. Montrose, about 1830.

BARCLAY, HUGH. Edinburgh, 1717-49.

"Son to the deceast George Barclay, minister of the Gospel at Sprouston, was booked apprentice to Thomas Gordon, Edinburgh, 11th April 1717. Compeared on 5th August 1727 and presented his essay, viz., an eight-day pendulum clock and a lock to the door, which was found a well-wrought essay, etc., and was accordingly admitted an ordinary freeman clock and watch maker of the Incorporation of Hammermen, Edinburgh. His essay masters were Alexander Brownlee and George Aitken. His essay was made in Patrick Gordon's shop."

27th November 1731.—"There being a complaint given in by William Sherriff, apprentice to Hugh Barclay, against his master for want of work and craving to be transferred. The house names Deacon Boswell, Deacon Bunkill, Walter Davidson, Alexander Brown, James Wilson, Thomas and Patrick Gordon, John Brown, clockmaker, and Alexander Brand, with the Deacon and Boxmaster, to be a committee to consider the above complaint and ordains Hugh Barclay to see and answer the complaint against this day sennight."

18th January 1732.—"The house being met, they continue the Committee on Hugh Barclay's apprentice complaint with the addition of David Hodge, and they to report their opinion on betwixt and the next quarter day."

12th February 1732.—"The Committee upon the complaint of Hugh Barclay's apprentice and the answers thereto, gave in their report, that they had considered into the same and examined both master and apprentice. And that they had found the apprentice to have been an idle inclined boy and that his complaint was not altogether right founded. And that therefore they had enjoined him to return back to his master and serve him faithfully the remaining time of his indentures, otherwise he should have no title to his freedom (of the Hammermen Incorporation) and recommended to his master to give all the insight and encouragement imaginable. The House approves of the Committee's procedure yairin."—*E. H. Records.*

The City Treasurer ordered to pay Hugh Barclay £2, 8s. for mending the clock in the Tron Kirk steeple (*see* p. 24, *History of the Tron Kirk*, by Rev. Dugald Butler).

Hugh Barclay died 20th June 1749.

BARCLAY, PETER. Lochwinnoch, 1706.

His name appears as one of the subscribers for the work entitled *The travels of true godliness from the beginning of the world to this present day*, by Benjamin Heach, Glasgow, printed by Archibald M'Lean for Alexander Weir, bookseller in Paisley. This volume is believed to be the first work published in Paisley.

BARCLAY, THOMAS. High Street, Montrose, 1811-22.

"Thomas Barclay, watchmaker, Montrose, served Heir of Provision General to his father, James Barclay, Mason there, dated 5th December 1811. Recorded 17th December 1811.—*Services of Heirs.*

BARR, FIDELE and THOMAS. 25 Greenside, Edinburgh, 1850.

BARR, MARK. High Street, Lanark, 1836.

BARR, THOMAS. Lanark, died 27th April 1890, aged 71 years.

BARR, WILLIAM. Muir Wynd, Hamilton, 1808-37.

"FIVE GUINEAS REWARD.—Whereas early on Tuesday morning, the 13th curt., the shop of Wm. Barr, watch and clock maker in Hamilton, was broken into and nine watches carried off, makers' names and numbers as follows :—

D. Williamson, London, No. 371.
N. Preston, London, No. 6013.
B. Richardson, London, No. 5577.
A. Anderson, London, No. 243.

" A hunting watch with a small glass by Richardson, London. A close hunting watch, Wm. Barr, Hamilton ; a new watch, Edmonds, flat chapter dial, and other two watches, names and numbers unknown.

" This is to give notice that whoever will give such information to Wm. Barr, in Hamilton, as will lead to the detection of the above articles will receive five guineas' reward and no questions asked."—*Glasgow Courier*, 15th September 1808.

BARRIE, ANDREW. 3 South St Andrew Street, Edinburgh, 1840; died 1907.

" The board of directors of the Edinburgh and Leith Gas Light Company are about to confer a boon on the inhabitants of the New Town and the Public generally, by lighting gratuitously the handsome clock lately erected by Mr Barrie at his premises in South Saint Andrew Street. From its elevated position in one of the greatest thoroughfares and its proximity to the railway terminus, this clock will no doubt be found more generally useful than any other public time-piece in that part of the city."—*Edinburgh Evening Courant*, 11th November 1850.

BARNETT, JOHN. Nicolson Street, Edinburgh, 1846.

BARRON, JOHN, Aberdeen, 1801 ; died 30th May 1852, aged 87.

BARRON, JOHN, & SON. 11 Nether-Kirkgate, Aberdeen, 1836.

BARRON & GREY. 11 Nether-Kirkgate, Aberdeen, 1846.

BATCHELOR, WILLIAM. Dundee, 1816.

BAXTER, JOHN. 72 South Street and Barrack Street, Perth, 1841-43.

BAXTER, JOHN. Dunkeld, 1836.

BAXTER, JOHN. Edinburgh, 1797.

BAYNE OR BANE, JOHN. Stirling, 1777-90.

BEGG, JOHN. New Town, Glasgow, 1800.

" John Begg, Watch-maker, Glasgow, Agent for the Gum Company, has got a fresh cargo of that well-known article for printfields. It is unnecessary to say anything with respect to its superior quality to any hitherto imported, the quick sales are sufficient. His customers may depend on being regularly supplied. Those who wish to purchase should apply as soon as possible. Terms of sale, above ten pounds, a Bill of two months; under, ready money."—*Glasgow Courier*, 17th May 1800.

BEGG, JOHN. Edinburgh, 1804-7.

"Mr John Begg, watchmaker to His Majesty, respectfully informs the Nobility, Gentry, and the Public, that he has commenced business in the Watch and clock line, in his chronometer workshop at the King's Arms, Parliament Square, Edinburgh, where may be had on the most approved principles, Time-pieces, viz., Longitudinal to go at sea, Duplex and detached escapements with ruby cylinders, going fusees, of which he has a large assortment. Likewise a variety of portable time-pieces in imitation of marble, with or without movements. J. B. was regularly bred to the business, having served his apprenticeship with a pupil of the celebrated George Graham, London, and since improved under the first workmen in that city. He had the honour of being introduced to His Majesty, who is, without exception, the first amateur in Europe, as also into the presence of all the Royal Family, in consequence of a curious watch invented by himself, and was immedi-ately dignified with His Majesty's authority appointing him his watchmaker in Scotland. The public can have any kind of clock or watch, as he has the making within himself, and has some of the first hands in Europe employed for this purpose." — *Edinburgh Evening Courant*, 7th July 1804.

"John Begg, the only watchmaker to His Majesty for Scotland, announces he has removed his chronometer workshop from Parliament Square to 17 Leith Street Terrace. Time-pieces, viz., Longitudinal to go at sea, Duplex and detached escapements with ruby cylinders, going fusees, and also a variety of portable time-pieces. J. B. calls attention to a new and singularly constructed watch, his sole invention, which some of the most competent judges admire as an uncommon production, being unrivalled by any professional artist whatever."— *Ibid.*, 1806.

These advertisements bring out better than anything else the pretensions and recommendations of this individual. Overshowed by his near neighbours, such as Thomas Reid, James Gray, and others, who, being all members of the Incorporation of Hammermen,

PARLIAMENT SQUARE, EDINBURGH, IN THE EIGHTEENTH CENTURY.

The centre of the Clockmaking art during that period.

[To face page 42.

would no doubt look on this man as an interloper, he was only saved from legal proceedings by his royal appointment, which they dared not challenge. John Begg's thoughts about such a society are curiously brought out in the evidence that was led in a dispute that arose in Aberdeen in 1806. Previous to that date clockmakers were not fully under the jurisdiction of the Hammermen there, and it was not till that year that full control was obtained over them. This was not got without some opposition, and the losing side having consulted an Edinburgh lawyer, he, in turn, sent a communication from John Begg as being an expert, and well able to give an opinion. Begg states that there are few living that are better acquainted than himself with the trade monopoly of the Hammermen Incorporation, in consequence of their charter enabling them to force and compel watchmakers to join them.[1] He then goes on to say that "business is kept out of the country in consequence of the heavy dues exacted, and that the trade was driven into the hands of those who were not trained, so that there is scarcely a cloth shop or hardware shop that does not deal in watches, who know no more about a watch than a cow does of a new coined shilling, and that his trade being an art should be above the jurisdiction of any trade and not be shackled by any incorporated body." This plain speaking must have given offence to his fellow craftsmen, and may account for his short tenancy—one year—of the shop in Parliament Square. The Leith Street Terrace address is the last trace of him here, the surmise being that the opposition of the trade made his business efforts an uphill fight, and that he removed from Edinburgh shortly after 1807

BEGGS, Thomas. 145 Trongate, Glasgow, 1822-41.

BELL, Alexander. St Andrews, 1785.

"OLD ST ANDREWS.—The little collection of burghal antiquities in the Council Chambers has been

[1] In connection with this compulsion of watchmakers, it will be seen in the notes on Dallaway & Son, page 100, that no craft was favoured more than another.

recently enriched by three interesting additions. The first of these is a receipt, or, to be more strictly accurate, two receipts of different dates, written on the same page of paper, acknowledging payment of salary for two consecutive half years for looking after the town clock. In the town's safe there are many receipts, but this one is of special interest, because it is entirely in the handwriting of Bailie Bell, and proves that for a time he was keeper of the town clock, a fact which escaped the notice of Southey in writing the life of the Bailie's famous son, Dr Andrew Bell, the founder of the Madras College. Southey tells that the father, Alexander Bell, was a man of extraordinary abilities, and having acquired no inconsiderable degree of mechanical and practical science, added to his original trade of barber that of clock and watch maker, and regulated by observations the timepieces in the public library of the University. Surely the town clock was of much more importance to the public than the time-pieces in the University library. Bell was a bailie, but at that time, and long afterwards, magistrates and councillors were not debarred from serving the city for payment. The payment for looking after the town clock was three pounds sterling a year, a consider-able sum in those days, when the assistant teacher in the grammar school only received seven pounds a year.

"Although there is an intervening period of fully six months between the respective dates of the bailie's two receipts, it seems impossible to avoid the conclusion that both were drawn up and signed at the same time, for not only are they written on the same piece of paper, but that piece of paper has been folded and preserved as a voucher with this endorsature: 'No. 61, Bailie Bell's receipt for £3 sterling.' Why, it may be asked, did he write two receipts instead of one. The reason is more transparent than recondite. When the assistant teacher already referred to gave a receipt for a quarter's salary, £1, 15s., no stamp was required, but when he gave one for a half year's salary, £3, 10s., it bore an impressed twopenny stamp. The bailie was economical, hence the following reduplication :—

"'St Andrews, 10*th* *June* 1785.—Received from Mr Andrew Watson, Factor to the Town of St Andrews, the sum of one pound ten shillings for keeping the Town Clock from Martinmas Jai vijc. and eighty-four to Whitsunday Jai vijc. and eighty-five, and the same is discharged by Alex. Bell.'

"'St Andrews, 21*st* *December* 1785.—Received from Mr Andrew Watson, Factor to the Town of St Andrews, the sum of one pound ten shillings for keeping the Town Clock from Whitsunday seventeen hundred and eighty-five years to Martinmas same year, which is discharged by Alex. Bell.'

"The salary which was due to Bailie Bell at the time of his death was drawn by his daughter Agnes, who in 1792, with her sister Janet, sold the picturesque old house in which they had been reared. It is said to have consisted of two stories with an outer staircase supported by wooden pillars and a wooden projection into the street. The site is now occupied by the *Citizen* Office."—J. H. F., *St Andrews Citizen*, 20th February 1904.

BELL, ALEXANDER. Glasgow, 1791.

BELL, ANDREW. Haddington, 1769-90.

BELL, DAVID. Stirling, 1801-50.

BELL, HENRY. Canongate, Edinburgh, 1660.

BELL, JAMES. 32 Potterrow, Edinburgh, 1850.

BELL, JAMES. Cambusnethan, 1770-90.

BELL, JOHN. Canongate, Jedburgh, 1837.

BELL, MATTHEW. Edinburgh, 1680.
    Booked apprentice to Richard Mills, 1680.

BELL, WILLIAM, son of above. Cambusnethan, 1790-1820.

BELL, WILLIAM. Bridge Street, Wick, 1837.

BELL, ——. Camnethan, 1700.

BENSON, DUNCAN. Glasgow, 1843.

BERRY, JAMES. 52 Castle Street, Aberdeen, 1836-46.

BERRY, James.   Stonehaven, 1840.

BERRY, William.   Seal Cutter, Edinburgh, 1750.

"First stair below the Earl of Murray's lodging, Canongate, Edinburgh, cuts all manner of Seals on Stone, Steel, Silver, and Gold, or any other metal, after the best and neatest manner, where gentlemen and ladies may have their Arms, Crests, Cyphers, or Heads cut to pleasure, and all at the lowest rates.

"*N.B.*—He also cuts and sells all manner of Scots Pebbles at reasonable rates."—*Edinburgh Evening Courant*, 4th January 1750."

BEVERIDGE, George.   Claymire, Kettle, Fife, 1799-1842.

"Betsy Wemyss or Duff, Sinclairtown, served Heir Portioner to her grandfather, George Beveridge, Clockmaker, Shiells, Kettle, Fife. Dated 21st September 1842. Recorded 6th October 1842."—*Services of Heirs.*

BEVERIDGE, Robert.   Kirkcaldy, 1837.

"Betsy Wemyss or Duff, Sinclairtown, served Heir Portioner General to her uncle, Robert Beveridge, Clockmaker, Kirkcaldy. Dated 10th May 1843. Recorded 29th May 1843."—*Services of Heirs.*

BEVERIDGE, Robert.   Newburgh, Fife, 1835.

BINNY or BINNIE, Daniel.   Edinburgh, 1747-79.

"Son to the deceast James Binny of Garnclare, was booked apprentice to Andrew Dickie, watchmaker, Edinburgh, 11th June 1747."

23rd June 1757.—"A complaint having been made that Daniel Binny carried on the clock and watch making trade under pretence of being servant to Mrs Geddes, relict of James Geddes, clock and watch maker. The Incorporation recommended to the Convener to inquire at Mrs Geddes if or not Binny works to her as her servant, and, if not, to desire Binny desist from working within the privileges of this city, and upon his refusing so to do, to give proper orders for prosecuting him before the Magistrates."

6th August 1757.—"Daniel Binny, late apprentice to Andrew Dickie, clock and watch maker, presented a bill to be admitted freeman clock and watch maker in this

Incorporation, which being received, he was admitted to an essay, and essay masters appointed to him. The essay to be presented between and the first of January next to come. And this indulgence of so long a delay was granted to him in regard that the essay could not be well finished in shorter time. But declaring that this indulgence should be no precedent in time coming to the members of the other arts whose essays can be finished in shorter time, Daniel Binny made payment of £5 sterling as the first half of his upset money, and is to pay the other half at his admission."

4th February 1758.—"Compeared and presented his essay, being a watch movement made and finished in his own shop, as Andrew Dickie, landlord, and Robert Clidsdale, William Balfour, and Alexander Brand, essay masters to the said Daniel Binny, declared, which essay was found to be well wrought, etc., and he was therefor admitted a freeman clock and watch maker of the Incorporation, and he paid five pounds sterling as the last half of his upset dues."—*E. H. Records.*

"All persons addebted to the deceast Andrew Dickie, watchmaker, are hereby desired to pay what they owed him to Daniel Binny, watchmaker, his nephew and sole heir and executor, or to David Lindsay, writer in Edinburgh, who has full power to receive and discharge the same.

"Daniel Binny, who was educated by his uncle to the business, has moved from his house behind the City Guard to the house lately possessed by Mr Dickie in Wilson's Land, Lawnmarket, where the former customers of Mr Dickie, who are pleased to employ him, and his own customers, of whose favour he hopes the continuance, will be served with care and despatch."— *Caledonian Mercury,* 18th May 1765.

"Daniel Binny, clock and watch maker in Edinburgh, and nephew of the deceased Mr Andrew Dickie, clock and watch maker there, thanks his customers for former favours, and begs leave to acquaint them that he has moved at Whitsunday last from Mr Dickie's late shop in Wilson's Land, Lawnmarket, to a shop within the Nether Bow, north side of the street, where such as are pleased to favour him with their employment or commissions will be well and duly served with clock or watch work in all the different branches.

"It is hoped that all persons addebted to the said deceased Mr Dickie, or the said Daniel Binny, his heir and executor, either by accompt or otherwise, will pay up what they are owing either to the said Daniel Binny or to David Lindsay, writer in Edinburgh, who has power to receive and discharge the same, and thereby prevent the disagreeable necessity of a pursuit if this notice is not speedily complied with."—*Edinburgh Evening Courant*, 8th June 1767.

BINNY & GORDON. Nether Bow, Edinburgh, 1774.

BISHOP, JAMES. Musselburgh, 1787.

BISHOP, JAMES. Foot of Pleasance, Edinburgh, 1794.

BISSET, DAVID. Perth, 1765.

BISSET, WILLIAM. Perth, 1808.

BISSET, WILLIAM. Dundee, 1781.

BLACK, ANDREW. Leslie, 1837.

BLACK, ANDREW. Colinsburgh, 1837.

BLACK, ANDREW. Alloa, 1830-72.

BLACK, ANDREW. 146 Saltmarket, Glasgow, 1818.

BLACK, ANDREW. Leslie, Fife, 1838.

BLACK, DAVID. Colinsburgh, Fife, 1830.

BLACK, JAMES. Links, Kirkcaldy, 1820-37.

BLACK, JAMES. Church Street, Berwick-on-Tweed, 1836.

BLACK, JOHN. 16 Longacre, Aberdeen, 1846.

BLACK, JOHN. Edinburgh, 1771-77.

"Booked apprentice to William Downie, 17th July 1771; required to serve out the remainder of his time with Norman Macpherson, 18th February 1777."—*E. H. Records.*

BLACK, THOMAS. 17 Castle Street, Dumfries, 1837.

BLACKIE, GEORGE. Musselburgh, 1796-1844.

The author of these notes is in possession of an eight-day clock made by this maker. Made for an ancestor in the year 1800, the receipt given on payment, which is preserved also, shows that seven guineas was the cost.

"On Monday night Mr George Blackie, watchmaker, Musselburgh, presented a handsome clock to the Free Church congregation of that place. Mr Blackie is one of the oldest men in the congregation, being about 70 years of age. 'And that he might live to finish the clock' has been of late with him a frequent wish."—*The Witness*, 21st August 1844.

"George Blackie, watchmaker, New North Parish, Edin., was married to Isobel, Lady Yester's Parish, daughter of the deceased David Easter, Musselburgh, 22 Decr. 1795."—*Edinburgh Marriage Register*.

BLACKIE, JOHN.   Meadow Bank, Edinburgh, 1848.

"ROYAL SCOTTISH SOCIETY OF ARTS, 27*th November* 1848.—At a meeting held on this date there was read a description of an electric clock on an improved principle by Mr John Blackie, electric clock maker, Meadow Bank Station, North British Railway, Edinburgh.

"The clock was exhibited in action. This clock was stated to be an improvement on Mr Bain's electric clock, both in the mode of adjusting the permanent magnets and in the mode of breaking and re-establishing the circuit; the break being less liable to oxidise. It was also stated that the electric current acted to greater advantage on the coil of the pendulum. Mr Blackie also claimed as new the simple train of the movement, which consists of very few wheels, and he also claimed a delicate method of adjusting the length of the pendulum."

BLACKIE, J. R., 36 Bridge Street, Leith, 1850.

BLACKWOOD, THOMAS.   Bridgend, Kinnoul, Perth, 1798.

BLAIKIE, WILLIAM.   Edinburgh, 1726.

"William Blaikie, watchmaker, married Margaret Swinton, 13 Novr. 1726."—*Edinburgh Marriage Register*.

BLAIR, ANDREW.   Edinburgh, 1775.

Booked apprentice to James Howden 27th December 1775.

BLAIR, JAMES.   Kilwinning, 1836.

BLAIR, THOMAS.   Perth, 1746.

BONNAR, MRS.   Portsburgh, Edinburgh, 1802.

"To be sold by Public Roup within the Royal Exchange Coffee-house upon Friday, the 5th day of February 1802, at one o'clock afternoon, that tenement of houses on the north side of Portsburgh with a large area behind, possessed by Mrs Bonnar, watchmaker, and others, yielding £20 per annum."—*Edinburgh Evening Courant*, 1st February 1802.

BONNAR, ROBERT.   Dunfermline, 1733, page 254.

BOOKLESS, PETER.   Canongate, Edinburgh, 1798.

BOOTH, G. & SON.   36 Union Street, Aberdeen, 1820-46.

BOOTH, JAMES.   Auchinblae, 1837.

BOOTH, JOHN.   41 Upper Kirkgate, Aberdeen, 1820-46.

BOVERICK, SOBIESKI.   Edinburgh, 1768.

"S. Boverick, watchmaker from London, having had the honour of exhibiting his collection of miniature curiosities to the nobility some few years since, thinks it is his duty to acquaint them that he works family hair with a needle in so extraordinary a manner that the newness of the taste and the delicacy of the work have been admired by all who have seen it. Specimens of which, with the prices, may be seen at his lodgings, Mrs Wilson, Anchor Close, second story, Edinburgh. Where likewise may be seen the above-mentioned curiosities."—*Caledonian Mercury*, 3rd September 1768.

Admitted a member of Lodge St David, Edinburgh, 20th September 1768.

BOWDINGIS OR BOWDOWINGIS, ADRIAN.   Edinburgh, 1595.—*Edinburgh Baptismal Register*.

BOWER, JOHN.   Kirreymuir, 1802.

BOWERS, ANDREW.   Cupar-Fife, 1842.

BOWIE, JAMES.   Kirkcaldy, 1825.

BOWIE, JOHN.   Stirling, 1811.

BOWIE, WILLIAM.   Canongate, Edinburgh, 1719.

"Admitted a freeman clock and watch maker in Canongate Hammermen, 11th September 1719, his essay being ane balance of ane watch and ane pendulum spring clock."—*C. H. Records*.

BOWIE, Kirkcaldy, 1779.

"WATCH LOST.—Lost a few days ago between Gallatown and Kinghorn, a silver watch, maker's name, James Gabyd, London, No. 21968. Whoever has found the same may apply to Mr Bowie, watchmaker, Kirkcaldy, who will give a suitable reward."

BOYD, JAMES. Cupar-Fife, 1818.

"Stolen on the 23rd instant a plain gold watch, maker's name, Charles Walker, Coventry, No. 3290. Anyone stopping her will be handsomely rewarded by applying to Mr Boyd, watchmaker, Cupar-Fife."— *Edinburgh Advertiser*, 30th June 1818.

BRACKENRIDGE, ALEXANDER. Market Lane, Kilmarnock, 1820.

BRACKENRIDGE, JAMES. Kilmaurs, 1726.

BRAND, ALEXANDER. Edinburgh, 1711-57.

Married Margaret Tarbet, 23rd Nov. 1711.

"Admitted a freeman clock and watch maker in Canongate Hammermen, 12th April 1716, his essay being ane balance of ane watch and ane pendulum spring clock."

"There was stolen out of a gentleman's chamber on the 27th May last, an old silver watch and pendulum, with hour and minute hands, made by Andrew Brown, Edinburgh, having a loose pendant and a ribbon instead of a chain. Any person who can give notice thereof to Mr James M'Ewen, bookseller, or Mr Brand, watchmaker, in the Mint, so as the watch may be recovered, shall have a suitable reward and no questions asked."— *Edinburgh Evening Courant*, 1st June 1721.

29th December 1726.—"The which day the general committee convened, the Deacon laid before them that my Lord Provost of Edinburgh had called for him and told him that he was resolved to apply to the Incorporation, by way of letter, that the Incorporation would do him the favour, and make him the compliment of receiving into the Incorporation Alexander Brand, Clockmaker, an freeman among them though not entitled yairto, but more as a favour done him. And yairfor craved the committee's opinion whether he should receive the said letter in order to lay it before the whole house. The committee by plurality of votes are of the opinion that the Deacon should receive the said letter from my Lord Provost and lay the same before the whole Incorporation at ye next meeting.

3rd January 1727.—"The Deacon, conform to the opinion of the committee at last meeting, produced a letter to the Incorporation from my Lord Provost as follows :—

"EDINBURGH, 30*th* *December* 1726.—Alexander Brand, Clockmaker in the Mint, being very well recommended to me by a great many persons of distinction and good friends to the city, I must give you and the Incorporation the trouble of interceding on his behalf that he may be received as one of your number upon your finding him qualified, and his paying what dues of upset you think reasonable. If the Incorporation is pleased to grant this request, I am very sensible it will be an act of very great generosity and good nature to him, and of condescension to me. I shall always be found to make suitable returns, being sincerely, Sir, the Incorporation's faithful friend and most humble servant, GEORGE DRUMMOND."[1]

"The said letter is directed to Thomas Giffard, Deacon, and his brethren the Incorporation of the Hammermen of Edinburgh :—

"The Deacon yairfor craved the Incorporation's opinion of the said letter, and whether they would grant the favour desired and upon what terms. The Incorporation having taken the same into yair consideration and reasoned yair upon for some time, it is put to ye vote whether they should grant the desire of the Provost's letter by receiving the said Alexander Brand a freeman to ye Incorporation or not. Carried without a contrair vote that the said Alexander Brand shall be received, and yairfor, in compliment to my Lord Provost, they admitted the said Alexander Brand to ane essay, viz.,

[1] This George Drummond, as is well known, was one of the most able Lord Provosts the city of Edinburgh had during the eighteenth century, and his name will always be remembered for the part he took in the erection of the first North Bridge, an enterprise which was productive of much prosperity to the city.

ane eight days' pendulum clock and a lock to the door with a key. The essaymasters are Alexander Brownlie and William Richardson. His essay to be made in John Brown's shop, and presented betwixt and Whitsunday next. He payed the boxmaster £53, 6s. 8d (Scots) as the half of his upset and ten merks as the half of the (Trades) Maiden Hospital, and he is to pay the other half when he presents his essay."

6th April 1727.—"The which day the house being met, compeared Alexander Brand, Clockmaker in Edinburgh, and presented his essay conform to the minutes of January last, viz., ane eight days' pendulum clock and a lock to the door with a key, which was found a well wrought essay, etc."

These extracts from the *E. H. Records* give faithfully a complete account of what was then considered as a most uncommon request, it being almost impossible for an outsider to obtain admission into this close incorporation unless he had either the right by marriage or else had first served an apprenticeship to one of their own number. Two points are brought out in the successful issue, viz., the powerful influence that Lord Provost Drummond had with the craftsmen citizens of Edinburgh, and the popularity and respect Alexander Brand was held in. He appears to have been grateful for the privilege for the clock he made, for his essay was presented by him to the Incorporation, who placed it in the Magdalen Chapel, their meeting place, where it still remains to this day, unfortunately now silent from neglect. The surmise is that Brand died about 1757.

BRAND, JAMES. Edinburgh, 1732-93.

"Son of Robert Brand, wright in Brocklaw, in the shire of Mearns, is booked apprentice to Alexander Brand, Clock and Watch maker, 5th August 1732."— *E. H. Records.*

BRAND, JOHN. Dumfries, 1790-1802.

BRANDER, JAMES. Keith; died 11th March 1835, aged 47.

BREAKENRIG, ALEXANDER. Edinburgh, 1800-26. *See* p. 55.

BREAKENRIG, JAMES. Lawnmarket, Edinburgh, 1802-6.

Son of Robert; succeeded to his father's business in the Grassmarket, which he removed to the Lawnmarket; but at what date is unknown. He, different from the father, was regularly apprenticed to the trade, as on the 12th February 1802 he compeared and presented his essay, being a clock movement begun and finished in his own shop in presence of David Murray, landlord, James Howden, Robert Hinmers, and Ebenezer Annan, essay masters, as they declared, and he was accordingly admitted a freeman clock and watch maker in the Incorporation of Hammermen, Edinburgh.

"Lost at the Queensferry, on Monday 12th of June, a silver watch, maker's name, Charles Thompson, London, No. 11336. Whoever will restore the same to James Breakenrig, watchmaker, Lawnmarket, Edinburgh, or to John Brown, innkeeper, Queensferry, shall receive a suitable reward."—*Edinburgh Evening Courant*, 2nd July 1802.

James Breakenrig died in 1806, the business being continued on till 1817 by his widow.

"UNCLAIMED WATCHES.—There was found among the effects of the late Mrs Breakenrig, watchmaker, Lawnmarket, several silver watches given in to her to be repaired, some of which have never been applied for and the owners are unknown. If therefore those to whom these watches belong do not apply for them to William Lothian, writer, Milne's Court, within one month from this date, they will be sold for behoof of the deceased creditors."—*Edinburgh Advertiser*, 16th January 1818.

BREAKENRIG, JOHN. West Port, Edinburgh, 1767-1800.

This we take to be the brother of Robert Breakenrig, Grassmarket. It is probable that he was employed by his brother, and on the latter's death was forced to commence work on his own behalf, for his brother had left a son, James, to carry on his business. Not having the qualifications of Robert in the way of special services to further his interests, the only other way was to become a freeman Hammerman, and he therefore compeared on 14th November 1767 and presented a bill craving to be admitted a clock and watch maker freeman in Portsburgh. This application was favourably received and his essay and essay masters were appointed. He compeared on 30th January 1768 and presented his essay, being the movement of a clock, begun, made, and finished in his own shop, in presence of James Hutton, landlord, John Chalmers, and John Safely, essaymasters, as they declared, etc.

He commenced business in what came to be known as No. 107 West Port, which he carried on till about 1800. Probably dying about this date, the business was continued by his son, Alexander Breakenrig, till 1826. This shop had as a sign above the door a large gilded watch with the following : " Established 1768." In 1826 the business fell into the hands of James Webster (q.v.), who carried it on till 1868, thus continuing a connection which had lasted nearly a century.

" EXCHEQUER CHAMBERS, 15*th May* 1804.—Notice is hereby given to all concerned that Margaret Chalmers, sometime spouse and afterwards relict of John Breakenrig, clock and watch maker in Portsburgh of Edinburgh, has applied to the Right Hon. the Barons for a gift of ' Ultimus Haeres ' of the estate and effects of the deceased Janet Kelly, shop-keeper in North Leith."

BREAKENRIG, ROBERT. Edinburgh, 1757-1762.

This unusual surname admits of quite a variation in the way of spelling. On a large number of dials it is to be found as Brakenrig, Braikenrig, Brackenrig, Breakenrig, and Breakenridge, this second last being the usual spelling of at least two of the family. The surname occurs in the *E. H. Records* as early as 1677 when one Charles Breakenrig is allowed a sum of £12 (Scots) as his yearly pension. What his trade or craft was does not appear, and there is no mention of the name until the year 1757, when Robert Breakenrig comes into authentic history. We therefore commence with what is to be found concerning him as he is really the first of the family known as clockmaker.

5th February 1757.—" On this day there was given in a complaint against Robert Breakenrig for working within the privileges of the city, being an unfreeman, and he was desired to desist from working, and in case of refusal to give proper orders for prosecuting him before the magistrates."

7th May 1757.—" Robert Breakenrig had, during the late press for land forces into his majestey's service, produced a discharge bearing that he had served as a soldier in the late war, and which, the magistrates were of opinion, not only protected him from being adjudged into his majestey's service, but also entitled him to the freedom of any incorporation."—*E. H. Records.*

He was safe under this " permit," but had to pay what was known as stallenger's dues, generally a sum of £2 sterling yearly. Thomas Reid, in his treatise on *Clock and Watch Making*, refers to him as being an excellent worker, and notes that he made a small spring clock with a duplex escapement a few years after Throut's treatise was published. Might we not surmise that Breakenrig had stumbled on the same improvement without knowing the value of his discovery. The last mention that I have been able to discover occurs in an advertisement in the *Edinburgh Evening Courant* of the 19th July 1762.

" Stolen or lost at Hamilton, a silver watch, curved round the border of the plate between the figures, maker's name, Richard Trapp, marked on both the out and inside No. 5696. Whoever has found the said watch and will restore it to Mr Breakenrig, watchmaker in the Grassmarket, Edinburgh, shall be sufficiently rewarded."

BREAKENRIG, ROBIN. Edinburgh, 1761.

BRECKENRIDGE, ALEXANDER. Market Lane, Kilmarnock, 1799.

BRECKENRIDGE, A., & SON. Kilmarnock, 1799-1848.

" He began business in 1799, his premises being in Market Lane on part of the site now occupied by the Market Hotel; in 1836 he removed to King Street, the firm name being A. Breckenridge & Son. Mr Breckenridge died in 1848 and the business was continued by the son and afterwards by a daughter under the same firm name until about 1898."—*Kilmarnock Standard*, 28th May 1913.

BRECKENRIDGE, WILLIAM. King Street, Kilmarnock, 1850.

BREMNER, WILLIAM. High Street, Kirkwall, 1835.

BRIDGES, THOMAS. Edinburgh, 1691.

An Englishman; booked journeyman to Andrew Brown, present boxmaster, on 9th September 1691. He paid 40 shillings and the other dues."—*E. H. Records*.

BRIGGS, ALEXANDER. Edinburgh, 1762.

"Bound apprentice to John Dalgleish, 5th July 1762." —*E. H. Records*.

BROTHERSON & MACKAY. Dalkeith, 1830-44.

BROWN, ALEXANDER. Arcade, Glasgow, 1836.

BROWN, ALEXANDER. Coatbridge, 1847.

BROWN, ALEXANDER & Co. 3 Union Street, Glasgow, 1837-41.

BROWN, ANDREW. Edinburgh, 1665-1712.

"The second day of February 1665. The quilk day, Andro Broun, sone lawfull to umquhil Jon Broun, in Lang Newtone, is booked prentice to Umpra Milne, clock maker."

7th August 1675.—"The quilk day, in presence of the Deacon and brethren, compeared Andrew Brown, Knokmaker, sometime prentice to Humphrey Milne, knokmaker, burgess of Edinburgh, and presented his essay, to wit, ane knok with a watch larum and ane lock upon the door, which was found to be a weill wrought ane essay, able to serve His Majesty's leigis, and yairfor they admitit and received him to be ane ordainary freeman amongst them in his airt and trade of knokmaking. His essay masters Jon Alexander and Jon Callender, his essay was made in Jon Alexander his house. He payet to the boxmaster £100 Scots, etc."

Elected boxmaster or treasurer to the Incorporation of Hammermen, Edinburgh, 14th September 1689.

22nd February 1692.—"The whilk day the Deacon, Boxmaster, and Patrick Drysdaill, John Harvie, and John Alexander, being convened as a committee appointed by the haill house, and having considered the late boxmaster, Andrew Brown, his accompts, and that therein he hath charged himself of £46 of ground annuell, due out of Mylne's land at the New well proceeding Whitsunday 1691, and that he hath only received £10 yairof from Walter Glendenning, one of the tenants, and given his receipt therefor. So that there is resting to him £36, 6s., quilk he has compted for. It is their opinion that the foresaid sum due as ground annuell should be defalked off Andrew Brown's compt, and the present boxmaster appointed to get a decreet against those liable in ground annuell."

17th May 1711.—"The house, by plurality of votes, appoints the boxmaster to lend to Andrew Brown, clockmaker, one thousand pounds (Scots), upon his granting to them an heritable bond, bearing infefment for the annual rent yair out of his cellar. The principal sum to be payable at Martinmas, with a rent from Whitsunday last, and two hundred merks of penalty."

12th April 1712.—"There being a petition given in by Andrew Brown, son to the deceast Andrew Brown, clockmaker, craving the Incorporation would give him some money for defraying his charges to London, and mentioning the great wants, straits, and necessity he lay under, and declaring he should never be more troublesome to the Incorporation. Which being read and considered by the house, they unanimously ordain the boxmaster to give thirty pounds Scots to the said Andrew Brown, to help in manner as mentioned, and take his discharge of the same."—*E. H. Records.*

For further particulars about this able man, see notes on Magdalen Chapel, Clock and Bell, page 246.

In trying to get some contemporary notices about him, two advertisements printed in the *Edinburgh Gazette* of the year 1699, an Edinburgh newspaper of

LONG CASE CLOCK,

In marquetry case. By Andrew
Brown, Edinburgh, 1665-1712. The
property of the Faculty of Advocates.
(See p. 58.)

LONG CASE CLOCK,

In walnut case. By Thomas
Gordon, Edinburgh, 1688-1743.
The property of the Bank of Scot-
land, Edinburgh. (See p. 107.)

exceeding rarity (only one volume is believed to be extant, and that now in private hands), we get a peep at something more than the information contained in the official books of his incorporation.

"Lost between Edinburgh and Dalkeith, a plain silver watch with a shagreen pin'd case, goes with a therm, having the day of the month on the dyal plate hanging on an old flour'd ribbon. Whoever brings the said watch to Andrew Brown, watchmaker in Edinburgh, shall have half a guinea reward."

"James Barrow, aged about twenty, of a low stature, a little pock-marked, speaks the English accent, had on when he went away a short flaxen coll cut wig, in an ordinary habit; run away from his master the nineteenth instant, with a plain gold watch without a christal, with an enambiled dial, the enembling on the figures is broken off, a silver pendulum watch with a minute hand made by William Young, at Charing Cross, London, with a shagreen case, the centre and balance wheels pierced, a plain silver watch and an oval brass watch, with several other things. Whoever can secure the said youth and give notice thereof to Captain Andrew Brown, watchmaker in Edinburgh, shall have two guineas reward."

It will be noticed in the last advertisement that he is designated "Captain." This title he acquired in 1685 when he was made Captain of the Red and Yellow in the Trained Band, which did duty then in guarding and watching the city. This position was bound to have made him a well-known figure in Edinburgh, but he never appears to have sought municipal honours. This duty and attention to his extensive business filled up a useful life till 1711.

In view of the long time he was in business—thirty-five years—it is remarkable how exceeding scarce are specimens of his art. Only three have come under our notice: one being the splendid clock in the lobby of the Advocates' Library; another which was exposed for sale in the window of a dealer in Queen Street, Edinburgh—both these two having cases of beautiful and chaste marquetry; and the third one in possession of a private party in Linlithgow.

BROWN, Charles. Stranraer; died 1844.

BROWN, Charles. 4 Bristo Street, Edinburgh, 1850.

BROWN, Daniel. High Street, Glasgow, 1783.

BROWN, Daniel. Mauchline.

Maker of the clock which was sold on the dispersal of the poet Burns's furniture on 17th April 1834 for £35.

BROWN, David. Edinburgh, 1772-81.

Booked apprentice to James Cowan, 31st October 1772.

BROWN, George. Edinburgh, 1772-1825.

Bound apprentice to James Gray, 3rd December 1772, and discharged of his indentures by him, 22nd June 1779.

1st February 1812.—"Compeared and produced his essay, viz., a clock movement begun, made and finished in his own shop, in presence of James Ramage, landlord, and James Clark, essay masters, as they declared."— *E. H. Records.*

Was in business at Nicolson Street, 1794; head of Canongate, 1804; 92 High Street, 1821. Died 28th March 1825, aged 65 years.

BROWN, George. Linlithgow, 1710. *See* note on Linlithgow Town Clock.

BROWN, George. Airdrie, 1817-37.

BROWN, George. Glasgow, 1830.

BROWN, George B. 38 Shore, Leith, 1836.

BROWN, George. West Port, Arbroath, 1834.

BROWN, James. Elgin, 1726-68.

BROWN, James. Aberdeen, 1720-33. *See* note on Elgin Clocks, page 137.

BROWN, Mrs J. 35 South Bridge Street, Edinburgh, 1837.

BROWN, JOHN. Edinburgh, 1680-1710.

"Son to Andro Broun, Tailor, burgess of Edinburgh, was booked apprentice to Andrew Brown, 21st October 1680."

24th August 1689.—"Compearit John Brown, late prentice to Andrew Brown, clockmaker, burgess of Edinburgh, and presented his essay, viz., a house clock with a watch larum, and locks upon the doors, which was found a well wrought essay, etc. His essay masters were Richard Mills, David Cockburn, and John Alexander. The essay was made in Andrew Brown's shop. He payed to the boxmaster 'ane hundreth' pounds (Scots) for his upset and ten merks for the firelock and bandeliers."

This last refers to a statute issued by the Town Council requiring the various craft incorporations to furnish so many defensive weapons for either watching or defending the city.

24th July 1710.—"The which day the Incorporation of Hammermen being met, they ordain the boxmaster to give to Grisel Dalrymple, relict of John Brown, clockmaker, ten shillings sterling to help her in her present straits."—*E. H. Records.*

BROWN, JOHN. Edinburgh, 1720-50.

21st May 1720.—"Compeared John Brown, son to the deceast John Brown, Clockmaker, and presented his essay, viz., ane eight-day pendulum clock and a lock to the door with a key which was found a weill wrought essay, etc. His essay masters were Patrick Gordon and George Auld. His essay was made in Alexander Brownlie's shop."

"John Brown, watchmaker, North Kirk Parish, married Margaret Syme, daughter to the late John Syme, Captain of the City Guard, 25 Feby. 1733."—*Edinburgh Marriage Register.*

27th July 1745.—"The which day the house unanimously continued John Brown, watchmaker, to represent the Incorporation and be one of the managers of the Charity Work House of this city for the ensuing year."

10*th* *September* 1745.—"Thereafter the house proceeded to the election of their treasurer for the ensuing year, and the Deacon named George Boswell John Brown, and Malcolm Brown, to be the leet of three for that office ; and the vote being stated, George Boswell, ten, John Brown, thirty-nine, Malcolm Brown, nine, the house unanimously made choice of John Brown, watchmaker, to be treasurer to the Incorporation, who accepted thereof and give his oath for faithful administration, and took his chair accordingly."

He filled the same office 1746-47-48.

4*th* *May* 1754.—"Kathrine Brown, daughter to the deceast John Brown, late watchmaker, freeman of this Incorporation, was by a great majority elected and nominated to supply the place of —— Jackson in the Trades Maiden Hospital at the gift of the Incorporation. She was born the 16th June 1744, as appeared by a certificate produced under the hand of James Craig, Session-Clerk, and of this election the clerk is appointed to give to the said Kathrine Brown an extract gratis."

2*nd* *November* 1771.—"It being motioned that the widow of John Brown, Clock & Watchmaker, had a view of getting into the Trinity Hospital, by private presentation, provided the Incorporation continue her as a pensioner, or give the money to her daughter. The Incorporation, considering that this would be no prejudice to them, on the contrary was providing for a family which their small bounty was not sufficient for, agreed that the quarter pension should continue to be paid to her or her daughter, if she should desire it."

These minutes from the Hammermen's Records give faithfully the position John Brown took in the conduct of the affairs of his society, and it is interesting to note that his services were appreciated by his fellow brethren, as is revealed in the last two minutes, which bring out clearly their anxiety to do what was in their power for his wife and family. That he was a well-known citizen in Edinburgh is easily seen in the following selection of advertisements issued during his lifetime, which incidentally bring out where his business premises were situated :—

"That upon the 5th there was lost by the way leading from Coupar to Piddoch-hall a silver watch of L. Esturgeon's make. Any person that has found or can give notice thereof may acquaint John Annan, writer in Coupar, or John Brown, watchmaker in Edinburgh, and the first discoverer shall have from the loser a sufficient reward and his good wishes."—*Caledonian Mercury*, 16th March 1730.

"Lost on the 7th a silver watch made by Thomas Best, London, engraved upon the dial plate, but no engraving on the inner plate, and the hook out of the barrel of the main spring. Whoever will return the watch to John Brown, watchmaker in Edinburgh, shall have half a guinea reward."—*Ibid.*, 9th January 1735.

"Whereas there was lost upon the 8th March last, about a mile from Montrose, a silver watch of a middle size, maker's name is Ingram, upon the dial plate No. 2589, with a black leather string, and at it a steel seal with three impressions, a little bruised in the case without. This is to give notice to all watchmakers or others into whose custody the watch with any of the above marks may come to hand, or to any who can inform in whose custody the said watch can be found, so as to be returned to the owner, let them call for John Brown, watchmaker, at his shop a little above the main guard, north side of the street, Edinburgh, or for Daniel Stewart Vinter at his house in Montrose, where they shall have a sufficient reward."—*Ibid.*, 16th May 1743.

"Lost on the 12th December, betwixt Edinburgh and Cockpen, a silver watch with hour and minute hands, maker's name, J. Thomas, No. 1418. Whoever can give notice of the said watch to John Brown, watchmaker in Edinburgh, shall be sufficiently rewarded."—*Ibid.*, 17th December 1744.

BROWN, JOHN.   Edinburgh, 1758-72.

20*th July* 1758.—"John Brown, son of John Brown, clock and watch maker, booked apprentice to James Cowan."

10*th July* 1771.—"John Brown, son of the deceast John Brown, watchmaker, presented a bill craving to be admitted a freeman clock and watch maker."

2nd May 1772.—"Compeared and presented his essay, being a watch movement begun, made, and finished in Samuel Brown's (his brother) shop in presence of Samuel Brown, landlord, John Gibson, John Murdoch, and William Auld, essay masters, as they declared."—*E. H. Records.*

The above makes the third John Brown all of the same family who were watch and clockmakers in Edinburgh, but this last does not appear to have been in business for himself. The probability is that he was employed as a workman by his brother, Samuel Brown (q.v.), who succeeded to the father's business in 1750.

BROWN, JOHN. Back of City Guard, Edinburgh, 1763-76.

13*th June* 1763.—" Son of James Brown, journeyman mason in Edinburgh, and one of the boys educated in George Heriot's Hospital, booked apprentice to James Duff."

5*th August* 1769.—"Discharged of his indentures on this date by James Duff."—*E. H. Records.*

BROWN, JOHN. Port Glasgow, 1785.

BROWN, JOHN. Irvine, 1829.

"James Brown, sailor in Irvine, served Heir in General to his father, John Brown, Clock and Watch Maker there, dated 26th October 1829. Recorded 1st December 1829."—*Services of Heirs.*

BROWN, JOHN. Elgin, 1743.

BROWN, JOHN. St Andrews, 1783.

BROWN, JOHN. Bishop Mill, Elgin, 1837.

BROWN, JOSEPH. Kirkcaldy, 1769.

" To be sold by Joseph Brown in Kirkcaldie, four spring table clocks, two of which play four different tunes each. They are executed in the best manner and go eight days. They will be sold at reasonable rates."— *Edinburgh Advertiser*, 27th May 1769.

BROWN, MALCOLM. Edinburgh, 1778.

Discharged of his indentures by Laurence Dalgleish, 21st March 1778.

BROWN, MURDOCH. Edinburgh, 1772.

Admitted a member of Lodge St David, Edinburgh, 12th November 1772. Minutes state admitted gratis, being an Artist and Musician.

BROWN, PETER. Ayr; died 1847.

BROWN, ROBERT. Edinburgh, 1702.

Booked journeyman to Andrew Brown, clockmaker, 7th February 1702. Married Margaret Cleghorne in the parish of North Leith, 5th September 1704.

BROWN, SAMUEL. Edinburgh, 1750-87.

" John Brown (q.v.), watchmaker in Edinburgh, being lately deceast, the business is carried on as formerly by Samuel Brown, his eldest son, for behoof of his mother-in-law and four infant children, at their house, a little above the Guard, north side of the street, Edinburgh.

" Such persons as are indebted to the deceast are intreated to pay their debts to the widow who is fully empowered to receive the same. Commissions from the country shall be done with great care and accuracy."— *Caledonian Mercury*, 8th January 1750.

" Just published, and to be delivered to the subscribers by Samuel Brown, watchmaker. opposite to the Guard. Edinburgh, a popular treatise on Astronomy by James Ferguson (q.v.)."—*Ibid.*, 25th September 1756.

6th August 1757.—" Samuel Brown, son to the deceast John Brown, clock and watch maker, compeared and presented a bill to be admitted a freeman clock and watch maker of the Incorporation, which was received, and an essay and essay masters were appointed. The essay to be presented between and the fourth of January next to come. And this indulgence of so long a delay was granted to him in regard that the members of the watchmaker's art declared that the essay could not be well made in shorter time. But declaring that this indulgence should be no precedent in time coming to the members of the other arts, whose essay could be finished in a shorter time. He made payment to the treasurer of £3, 12s. 2½d., as the half of his upset money and is to pay the other half at his admission.

4th February 1758.—" Compeared and presented his

essay, being a watch movement made and finished in his own shop, as William Nicol, landlord, Deacon Dalgleish, William Auld, and James Cowan, essay masters declared, which essay was found to be a well wrought essay, etc., and he was therefore admitted a freeman clock and watch maker in the Incorporation. He made payment to the treasurer of three pounds twelve shillings and two pence, and two thirds of a penny as the last half of his upset dues."—*E. H. Records.*

He entered into partnership with George Skelton (q.v.) in 1784, which partnership was continued till his death in 1787.

"Agnes Cunningham or Milne, served Co-Heir of Provision General to her Grandfather, Samuel Brown, watchmaker there, dated 9th March 1835. Recorded 18th March 1835."—*Services of Heirs.*

"James Thomas Alexander, Surgeon, Edinburgh, served Co-Heir of Provision General to his Great Grandfather, Samuel Brown, watchmaker there, dated 9th March 1835. Recorded 25th March 1835."—*Services of Heirs.*

Admitted a member of Lodge St David, Edinburgh, 6th July 1753. Gavin Wilson, the poet of the Lodge, in his "New Song of St David's," refers to him as follows :—

> "There social brother Brown does sing
>   Igo and ago,
>   A song that makes our glasses ring
>   Iram coram dago."

BROWN, Thomas.   Auchtermuchty, 1825 (?).

BROWN, Thomas.   Berwick-on-Tweed, 1849.

BROWN, William.   Dumfries ; died 14th November 1795.

BROWN, William.   Edinburgh, 1733.

"Son to William Brown, stabler, burgess of Edinburgh, booked apprentice to John Brown, Clockmaker, 15th September 1733."—*E. H. Records.*

BROWN, ——.   Elgin, subsequent to 1820.

BROWN & CHALMERS.   Leith, 1842.

BROWN & SKELTON. Edinburgh, 1784-87.

"Lost upon the Red Brae near Channelkirk, some weeks ago, a Pinchbeck watch with a green shagreen case, maker's name, John Stellas, London, No. 188. Whoever has found the same will please restore it to Brown and Skelton, opposite the Guard, Edinburgh, who will give a handsome reward."— *Caledonian Mercury*, 2nd November 1785.

BROWNLEE, ALEXANDER. Edinburgh, 1740.

Son to James Brownlee, merchant in Edinburgh; booked apprentice to Archibald Straiton, watchmaker, 3rd May 1740.

BROWNLEE, WILLIAM. Hamilton, 1800.

BROWNLIE, ALEXANDER. Edinburgh, 1710-39.

5th April 1710.—"Booked apprentice to Robert Alexander."

29th March 1718.—"On which day he compeared and presented his essay, viz., the movements of a watch, which was found a weill wrought essay, etc. His essay masters were Alexander Hay and Patrick Gordon. The essay was made in William Sutor's shop."

"Alexander Brownlie, watchmaker, married to Margaret Graham, daughter of the late W. Graham, merchant, 17 Decr. 1719."—*Edinburgh Marriage Register*.

2nd December 1721.—"The house being met, the Deacon represented to the house that yesterday, in the forenoon, Alexander Brownlie, clockmaker, had made a seizure of a part of the dial work of ye town clock (this was a new clock that was being erected in St Giles Church, the manufacture of L. Bradly, London), as being wrought by an unfreeman, and that this day the Magistrates had summarily fined and imprisoned the said Alexander Brownlie for the seizure, and therefore the opinions and sentiments of ye incorporation is demanded, and what resolutions they will take. The house are unanimously of opinion that the procedure of the Magistrates against the said Alex. Brownlie is not only illegal against the said Alex. Brownlie, but likewise tends to ye breach and overthrowing the privileges of this Incorporation, confirmed to them by advice of the Town Council, the said Alex. Brownlie having done nothing but what is consistent and to the support of ye Incorporation's privileges.

"Therefore the house unanimously resolve, for ye preservation of their privileges, to enter a process against the Magistrates for yair illegal procedure against the said Alex. Brownlie, and for that effect appoint the Deacon and Boxmaster, Deacon Herring, Deacon Boswall, Edward Bunkle, Alexander Brown, and Thomas Gordon to meet with Mr Boswall of Affleck, advocate, and consult him anent the method of procedure in the law process, and likewise are of opinion that ye concurrence of the fourteen Deacons be demanded, and in order yairto appoint their clerk to draw up a petition to them for that purpose. It is put to the vote whether the incorporation will approve of this act, which, without a contrair vote, is approved of."—*E. H. Records.*

Admitted a member of the Lodge of Mary's Chapel, No. 1, 28th January 1727.

BROWNLIE, ARCHIBALD. Strathaven, 1844.

"Mary Brownlie, Coldstream, served Heir Special to her father, Archibald Brownlie, clockmaker, Strathaven, who died 16th April 1844, in half of house and ground at Strathaven, Lanarkshire, dated 22nd July 1859. Recorded 26th July 1859."—*Services of Heirs.*

BROWNLIE, JAMES. 22 Stobcross Street, Glasgow, 1836.

BRUCE, JAMES. Edinburgh, 1718.

"Son to Mr Alexander Bruce, advocate, is booked apprentice to Alexander Brownlee, 8th November 1718."—*E. H. Records.*

BRUCE, DAVID. Aberdeen, 1538, page 2.

BRUCE, ROBERT. Edinburgh, 1797.

"Robert Bruce, clock and watch maker, married Mary Gowans, 12 Decr. 1797."—*Edinburgh Marriage Register.*

BRUCE, WILLIAM. Edinburgh, 1757.

BRUCE, WILLIAM. Portsburgh, Edinburgh, 1743.

BRUNTON, PATRICK. Dalkeith, 1788.

BRUNTON, WALTER. Edinburgh, 1771-1808.

BRYDEN, THOMAS. Johnshaven, 1837.

BRYSON, CHARLES. 31 Trongate, Glasgow, 1837.

BRYSON, JOHN. High Street, Dalkeith. 1836-82.

BRYSON, ROBERT, & SONS. See page 70.

BRYSON, ROBERT, F.R.S.E. 66 Princes Street, Edinburgh, 1810-52.

"Commenced business first at the Mint, High Street, Edinburgh, 1810; did not become a member of the Hammermen's Incorporation till 1815, when the entry money and other dues amounted to £70, which he paid. That same year he issued the following advertisement:—

"Robert Bryson, Clock and Watch Maker, announces to his friends and the public that he has removed from the Mint to that commodious house, No. 5 South Bridge Street, opposite to Hunter's Square, where he will be happy to see those friends who so liberally patronised him at the Mint."—*Edinburgh Evening Courant*, 6th June 1815.

This South Bridge place of business he tenanted till 1840, and while there he became closely allied with Mr Horner in the foundation of the Watt College, now known as the Heriot-Watt College, an institution which to-day occupies a foremost place in technical education. That this College was a matter congenial to his tastes, is easily seen in the trouble he took to ensure its success. Early advertisements show that he made his place of business an office for enrolling students, and from his self-sacrificing labours undoubtedly contributed largely to put the institution in a satisfactory condition.

Removing to 66 Princes Street in 1840, he continued to turn out work of the highest class. A number of his clocks and watches are in existence yet, particularly a splendid sidereal clock which he made in 1832 for the Royal Observatory, Edinburgh.[1] This clock was used by the late Professor Henderson for all his observations

---

[1] For these particulars I am indebted to the late Professor Copland, Royal Observatory, Blackford Hill.

on Calton Hill, and afterwards by the late C. Piazzi Smyth for the same purpose up to 1855, being only superseded by the gift of a new sidereal clock made by Dent of London. This clock by Bryson became the property of the city of Edinburgh in 1895 and is still in use.

He became a member of the Royal Society of Arts, Edinburgh, and his first printed communication in the *Transactions* of that body, as far as we can glean, was read on the 12th December 1842. It was a description, with a drawing of the apparatus invented by him, for turning on and shutting off the gas which illuminated his translucent dial. The Society's Honorary Silver Medal was awarded him for this paper.[1]

He died on 8th August 1852, aged 74 years, and was interred in the New Calton Burying Ground, Edinburgh, where it is recorded on a large and handsome monument that he was for a period of nearly fifty years watchmaker in Edinburgh. He was succeeded by his two sons, Alexander and Robert, the firm being known as Robert Bryson & Sons.

We have not succeeded in getting the exact year when the copartnery was entered into, but doubtless long before the senior partner's death in 1852 these two talented men were closely associated with their father.

BRYSON, ALEXANDER, F.R.S.E.,[2] the elder son of the above, occupied an unique position, being not only a skilled horologist but also possessed of considerable scientific attainments. Becoming a member of the Royal Society of Arts, his entry into that body was of material benefit to the usefulness and conduct of its transactions. Occupying the highest posts they could appoint him to, he favoured his brother associates and the public with

---

[1] His next was a description of a self-registering barometer invented by himself in 1844, followed by another in 1845, "On a Method of rendering Baily's Compensation Pendulum insensible to Hygrometric Influences," for which he was awarded the Society Silver Medal or Plate to the value of ten sovereigns.

[2] Admitted a member of Lodge St David, Edinburgh, 28th May 1839.

papers and notes of inventions of the greatest usefulness and originality.

A brief summary of these are now given, which, however, do not exhaust his activity in scientific research, but they are enough to show the wide range of his attainments. All of them were read or described by himself at the various meetings of the Royal Society of Arts; date of delivery of each are appended :—

8th May 1843.—" At the request of the Council an Exposition of the Mechanism of Clocks and Watches, including the various Escapements, Pendulums, and Balances, was given by Mr Alexander Bryson, F.R.S.S.A., M.G.S.E., Chronometer Watch and Clock Maker, Edinburgh."

12th May 1845.—" Additional notice of Mr R. Bryson's self - registering Barometer with remarks showing that no corrections for Temperature will be necessary in this instrument. The instrument was exhibited.

" Mr Bryson also exhibited an accurate method of determining the expansion of Mercury from increased temperature in the standard barometer, and demonstrated that the syphon barometer, used as a self-registering instrument (as formerly described to the Society) and observed by the shorter limb of the syphon, requires only a correction of 0·006 inches for 60 degrees Fahrenheit.

" Mr Bryson also described the results obtained from his hourly barometric register kept during two years, and remarked the extreme similarity existing between these and the observations of Professor Forbes during three years at Colinton."

9th February 1846.—" Description of a new Clock impelled by a combination of Gravitation and Electro Magnetism, invented by Mr Alexander Bryson, Councillor, R.S.S.A., M.G.S.E.

" In this clock the common pendulum is used. It is kept vibrating in equal arcs, by a small falling bar or detent, which is raised every alternate second by the attraction induced in a soft electro magnet. The magnetism is excited by constant batteries placed in the bottom of the clock case, which may be kept in action for any desirable period, and when changed it is not necessary to stop the clock, as before the spent battery is out of action the other, which is newly charged, is in full operation. The wheelwork showing minutes and seconds is moved by the gravitation bar or detent immediately on its being attracted by the electro-magnet. When this clock is made to show minutes and seconds only, as in observatory clocks, it consists of two wheels only, and when it is made to show hours three wheels are necessary. The contract-breaker is suspended on knife edges immediately above the pendulum bob, having a gold concentric arc, on which press two very slight gold springs. In this arc is inserted a piece of ivory which breaks the current and permits the falling bar or detent to fall on the pendulum, so as to keep up its vibration.

"By the method of coincidences it was stated the pendulum was found to keep its motion with the utmost steadiness as compared with a compensation mercurial pendulum beating seconds."

27th April 1846.—"A letter from Mr Alex. Bryson was read, withdrawing his communication as above, in respect he now finds that he has been anticipated in this invention by Mr Alexander Bain, of South Hanover Street, Edinburgh."[1]

13th December 1847.—"Specimens were exhibited and described of the teeth of Wheels of Steeple Clocks cut and finished on the Engine."

10th April 1848.—"'On a New Lubricant for Machinery.' This paper described a new compound possessing properties which seem to render it a better lubricant than those in use for large machinery. It is a compound of oil, sulphur, and vulcanized caoutchouc."

8th January 1849.—"The Aneroid Barometer was exhibited and described."

26th January 1852.—"By permission of the Society a letter from Mr Alex. Bryson, F.R.S.S.A., was read, containing his suggestions as to the origin of the Fire which caused the loss of the steam-ship *Amazon*."

12th April 1852.—"The patent striking Electro-Magnetic Clock, invented by Mr Charles Shepherd, of London, was described by Dr George Wilson, F.R.S.

---

[1] Mr Bryson read the description of Mr Bain's clock (see page 32) on 14th April 1845.

The clock was put in working order and taken charge of at the meeting by Alex. Bryson, Esq."

22nd January 1855.—"The Society's Silver Medal was awarded to him for his notice of a simple Compressible Syphon of his own invention."

12th November 1855.—"At the special request of the Council, 'An Exposition of the Mechanical Inventions of Dr Robert Hooke.'"

10th December 1855.—"'On an Improved Method of preparing Siliceous and other Fossils for Microscopic Investigation,' and also a description of a new Pneumatic Chuck."

11th April 1859.—"'On the Injurious Effects of Cedar-wood Cabinets,' by Alexander Bryson, F.R.S.S.A., Her Majesty's Clockmaker for Scotland. Specimens exhibited."

25th April 1859.—"'On a New Method of Measuring Watch Glasses.' Awarded the Society's Silver Medal."

26th March 1860.—"'On a New Lime Light and Lamp,' exhibited in action."

24th April 1862.—"Communication on the recent frequent accidents from hydrocarbon liquids."

24th April 1864.—"On the means of determining the presence and position of Icebergs during fogs or darkness at sea."

This last paper was awarded the Hepburn Biennal prize, value twelve sovereigns, and crowned, so to speak, a career which, as our readers may see, was full of activity and study. The list given of his works is necessarily imperfect, for his abilities were so varied that his advice and counsel were sought by the most eminent scientific men of his day, and his early death at Hawkhill, near Edinburgh, on the 7th December 1866, aged 50 years, created a blank not only in the Society of which he was so illustrious a member but throughout all Scotland. His death left his brother, Robert, the only partner of the large and prosperous business which had been so successfully carried on. Extensive as the business was he yet found time to be of use to his fellow citizens. His advice was highly valued in the management of a number of Public Institutions, and becoming a member of the Merchant Company he was made

Master, and, while filling this honourable position, had a good share in the foundation of the successful educational institutions which under the name of the Merchant Company Schools have helped to make Edinburgh famous for its educational advantages. He died in 1886, the business passing into the hands of Messrs Hamilton & Inches, 88 Princes Street, who still retain the royal appointment.

BUCHAN, ALEXANDER. 41 George Street, Perth, 1833.

Possibly a son of the immediately succeeding, whom he succeeded on 8th January 1833, being then located at Bridgend.

BUCHAN, ARCHIBALD. Kinnoull, Perth, 1800-32.

BUCHANAN, ANDREW. 8 William Street, Greenock, 1836.

BUCHANAN, ROBERT, jun. 37 Dundas Street, Glasgow, 1835.

BUGLAS, C. Berwick-on-Tweed, 1787.

"Watch supposed to be stolen, and found in the custody of William Tennent, apprehended in North Berwick, on the 22nd July last, when he broke prison. A large silver watch, seemingly new, maker's name, George Creak, London, No. 1358; on the dial plate is engraved 'C. Westwood,' and within the case there is a watchmaker's label, 'C. Buglas, Clock and Watch Maker, Berwick.'"—*Edinburgh Advertiser*, 30th October 1787.

BURBIDGE, ——. Edinburgh, 1673.

BURGES, JOHN. Stirling, 1806.

BURN, DAVID. Bathgate, 1798.

BURNET, JOHN. Tarves, 1810-46.

BURNS, DAVID. Mid-Calder, 1797.

BURNS, ROBERT. Melrose, 1832.

"James Burns, Clockmaker, London, served Heir in General to his father, Robert Burns, Clockmaker, Melrose, dated 30th May 1832. Recorded 4th June 1832."—*Services of Heirs.*

BURTON, WILLIAM. Dunse, 1824.

BUTLER, ROBERT. 48 Hamilton Street, Greenock, 1836.

CAITHNESS, DAVID. Dundee, 1787.

CALDER, JOHN. High Street, Glasgow, 1775-1816.

CALDER, JOHN, jun. 110 High Street, Glasgow, 1814-28.

CALDER, JOHN. 326 Lawnmarket, Edinburgh, 1819; 85 West Port, 1825.

31st July 1820.—"He appeared and presented a petition craving to be admitted a freeman clock and watch maker in the Incorporation, which being received, an essay was appointed, viz., a clock movement to be begun and finished in his own shop, James Ramage, landlord, James Gray, Richard Millar, and James Ritchie, essay masters, and to be finished this day six months. He paid the treasurer ten pounds, being the first half of his entry money. Admitted as above on 5th February 1821.—E. H. Records.

CALDWELL, JOHN. Glasgow, 1812.

CALDWELL, WILLIAM. 5 Malta Street, Glasgow, 1820-37.

CALLAM, CHARLES. Nicolson Street, Edinburgh, 1804.

CALLAN, ARCHIBALD. Douglas, 1834.

"Marion Callan or Haddow, in Douglas, served Heir of Provision General to her father, Archibald Callan, watchmaker there, dated 6th June 1834. Recorded 17th June 1834."—Services of Heirs.

CALLENDER, JAMES. Edinburgh, 1731.

Booked apprentice to George Scott, Canongate, 1731.

From a note kindly forwarded by A. M. Mackay, Esq., Past Master of Lodge of St David's, Edinburgh, No. 36, there is every probability that this James Callender was one of the founders of the Lodge on 2nd March 1738. He is recorded as being in very poor circumstances in the years 1753-54 and 1756, when he received pecuniary assistance from the Lodge. In 1758 he published a collection of Masonic Songs. He died in 1762 and was buried at Leith at the expense of the Lodge.

CAMERON, ALEXANDER. Selkirk, 1816.

CAMERON, ALEXANDER. High Street, Dundee, 1823-37.

"A. C. begs to announce that he has fixed a Sidereal Clock, and procured a Transit instrument divided into N.P.D. from a workman recommended by the Astronomer Royal at Greenwich Observatory, for rating chronometers and watches.

No chronometer or watch will receive a certified rate unless the maker's name and box number are engraved upon it. Those watches that are left blank or without the maker's name are generally got up as traffic upon sale or return but cannot be exported.

A. C. purposes being in the English market in a few weeks, and solicits orders for himself or his English connection, which may be executed direct from the different manufacturers. His friends in the south and north of Scotland will be waited upon at the usual times with a new set of patterns."—*Edinburgh Evening Courant*, 6th January 1828.

CAMERON, HUGH. Johnshaven, 1780-90.

CAMERON, JAMES. Rigg Street, Stewarton, 1837.

CAMERON, JAMES. Edinburgh, 1776-77.

"Bound apprentice to John Cleland, 11th May 1776. Bound apprentice to Samuel Brown on 19th March 1777. He paid nothing for booking on account of having paid as an apprentice, but is still to pay in case the incorporation shall appoint him to do so.—*E. H. Records.*

CAMERON, JAMES. Selkirk, 1832.

CAMERON, JAMES. 85 Murraygate, Dundee, 1828-50.

CAMERON, JOHN. Perth, 1795.

Apprenticed to James Young.

CAMERON, JOHN. Victoria Place, Kilmarnock, 1850.

CAMERON, JOHN. Barrhead, 1836.

CAMERON, JOHN. Aberfeldie, 1836.

CAMPBELL, ARCHIBALD. Gourock, 1805.

"Died at Gourock on Wednesday evening, Archibald Campbell, Watchmaker, aged 107 years."—*Edinburgh Evening Courant*, 3rd June 1805.

CAMPBELL, CHARLES. Borrowstounness (Bo'ness), 1770-1812.

"Died at Borrowstounness on the 25th November, aged 75 years, Mr Charles Campbell, many years clock and watch maker there."—*Edinburgh Evening Courant*, 27th November 1812.

CAMPBELL, HUGH. Edinburgh, 1692.

Booked apprentice to Humphrey Mylne, 6th August 1692.

CAMPBELL, JAMES. Edinburgh, 1803-10.

Bound apprentice to Robert Green, 17th June 1803. Discharged of his indentures, 3rd February 1810.

CAMPBELL, JAMES. 51 High Street, Johnstone, 1836.

CAMPBELL, JOHN. 18 North Bridge, Edinburgh, 1799-1819.

"Bound apprentice to Robert Hinmers, 4th May 1799. Discharged of his indentures 3rd May 1806.

4th November 1809.—"Compeared and produced his essay, being a watch movement begun, made, and finished in his own shop in presence of James Howden, landlord, Robert Hinmers, Robert Logie, and William Thomson, as they declared."—*E. H. Records.*

"John Campbell, watchmaker and jeweller, respectfully announces to the Public that he has opened the shop lately possessed by Mr Dalgleish (q.v.), with an entire new stock of the very best quality and most exquisite workmanship, and by unremitting attention to business and earnest endeavours to please, hopes to merit a share of public favours. J. C. has been regularly bred in the profession and personally acquainted with the first manufactures in England, where he has selected his present assortment, which he may confidently say is not surpassed in beauty and quality to any in town. 18 North Bridge."—*Edinburgh Evening Courant*, 30th July 1808.

"Watch stolen from a house back of Fountain Well. A silver watch, maker's name, P. Hopkins, No. 12512. If offered for sale please inform Mr Campbell, watchmaker, North Bridge."—*Ibid.*, 26th May 1810.

"GOLD WATCH STOLEN.—On the evening of Thursday last from a house in Rose Street, a gold watch, maker's name, John Pinkerton, Haddington, No. 6395. It is requested that any person to whom the same may be offered for sale will secure it, and give intimation to Mr Campbell, Clock and Watch Maker, North Bridge, by whom he will be handsomely rewarded."—*Edinburgh Evening Courant*, 16th January 1813.

CAMPBELL, JOHN. 95 Hutcheson Street, Glasgow, 1823.

CAMPBELL, MARSHALL. Colmonell, Ayrshire, 1850.

CAMPBELL, ROBERT. Canal Street, Edinburgh, 1778-94.

CAMPBELL, WILLIAM. Stirling, 1745.

Booked journeyman to Robert Melvill Stirling, 13th June 1745.

CANT, JAMES. Perth, 1824.

CARMICHAEL, JAMES. 42 Hanover Street, Edinburgh, 1796.

"James Carmichael, Clock and Watch Maker, respectfully informs his friends and the public that he has opened that shop, No. 42 South Hanover Street, New Edinburgh, where he intends to carry on the business in all its various branches. He trusts he shall merit the patronage of the Public by carefully and punctually executing their orders." — *Scots Chronicle*, 3rd June 1796.

CARMICHAEL, JOHN. New Street, Greenock, 1750-1800.

Maker of the first clock in Greenock Parish Church, 1786.

"GREENOCK.—A most daring robbery was committed here between Saturday night and Sunday morning. The shop of Mr Carmichael, watchmaker, was entered into by picking the locks, and property mostly consisting of gold and silver watches to the amount of several hundred pounds carried off. A most diligent search is being made for the thieves, and already several persons have been apprehended on suspicion."— *Edinburgh Evening Courant*, 28th April 1800.

CARNEGIE, ——. Arbroath, 1850.

CARNEGIE, ROBERT, and two brothers. Kineff and Drumlithie, 1838.

CARNEGIE, ROBERT. Auchinblae, 1837.

CARRUTHERS, DAVID. Ecclefechan, 1840.

CARRUTHERS, GEORGE. Langholm, 1836; died 1866, aged 76.

CASSELS, JAMES. Lanark; born 19th May 1833; died 19th February 1906.

CATHRO, ——. Dundee, 1823.

"The Lords Commissioners of the Admiralty having advertised a premium of £300 for the best chronometer which should be kept at Greenwich for one year, thirty-six were sent thither by the principal chronometer makers in London and were kept in 1823. It was announced that if any chronometer varied six seconds it could not obtain a prize. At the end of the year the second best chronometer, of which the variation was about five seconds, was made by Mr Cathro, a native of Dundee. Such perfection was never before attained, and it justly excited the astonishment of all astronomers and of the Board of Admiralty.—*Glasgow Mechanics' Magazine*, 1826, vol. ii., page 145.

CHALMERS, ALEX. THOMSON. Aberdeen, 1836.

CHALMERS, DAVID. 12 Catherine Street, Edinburgh, 1803-19.

CHAPMAN, FRANCIS. Main Street, Pollokshaws, 1836.

CHAPMAN, FRANCIS. 55 Brunswick Street, Glasgow, 1840.

CHARLTON, JOHN. Edinburgh, 1792.

"John Charlton, Watch and Clockmaker, married to Margaret Aitkinson, 20th March 1792."—*Edinburgh Marriage Register*.

CHARRAS, CHARLES. Glasgow, 1717.

CHARTERS, DECKFORD. Edinburgh, 1783.

Bound apprentice to Normond Macpherson, 26th February 1783.

CHARTERS, WILLIAM. 68 High Street, Dumfries, 1837.

CHISHOLM, ADAM. 5 St Andrew's Street, Dumfries, 1780-1821.

CHRISTIE, GABRIEL. Edinburgh, 1736.

Son of James Christie, merchant in Stirling, booked apprentice to Andrew Dickie, 6th December 1736.

CHRISTIE, JAMES. Perth, 1820-48. 82 High Street, Perth.

"James Christie, watch and clock maker, Perth, served Heir in General to his father, James Christie, Meal Dealer there, dated 30th August 1820. Recorded 11th September 1820."— *Services of Heirs.*

CHRISTIE, JAMES. 52 St John Street, Perth, 1820-43.

CLAPPERTON, GIEDON. Edinburgh, 1777.

Bound apprentice to Laurence Dalgleish, 29th January 1777.

CLARK, ANDREW. Canongate, Edinburgh, 1753-64.

Booked apprentice to James Nicoll, Canongate, 27th February 1753. Admitted a freeman clock and watch maker of Canongate Hammermen, 3rd May 1760, his essay being the inside of a watch movement.

Married Grizal Doig, 28th February 1761.

CLARK, CHARLES. Edinburgh, 1814.

31*st August* 1814.—"Compeared on this date and presented a petition craving to be admitted a freeman locksmith in right of James Clark (q.v.), clockmaker in Edinburgh, his father, which was granted, and he paid the treasurer six pounds."

4*th August* 1815.—"Compeared and produced his essay, being a timepiece begun, made, and finished in the presence of James Clark, sen., as landlord, and James Paterson and John Picken, as they declared, and was accordingly admitted. He paid the treasurer six pounds."—*E. H. Records.*

CLARK, GEORGE. Aberdeen; died 1852, aged 36.

CLARK, JAMES. Edinburgh, 1791-1835.

Married Elizabeth Thomson, 23rd August 1791.

29*th June* 1807.—"Compeared and presented a petition craving to be admitted a freeman member of the Incorporation, for which he was willing to pay Seventy pounds Sterling. The prayer of which was granted, and an essay appointed to him to be produced at the Martinmas quarter. He paid the treasurer thirty-five pounds, being the first moiety of his entry money."

30*th January* 1808.—"Compeared and produced his

essay, a clock movement, begun, made, and finished in his own shop, in presence of James Ramage, landlord, George Skelton, Robert Foot, and Andrew Wilson, essay masters, as they declared. He paid thirty-five pounds as the second moiety of his entry money."—*E. H. Records.*

"CLOCKMAKERS WANTED.—A few journeymen will receive good encouragement and constant employment. Personal application to James Clark, Clock and Watch Maker, Mint Close, is expected, where clocks and machines of all kinds are executed with neatness and despatch.—*Edinburgh Evening Courant,* 23rd November 1805.

"James Clark, Clockmaker, a little below the Tron Church, returns thanks for the orders he has been favoured with for steeple clocks from various parts of Scotland.[1] He makes clocks for one or more dials of excellent workmanship, which is offered on moderate terms."—*Ibid.,* 18th November 1809.

"An elegant small steam engine, valued at 200 guineas. To be disposed of by 200 shares at one guinea each. James Clark, Clock and Machine Maker, proposes disposing of the above elegant engine by 200 shares at one guinea each, to be determined by ballot on Wednesday, the 19th January 1814, in M'Ewan's Rooms, Royal Exchange, at one o'clock P.M. The engine may be examined every lawful day at Mr Clark's house, entering from No. 8 High Street, where shares may be had. J. C. executes with the greatest accuracy, attention, and expedition, every kind of machinery in brass and steel."—*Ibid.,* 8th January 1814.

The Edinburgh Town Council, on 19th December 1827, accepted an estimate by James Clark to furnish an eight-day clock for the Tron Church Steeple to carry four sets of minute and hour hands for dials from 6 to 8 feet diameter, and of sufficient strength to raise a hammer to strike a bell of 15 cwts.

"SOCIETY OF ARTS FOR SCOTLAND.—Prizes gained and presented on 17th June 1829. To Mr James Clark, Steeple-Clock and Machine Maker, Edinburgh. The Society's Gold Medal, value £15, 15s., for his description and relative drawings of a method of cutting screws. The great importance of the subject, the care which

---

[1] See Haddington Town Clocks, page 180.

F

had been bestowed in the construction of the expensive apparatus, and the attention which was paid to the laying of the matter in a proper manner before the Society appeared to the Committee to deserve the highest mark of the Society's approval."—*Transactions of the Royal Society of Arts for Scotland*, 1829.

"TURRET CLOCKS AND MACHINERY MANU-FACTORY. — James Clark has always on hand a number of turret clocks suitable for public offices or church spires where one or more dials may be wanted. J. C. makes all kinds of models in brass or steel, and from the long experience in the above branches, he assures those who may favour him with their orders that they will find his charges moderate."—*Edinburgh Evening Courant*, 22nd May 1834.

CLARK, JAMES. Kirkcaldy, 1843.

CLARK, JOHN. 54 Cathcart Street, Greenock, 1820-36.

CLARK, JOSEPH. Kirkcaldy, 1843.

CLARK, ROBERT. Market Lane, Kilmarnock, 1850.

CLARK, ROBERT. Newburgh, Fife, 1836.

CLARKE, JOHN. Greenock, 1822-37.

CLARKE, WILLIAM. Greenock, 1805.

CLELAND, JOHN. Edinburgh, 1761-84.

"Booked apprentice to James Duff, 24th March 1761."

7th May 1763.—"The incorporation, with the consent of James Duff, transfers John Clelland, his apprentice, for the time yet to run of his indentures to Daniel Binny. Discharged of his indentures by Daniel Binny, 1st March 1767."

"Presented a bill craving to be admitted a freeman watchmaker, 26th July 1771."

25th January 1772.—"Compeared and presented his essay, being an horizontal watch begun, made, and finished in presence of James Gibson, landlord, Robert Clidisdale, James Duff, and Robert Cairriton, essay masters, as they declared."—*E. H. Records.*

"The copartnery of Gibson and Cleland, watch-makers in Edinburgh, being now dissolved, John

PINCHBECK WATCH,

With enamelled back. By John Cleland, Edinburgh, 1761-84.
In the Museum of the Society of Antiquaries of Scotland,
Edinburgh. Reproduced by permission.

Cleland begs leave to acquaint the public that he carries on the clock and watch making business in all its branches in the fore shop, first storey of Galloway's land, opposite to Libberton's Wynd, Lawnmarket, Edinburgh.

"As Mr Cleland has for some years applied himself to finishing, and for a considerable time conducted the business of one of the principal shops in London, those who are pleased to favour him with their employment may depend upon being served with the greatest exactness and despatch.

"*N.B.*—Commissions directed as above will be carefully executed." — *Edinburgh Evening Courant*, 26th June 1773.

"There was lost on Saturday the 22nd of May 1784, either in the playhouse or betwixt it and the Exchange Coffee House, a single cased Gold Watch, maker's name, Thomas Hill, London, No. 932, with a leather string and key. If the same comes to hand, please acquaint John Cleland, watchmaker, who will give a handsome reward."—*Caledonian Mercury*, 24th May 1784.

A capital example of his skill, namely a lady's watch, is now in the museum of the Society of Antiquaries of Scotland, Queen Street, Edinburgh. *See* illustration facing page 82.

CLELAND & MOLLISON. Edinburgh, 1785-90.

"Margaret Guthrie, relict of John Cleland, watch and clock maker in Lawnmarket, Edinburgh, begs leave to inform her friends and the customers of her late husband that the business is carried on by Charles Mollison (q.v.), an experienced watch and clock maker, for the behalf of her and her small family under the firm of Cleland and Mollison. Commissions from the country will be punctually and faithfully executed. Those to whom John Cleland was indebted will please give in notes of their debts to the said Margaret Guthrie."—*Caledonian Mercury*, 12th September 1785.

CLELAND, Mrs. Edinburgh, 1790-96.

"Lost, a plain gold case of a watch between Edinburgh and Leith. Any person who has found the same and will bring it to Mrs Cleland, watchmaker, Lawnmarket, Edinburgh, shall be handsomely rewarded." —*Edinburgh Evening Courant*, 6th October 1791.

"Found, a Pinchbeck watch. Any person who has lost the same will please apply to Mrs Cleland, watchmaker, below the Cross, Edinburgh."—*Ibid.*, 14th April 1796.

"CLOCK AND WATCH MAKING.—Mrs Cleland, Head of New Assembly Close, Edinburgh, acknowledges her gratitude for past favours, and respectfully begs leave to acquaint her friends and the public that she still continues to carry on the clock and watch making business in all its branches, under the direction of a young man who has had long experience in that line. She therefore solicits her friends and the public at large for a continuance of their favours.

"*N.B.*—A neat assortment of Clocks and Watches always on hand."—*Ibid.*, 11th June 1796.

See also Robert Hinmers, page 190.

CLIDSDALE OR CLYDSDALE, ROBERT. Edinburgh, 1738-86.

"Son of Archibald Clidsdale, Schoolmaster, Kennoway, Fife; booked apprentice to Alexander Brand, 15th September 1738. Compeared on 17th November 1753, and presented his bill for being admitted a freeman clock and watch maker, which was received, and an essay and essay masters were appointed him. The essay to be presented betwixt and Michaelmas next. He paid the treasurer five pounds sterling as the half of his upset dues."

2nd October 1754.—"Compeared and presented his essay, being the movement of a watch begun and ended in his own shop, in presence of John Dalgleish and Andrew Dickie, watchmakers, and George Aitken, smith, essay masters, and Alexander Brand, landlord, as they declared, which was found a well-wrought essay, etc. He paid the treasurer five pounds sterling, as the last half of his upset money, and he also paid the clerk and officers dues."—*E. H. Records.*

"Lost on the 21st, at Musselburgh, a silver watch, maker's name, Robert Clidsdale, No. 141. Whoever returns the said watch to the said Robert Clidsdale, or the publisher of this paper, shall be handsomely rewarded.

"*N.B.*—The watch has a steel chain with a steel hook in the form of a fish."—*Caledonian Mercury*, 21st April 1764.

" A WATCH LOST.—There was stolen or lost on Tuesday, the 30th of October 1781, betwixt the Parliament Close and the head of the Canongate, a small-sized gold watch, maker's name, R. Sanderson, London, No. 415. It is entreated if said watch is offered for sale or mending to stop her and acquaint Robert Clidsdale, watchmaker, opposite head of Niddry's Wynd, who will give a sufficient reward."—*Ibid.*, 3rd November 1781.

" James Clidsdale, served Heir General to his father, Robert Clidesdale, watchmaker in Edinburgh, dated 15th June 1786. Recorded 22nd June 1786."—*Services of Heirs.*

" To be sold by public roup within John's Coffee-house, on Wednesday the 18th January 1804, the whole feu-duties and casualties of superiority at St John's Hill, South Back of the Canongate, which belonged to the deceased *Robert Clidsdale, watchmaker* in Edinburgh. The feu-duties amount to £30 annually."—*Edinburgh Evening Courant*, 7th January 1804.

CLIDSDALE, HUGH. Edinburgh, 1762-1821.

Booked apprentice to Robert Clidsdale, 6th December 1762. Discharged of his indentures by Robert Clidsdale, 22nd December 1769.

" Hugh Clidsdale, watchmaker in London, served Heir General to his uncle, Robert Clidsdale, watchmaker in Edinburgh, dated 18th November 1808. Recorded 28th November 1808."—*Services of Heirs.*

" Hugh Clidsdale, watchmaker in Edinburgh, served Heir General to his sister Rebecca Clidsdale there, dated 30th January 1821. Recorded 7th February 1821."—*Services of Heirs.*

COATS, ROBERT. Hamilton, 1745-61.

COCHRANE, THOMAS. Edinburgh, 1754-62.

" Son to Captain Basil Cochrane, Governor of the Isle of Man ; booked apprentice to John Dalgleish, watchmaker, 3rd July 1754. Discharged of his indentures by John Dalgleish 24th July 1762."—*E. H. Records.*

COCHRANE, THOMAS. Glasgow, 1810.

COCHRANE, WILLIAM. 19 Smith Hills, Paisley, 1836.

COCKBURN, ADAM. Haddington, 1804-43.

Adam was a bit of a poet, and the following lines hit off one of his characteristics, namely, that of never staying long in one's shop:—

> "See, Adie Cockburn shifts again ;
> His work and toil are all in vain.
> What's made in eident sitting
> Is lost in constant flitting.
> Soon bakers' warm and smoking batches
> Will take the place of Cockburn's watches."
> MARTINE'S *Annals of Haddington.*

Adam Cockburn went to Canada in 1843.

COCKBURN, ANDREW THOMPSON. Berwick-on-Tweed, 1843.

COCKBURN, WILLIAM. Haddington, 1814.

COGHILL, JAMES. Glasgow, 1811.

COLEMAN, THOMAS. Foot of Leith Walk, Leith, 1811.

COLLISON, ALEXANDER. Stonehaven, 1834.

COMMON, JAMES, sen. Coldstream ; died 1849.

COMMON, JAMES, jun. Coldstream, 1849.

"James Common, Clock and Watch Maker in Coldstream, served Heir General to his Grandfather, James Common, watchmaker there, dated 18th June 1849. Recorded 26th July 1849."—*Services of Heirs.*

CONQUER, PATRICK. Perth, 1790.

Booked apprentice to Joseph Taylor, Perth, 1790.

CONQUEROR, PETER. Hide Hill, Berwick-on-Tweed 1806-22.

CONSTABLE, ALEXANDER. Dundee, 1838.

CONSTABLE, GEORGE. Cupar-Fife, 1814.

CONSTABLE, WILLIAM. Dundee, 1806.

CONSTABLE, WILLIAM. 7 High Street, Dundee, 1812-28.

COOK, JAMES. Strichen, 1846.

COOK, JAMES. Dumfries; died 2nd January 1874, aged 62 years.

COOK, WILLIAM. Aberdeen, 1651, page 6.

COOPER, THOMAS. Castle Street, Hamilton, 1836.

COOPER, WILLIAM. Castle Wynd, Hamilton, 1808-24.

"Robbery on Thursday last, the 31st ult., betwixt the hours of eleven and twelve at night. John Lechone, farmer in Glasfurd, on his way home was knocked down and robbed of his pocket book and watch, maker's name, Bradshaw & Ryley, Coventry, No. 720. A handsome reward will be given for recovery of said watch or such information as may lead to a discovery of the perpetrators of the robbery by applying to William Cooper, Clock-maker, Hamilton."—*Glasgow Courier*, 7th July 1808.

"Mechanical wonder in Horology, invented by Mr William Cooper, Hamilton. Eight-day clock, lately invented by him, that will show the hours, minutes, and seconds with only three wheels and two pinions. Illustrated and described in the *Glasgow Mechanics' Magazine* for Saturday, 12th July 1824."

CORBET, ROBERT. 27 Slockwell Street, Glasgow, 1822-41.

CORDINGLEY, THOMAS. High Street, Wick, 1836.

CORRIE, PHILIP. Langholm, 1800-17.

COULTER, WILLIAM. Dockhead Street, Saltcoats, 1837-50.

COUPER, ANDREW. Clock Case Maker, Edinburgh, 1836.

"Andrew Couper, Clockcase Maker, Edinburgh, served Heir of Conquest, etc., to his brother, Thomas Couper, wright in St Andrews, dated 29th March 1836. Recorded 6th April 1836."—*Service of Heirs*.

COUSTEILL, JOHN. Edinburgh, 1694-1715.

"Son to Peter Cousteill, tailor and burgess of the Canongate, booked apprentice to Paul Romieu, 28th August 1694."

6th *November* 1714.—"There being a petition given in by John Cousteill, late prentice to the deceast Paul Romieu, watchmaker, craving that the house would grant warrand to the Deacon and Boxmaster to discharge his indentures. To the effect he may get his freedom yairby for the reasons yairin contained. It being put to the vote whether the desire of the petition should be granted or not, it was granted by plurality of votes."

15*th April* 1715.—"The which day the haill

Incorporation being met, compeared John Cousteill, late apprentice to the deceast Paul Romieu, watchmaker, and presented his essay, viz., the movements of a watch, which was found a weill wrought essay, etc. His essay masters were Robert Alexander and John Fraser. His essay was made in William Sutor's shop."—*E. H. Records.*

COUTTS, JAMES. Perth, 1800—Barosa Street, Perth, 1837-48.

COWAN, HUGH. Duerness Street, Thurso, 1837.

COWAN, JAMES. Edinburgh, 1744-81.

"Son of George Cowan, wright in Edinburgh; booked apprentice to Archibald Straiton, watchmaker, Edinburgh, 4th February 1744."

13*th June* 1753.—"Presented his bill for being admitted a clock and watch maker in right of his service, which was admitted and received, and an essay and essay masters appointed him. He paid unto the Treasurer five pounds sterling as the half of his upset, the other half to be paid at his admission."

2*nd February* 1754.—"Compeared and presented his essay, being a movement of a watch begun and ended in his own shop in presence of James Geddes, William Nicol, and William Aitken, essay masters, and Archibald Straiton, landlord, as they all declared, which was found a well wrought essay, etc. He paid the Treasurer five pounds sterling, as the last half of his upset money, and he also paid the clerk and officers dues."—*E. H. Records.*

"Lost at Dalkeith, on the 4th of October last, a silver watch, maker's name, D. Walker, London, No. N.C.N. Any person who has found the same may apply to James Cowan at his shop, west end of Luckenbooths, Edinburgh, and they shall be sufficiently rewarded."—*Caledonian Mercury,* 6th November 1756.

Elected Deacon of the Incorporation of Hammermen of Edinburgh, 17th September 1759-60-61.

"Stolen a small-sized silver watch, maker's name, James Miln, St Ninians, No. 995, the glass a little cracked, having a seal in the form of a compass hung by a black ribbon knotted in the middle. Whoever can give account of the said watch so as it may be recovered to Mr James Cowan, watchmaker, Lawnmarket, Edinburgh, shall have a guinea reward."—*Ibid.*, 19th December 1761.

"Lost on Saturday last, between Edinburgh and Penicuik, a Pinchbeck watch, with green case, maker's name, J. Jackson, No. 8105, with a steel chain and two seals. Whoever has found it and returns it to the Publisher of this paper or Mr Cowan, Parliament Square, shall be handsomely rewarded."—*Ibid.*, 14th June 1779.

"Lost on the 12th of October on the road from Dalkeith to Newbattle, from thence to the eight mile stone on the London road, returning to Dalkeith by the village of Lasswade, a small single cased French watch, maker's name, Charles Versen, Paris. Whoever has found the same and will bring it to Mr Cowan, watchmaker, Edinburgh, will receive a reward."—*Edinburgh Evening Courant*, 14th October 1780.

For further information regarding this clever and capable craftsman, see notes on William Auld, p. 22, and p 310 for Thomas Reid who succeeded to his business at his death, which took place in 1781. A splendid specimen of his skill is now located in the entrance hall of the Signet Library, Parliament Square, Edinburgh, the situation being only a few yards away from where it was originally made.

"Ann Cowan or Pringle, wife of Dunbar Pringle, currier, Edinburgh, served Heir General to her brother, James Cowan, watchmaker there, dated 9th July 1783. Recorded 12th July 1783."—*Services of Heirs.*

COWAN, WILLIAM. 8 High Street, Glasgow, 1806-22.

"On Friday night last a gentleman was stopped in Candleriggs Street by some persons who robbed him of a silver watch, large size, flat face, gold hands, maker's name, John Brown, London, No. 2676, having a brown ribbon with a gold key. Whoever will bring said watch and key to Mr William Cowan, watchmaker, High Street, or give information where the same may be found, will be handsomely rewarded."—*Glasgow Courier*, 25th May 1812.

COWAN, WILLIAM. Main Street, Lennoxtown, 1836.

CRAIG, DAVID. Ford, Pathhead, Dalkeith, 1798-1804.

"Lost or stolen on Wednesday night last a silver caped and jewelled day of the month watch, maker's name, David Craig, Ford, Pathhead, No. 765. Whoever will bring the same to Robert Logie, watchmaker, Richmond Street, Edinburgh, shall have forty shillings of reward."—*Edinburgh Evening Courant*, 9th June 1804.

CRAIG, JAMES. Glasgow, about 1760.

A capital specimen of this man's work was shown at the Glasgow Exhibition, 1911. It indicated the hours and the minutes, the day of the month, the moon's age, the signs of the Zodiac, the phases of the moon and her position in the heaven, An-astrolabe showing the stars of the principal constellation varying their position with the Calendar.

CRAIG, PETER, Clock Dial Maker. Glasgow, 1837.

CRAIG, ROBERT. Kilmaurs, 1740.

CRAIG, ROBERT. Kilmarnock, 1748.

"It is with pleasure we, the Magistrates and Town Council of Air (Ayr), inform the public that we have got iron or steel mills here for grinding malt, lately erected by Robert Craig, watchmaker in Kilmarnock, which appears to be a considerable improvement of its kind, and is in a great measure his own invention. The mills go by water, have one outer and one inner wheel of the usual form. The cogs of the inner wheel play upon the pinion of a horizontal wheel which drives two iron machines, whose cutters or teeth are made of steel, and so fitted with screws that they can be easily taken out and sharped when occasion requires, which will not, however, as we are assured, be necessary to be done oftener than once in two years. The tridle boards are commanded by strong steel springs which are able to stop the machine and prevent its being hurt by nails or stones among the malt. The mills go with as little water as any ordinary corn mills and grind with ease 16 bushels in 7 minutes. They have been going now for two months past and answer extremely well."— *Glasgow Courant*, 24th to 31st October 1748.

CRAW, JAMES. High Street, Forfar, 1837.

EIGHT-DAY CLOCK.
In mahogany case. By James Craig, Glasgow.
1760. The property of Sir John Stirling-Maxwell,
Bart., of Pollok.

[To face page 90.

CRAWFORD, ARCHIBALD. 6 Manse Court, Main Street, Largs, 1836-50.

CRAWFORD, GEORGE. High Street, Falkirk, 1836.

CRAWFORD, JAMES. 51 High Street, Johnstone, 1836.

CRAWFORD, ROBERT. Foulden, Dunse, 1803.

CRAWFORD, WILLIAM. Markinch, 1837.

CRAWFORD, WILLIAM. Glasgow, 1799.

"Watch lost on Wednesday, the 30th of October last, in the town of Rutherglen. An old silver watch, maker's name, William Crawford, Glasgow."—*Glasgow Courier*, 26th November 1799.

CREE, JOHN. 47 Stockwell Street, Glasgow, 1829-41.

CREIGHTON, DAVID. 28 Hamilton Street, Greenock, 1821.

CREITH, ROBERT. Leith, 1554. *See* pages 134-5.

CREYCH, ROBERT. Edinburgh, 1570 (probably same as above).

CRICHTON, DAVID. Glasgow, 1822.

CRICHTON, GEORGE. Mid-Calder, 1829.

"Agnes Crichton, in Mid-Calder, served Heir General to her mother, Barbara Stuart, wife of George Crichton, watchmaker there, dated 14th December 1829. Recorded 21st December 1829."—*Services of Heirs.*

CRICHTON, JOHN. Shore, Leith, 1793-1800.

CRIGHTON, JOHN. Dundee, 1795.

CRIGHTON, WALTER. Nungate, Haddington, 1850.

CROLL, COLIN. 16 South St Andrew Street, Edinburgh, 1804-8.

This maker does not appear to have been a freeman of the Edinburgh Hammermen Incorporation, but the omission occurring in his case will be found in that of a large number of others who were in business after 1800. This was brought about by the action of the members of these old-world societies, who by a short-sighted policy some years previous had increased the entry money and other dues for freemen, in some cases £70 being asked, and ultimately £100 being demanded and paid for admission. This was prohibitive in the case of any but the wealthy, the consequence being that men of undoubted talent who lacked this amount of ready money trusted to their own exertions rather than undergo this exaction. To attempt to start business within the jurisdiction of these incorporations was next to impossible, as they had all the powers of the law at their command ; but in the case of a city like Edinburgh the march of progress was a factor that baffled their powers. The extension of the city by the opening of the North Bridge made a loophole which, by the wisdom of the Magistrates, was declared to be outside the scope of the Incorporation's bounds, and rendered it possible for a competent craftsman to commence business, of course suffering all the disadvantages of being outside of the recognised districts of particular trades. Croll evidently knew all these risks and commenced business at 16 South St Andrew Street, Edinburgh, in 1806. His abilities and stock may be judged of by the articles he dealt in, viz., box and pocket chronometers, repeating and horizontal watches, musical, spring, quarter, and common eight-day clocks. Not only these "but any part or movement of them is executed at the shortest notice, complete satisfaction being guaranteed." Notwithstanding all these qualifications Croll could not hold on, and by the year 1808 his name disappears as a watch and clock maker in the city of Edinburgh.

CROLL, COLIN. George Street, Perth, 1818.

This is, in all probability, the same maker as above, who, profiting by his experience, found it a difficult matter to make a business without becoming a Hammerman, and, accordingly, a Colin Croll was admitted a freeman of the Perth Hammermen in 1818.

CROLL, WILLIAM. West Port, Dundee, 1837.

CRONE, WILLIAM. Upper Denburn, Aberdeen, 1846.

CROOKS AND BURN. High Street, Edinburgh, 1796.

"To WATCHMAKERS AND DEALERS IN WATCHES.—Crooks and Burn respectfully announce that they have

formed a connection with two of the most eminent watch manufacturing houses in London, and supply dealers at the London wholesale prices, adding only a small commission for trouble and risk of carriage to Edinburgh. They also intimate to the public that this establishment obviously enables them to sell on the most favourable terms, and their liberal plan of warranting all watches at Three Guineas price and upwards, securing satisfaction to a certainty, is a material object. The most pointed attention to orders from the country."
—*Edinburgh Evening Courant*, 17th November 1796.

CROSS OR CORSE, JAMES.   Perth, 1800-31.

Booked apprentice to Patrick Gardiner, Perth, 1800.

"John Corse or Cross, at Teuchithill, served Heir General to his brother, James Corse or Cross, clockmaker, Perth, dated 30th September 1831. Recorded 11th October 1831."—*Services of Heirs*.

CROSS & CARRUTHERS.   21 Elm Row, Edinburgh, 1837.

CROUCH, WILLIAM.   40 North Bridge, Edinburgh, 1850.

CRUICKSHANKS, GEORGE.   Elgin, 1820-37.

CRUKSHANKS, JOHNE.   Aberdeen, 1453.   Page 1.

CUMMING, ALEXANDER.   London, 1733-1814.

Mathematician and Mechanic, was a native of Edinburgh. He was apprenticed to the watchmaking business, which he carried on with great reputation for many years in Bond Street, London. On retiring from trade he settled in Pentonville, where he had several houses. He was appointed a magistrate, and elected a Fellow of the Royal Society. Died 8th March 1814.

"To be disposed by lottery by Robert Hay, Auctioneer, at the Edinburgh Vendue, second fore stair below the cross well, south side of the High Street, Edinburgh, a very fine eight-day clock with a mahogany case, dead seconds from the centre, made by Mr Cumming, clock and watch maker to His Majesty at London."—*Edinburgh Advertiser*.

CUMMING, ALEXANDER.   Inveraray, 1775.

CUMMING, CHARLES. Edinburgh, 1772-78.

Booked apprentice to Walter Brunton, Edinburgh, 1772.

CUMMING, JAMES. Edinburgh, 1761.

Booked apprentice to Deacon James Cowan, clock and watch maker, Edinburgh, 7th February 1761.

CUMMING, JOHN. Edinburgh, 1737.

Son to Arthur Cumming, barber in Edinburgh; booked apprentice Patrick Gordon, 5th February 1737.

CUNNINGHAM, JAMES. Haddington, 1776.

CUNNINGHAM, WILLIAM. Sanquhar, 1837.

CUNNINGHAM, W. AND A. 79 George Street, Edinburgh, 1790-1845.

CURRER, JOHN. Peebles, 1840.

CURRER, ROBERT. High Street, Peebles, 1836.

CURRIE, THOMAS. Edinburgh, 1793-1804.

Castle Wynd, 1793; Hay's Close, Grassmarket, 1804.

CUTHBERT, JAMES. Perth, 1735-55.

Admitted a freeman clock and watch maker in Perth Hammermen, 1735.

"That in the night betwixt the 2nd and 3rd December last, there was stolen out of James Cuthbert, clock smith in Perth, two silver watches: the one No. 2113, maker's name David Lasturgeon, London, which has the regulator on the dial plate blued, casts up the day of the month in the dial plate at winding up, single cased, and winds up on the back of the case, covered with a shutter, hath a bridge instead of a cock of a large size, with the main spring within her broke; the other an old watch, the maker's name and number unknown, having only an hour hand double cased. If any person can give notice of the above two watches so as they can be returned to the said James Cuthbert or to the publishers of this paper, they shall have one guinea reward and no questions asked, and if they come to any watchmaker's hand, they will be so good as detain them."—*Edinburgh Evening Courant*, 30th January 1755.

CUTHBERT, JOHN. Perth, 1764.

Admitted a freeman clock and watch maker in Perth Hammermen, 1764.

DALGARNO, ALEXANDER. Aberdeen; died 1852.

DALGLEISH, JOHN. Edinburgh, 1742-71.

8th May 1742.—" Son of John Dalgleish, late freeman and Deacon of this Incorporation, presented his bill for being admitted freeman watch and clock maker, which was received accordingly. He paid Three pounds, twelve shillings, and two pence and two thirds of a penny Sterling, as the half of his upset and dues for the Maiden Hospital, and is to pay the other half at his entry."

12th November 1742.—" Compeared John Dalgleish, son to John Dalgleish, deceast, locksmith, and late Deacon of this Incorporation, and presented his essay, viz., a white movement of a watch, which was found a well wrought essay, etc. His essay masters were John Richardson and John Brown. His essay was made in his own shop and Hugh Barclay, landlord."—*E. H. Records.*

" John Dalgleish, watchmaker, burgess, North Kirk Parish, married to Hannah Johnston, daughter of John Johnston, merchant and late baillie in Culross, 19 Decr. 1742."—*Edinburgh Marriage Register.*

" Lost last night betwixt the Abbay and the Meal Market, a small-sized silver watch, maker's name, Ellis, London, with a green silk string and a key. Whoever has found it let them call at John Dalgleish, watchmaker in Edinburgh, who will give half a guinea of a reward."—*Caledonian Mercury,* 7th June 1744.

15th September 1749.—" At a meeting of the Incorporation, called on the above date for the purpose of voting on the names submitted as candidates for the office of Deacon, objections were taken to John Dalgleish's vote. James Clausen protested that John Dalgleish should not be allowed to vote because he had a benefice and office from the Town Council for keeping the town clocks, and an act of Council for that purpose with an annual salary, to which Deacon Gifford and others adheared.

"John Dalgleish answered he had no such office as either from the nature of the thing or by any law could disqualify him from his right of voting as any other free member, and protested his vote might be received and held good, to which Deacon Wilson adheared.

"John Dalgleish then voted under such conditions, and, briefly, it may be stated that he had the satisfaction of seeing five of the six names he voted for elected to be presented to the Town Council for revisal, his own name making the sixth. Next day a meeting being called, the members agreed that the protest taken against John Dalgleish's vote shall go no further than among themselves, and the Deacon then presenting the amended lect from the Town Council (three names in number), voting took place, and John Dalgleish was practically unanimously elected Deacon of the Edinburgh Hammermen for the ensuing year, and as usual the minutes of this meeting are signed in his own handwriting."—*E. H. Records.*

"A gold watch lost, the dial plate gold, maker's name Johnson, and the day of the month cast up on the dial plate. The watch is pretty large, has only a single case, and winds up on the back of the case. It had a steel chain and a steel seal with a coat of arms. If any person has found it and will return it to Mr John Dalgleish, watchmaker, in the Parliament Close, Edinburgh, shall be sufficiently rewarded." — *Caledonian Mercury*, 23rd May 1753.

"To be sold on the 10th February next, betwixt the hours of four and five afternoon, within John's Coffeehouse, a house, fifth story of Paterson's Court, possest by John Dalgleish, watchmaker, consisting of kitchen and three fire rooms, rent £7."—*Edinburgh Evening Courant*, 30th January 1767.

We now give an account of an episode in John Dalgleish's life, which, no doubt, affected many others beside him, namely, the visit of Prince Charlie and his Highland host to Edinburgh in the ever-memorable year of 1745, but was curiously enough brought home to him in a manner that gave him some concern. This was owing to the inquiry by the Government into

the matter after the Rebellion was over, and in Vol. 18
of *State Trials*, page 102-6, will be found an account of
the "Trial of Archibald Stewart, late Lord Provost
of Edinburgh, for neglect of duty and misbehaviour
in the execution of his office as Lord Provost, before
and at the time the rebels got possession of the city,
in the middle of September 1745." John Dalgleish
had the unique experience of being summoned as a
witness for both sides of the inquiry, his testimony
being as follows :—

"John Dalgleish, watchmaker in Edinburgh, depones,
That he was a captain of the trained bands on duty
upon the evening of Monday, the 10th of September
1745, and between seven and eight o'clock at night,
he received a message by one of the town's officers,
containing orders to him to cause his company to
lay down their arms and to dismiss them, which he
did not incline on that message to do, but sent his
ensign, William Sibbald, tailor, with orders to find out
the Provost wherever he was and to acquaint him,
and if he could not be found, the captain commandant ;
that he the deponent had received the above message,
as from the panel or some of the council, and to
enquire at one or either of them if such a message
was sent, and what he would do in relation to the
subject thereof. That his ensign accordingly went
and returned to him between eight and nine o'clock,
with orders as from the panel to dismiss his guard
and lay down their arms, and the deponent being then
standing at the door of the Weigh-house, which was
his post, and where he had planted two sentries, his
men rushed out upon him leaving their arms behind
them. And depones, That he received no direction
from any person in what manner these arms should
be disposed of or secured. Depones, That he first
mounted guard upon the evening of the fast day,
which was held two weeks before the rebels came
to town, and mounted guard again upon the 16th
day of September, about seven o'clock in the morning,
and just before that saw Panel in the Goldsmith's Hall,

who acquainted the deponent that he would get powder
and ball and cartridge boxes from John Hislop, the
city store keeper. That about nine o'clock he sent
to Mr Hislop, desiring to have them, but he not being
in the way the said ammunition was not brought
till about eleven o'clock, when as much as was
thought would be useful was delivered to him for
his company.

"Being interrogate for the panel depones, That
betwixt nine and ten of the Sunday morning, the
15th, the officers of the trained bands were called
by the captain commandant, by the panel's orders,
to the Crown tavern, where he and the rest of the
captains, who were all in one room together, received
orders from their commandant to be ready to draw
out their companies on a minute's warning, which
each captain communicated to his subaltern with orders
to such of them as were there not to leave that tavern
without leaving word where they might be found.
That about three o'clock of the afternoon of this day
the captains got orders to repair to their respective
bounds and draw out their companies, which they
accordingly did, and then the deponent's company
had arms distributed among them, and, as far as he
could observe, arms were delivered to the other companies, and that before the companies were dismissed
they received orders to be ready to march at tuck
of drum."

These scattered but authentic notices of this craftsman exhibit the part he played in the common affairs
of his fellow citizens. Useful in his day and generation
he had the satisfaction of handing on his flourishing
business to his son Laurence (q.v.) some years before
his death, which took place at the close of the year
1771.

DALGLEISH, LAURENCE. Edinburgh, 1771-1821.

23rd *March* 1771.—"Compeared and presented a
bill craving to be admitted a freeman clock and watch
maker in right of his father. The prayer of which was

granted. The essay to be presented between and the first Martinmas meeting. He paid the Treasurer sixty-five merks as the first half of his upset money."

25th January 1772.—" Laurence Dalgleish, son of the deceast John Dalgleish, compeared and presented his essay, being a watch movement begun, made, and finished in his own shop, in presence of James Cowan, landlord, Robert Clidsdale, William Downie, and Thomas Letham, essay masters."—*E. H. Records.*

"Christina Dalgleish, wife of L. Dalgleish, watchmaker, Edinburgh, served Heir General to her father, Patrick Geddes, Surgeon, Culross, dated 26th July 1791. Recorded 28th July 1791."—*Services of Heirs.*

"Laurence Dalgleish retires from business; he goes to reside at Torryburn, where he will be able to supply his customers on more moderate terms than formerly. Although L. D. has no successor to his business, yet from the friendship he bears to Mr George Skelton (q.v.), watchmaker at the Cross, he takes this opportunity of recommending him to his customers for repairing their watches, and that they may be assured that he is a man of integrity and completely master of his business, and he has not the least doubt of his giving entire satisfaction to L. D.'s friends."—*Edinburgh Evening Courant,* 18th June 1808.

He died at West Grange in 1821.

DALGLEISH, ROBERT. High Street, Falkirk, 1820.

DALGLEISH & DICKIE. North Bridge, Edinburgh, 1791.

"A watch lost on Wednesday, the 19th current, between seven and eight in the morning. A silver watch was lost between the west end of the links of Kirkcaldy and Pettycur Harbour, maker's name, Thomas Stroud, London, No. 451. If the person who has found the same will restore it to Messrs Dalgleish and Dickie, watch makers, North Bridge Street, Edinburgh, they will be handsomely rewarded, and it is requested it may be stopt if offered for sale."—*Edinburgh Evening Courant,* 20th October 1791.

DALL, THOMAS.   Dundee, 1819.

"Lily Anderson or Dall, wife of Thomas Dall, watchmaker, Dundee, served Heir Portioner General to her father, Walter Anderson, weaver there, dated 12th August 1819.   Recorded 17th August 1819."
—*Services of Heirs.*

DALLAS, ALEXANDER.   Inverness, 1850.

See note on William Smith, Inverness, pages 366-7.

DALLAS, JOSEPH.   Perth, 1760.

17*th May* 1760.—"Joseph Dallas, a stranger, is admitted to be a freeman clock and watch maker in the Incorporation of Hammermen, Perth, for payment of five pounds sterling."

"Prosecuted in 1763 for encroaching on the trade privileges."—*Perth Hammermen Records.*

DALLAWAY & SON.   Edinburgh, 1785-1812.

Though not clockmakers, yet are entitled to a place in these lists, seeing that nearly all the painted and enamelled clock dials produced in Edinburgh near the end of the eighteenth century were the work of this firm.   The earliest notice of the name occurs in an advertisement in the *Edinburgh Evening Courant*, dated 18th June 1785.

"A feu-duty of Four pounds ten shillings, upliftable forth of a piece of ground lying on the north side of the Canongate at the foot of Tolbooth Wynd, with a work house built thereon as presently possessed by Mr William Dallaway, Japanner."

This William was the first in Edinburgh to introduce the art of japanning, and from about 1780 up to 1800 had the monopoly of the manufacture in the district. It is highly probable that he was also the designer and draughtsman of a number of these painted dials as the following seems to imply :—

"JAPANNING.—William Dallaway returns his grateful acknowledgments to such as have employed him, and solicits a continuance of their favours.   He has taken in partnership his son, who has been in London and Birmingham for the improvement of that art.

Informs their employers that he has procured the secret of inlaying stove fronts, dressing-cases, candlesticl s, etc which is a thing never attempted here before. The merchants in that line must see the utility of such an art as they can have whatever pattern executed in less time than they could bring them from London. There tortoiseshell and Pontipool work exceeds every thing of the kind attempted here both for beauty in varnish and regularity in striping.

" W. D. & Son beg leave to mention that they have greatly enlarged their shops for the carrying on the chair japanning and that they have procured some of the finest varnishes for wood. They have a varnish for mahogany tables and tea-trays that will not fly although ever so hardly handled. W. D. & Son flatter themselves that their work upon trial will give satisfaction. Commissions from the country carefully executed. W. D. still continues to teach drawing in all its branches as usual.—Foot of Tolbooth Wynd, Canongate."—*Ibid.*, 2nd February 1793.

William Dallaway dying after this date, the business became known as H. Dallaway & Son. To give an idea of the trade they carried on, an advertisement from the same newspaper, and dated 18th May 1797, follows :—

" H. Dallaway & Son, Japan Manufactory, North Back of Canongate, Edinburgh.

" H. D. & Son return their grateful acknowledgments for past favours. They beg leave to inform their friends and the public that they have on hand a complete assortment of the following articles which they continue to sell Wholesale, Retail, and for Exportation :—

" Japanned Fire Screens of black iron, a capital invention, and for elegance and neatness nothing can excel them ; Clock Dials, a fine collection ; Tea Trays, Waiters, Candlesticks, Snuffer Stands, Knife Slips, Bread Baskets.

" H. D. & Son cannot let slip this opportunity of particularly recommending their Tea Trays, Waiters, etc., as they have now brought them to that perfection as would do honour to an English Manufactory. They flatter themselves that from their perseverance and attention they still will merit a continuance of past favours. Commissions from the country in the Japanning line or for any of the above articles will be carefully attended to."

How long after this date the Japanning Manufactory was carried on we have been unable to discover, but another brother named Patrick Dallaway opened an ironmonger's business in the High Street about 1807, which, as the following correspondence shows, was in active existence at that date. We may be pardoned for bringing this brother's name into our lists, seeing he is in no way entitled to be classed as a clockmaker, but it is given chiefly to bring out the arbitrary manner which the Hammermen of Edinburgh adopted in coercing a citizen whose only fault was that he dared to open a shop within their jurisdiction without first joining the Incorporation. The correspondence from their Records here given shows the jealousy that existed even as late as the nineteenth century among the trade burgesses of Edinburgh.

29th July 1809.—"Remitted the case of Patrick Dallaway, stated to be guilty of an encroachment, to the quartermaster to call him to account, and with powers to proceed against him if he does not give them satisfaction."

4th November 1809.—"William Lochart, from the Quartermaster's, reported that they had waited on Mr Dallaway relative to the encroachment made by him on the rights of the Incorporation, but had received no satisfaction nor had he thought proper to return any answer to a letter written to him on the subject. It was agreed, however, to delay any proceedings against him until next quarter, and direct intimation to be made to him that if he fails to enter with the Incorporation against that time, that they will direct he to be prosecuted."

2nd April 1910.—"Letter from P. Dallaway, which was received previous to the meeting of the 3rd February, but wants a date.

"To the Deacon and Incorporation of Hammermen of Edinburgh :—

"GENTLEMEN,—On the 22nd instant I received a letter from your clerk, Mr C. Cunningham, informing me unless I entered with the trade at first meeting a prosecution would be commenced against me under a pretence that I was infringing on their rights. I have to inform you I do no more than the Greenside Company and not so much as Mr Thomson. Notwithstanding this, I mean to settle with the Incorporation of Hammermen in an amicable manner. I now make an offer of the sum that was paid by Mr Sanderson to be allowed the privilege of keeping warehouse within the city. At present I do not; I only exercise the profession of a merchant. The few articles that are manufactured by William Dallaway & Son in the Canongate, and the small quantity that is bought by me from that concern, is very trifling indeed. Should my offer not be accepted I have, on the other hand, no objection to become bound that no article manufactured by that company shall be sold or retailed within the city, that will in the least infringe on the rights and privileges of the Incorporation of Hammermen. I have also to observe that there is not an article that is manufactured by that concern that is not as regularly paid for as if it had been brought 1000 miles distant, and really, considering that I am no Hammerman bred, and as you have already a precedent in your books, wherein you have admitted the exercise of the trade to an individual without granting the rights or privileges of the chapel, or anything that may belong to the Incorporation, except the free exercise of his business within the city. In Mary's Chapel there are several instances of the same nature. Some time ago I mentioned to Messrs Smith and Lochart that I was willing to submit my case to arbitration, but to this I never received an answer, but peremptorily demanding me to enter without ever convincing or instructing why I should do so.

"I think after making this offer my case might be

seriously considered, and I make no doubt all of you will be convinced of the fairness of my conduct towards the Incorporation of Hammermen.

"Your accepting of my offer will much oblige, etc.,

"P. DALLAWAY."

2nd April 1810.—"Which letter and the proposition therein contained having been fully considered by the committee, they are of opinion that the terms he offers ought not to be accepted of. But if Mr Dallaway shall, at or before the term of Whitsunday next, pay to the treasurer the sum of £35, they would propose that he shall be allowed twelve months more to consider whether he will pay the other £35, make an essay and become a member, or pay only £15 more, for which sum of £50 he should have the privilege of carrying on the tinsmith art within the city, but to have no title or interest in the other rights and privileges of the Incorporation."

22nd May 1810.—"The committee having reconsidered their former report in terms of the minute from last quarter meeting, are of opinion that although in general a less sum than £50 should not be taken for allowing any person to practise an art which interferes with the privileges of this Incorporation, yet as the father of Mr Dallaway had introduced the Art of Japanning into this quarter, which had turned out to be beneficial to the trade of the country, they therefore recommend that out of respect to his memory his son should be allowed to carry on the tinsmith trade within the city for the sum of forty pounds during his life, but to enjoy no other privileges belonging to the Incorporation, and for the same reason if Mr Dallaway prefers entering with the Incorporation, and being admitted in common form, that he should be received upon paying sixty pounds sterling."

"Letter read from P. Dallaway, dated 29th November 1810, on 2nd February 1811 :—

"In answer to yours of the 3rd, enclosing an extract of the Hammermen of Edinburgh, I have, in the first place, to return them my most respectful compliments

for the very handsome manner they have offered me
to become a member of their Incorporation, on account
of my father having introduced the japanning trade,
and, believe me, nothing would have given me more
pleasure than to have become a full member of so
respectable a body. But from the death of my father,
I find I cannot carry on the ironmongery business and
follow the japanning also; therefore I must relinquish
one of them. I have now come to the resolution of
giving up the said ironmongery and mean to devote my
attention to my manufactory. I trust this will be a
sufficient apology to the Incorporation for my not
entering with them, and I am, with gratitude, your most
obedient servant, P. DALLAWAY."

(Same date).—".And the meeting having considered
the same, are of opinion that as he has carried on
business for two years, that the treasurer should apply
to him for eight guineas as Stallanger's fees to the term
of Whitsunday next."

3rd August 1811.—"Read letter from P. Dallaway
and direct the clerk to write him and insist for payment
of £8, 8s. as a Stallanger fee to Whitsunday last,
acquainting him at same time that unless he come
forward to enter with the Incorporation or remove his
shop between Whitsunday and Martinmas next that the
prosecution will be proceeded in, and the clerk is
authorized accordingly."

2nd November 1811.—"Patrick Dallaway compeared
on this date, and presented a petition craving to be
admitted a freeman tinsmith for payment of sixty
pounds, as fixed by minute of the Incorporation, dated
22nd May 1810; and the prayer thereof being granted,
it was agreed that the eight guineas already paid by
Mr Dallaway of Stallanger fees should be allowed out
of the first moiety of his entry money. He accordingly
paid the treasurer £21, 12s., and was appointed to
produce his essay at the next quarter."

1st February 1812.—"Compeared and produced his
essay, a drainer, begun, made, and finished in his own

shop in presence of Adam Anderson, landlord, and John Steel and Robert White, essay masters, as they declared. He paid the treasurer thirty pounds, being the second moiety of his entry money, and was accordingly admitted."

DALRYMPLE, WILLIAM. Edinburgh, 1781.

Booked apprentice to Robert Aitchison, Edinburgh, 3rd November 1781.

DALZEIL, JAMES. Fraserburgh, 1798-1815.

DANKS, ——. Watch Case Maker, Edinburgh, 1819-35.

84 High Street, 1819; 1 Carrubber's Close, 1835.

DARLING, ROBERT. Canongate, Edinburgh, 1788-1825; 4 West Richmond Street, 1825.

DARLING, ROBERT. Haddington, 1796.

DARLING, ROBERT. Lauder, 1797.

DAVIDSON, ANDREW. George Street, Stranraer, 1820.

DAVIDSON, ——. Dunse, 1808.

"CURIOUS FIND IN A CLOCK.—A curious find was made the other day in the works of the old clock, which for many years was in the 'briest o' the laft,' or perhaps nowadays more intelligibly the front of the gallery, in the old Free Church, Newton Port. When, more than twenty years ago, the church was deserted for the new St John's Church at the West Port, the clock was removed, on instructions, by Mr D. M. Rose, Market Street. The old recorder of time, which had served its day and generation well, was of no use, but it lay unbroken-up till a few days ago. It was believed to have been made by a Haddington clockmaker, but strangely enough, this point was settled in its hour of dissolution. On opening what is known as the 'barrel' of the works, Mr Rose found a small bit of old-fashioned hand-made paper, bearing on both sides faded writing. The paper is about $3\frac{1}{2}$ inches by $2\frac{1}{2}$ inches. The writer has been somewhat illiterate. The following, as closely as the writing can be made out, is an exact copy:—' Dunse, May 6, 1808.—I can't say when this is putin in, but Lord knows when it will be taken out again we'll (the two ll's are somewhat scratched out) will be all Dead and rotten be that time.

James Gray, Boren in Blincarne (or Blinearne), Aged
22 years, prentice to Mr Davidson, Dunse, May 6th
1808, Mr Davidson's Shop. With the jornaman and
prentices Names. James Davidson, son to Billie; Thos.
Gray, prentice; Jno. Paxton, pre.; Jas. Atkinson, jor.;
Wm. Walker (or Walter), jor.; James Gray, prens.;
Thos. McGregor, prs.; Alexr. McGregor, Maker, jornn.
Mr A. McGregor going to Yenmouth' (word doubtful).
Apparently the word 'can't' in the opening line was
meant to be 'can'; 'pre' means 'prentice'; and 'jor,'
'journeyman.' Almost to a day the paper lay in its
hiding-place for 108 years. The writer, Thomas Gray,
must have been born in 1786, the year when Robert
Burns first published his poems."—*Haddington Courier*,
19th May 1916.

DAVIDSON, CHARLES. Forfar, 1798-1815.

DAVIDSON, JAMES. Dunbar, 1813-37.

DAVIDSON, JAMES. Old Deer, Aberdeenshire, 1836.

DAVIDSON, JAMES. High Street, Girvan, 1820-37.

DAVIDSON, JOHN. 21 Oxford Street, Glasgow, 1836.

DAVIDSON, JOHN. Wick, 1892. Page 26.

DAVIDSON, NEAN. Dunse, 1798-1820.

DAVIDSON, ROBERT. Lerwick, Shetland, 1836.

DAVIE, CHRISTOPHER. Linlithgow, 1783-1832.
     Son of below, and for many years Dean of Guild
of Linlithgow.

DAVIE, JOHN. Linlithgow, 1753-84. *See* notes on
     Linlithgow Town Clocks.
     "James Bryce, flaxdresser in Linlithgow, married
     Margaret, daughter of John Davie, watchmaker there,
     29th April 1778."—*Edinburgh Marriage Register*.

DAWSON, DAVID. Tarbolton, 1837.

DAWSON, MATTHEW. Haddington, 1798-1843.

DEAN, THOMAS. 25 New Bridge Street, Glasgow, 1841.

DEANS, JOHN. Haddington, 1803.

DEVERLEY, HUGH. 232 High Street, Perth, 1843.

DEVLIN, PATRICK.   Greenock, 1840.

"On Friday night or Saturday morning the shop of Mr Patrick Devlin, watchmaker, situated in William Street, Greenock, was entered by thieves, and no fewer than sixty-four watches, seven of them which were of gold, carried off, besides a quantity of jewellery, the extent of which has not yet been ascertained.   There were also taken three American eagles (gold), one old guinea, a sovereign and a half, and about thirty ounces of dollars and old coins.   The value of the watches alone is about £500.   No trace of the thieves had been obtained up to Saturday night.

"We noted some time ago that a jeweller's shop was broken into in Greenock and gold and silver watches carried away to the value of £500.   In consequence of information communicated to the Carlisle Police, they succeeded in taking into custody a broker from Glasgow who was attempting to dispose of some of the stolen watches.   Upwards of twenty were found in his possession, and the prisoner and property were brought to Glasgow by Mr Mann, Superintendent of the Greenock Police."— *Edinburgh Evening Post*, 11th and 25th July 1848.

DEWAR, DAVID.   West Street, Doune, 1837.

DICK, JAMES.   Ayr; died 11th June 1800.

DICK, ROBERT.   Dailly, Ayrshire, 1850.

DICK, WILLIAM.   96 Jamaica Street, Glasgow, 1841.

DICKIE, ALEXANDER.   Edinburgh, 1762-1808.

"Bound apprentice to Daniel Binny, watch and clock maker, 20th June 1762.   Discharged of his indentures on 26th December 1769.   Compeared on 26th December 1776, and presented a bill craving to be admitted a freeman clock and watch maker."

3rd May 1777—"Compeared and produced his essay, being a watch movement begun and finished in his own shop, in presence of Robert Clidsdale, landlord, John Skirving, Thomas Morgan, and Thomas Sibbald, essay masters as they declared, etc."—*E. H. Records.*

"Lost this morning in the town of Leith or on the pier, a gold chased watch, No. 219, maker's name, Thomas Harvey, London.   Whoever has found the said watch and will remit it to Mr Dickie, watchmaker,

BRACKET CHIMING CLOCK,

In walnut case, with ormolu mountings. By Alexander Dickie, Edinburgh, 1762-1808. The property of the Bank of Scotland, Edinburgh.

[To face page 108.

Bridge Street, or the publisher of this paper shall be handsomely rewarded."—*Edinburgh Evening Courant*, 18th August 1781.

In all probability this is the same individual who was in partnership with Laurence Dalgleish. *See* page 99. A beautiful bracket clock of his production is now located in the Bank of Scotland, Edinburgh. *See* illustration.

DICKIE, ANDREW. Edinburgh, 1736-52.

9th January 1736.—" The committee having taken into their consideration the possibility of admitting strangers to be freemen, it being a tender point to the generality of the arts to determine that point absolutely at present, but leaves it to the consideration of the particular art when application is made to them upon that account. And as to giving an answer to Mr Dickie's letter, they upon desire of clockmakers present, delay giving their opinion till the clockmakers meet with Mr Dickie this night, and give in their report after they have communed with Mr Dickie against to-morrow morning."

10th January 1736.—" The house having met, the Deacon reporting from the meeting of the clockmakers that they were willing to receive Mr Dickie in the terms of his letter, John Brown, clockmaker, protested that in case this house is not able to protect the clockmaker's art in their privileges against any stranger, the house shall be obliged not only to refund the money paid by Mr Dickie but also what money has been paid by any of the art, to whom Patrick Gordon, Alexander Brand, and Hugh Barclay adhered."

(Same date).—" The Incorporation having considered the letter from Andrew Dickie, clockmaker, craving to be admitted a freeman clockmaker upon his paying Thirty pounds Sterling, providing the Incorporation will provide him his burgess-ship and free him of all the expenses of getting it, and also the report from the clockmakers of their being willing and consenting to his being admitted on these terms, the house unanimously agree to receive him upon these terms and recommend to the Deacon to get him made burgess as easy as possible."

28th September 1736.—"Compeared and presented his essay, viz., an eight-days' pendulum clock, which was found a well wrought essay, etc., and therefore they admitted him to be a freeman clock and watch maker among them. His essay masters were John Brown, clockmaker, Alexander Brand, and George Aitken. His essay was made in Hugh Barclay's shop. He paid the boxmaster Thirty pounds Sterling for his upset, and, in token of his consent to the Incorporation's Act, had subscribed their presents. *Sic subita*, Andw. Dickie." —*E. H. Records.*

" There was lost on Thursday, the 15th current, at the Head of the Canongate, a watch with an enamelled dial plate in a single case covered with Shagreen, maker's name, Etherington, London, No. 2090. Any person who can give notice thereof are desired to acquaint Andrew Dickie, watchmaker in Edinburgh, and they shall be handsomely rewarded and no questions asked."— *Edinburgh Evening Courant*, 30th January 1750.

" There was lost on the 9th July between Bilston and Papermill, a watch in a gold inner case and enamelled dial, its outer case shagreen of a green colour neatly studded, within which case is an Equation table with the following direction on it : ' Andrew Dickie, at the Blackmoor Head and Star, in West Smithfield, London.' Whoever has found the same and will bring it entire to Mr Andrew Dickie, watchmaker, Edinburgh, shall have 3 guineas reward."—*Caledonian Mercury*, 15th July 1755.

As will be seen by the above minutes from the *Hammermen's Records*, no information is to be found where this maker came from. It is clear from the comparative easy manner he gained admission into the Incorporation that his credentials and skill were of a high order, a fact brought out by reference to the notes on Dunfermline Town Clocks, page 128, where he was selected to make and fit up a new clock for the Kirk Steeple in 1743-45. He was in business at Wilson's Land, Lawnmarket, Edinburgh, which he occupied till 1765, the year of his death ; his nephew, Daniel Binny (q.v.), succeeding to his business at that date.

DICKIE, ANDREW. Dunfermline, 1752.

In Henderson's *Annals of Dunfermline* it is stated that one Andrew Dickie was the first clockmaker to commence business in that town.

DICKIE, ANDREW. Stirling, 1723-39.

DICKIE, WILLIAM. Dunfermline, 1780.

"A WATCH STOLEN.—There was stolen within these few days from a house in the town of Dunfermline, a silver watch with an enamelled dial plate, maker's name, David Hastings, Alnwick, No. 150. Any person who will bring the same or give information as shall lead to the recovery of it to Mr William Dickie, watchmaker, Dunfermline, or to the publisher of this paper will be handsomely rewarded."—*Edinburgh Evening Courant*, 27th September 1780.

DICKMAN, JOHN. Leith, 1800-50.

Bernard Street, 1800; 36 Shore, 1825; 4 Charlotte Place, 1850.

DICKMAN, JOHN. Edinburgh, 1842.

At a meeting of the Royal Society of Arts held on 12th December 1842, a timepiece constructed on the principle of the rotary pendulum without an escapement was exhibited by Mr John Dickman, chronometer, watch, and clock maker, 142 George Street, Edinburgh.

DICKSON, CHARLES. Dundee, 1722.

DICKSON, JOHN. Edinburgh, 1790.

Apprenticed to Laurence Dalgleish, 10th February 1790.

DIXON, THOMAS. High Street, Haddington, 1837.

DOBBIE, ANDREW. Glasgow, 1820-48.

"Serious Riot in Glasgow on Monday, 5th March 1848. Mob attacked the shop of Mr Dobbie, Clyde Place, watchmaker, and presented a pistol at the head of the shop boy, threatening to shoot him if he dared to offer any resistance. They then proceeded to rifle the shop of the gold and silver watches it contained; some of the marauders were observed running out of the shop with their pockets full of watches. Mr Dobbie himself was wounded in defending his property."—*Edinburgh Evening Courant*, March 1848.

DOBBIE, GEORGE. High Street, Falkirk, 1821-50.

DOBBIE, John.   Prestonpans, 1820.

DOBBIE, John.   275 High Street, Glasgow, 1802-26.

"Watch lost about a month ago in the village of Milngavie, a silver watch with concrete seconds, silver caped stop point broken, maker's name, C. Davidson, London, No. 6098, both upon the cape and work. Those who have the said watch and will return it to Mr John Dobbie, watchmaker, High Street, Glasgow, will receive a genteel reward."—*Glasgow Courier*, 23rd October 1802.

DOBBIE, John.   Edinburgh, 1783.

DOBBIE, Thomas.   51 Adelphi Street, Glasgow, 1828-48.

DOBBIE, William.   Falkirk, 1768.

"Lost or stolen betwixt Falkirk and Carron works, a silver watch with a brass pendant, bow and stud, and a silver face, maker's name, Phillips, London, number not known. If the said watch come to any watchmaker or merchant's hand, they will please stop the same, and write to William Dobbie, Clock and Watch Maker, Falkirk. If any person delivers it to the said William Dobbie, they will be sufficiently rewarded."—*Caledonian Mercury*, 17th September 1768.

"John Bowie, malster, St Giles Parish, married Eupham, daughter to the deceased William Dobbie, watchmaker, Falkirk, 18th Decr. 1783."—*Edinburgh Marriage Register*.

DOBBIE, William.   Falkirk, 1821-45.

Probably son of above.

"Watchmaker and Jeweller and Clockmaker to the Queen, opposite to the Steeple, High Street, Falkirk, respectfully announces that he has just got to hand a large assortment of Gold and Silver patent lever and other watches, and has much pleasure in recommending them to the public, feeling assured that he never had it in his power to supply them with watches of such superior quality at the same moderate prices.

"His stock of warranted eight-day clocks being made under his own inspection, they are of the best workmanship and just such as were made by his forefathers. W. D. has just completed two of Russell's splendid and celebrated royal Barometers (now scarce), warranted identical with those made by the original constructor. The dial presents two indexes, the one of common range and the other indicating the thousands of an inch in the rise or fall of the Mercury.

"Mr Russell had the honour of presenting one of these barometers to his late Majesty, George the Third, and another to the then Prince of Wales, who were both pleased to express their approbation of them."—*Alloa Monthly Advertiser*, 7th February 1845.

DODS, ANDREW. Selkirk, about 1785.

DOIG, ALEXANDER. 6 Ann Street, Edinburgh, 1811.

DOIG, ALEXANDER. Musselburgh, 1814-36.

"SOCIETY OF ARTS FOR SCOTLAND.—Prize gained and presented to Mr Alexander Doig, watchmaker, Musselburgh, the Society's Silver Medal, value £5, 5s, for his description of the model of a clock pendulum without the crutch.

"*Note.*—The great perfection to which the art of clockmaking is carried renders any attempt at a further improvement both extremely difficult and highly interesting, and it is thus peculiarly the province of the Society to encourage any contrivance for obviating a known difficulty."

DOIG, WILLIAM. Polmont, 1825; clockface in Grand Lodge Museum, Edinburgh.

DON, GEORGE. Glasgow, 1804.

DONALD, JAMES. Edinburgh, 1815.

Apprenticed to Robert Bryson, 4th November 1815.

DONALD, WILLIAM. Rhynie, Aberdeenshire, 1837.

DONALDSON, ANDREW. 25 High Street, Airdrie, 1836.

DONALDSON, DAVID. 4 Dalrymple Place, Edinburgh, 1822.

DONALDSON, JAMES. Meigle, 1837.

DONALDSON, JOHN. 48 Glassford Street, Glasgow, 1839.

DOUGAL, ALEXANDER. Strathaven, 1836.

DOUGAL, ALEXANDER. Trongate, Glasgow, 1846.

DOUGAL, GEORGE. 78 Candlemaker Row, Edinburgh, 1819.

DOUGAL, JOHN. Kippen, 1836.

DOUGAL, ——. Brunswick Street, Glasgow, 1849.

DOUGLAS, ALEXANDER. Canongate, Edinburgh, 1817.

DOUGLAS, GEORGE. Holytown, 1847.

DOUGLAS, GEORGE. Bonhill, 1837.

DOUGLAS, JAMES. Dundee, 1794.

DOUGLAS, JAMES. Edinburgh, 1759.

Son of Alexander Douglas, Edinburgh; booked apprentice to William Nicol, 24th February 1759.

DOUGLAS, JAMES. 65 Gallowgate, Glasgow, 1841.

DOUGLAS, JOHN. Dumbarton, 1824.

DOUGLAS, WALTER. Dollar, 1795.

DOUGLAS, WALTER. Douglas, 1820.

DOUGLAS, WALTER. Polwhat Street, Galston, 1837.

DOUGLAS & SON. Greenock, 1842.

DOUGLASS, ALEXANDER. Bowmore, Islay, 1837.

DOW, ANDREW. 22 Argyle Street, Glasgow, 1837.

DOW, JOHN. 132 Trongate, Glasgow, 1837.

DOWNIE, DAVID. Edinburgh, 1812.

1st October 1812.—"Compeared and presented his petition craving to be admitted a freeman in right of his father, William Downie (q.v.), late clock and watch maker in Edinburgh and member of the Incorporation. Petition granted, and he paid the treasurer six pounds sterling."

31st October 1812.—"Compeared and produced his essay, being a clock movement, begun, made, and finished in the shop of George Skelton, landlord, in presence of James Ramage and Andrew Wilson, essay masters as they declared."—*E. H. Records.*

DOWNIE, JOHN. About Edinburgh, 1745. *See* William Downie.

DOWNIE, WILLIAM. Edinburgh, 1745-76.

"Son to John Downie, watchmaker, about Edinburgh; booked apprentice to James Geddes, watchmaker, 2nd February 1745. Discharged of his indentures on the 7th February 1756 by the Incorporation, owing to the death of James Geddes."

2nd November 1765.—"Presented a bill for being admitted a freeman clock and watch maker, which was received, and he appointed to give in an essay, being a spring clock to be made and finished in his own shop, and to be presented between and Whitsunday next —William Nicol, landlord, James Duff, Normand Macpherson, and William Richardson, essay masters. He made payment of Five pounds to the treasurer as the half of his upset."

3rd May 1766.—"Compeared and presented his essay as above."—*E. H. Records.*

"Lost on Saturday night, the 28th instant, betwixt Heriot's Hospital and Blackfriar's Wynd, a watch with a gold inside case and a pinchbeck gilt outside case, a steel chain, and gold seal key. If the same comes to hand acquaint William Downie, watchmaker, Luckenbooths, who will give a handsome reward."—*Edinburgh Evening Courant*, 30th January 1775.

"A rouping of Clocks and Watches and Watchmakers' tools. To be sold upon Wednesday the 19th of March 1777, at the house of Mrs Downie, Gavenlock's Land, head of the Luckenbooths, Edinburgh, the whole stock in trade belonging to the deceased William Downie, clock and watch maker in Edinburgh, consisting of a variety of both new and second-hand clocks and watches, as also the whole working utensils consisting of all sorts of watchmakers' tools, such as clock and watch engines, vices, turn-benches, etc."—*Edinburgh Evening Courant*, 12th March 1777.

In 1794 Mrs Downie issued an advertisement about a lottery of a musical clock made by her late husband, which is interesting. The description affords a good idea of the capabilities of William Downie as a craftsman.

"Lottery of a musical eight-day clock, the property of Mrs Downie, widow of the late William Downie, clock and watch maker in Edinburgh, under whose immediate inspection the clock was made, and is one of the most complete pieces of mechanism of its kind ever produced. It has dead seconds from the centre, moon's age, and a tide table. It chimes nine tunes upon eighteen bells and is in the most perfect order, having only been set agoing within these few months, and was valued by Mr Downie himself at forty guineas, being the sum now fixed for it by issuing eighty tickets at half a guinea each.

"*N.B.*—The clock presently stands in the wareroom of William Lamb, upholsterer. The number of tickets being nearly subscribed for, the drawing will take place on Thursday, 22nd January 1795. It is hoped those who mean to adventure will apply early."—*Edinburgh Evening Courant*, 20th December 1794.

"Very Valuable Musical Clock.—The adventurers in the Lottery of a Musical Clock belonging to Mrs Downie are most respectfully acquainted the delay of the drawing has been occasioned by some tickets remaining still unsold after every exertion to get them disposed of, but it is now fixed to take place assuredly on Tuesday, 12th January current, in that elegant room in Canongate, known by the name of St John's Chapel, at 12 o'clock noon, when every person interested is invited to attend. The clock still remains in the wareroom of Mr William Lamb, Upholsterer, and it is hoped the few remaining tickets, price 10s. 6d., will be sold in the interim; at same time the holders of tickets must observe that any not returned before Tuesday will be held as sold."—*Ibid.*, 9th January 1796.

"Mrs Downie begs leave to return her very grateful thanks to those who were so good as adventure in the lottery of her valuable musical clock (every ticket having been sold) to acquaint them that the drawing took place agreeable to the former notice on Tuesday last, when number forty-five turned up the fortunate number entitled to the clock, the holder of which, upon presenting the ticket, will have it delivered, and it is presumed will not refuse paying the expense of this notice."—*Ibid.*, 14th January 1796.

William Downie admitted a member of Lodge St David, Edinburgh, 15th December 1767. He, along with Samuel Brown, had the honour of his name being included in Gavin Wilson's "New Song of St David's," as follows :—

"There you'll hear brother Downie sing
  Igo and ago.
Ye never heard a better thing,
  Iram coram dago."

DRENEY, SAMUEL. Girvan, Ayrshire, 1850.

DRESCHAR & ROBOLD (German). 2 New Street, Paisley, 1836.

DRUMMOND, FRANCIS. Shilling Hill, Alloa, 1837.

DRUMMOND, JOHN. Brechin, 1789.
Maker of the new clock in the Town Hall there.

DRUMMOND, JOHN. Rose Street, Edinburgh, 1794.

DRYSDALE, JAMES. Edinburgh, 1742.
Admitted a freeman clock and watch maker, Edinburgh Hammermen, 7th August 1742.

DRYSDALE, WALTER SCOTT. Greenside, Edinburgh, 1812-29.

Son of William Drysdale (q.v.), but no mention of his name is to be found in the *Hammermen's Records*. The same year that his father adopted him as partner he retired from that concern, and having commenced business in Greenside Place in 1812, he advertises that "he has had long experience in London, and that no apprentice should be allowed to clean and repair watches, and that it will be a great pleasure to him to serve the public personally." In the year 1818 he had his premises entered by thieves; the story and its sequel, as reported in the *Edinburgh Advertiser*, is as follows :—

"Between Saturday night and Sunday morning the shop of Mr Drysdale, watchmaker in Greenside Street, was broken into by cutting the window shutters with a centre bit. Upwards of twenty watches were stolen. Every exertion is making to discover the depredators."
"The perpetrators of the theft of watches from Mr Drysdale's shop in Greenside Place were discovered, and prove to be two individuals who were taken into custody the day after the shop was broke into, who denied all knowledge of the transaction. The superintendent of police has been indefatigable in his exertions on this occasion, and by travelling over a great part of Roxburghshire has accomplished a discovery of the stolen watches built up with stone and lime in the side of a kitchen grate."

" Persons of the name of Stewart, who keep a public house in the Canongate, and who have been long notorious as resetters of stolen goods, are also in custody as being implicated in the above crime, and an investigation before the Sheriff is now going on."

" High Court of Justiciary—Yesterday came on before the Court of Justiciary the trial of Catherine Stewart or Ferrier and Robert Stewart, both lately residing at the Russian Tap Room in the Canongate, Edinburgh, and Margaret Cowan, lately residing in said Russian Tap Room, and widow of the deceased Thomas Ferrier, tacksman, of Melville Muir Colliery, charged with twelve different acts of reset of theft, aggravated by their being persons habit and repute resetters of stolen goods. Margaret Cowan was outlawed for not appearing, and the trial proceeded against Stewart and his wife, who were both found guilty to seven charges in the indictment. The Court, after an impressive address from the Lord Justice Clerk, sentenced the prisoners to transportation for life."— *Edinburgh Advertiser*, 3rd-13th February and 9th June, 1818.

Walter Scott Drysdale died at 4 Lothian Street, Edinburgh, 27th September 1829. The following notice was issued by his widow :—

" Mrs W. S. Drysdale begs to return her kindest thanks for the patronage her lamented husband enjoyed for so many years, and takes the liberty to intimate that, having resolved upon relinquishing the business, she will, on Monday first, commence a sale of her valuable stock, consisting of clocks, watches, jewellery, etc., at such prices as will make it an object to the purchaser, more particularly as the whole must be cleared before Martinmas. All accounts or debts due by her late husband must be immediately lodged, and all accounts due him are requested to be settled without delay."— *Edinburgh Evening Courant*, 10th October 1829.

DRYSDALE, WILLIAM. Lothian Street, Edinburgh, 1786-1823.

4th November 1786.—" Appeared and presented a petition craving to be admitted a freeman in Portsburgh."

13th February 1800.—"The Deacon presented a letter from William Drysdale craving to be admitted a freeman, if found properly qualified, for which he was willing to pay £50 sterling. The request was granted, and an essay and essay masters appointed, the essay to be presented between and Lammas. He paid £25 as the first moiety of his entry money."

2nd August 1800.—"Compeared and presented his essay, being a clock movement begun and finished in his own shop in presence of David Murray, landlord, and James Howden, Robert Hinmers, and Ebenezer Annan, essay masters as they declared, etc. He paid £25 as the second moiety of his entry money."—*E. H. Records.*

"W. Drysdale, Clock and Watch Maker, begs leave to acknowledge with peculiar sensations of gratitude the liberal patronage he has experienced from his friends and the public, and to acquaint them that he has removed from Bristo Street to a commodious shop, south end of the Potterrow, nearly opposite Crichton Street, where he makes, sells, and carefully repairs all sorts of Clocks and Watches, of which he has on hand an elegant assortment, also a large quantity of hardware with a variety of articles too tedious to mention.

"*N.B.*—Watch glasses put in at threepence each."
—*Edinburgh Evening Courant,* 17th April 1794.

"W. Drysdale begs leave to inform his customers and the public that he has moved from the Potterrow to 14 North Bridge, where he carries on the watch and clock making business in all its branches. Has always on hand an elegant assortment of Watches and Clocks."
—*Ibid.,* 2nd June 1800.

"William Drysdale, sen., begs leave to acquaint his numerous customers and the public that in consequence of his son Walter having separated from him in December last, he has assumed his son William as a partner under the firm of Drysdale and Son. His son having been taught by and practised under some of the most eminent workmen in England, particularly in manufacturing lever watches and others of the first quality, and they have added considerably to their former stock, particularly lever watches, and can with confidence recommend them to the Public. Those who honour them with their watches to repair may depend upon the utmost attention being paid as they do them with their own hands."—*Ibid.*, 7th March 1812.

"William Drysdale begs leave to announce that he retires in favour of his son Thomas, who is an excellent workman, having in addition to his father's instruction had for some time the benefit of working in the shop of one of the first watchmakers in London."—*Ibid.*, 2nd June 1823.

These advertisements, affording as they do a glimpse of the business life of William Drysdale, yet do not show all sides of his career. That his fellow-citizens had some faith in his other capabilities is best shown by the following account of a public meeting held in Edinburgh on the 7th December 1816. This meeting was convened in order that steps should be taken to alleviate the suffering caused by the war which culminated in the victory of Waterloo, 1815.

"Meeting of the inhabitants of Edinburgh held within the Parliament House, 7th December 1816.

"That this meeting, deeply sensible of the pressure of the times and the exemplary manner in which it has been borne by those upon whom it has chiefly fallen, resolve that a subscription shall be immediately entered into for the purpose of affording relief of a number of artisans and labourers in this city and immediate vicinity, and now out of employment. That the following gentlemen be appointed a committee for superintending the application of the money subscribed, and that they shall be authorised to adopt such measures as shall appear to them most expedient for providing suitable employment for such persons belonging to the city and suburbs as are able to work, and for administering relief to those who, by sickness or infirmity, are unable to support themselves. A large committee appointed, among which are the names of Mr William Drysdale, watchmaker, and Mr James M'Gregor, watchmaker."

William Drysdale died 11th August 1823, aged 62 years, his remains being interred in the Old Calton burying-ground, where a neat marble tablet on the north-east wall marks the spot.

"Alison Murray Drysdale, Portobello, Thomas Drysdale, watchmaker, Quebec, and William Drysdale, watchmaker, Philadelphia, were each of them served Heir of Provision General to their father, William Drysdale, watchmaker, Edinburgh, 28th September 1835. Recorded 2nd October 1835."—*Services of Heirs.*

DRYSDALE, WILLIAM. Dunbar, 1791.

In business at foot of West Bow, 1800; died 1839. *See* note on Charles Smeaton, Dunbar.

DRYSDALE, WILLIAM. High Street, Falkland, Fife, 1832.

DUFF, DANIEL. 38 New Street, Paisley, 1836.

DUFF, DAVID. Hyndford's Close, Edinburgh, 1806.

DUFF, JAMES. Burntisland, 1812.

DUFF, JAMES. Edinburgh, 1758-74.

6th May 1758.—"A petition was presented for James Duff, late apprentice to John Dalgleish, watchmaker in Edinburgh, and son of Alexander Duff, freeman of this incorporation, praying to have an essay and essay masters appointed, which being considered they granted the desire thereof."

11th November 1758.—"Compeared and presented his essay, being an eight-day clock made and finished in his own shop as John Dalgleish, his landlord, and Andrew Dickie, Robert Clidsdale, and Thomas Donald, his essay masters, declared, which was found a well wrought essay, etc., and they therefore admitted him a freeman clock and watch maker of this Incorporation."—*E. H. Records.*

"Stolen out of a gentleman's house in the Causeyside on Tuesday night last, a gold chessed watch jewelled, maker's name, Wm. Martin, London, with a lady's steel chain and two gold seals. Whoever will give information so as the same may be recovered shall receive a handsome reward by applying to James Duff, watchmaker in Edinburgh, and it is hoped that if the said watch is offered for sale the same may be stopped, for which a proper reward will be given by the said James Duff."—*Caledonian Mercury,* 6th January 1765.

DUNBAR, JAMES. Edinburgh, 1710.

> 16th December 1710.—"Late servitor to Mr George Frazer, sub-principal of the old town college of Aberdeen; booked apprentice to Andrew Brown, Edinburgh."— E. H. Records.

DUNBAR, JAMES. High Street, Perth, 1820.

DUNCAN, ALEXANDER. Elgin, 1785. See Elgin Town Clocks, page 137.

DUNCAN, ANDREW. Edinburgh, 1727.

> 27th April 1727.—"Son to John Duncan, merchant, and late Dean of Guild; booked apprentice to Alexander Brand."—E. H. Records.

DUNCAN, ANDREW. Aberdeen, 1824.

> "Andrew Duncan, clockmaker, Aberdeen, served Heir in General to his father, Andrew Duncan, square wright in Huntly, dated 21st February 1824. Recorded 26th February 1824."—Services of Heirs.

DUNCAN, D——. St Catherine's Street, Cupar - Fife, 1835-50.

DUNCAN, GEORGE. 25 Bridge Street, Banff, 1827-46.

DUNCAN, JAMES. Old Meldrum, 1785-95.

> Maker of the old town steeple clock at Stonehaven.

DUNCAN, THOMAS. Edinburgh, 1729.

> Booked apprentice to James Nicoll, Canongate, 1729.

DUNCAN, ——. Dalbeattie, about 1840.

DUNCAN, ——. Glasgow, 1849.

DUN, WILLIAM. John Street, Glasgow, 1779-1803.

> "William Dun, son of William Dun, watchmaker in Glasgow, served Heir of Provision General to his uncle, Archibald Napier, druggist, Edinburgh, dated 27th May 1803. Recorded 1st June 1803."—Services of Heirs.

DUNDEE. Notices regarding Saint Mary's Clock, from 1540 to 1664.

> It is evident that the tower of the church has not been originally intended to contain a clock, seeing that

no suitable central position has been designed for dials, these until a recent time having been placed against windows on the east and west. When a clock was erected originally cannot now be determined, but it is certain that probably not long after it was built, which all accounts make out to have been about the end of the fourteenth century, a clock was placed within it which struck the hours for service. It had by the year 1540 become so worn and untrustworthy that the Town Council entered into a contract with William Purves, burgess of Edinburgh, for the construction of another in its place.

By this contract it was agreed that William should make "ane sufficient and substantious knok with all instruments of iron work necessary and pertaining thereto, justly ganging, to strike hour and half hour complete and justly, the twenty-four hours day and night, with three warnings to contain six score and nine straiks (strokes), the first at four hours in the morning, the next at twelve hours at noon, and the third at nine hours at even" (these were the times of matins, mass, and evensong), "upon the five bells of the steeple, for the sum of seven score and seventeen pounds, ten shillings; the weight to be four score of stanes or thereby, and gif it happens the knok to weigh ten stone more or less, what she weighs mair to be payed to William, and what she weighs less to be defaulted to him." Thereafter he made the knok and set up the same in their steeple on Palm Sunday, 1543, weighing of wrought work through her proportions and "substantiousness" one hundred and thirteen stones.

For the extra weight he claimed payment at the contract rate; this the Council refused to pay, but gave him a sum to account. After considerable delay, he in 1546 raised an action against them before the Lords of Council and Session, concluding for the whole of his claim, and alleging that James Scrymgeour, constable, and Provost of Dundee, after the making of the contract, bade him make the knok gude and substantious, and whatever she weighed or drew above the contract he

should be "weill payit." He alleged besides that, until
the clock was complete and set up, he "gart their auld
knok in the steeple strike hours for service, and keep
gude rule." The Lords of Council having heard the
parties, decreed that the Town Council pay William the
sum of one hundred and ninety-seven pounds fifteen
shillings, which was equal to a deduction of ten stones
off the gross weight.

This clock was destroyed by fire in 1553, and the
next year means were taken for providing a clock and
bell. "It is ordered by the Council and Deacons of
Crafts that an tax of two hundred pounds be set and
gathered for payment of the knok, and bringing hame
of ane bell for the same." The clock, which was then
made by David Kay,[1] probably an Edinburgh craftsman,
did not have the elaborate and substantial character of
the one constructed ten years before by William
Purves. During its long term of service it often went
wrong and needed much repair, yet its remains, which
still stand in the corner of the tower, show that it is a
good example of the honest hammermen work of the
period. At first it had only one dial. Robert Gagy is
"conducit" to paint the orloge of the steeple for thirty-
twa pence ilk day for his wages, and the kirkmaster is
instructed to provide five pounds to furnish gold and
colours to the orloge, and to pay Robert daily wages.

On 11th September 1554, David Kay, knokmaker,
had occasion to leave the town before it was completed,
so he required the bailies that "he might have John
Corntoun (the acolyte) licensed to keep the knok in his
name and behalf for the space of forty days unto his
return; the whilk desire the bailies granted under
protestation that what skaith or danger come unto the
knok suld nocht lie nor be impute to the town's charge."
When finished, it was entrusted to Sir James Kinloch,
the parish clerk, and his brother William became surety

---

[1] This surmise we give as occurring in the account from which these
notes are taken, but if the notices on the town clocks of Glasgow (see
p. 160) are compared, the David Kay, Crail, mentioned there, is without
doubt, the same clockmaker who made the above.

for him that " he shall do his exact diligence in keeping
of the knok for his fee of five merks yearly. And that
if any damage chances come unto the knok through
his negligence, William shall refund the skaith to the
town."

After the death of Sir James in 1558 the kirkmaster
granted him to have received the common knok in
the steeple from William sufficient, and released him
of the suretyship. But William's youngest son, having
been put into the office of parish clerk which his uncle
held, the father became bound to " uphald the knok
ganging justly" and cause the bells to be rung at times
convenient and used, until his son be able and qualified
to serve in the office. And the treasurer was instructed
to deliver to William yearly, to be given to the keeper
of the knok, " ane stand of claiths."

12th June 1564.—" The Council disponed five merks
of the feu mail of Sanct Agatha's Chaplinne to John
Broun, who had been one of the Gray Friars, so long
as he in time coming serves ·the township in keeping
of their knok. In 1573 a commission of the General
Assembly made inquiry into how the duties and rents
which had been recovered were being appropriated, and
they found at this date that John Broun, quha wes ane
of the Gray Friars, was receiving sixteen pounds
yearly."

1588. —" Patrick Ramsay, smith and gunmaker,
did thankful service by his good attention on the
knok and steeple, and got his stipend enlarged in 1604
to twenty pounds, and afterwards to forty, besides
being exempt from the payment of all taxation except
such as the crafts shall take. He did not escape the
tongue of calumny, which turned out that Patrick had
been very wrongously slandered." On 27th June 1609
he wrote to the Council a characteristic letter, describing
the state the knok was in, which was as follows :—

" Unto your worships humblie meanis your daylie
servitour Patrick Ramsay, Smith.

" That quhair it is not unknown to your worships
that I, after returning to this town when it pleased

God to withdraw his visiting hand[1] therefrom, at your worship's desire, was moved to undertake my auld service in attending upon the knok, at which times your worships promised to have an consideration of my great pains quhilk I was to sustain in the frequent visiting of the said knok and continued reparation of her, seeing now she is all broken and worn and decayed in all the pairts thereof. Upon expectation thereof I have continually attended with my sons and servants since, and thereby have been abstracted from my labour which I should sustain my wife and bairns.

" Therefore, now, I have taken occasion to remember your worships humbly, that order may be taken how I may be payed for my bypast service, and in time coming, gif your worships will give me reasonable augmentation to my former fee, I will bind and oblige myself to sustain the said knok and preserve her from decay and mend and repair her upon my own expense during my life, quhilk will be no little profit to the commoun weill."

This appeal was successful, and the Council on 2nd January 1610 agreed that if Patrick presently took down and repaired the knok sufficiently they would give him forty pounds for mending it, and in consideration of the great labour and pains continually taken by him in the ordering thereof they promised to augment his stipend with twenty pounds, to be paid by the minister and elders of the kirk, making " in the haill the soume of three score pounds for which he and his eldest son shall be haldin to uphold her during his own and his son's lifetime hereafter."

They on 6th October 1612 further agreed to give the son a stand of clothes yearly for his service, and as the old horologist himself continued to take great pains both day and night attending her, they augmented his fee with 10 merks.

The sons of Patrick Ramsay appear to have inherited a practical knowledge of the mysteries of

[1] He refers to a serious visitation of the plague which passed over Dundee at this date.

clock work. John, like him a hammerman, was trained from his youth up to help at the mending of the steeple clock and followed him as its keeper. Silvester chose another field of labour, and was appointed to the place of Doctor in the Grammar School with very moderate emoluments. In 1609 another clock having been obtained, it was placed in the Tolbooth. It is not known who had charge of it at first, but subsequently Silvester Ramsay attached himself to it, and by the attention which he bestowed upon its movements rendered the burgh much true and faithful service, and the Council finding him to be an experienced and qualified attendant, elected him on 8th August 1637, during all the days of his lifetime, keeper of the said clock at a yearly salary of four score merks. Of Silvester there is no further notice, but his brother became old in the public service; and in 1646 the Council, considering the weakness and inability of John Ramsay, clock-keeper, and his demission of that office, made choice of Andro Taileour, hammerman, to be keeper of both clocks, and ordered him the accustomed fees and duties.

Under Andro Taileour's charge the old clock in the steeple soon became disordered, and on 21st September 1648, "the council, having heard of the report of those who were desired to visit the knok in the steeple, how faulty she was, ordained James Alisone to take her down and help all defects in her, and at the perfecting of the work they promised to satisfy as they should his pains."

30th August 1664.—"The council ordains Robert Stratone and Thomas Davidson to draw William Smith to the lowest price they can for mending the steeple knok, and quhen they shall close with him, ordains the treasurer to pay the same, quhich shall be allowed in his accompts."—ALEXANDER MAXWELL'S *History of Dundee.*

DUNFERMLINE—Notices regarding the Common Clocks of the burgh of, from 1605 to 1876.

1605.—"To Johne and Harie Burrells for taking sundry the knok and putting it together again, and dichting the same, vijs."

5th February 1698.—"The said day the counsell agreed with Adam Stevinsoun (younger), smith, that he should not only daily row up and wait upon the knok, and also to mend and keep right all parts of her that shall become faulty, or make new wheels or other material, and to keep her going right, for which the council ordain their treasurer to pay him yearly the sum of twenty pounds (Scots), and siclike yearly hereafter, during his dressing, repairing, and keeping right said knok, and when he leaves, Adam to leave ye said knok in good condition and usual going."

4th December 1723.—"The said day Adam Stevinsoun having acquainted the council that he had turned the clock in the steeple into a pendulum clock, and desired the council might appoint some persons to visit her and report if ye clock be bettered yair by."

13th October 1733.—"The council considering that the time agreed with Robert Bonnar for keeping and taking care of the clock expired at Michaelmas last, they therefore called for Robert Bonnar, when he acquainted the council it was proper there should be made a crown wheel of brass for the clock in order to make her go well. Which being considered by the council, they agreed with him to make the same, and to pay him twelve pounds (Scots) thereof, and sett to him the keeping of the clock for six years to come at the old rent."

15th December 1743.—"The council ordered the treasurer to pay to Robert Bonnar, wright, thirteen pounds ten shillings (Scots) for his attending and rectifying the toun clock yearly."

26th June 1745.—"Which day the bailies informed the council that Mr Andrew Dickie, watchmaker in Edinburgh, was come over to this place, as he was desired by the council, anent a new clock to the Kirk steeple of this burgh, and that after the bailies and some of the members of the council had gone up with

Mr Dickie to the present clock in the steeple, which is reckoned quite useless and takes more expense to uphold the same than will go a good way to get a new clock. The bailies and these members heard Mr Dickie yairanent, and Mr Dickie offered to furnish a sufficient new clock to the said steeple, the two big wheels yairof to be fourteen inches in diameter and very nigh an inch thick, and these wheels and the other wheels to be of brass and the rest of the wheels to be in proportion to the two big wheels, to go for about thirty hours, and a minute hand within all, for Forty pounds Sterling. And that he declared he could do the thing cheaper, but could not attest a cheaper clock.

"Which being considered by the council, they appoint, warrant, and empower the two bailies and Dean of Guild in name of the town to contract with Mr Dickie for a new clock to the steeple at the said Forty pounds Sterling of price, and if they think fit to agree with Mr Dickie for a minute hand outside although the town should pay a guinea more for the said minute hand or so. And whatever the bailies and the Dean of Guild shall so contract, the council engages to relieve them yairof. And they enjoin the said bailies and dean of guild to agree with Mr Dickie to make the said clock to have an hour hand to the west, and the north brod or plate to have an hour and minute hand together. And allow them to contract with Mr Dickie in the cheapest way for the west hand also, and the whole price not to exceed forty-three pounds (Sterling)."

31st August 1745.—" Which day the bailies laid before the council a letter from Mr Dickie of the 28th current relative to the clock, signifying that it will be a troublesome job to pierce the hole in the west side of the steeple, and to put up the brod on the west side thereof, and wishing that the council would let it alone and he'll discount a guinea of the price.

"Which being considered by the council, they unanimously resolve and agree that there shall be no hand or brod on the west side of the steeple, and appoints the bailies or anyone of them to write Mr

Dickie to provide a sufficient dyall brod of good fir, and six feet in diameter, and to cause sufficiently paint the same with gold leaf of large figures for the hour hand, and the minute figures in proportion."

29th March 1746.—" Which day the bailies acquainted the council that Mr Andrew Dickie, watchmaker, informed them that the new clock made by him to the town, in virtue of the contract betwixt the town and him, is now placed in the church steeple, and that he says it goes, and that he is demanding twenty pounds four shillings and sixpence Sterling as the half price of the clock already due, with three pounds eleven shillings sterling as the price of making and gilding the dyall plate thereof, with seven shillings sterling as the expense of carriage of the dyall plate from Edinburgh to the ferry paid out by him. Which being considered by the council they warrant and empower John Knox, treasurer, to pay Mr Dickie the several sums extending in whole to twenty-four pounds two shillings and sixpence Sterling, but order the contract to be kept, that so Mr Dickie may fulfil the obligations thereof presentable by him thereby. As also the council order said John Knox to give to Mr Dickie's servant a crown of drink money.

" The same day the council agreed with Robert Meldrum, officer, to pay him half a crown for his due and regular and daily rolling up said clock for half of the year commencing this day, and for oiling the same during that space."

From a note affixed to Mr Dickie's letter of this date, it appears that there was a great number of people all round about gazing on the dial hands being fixed. When this was done and the hands set to the time, a loud and ringing hurrah arose from the multitude of lookers-on.

13*th March* 1756.—" Which day the council purchased from Alexander Richardson, late drummer, an old clock or movement at fifteen shillings Sterling, and delivered the same to William Inglis, present drummer, to use as long as he continues drummer, and to be answerable to the town therefor."

CLOCK FOR THE NEW TOWN HOUSE.—13*th January*
1773.—"Which day the Council agreed that the Dean
of Guild and Convener and Bailie Ireland transmit
copies of the several estimates given in for their new
clock to some proper person of skill, a clockmaker in
Edinburgh, or get an opinion which of the three
estimates is most proper to be executed, for the interests
of the town ; also his opinion which of the makers of
the estimates he judges properest for making said
clock."

3rd April 1773.—"This day the Council appointed
the Dean of Guild and Convener, Bailies Morrison,
Hunt, and Deacon Abercromby and Wilson, with the
Magistrates, as a committee, to commune with the
clockmakers in town anent the clock for the new steeple,
and to get an account of their cautioners. And in the
meantime the council agree that the clock shall have
four dial plates, and strike the quarters, and without
minute hands, and to report."

17th April 1773.—"Which day the council by a
majority of votes made choice of James Symsone, Clockmaker, to make the town clock for the new steeple, in
terms of his estimate and proposals formerly given in."

14th August 1773.—"This day the council by a
majority of votes agree that the clock for the new
steeple shall have four dial plates, without minute hands,
or striking the quarters."

29th December 1773.—"£36 to be paid to account of
new clock to James Symsone, Clockmaker, by John
Horn, old treasurer."

5th March 1774.—"The council order John Horn,
late treasurer, to pay James Symsone, clockmaker, five
pounds (Sterling) more upon his receipt, to account of
the town clock, and the said James Symsone immediately
to complete the clock with yettlin paises and sufficient
ropes, and to strike upon the present bell. On the
same day Mr Symsone offered to the council to put a
minute hand on the east dial of the clock if the council
would pay him for the expense of the dial plate and
hand."

April 1775.—"The new clock in the town house steeple appears to have been set in motion about the beginning of April 1775. The building of two additional stories to the town house began in July 1793, and was finished early in January 1795. There was also a new clock fitted up in the new clock turret, made by Matthew Parker (q.v.), in January 1795. The Town House was removed in 1876."—Extracts from the Burgh Records of Dunfermline, given in Henderson's *Annals of Dunfermline.*

DUNN, MALCOLM. Canongate, Edinburgh, 1764.

DUNN, THOMAS. Western Lane, Berwick-on-Tweed, 1820.

DURHAM, WILLIAM. High Street, Dunbar, 1820.

DURHAM, WILLIAM. Edinburgh, 1809-50.

Bound apprentice to James Howden, jun., 11th August 1809; was in business at 10 Brunswick Street, 1850.

DURHAM, WILLIAM. High Street, Thurso, 1837.

DURWARD, JOSEPH. Edinburgh, 1775-1819.

Admitted a freeman clockmaker, Canongate Hammermen, 20th October 1775, his essay being a balance wheel and pinion.

"Stolen from a chest of drawers in the house of Peter M'Queen, Head of the Canongate, Edinburgh, on Tuesday the 28th of November, a silver watch, maker's name, Lamont, London, No. 401. If any person or persons shall restore the same to Joseph Durward, watchmaker, Edinburgh, or give such information as it may be recovered, shall be handsomely rewarded. If said watch is offered for sale, it is requested she may be detained and notice given to Mr Durward."—*Caledonian Mercury*, 1st December 1783.

"Lost on the 30th November last betwixt the Head of Cowgate and the Tron Church, a silver watch, maker's name, R. Parker, London, No. 324. If offered for sale or otherwise it is entreated that the person be detected and information thereof sent to Mr Joseph Durward, Clock and Watch Maker, No. 4 Princes Street, Edinburgh. Whoever has found the same, by returning it to Mr Durward shall be handsomely rewarded."—*Ibid.*, 3rd December 1785.

"GOLD WATCH LOST.—There was lost on Tuesday night, the 13th current, betwixt the hours of 10 and 12 o'clock in South Bridge Street, a gold watch, maker's name, Rerxoll, Liverpool. Whoever will return the said watch to Mr Joseph Durward, No. 11 Leith Street, will be handsomely rewarded. There was a piece of black silk ribbon and a brass key at it."—*Edinburgh Evening Courant*, 19th June 1817.

" Joseph Durward announces with grateful acknowledgment the liberal encouragement with which he has been honoured for the last forty years, and begs leave now to intimate that he has now retired from business and most respectfully solicits the patronage of his numerous friends on behalf of Mr James Ritchie (q.v.), No. 29 Leith Street, whose professional abilities and attention to business will give every satisfaction to his employers."—*Ibid.*, 26th May 1819.

EADIE, ANDREW. Perth, 1794.

Apprenticed to Patrick Gardiner, Perth.

EARNS, JAMES. Edinburgh, 1712.

Son to the deceased James Earns, weaver in Anstruther ; booked apprentice to Captain Thomas Gordon, clockmaker, Edinburgh, 4th November 1712.

EDINBURGH—Notices regarding the Common Clock of the burgh of, from 1552 to 1861—" St Giles Kirk."

4th March 1552. — " The quilk day the provost, bailies, and council think expedient and ordain the common bell to have a string coming therefrom to the nether end of a pillar in the kirk, and to be locked in an almonry, and that, to have six keys, one thereof to the provost, four to the bailies, and the sixth to the bell man, that the said bell may be rung at all times (quhen tyme occuris)."

9th November 1552. — " The quilk day the provost, bailies, and council ordain that Patrik Guvane, keeper of the knok, have a key of the steeple door, to the effect that he may visit and keep the said knok and ring the common bell when he be chairgit thairto."

1552.—" To the keeper of the knok for his fee, iij. lib.

1552.—" For oil to the knok all year   viijs.

1554.—"The expensis made upon the mending of the knok and half hour at the town's command.

3rd February 1554.—"Given to a writer to write the indentures between Robert Creith and the comptr
xviijd.

"*Item, 6th February* 1554.—Given to three men for downtaking of the knok furth of the steeple to the cart
iijs.

"*Item*, for a close cart to carry down to Leith the great work of her
iijs. iijd.

"*Item*, to ane man to bare down her small work in a close creel to Leith
viijd.

"*Item*, for two fathom of a great cord to cause the great bell strike the hours quhen the knok is away
viijd.

"*Item*, given to Robert Creith or Creych, for up-putting of a little knok in the Tolbooth before the Lords quilk was borrowed from Master Johne Stevenson
vs.

"*Item*, given to Robert Creith quhilk he disbursit for a cut of a great tree to tow the pais cords of the knok of the hour and half hour
ijs.

"*Item, 25th February.*—Given to two men for downtaking of the half hour furth of the steeple and bearing of it to the cart
vjs.

"*Item*, for a close cart to carry all the works of the half hour to Leith
iijs.

"*Item*, to a man to bare down the vj hammers to Leith
iiijd.

"*Item, 18th March.*—Given for upbring of the knok and half hour again from Leith in two close carts and to a man to bare up the small work again
vjs. viijd.

"*Item*, to two pynors (labourers) to bare up the haill work again to the steeple
ijs.

"*Item*, for xij fathom of a great cord to bare the pais of the half hour, ilk fathom vjd.
suma vjs.

"*Item*, given to Sampsoun the painter to lay the haill knok and half hour all over with red lead to keep them from rusting
xlvs.

"*Item*, for two daillis to be a door and flooring

to that part of the steeple where the knok stands
to save it from wet and wind   vjs. viijd.

"*Item*, for saving of two daillis   xxd.

"*Item*, for nails   viijd.

"*Item*, to a wright for making of the door and
mending of the flooring   ijs. viijd.

"*Item*, for two crooks, two bands, a lock and key
to the said door to Johne Banx   iiijs.

"*Item*, 25*th March* 1555.—Paid to Robert Creith
for his haill labours of the knok and half hour

xxxiij lib.

"The haill sum of the expensis made on the knok
and half hour is   xxxix lib. vs. vjd."

8*th May* 1560.—"The provost, bailies, and council
understand that the kirk might be served with three
bells, one rung to the prayers, another for serving
the knok, and the third to be the common bell."

27*th November* 1566.—"The provost, bailies, and
council ordain Mr John Preston, dean of guild, to cause
mend the prik of the sun orlege on the south side of
the kirk in the kirkyard, and draw the letters thairof
of new."

24*th April* 1567.—"The dean of guild ordained to
cause paint the letters of the orlage."

"Three persons appointed to talk with the man
that has the orlage to sell, desired to be set up at
the Nether Bow, drif it to ane price, and report to the
council."

19*th April* 1570.—"It is appointed and agreed betwixt
the bailies, dean of guild, and council on the one part,
and Robert Creych, knokmaker, on the other pairt, viz.,
the said Robert binds and obliges him to mend and
uphold the town knok, they furnishing iron (allanerlie),
for the quilk case they ordain the treasurer present
and to come to pay him yearly during his lifetime
xls."

19*th March* 1584.—"Finds expedient that at the
taking doun of the old knok in the steeple and placing
a new knok in the room thereof, and that the said
old knok be taken and set up in the bell house at the

High School until a more commodious place be prepared for the same."

21st April 1585.—"Ordained the dean of guild to pay £55 as the price of the knok of Lindores, and the said dean of guild to intromett with the said knok and be comptabill for the same."

23rd April 1585.—"Condescends and agrees that —— Smith, smyth in Blantyre (?), for repairing of the knok of Lindores bought by the town, setting up thereof, and dressing of the same, to have two hands, to be set in the high steeple, and doing all things necessary pertaining to his occupation, at the sight and desire of the dean of guild, Johne Watt, or ony of the council quhome they please to take with them, to have three score pounds money, or else be made burgess and free with his craft, and therewith to have forty merks money, the said two conditions being in his option."

23rd June 1585.—"The bailies, dean of guild, treasurer, and a part of the council being convened, understanding that the new knok is made ready and prepared, therefore finds it most expedient that the same be set up, and the great bell whereupon it strikes to be raised higher, by the advice of Andro Sclater, William Littill, George Smith, and Henry Blyth."

The foregoing extracts are taken from the volumes published under the auspices of the Burgh Record Society, and as none have been published dealing with Edinburgh later than 1882, Index 1892, unfortunately it has not been found possible to continue the subject later, as a personal search into the City of Edinburgh's MS. Records would entail the labours of a lifetime. We can only give a copy of the inscription engraved on a brass plate fixed near the clock in the tower of St Giles, which is as follows :—

"L. BRADLEY,[1] Londini, Fecit.   MDCCXXI.

"Repaired and minute hand put to by Thomas Reid, 1797—Thomas Elder, Lord Provost.

[1] *See* Alexander Brownlie, Edinburgh, page 67.

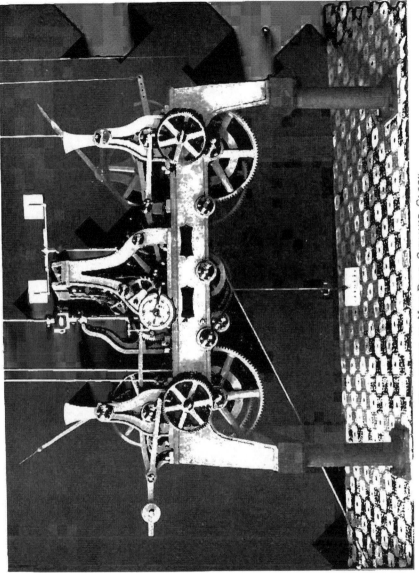

MOVEMENT OF NON-DIAL CHIMING CLOCK,

Installed in St Giles' Kirk, Edinburgh, 1912. Made and presented by
Messrs James Ritchie & Son, Leith Street, Edinburgh.

[To face page 136.

"Changed from 30 hours to an 8-day by Ritchie & Son, 25 Leith Street, 1861.

"New one altogether by James Ritchie & Son, Edinburgh, 1912."

EDWARDS, JOHN. Alloa, 1820.

EDWARDS, JOHN. Canongate, Edinburgh, 1725.

Booked apprentice to George Scott, Canongate, 1725.

ELDRICK, HAY. 1 Palace Road, Kirkwall, 1823 ; died 1832.

ELDRICK, JAMES. Son of above. Broad Street, Kirkwall, 1836.

ELGIN—Notices regarding the Common Clocks of the burgh of, from 1651 to 1785.

20th January 1651.—"Murray, Bellman—Anent Alexander Murray, bellman, his petition alleging he had 20 lib. more than was due by him for the customs the year preceding, and therefore desired allocation in the year succeeding. The council suspends their answer to the bill, until they see an amendment in the petitioner anent the ruling of the clock and ringing of the four hours and eight hours bell at morning and nights, and giff he fail in doing duty therein, he is to have neither payment or allocation, and himself be wairded (imprisoned)."

7th November 1681.—"The council has appointed that the twenty pounds (Scots) paid formerly to the bedler (beadle) for attending the knok, and ringing the great bell at four o'clock in the morning and at eight o'clock at night, and setting up the candle in the church, and other service done by the bedler and servant about the church, wherein the magistrates and council are concerned, shall no more be paid to any succeeding bedler, who only has the benefit of the little bell for doing thereof, who cannot exhort any inhabitant for the same, which, if he do, the magistrates and council are determined thereanent."

6th September 1703.—"The council constitutes and appoints James Russell, merchant in Elgin, to be their bellman, and the said James Russell obliges him that he shall keep the toun's clock so right in her going as that she shall not go half an hour backward or forward in twenty-four hours' time, as also he obliges himself to ring the eight hours bell at night and four hours bell in the morning punctually, and if he fail in either to lose his said office and be at the council's will, as also he dispenses with all the oil and tallow which the town was formerly in use, to pay quarterly for upholding and keeping right the clock and bells, which he shall now do so on his own charges; and also he dispenses with and shall crave no yearly salary from the town, in consideration of which he shall have the sole right to the dues of the little bell with the casualties of the great bell, besides what is payable to the treasurer, and the council appoints the treasurer to give to the said James Russell two dollars for bussing the clock."

21st January 1706.—" The council does hereby ordain that the great bell be rung every night at eight o'clock exactly, and the drum to begin and beat at nine o'clock every night precisely, and the clock to be wind up at twelve o'clock each day."

15th December 1706.—" The council appoints the treasurer to take such methods as may be efficient to preserve the town's clock from being spoiled by the injury of the weather, and blowing from the north and south open places of the steeple."

17th August 1713.—" The town's big bell, which is in the church steeple, which was first founded in 1593, and having been in this year 1713 rendered useless by a rent therein, was taken down by order of the Town Council, and upon the 13th August current was refounded within this burgh by Albert Gelly, founder in Aberdeen. The expense thereof was done upon the town's common good, and upon the 17th August the said bell was hung up and rung. The weight thereof consists of 638 pounds, and the whole price of the said bell extends to 325 pounds (Scots), including the price of what metal was furnished by the said founder."

13th June 1720.—" Agreement with James Brown, clockmaker at Aberdeen, to make and build an sufficient and weel goeing clock in the steeple of the Tolbooth, with two dial plates, and that for £18 sterling, to be paid out of the vacant stipends for 1716, and, if necessary, the common good."

19*th February* 1722.—"£27 sterling to be paid to James Brown, clockmaker, for the Tolbooth clock, it being well going and an eight day clock."

12*th June* 1724.—"The provost delivered to the treasurer an pass key that opens three doors in the Tolbooth, which was formerly made for the convenience of Mr Brown, clockmaker, when he was building the Tolbooth clock."

2*nd July* 1733.—"The council to treat with James Brown, watchmaker, to keep the Tolbooth and kirk clocks, which are not exactly keeped by James Watson, beddall."

"Wanted at Elgin a skilful clock and watch maker, who might reasonably expect proper encouragement, as there is none of that business here nor betwixt Inverness and Banff, being 50 miles distant. The Magistrates of Elgin would give a small salary for keeping the town's clocks in good order. Any well qualified clock and watch maker who inclines to come here and carry on business may signify the same by letter directed to Mr Patrick Duff, Town Clerk of Elgin."—*Edinburgh Evening Courant*, 17th June 1756.

13*th March* 1769.—"Alexander Gray appointed clock-keeper for seven years at a salary of £2 sterling yearly, with ropes and a pint of oil yearly, and, as the clocks are much in want of repair, he agrees to mend them and to keep in repair for seven years for £3 sterling."

21*st November* 1785.—"Alexander Duncan is appointed keeper of the clocks for five years at a yearly salary of £3, 10s., to keep the same in repair, except timber work and ropes; also, he is to furnish for the High Church a timepiece, on payment of £2, 10s. sterling, and admission as a freeman burgess of this Burgh."

ELLEIS, DAVID. Aberdeen, 1560. *See* page 3.

ESSEX, JOSEPH. Canongate, Edinburgh, 1711.

Admitted a freeman clockmaker, Canongate Hammermen, 11th April 1711, his essay being a pendulum clock.

This maker's name is the first clockmaker to be met with in the earliest volume that is now extant of the records of the Canongate Hammermen, the previous volumes having disappeared.

EUNSON, JAMES. Stromness, Orkney, 1836.

FAIRBAIRN, ANDREW. Edinburgh, 1807-34. 19 Chapel Street, 1807; 4 West Nicolson Street, 1825.

"ADVANTAGEOUS OPENING TO CLOCK AND WATCH MAKERS.—The house and shop, No. 4 West Nicolson Street, to let, with the goodwill of the business carried on by the late Andrew Fairbairn. The business has been in full and profitable operation for nearly thirty years; the situation is good, and such an opening to an industrious person with a small capital seldom occurs. The stock, consisting of clock and watch maker's tools, etc., is small and may be had at a valuation. Mr Fairbairn enjoyed the fullest confidence of all his employers, and it requires little more than diligence and application to business to render this a good and profitable concern. The terms of rent and goodwill of the business are moderate terms. Apply as above; if from the country, post paid."—*Scotsman*, 13th November 1834.

"Helen Fairbairn in Edinburgh, served Heir in General to her father, Andrew Fairbairn, clockmaker there, dated 25th May 1835. Recorded 1st June 1835."— *Services of Heirs*.

FAIRGREIVE, JAMES. Edinburgh, 1783-94.

Bound apprentice to David Murray, 19th July 1783. Discharged of his indentures, 23rd June 1791. In business, 18 North Bridge, 1794.

FAIRHOLM, ROBERT. Edinburgh, 1739.

3rd October 1739.—"Son of Thomas Fairholm of Piltoun; booked to Thomas Gordon."

5th February 1743.—"The house appoints Robert Fairholm apprentice to Thomas Gordon, watchmaker, now deceast, to be transferred to Patrick Gordon, watchmaker, for the time yet to run in the indentures. The said Patrick Gordon first paying the absents[1] due

---

[1] This means the times absent from the stated meetings of the Hammermen's Incorporation, and shows the punctilious manner they conducted their business as these two men were not only wealthy but citizens of some renown, and were quite good for the money.

by the said Thomas and himself, amounting to eleven shillings and sixpence Sterling."

12*th March* 1743.—"Patrick Gordon, watchmaker, in terms of the minute of last sederunt, paid eleven shillings and sixpence Sterling in full of the absents due by his deceast brother and himself."—*E. H. Records.*

FAIRN, JAMES. Clock Case Maker, Bristo Port, Edinburgh, 1800.

FAIRWEATHER, JOHN. Edinburgh, 1749.

Though not a clockmaker, was closely allied to the craft as his advertisement shows.

"TO THE CURIOUS. — John Fairweather, Lapidary, at Clockmill, in the corner of St Ann's Yards, cuts all kinds of Scots Pebbles after the best manner into all shapes at the lowest prices, and has, with his new invented machinery, lately made several pebble watch cases to the satisfaction of the most curious, and at so low a price as one guinea and a half the piece. He being the only Scotsman hitherto that has made any, notwithstanding there are other pretenders."—*Caledonian Mercury*, 7th September 1749.

FALCONER, WILLIAM. Laurencekirk, 1784.

"Clock and Watch Maker and Watch Material Manufacturer, returns his most grateful thanks to the noblemen, gentlemen, and watchmakers who have honoured him with their subscriptions, and also to those who have promised to do it, and in particular to the watchmakers of Edinburgh and Montrose for the encomiums they have wrote in the subscription paper on the undertaking, which undertaking is to establish on an extensive plan all the necessary branches of watchmaking in Scotland, as he makes the ·materials which used formerly to come from England, and he wishes the subscription papers filled up as soon as possible, for which reason he has lodged printed addresses to the public with the following gentlemen :—

Mr Macpherson, watchmaker, Edinburgh
" Downie, goldsmith,   "
" Hamilton, watchmaker, Glasgow
" James Milne,   "   Montrose
" Argo,   "   Peterhead
" Low,   "   Arbroath

Mr Young, watchmaker, Perth
„ Carmichael, „ Greenock
„ Brownlie, „ Hamilton
„ Mill, „ St Ninians
„ Turnbull „ Dunfermline

Silver watches to be offered as low as two pounds after the period of three years. He begs subscribers will not delay in honouring him with subscriptions to enable him to execute a business as necessary and beneficial to the country.

"One half of the subscription money is to lie in a banker's hand so that, in case of his failure, subscribers cannot lose half their money. He hopes the public will see the propriety of supporting his undertaking, as the manufacture of watches and all their materials in Scotland could not fail of saving and bringing much money to the country and giving bread to industrious mechanics ready to execute this undertaking."—*Caledonian Mercury*, 4th August 1784.

FARQUHAR, ANDREW. Marischal Street, Peterhead, 1837.

FARQUHAR, ANDREW. Edinburgh, 1768.

"On Wednesday the 6th April next, at eleven o'clock forenoon, in the auction room entering by the stair leading to High Coffee House, south side of the Cross, Edinburgh, there to be rouped and sold, a large parcel of good silver watches to be set up to sale in half dozens and sold to the highest bidder, and as they are sequestrate goods, once Andrew Farquhar's now the property of creditors, and certain to be sold, it is not doubted great pennyworths will be got. Good bills will be taken at six months, at the usual rate of interest above the purchase money, for the encouragement of merchants and country dealers. There is a variety of other goods to be sold at the same place."—*Caledonian Mercury*, 21st March 1768.

FARQUHARSON, ALEXANDER. Edinburgh, 1749-68.

Son of Charles Farquharson, writer in Edinburgh ; booked apprentice to John Dalgleish, watchmaker.

2nd July 1749.—"Presented a bill on 4th February 1764 craving to be admitted clock and watch maker, which was received, and an essay and essay masters were appointed to him."

28th July 1764.—"Compeared and presented his essay, being a watch movement in his own shop, as Robert Clidsdale, George Begbie, senior, and James Cowan, his essay masters, declared, which was found a well wrought essay, etc."—*E. H. Records.*

FARQUHARSON, CHARLES. Canongate, Edinburgh, 1722.

Bound apprentice to Alexander Brand, 1722.

FARQUHARSON, CHARLES. Dundee, 1733-42.

FARQUHARSON, LAUCHLIN. Perth, 1743.

Booked apprentice to David Thomson, Perth, 30th November 1743.

FARQUHARSON, ROBERT. 15 High Street, Dundee, 1847.

FAULDS, ALLAN. Kilmarnock, about 1830.

FAULDS, JAMES. Kilmarnock; died 1796.

FAY, JAMES and JOHN. 5 Stockwell Place, Glasgow, 1837.

FEAD, JAMES. 5 York Place, Edinburgh, 1843.

FENWICK, PETER, jun. Crieff, 1837.

FENWICK, FATHER and SON. Crieff, 1800-76.

FEREN, ——. Reform Street, Dundee, 1843.

FEREN & Co. 27 Irish Street, Dumfries, 1837.

FERENBACH, D. and C. 10 Nicolson Street, Edinburgh, 1850.

FERGUSON, ALEXANDER. Edinburgh, 1754-72.

"Discharged of his indentures by Deacon James Cowan on 17th June 1761."

This individual was probably the first apprentice that James Cowan trained.

10th July 1771.—"Presented a bill craving to be admitted a freeman clock and watch maker."

25th January 1772.—"Compeared and presented his essay, being an eight-day clock, begun, made, and finished in presence of James Cowan, landlord, and James Duff, Normand Macpherson, and George Begbie, essay masters as they declared, which was found a well wrought essay, etc."—*E. H. Records.*

FERGUSON, ALEXANDER. Dundee, 1777.

FERGUSON, ALEXANDER. Cupar-Fife, 1780.

FERGUSON, ARCHIBALD. 18 Houstoun Square, Johnstone, 1836.

FERGUSON, GEORGE. Perth, 1791.
Apprenticed to James Greig, Perth, 1791.

FERGUSON, JAMES. Banffshire, 1710; died in London, 1776.

"Astronomer and Mechanician. Was born at the Core of Mayer, near Rothiemay in Banffshire, on 25th April 1710. His father was a day labourer. In 1720 put to service, and in 1732 made a wooden clock and a watch with wooden wheels and a whalebone spring. In 1734 he came to Edinburgh to be trained as an artist, and he became a portrait painter, which he followed for twenty-six years. He afterwards went to London, and was buried in Marylebone Churchyard, 1776."—*Dictionary of National Biography.*

The reader is respectfully invited to consult the above volume, from which this short extract is taken, for more full and interesting details of this celebrated man, who, as an inventor of curious and useful clock movements, was never excelled. The following advertisement relating to his residence in Edinburgh will be found interesting, and shows the capabilities of the man :—

"There is an astronomical machine invented by James Ferguson, Limner in China Ink. This instrument is 18 inches long and 12 inches broad. It has four different pieces or wheels, by turning of which, according to direction, the true time and figure of all the eclipses are seen from 1732 to 1800 inclusive. Those of the sun as they will appear at Edinburgh, London, and Paris. It shows also during the above number of years the Sun's place and Moon's place in the Ecliptik, with their distance from one another, and from the Moon's nodes, every day of the year, with the temporary difference of most remarkable places of the earth from Edinburgh. It hath several tables besides, calculated for the above time, which shows by inspection the day of the month, Moon's age, Sun's rising and setting at Edinburgh, equation of time, and movable feasts, also the Magnitudes, Periodical Revolutions, Solar distances, Hourly velocities, etc., of the planets, and directions for finding the Moon's southing, and High Water in Moray Firth, and at the Ports of Aberdeen, Rochester, Dundee, Malden, Lisbon, Leith, and London for ever.

"This instrument is to be engraven on Royal paper, and the plate sold at a crown to any who are willing to subscribe for its publication, and they are requested to give in their names at the shops of Bailie Hamilton and Mr Symmer, Bookseller in Edinburgh, against the 1st of April 1742, and also from the author, James Ferguson, at his lodging in Nicol Somervail, painter, in the Flesh Market Close.

"If there be not a number sufficient to defray the expense of engraving the publication must be dropped."
—*Caledonian Mercury*, 26th January 1742.

See also notes on Samuel Brown, Edinburgh, page 65.

FERGUSON, MONTGOMERY. Mauchline, Ayrshire, 1837-50.

FERGUSON, WILLIAM STEPHEN. High Street, Elgin, 1837.

FERRIER, JOHN. King Street, Tain, 1836.

FIFE, WILLIAM. Edinburgh, 1780.
Bound apprentice to Thomas Morgan.

FINLAY, ANDREW. Gatehouse-of-Fleet, 1836.

FINLAY, JOHN & CO. 104 Trongate, Glasgow, 1837.

FINDLAY, JOHN. New Marflet Gallery, Aberdeen, 1836-46.

FLEMING, JOHN. Lyon's Lane, Port Glasgow, 1836.

FLETCHER, ROBERT GRAHAM. Edinburgh, 1825-51.
75 Princes Street, 1825; 24 George Street, 1836; 31 Frederick Street, 1846; died 1851.
See also note on Whitelaw and Fletcher.

FLETCHER & HUNTER. 31 Frederick Street, Edinburgh, 1850.

K

FLIGHT, ALEXANDER.　Cupar-Fife, 1820-35.

FLIGHT, BLAIR.　Kinross, 1775-99.

"WATCHES STOLEN.—On the night between Sunday the 5th and Monday the 6th March, curt., the shop of Blair Flight, Clock and Watch Maker in Kinross, was broken into and eleven silver watches, the silver cases of a watch, and some old silver carried off. The makers and numbers of eight of these watches are as follows, viz.:—J. Wallfo, London, No. 3346; Jas. Willis, Brighthampton, No. 801; Jhn. Laudern, without a number; Jo. Bond, London, No. 3210; C. Gratton, London, without a number (this watch had a copper case); Allan, London, No. 3519; C. Clay, London, No. 14860; Coburn, London, without a number.

"There is the greatest reason to suspect that the theft was committed by one John Fisher, a tinker or hawker. He was seen in Alloa on the 6th, where he was offering watches and old silver to sale, and left that place on the afternoon of that day, taking the road to Stirling, but he immediately returned to Alloa Glass House, inquiring if any person there had found a watch which he said he had lost; but getting no notice of it, he again set out the same road, and the watch was afterwards found by a country lad, and turns out to be the one marked C. Clay, No. 14860. Fisher was born in Alloa, where he resided till about six years ago, and since that time his residence is supposed to have been somewhere about Falkirk. His business of late was going through the country selling white iron tankards, brass candlesticks, and buying old metal. He is about 25 or 30 years of age, middle-sized, of a slender make, brownish complexion, has dark brown hair, and there is the mark of a cut on the left side of his upper lip. He had on when he left Alloa a blue duffle greatcoat with pocket lids on the outside, and wore a small round hat. Whoever apprehends him, or gives notice of him so as he may be brought to justice, shall receive a reward of Two Guineas from the above Blair Flight, to be paid upon his being secured. And it is entreated that all watchmakers or others will stop any of the watches above mentioned if offered to sale."—*Edinburgh Evening Courant*, 21st March 1775.

FLOCKHART, JOHN.　Edinburgh, 1797.

FOOT, ROBERT.   Edinburgh, 1755-98.

    3rd May 1755.—"Son of James Foot, workman in the Weigh House of Edinburgh ; booked apprentice to Archibald Straiton, clock and watch maker."

    3rd February 1759.—"Archibald Straiton did, with the consent of the Incorporation, transfer Robert Foot, his apprentice, to James Cowan, clock and watch maker, for the years yet to run of his indentures, and Robert Foot, cautioner, thereby became bound that he should serve Mr Cowan a year further after the expiry of the indentures."

    20th June 1762.—"Discharged of his indentures by James Cowan."

    12th May 1798.—"Compeared and presented his essay, being a plain eight-day clock, begun, made, and finished in the shop of James Howden, in presence of the said James Howden, landlord, and Robert Green, David Murray and Robert Cairnton, essay masters, as they declared, which was found a well wrought essay, etc., and they therefore admitted him as a freeman clock and watch maker in this Incorporation."—*E. H. Records.*

FORBES, DANIEL.   32 Shore, Leith, 1850.

FORBES, FRANCIS.   Edinburgh, 1741.

    "One Francis Forbes, Watch Chain Maker and gilder in water gold, lately come from London, lives at present at the fourth storey up the first forestair within the Netherbow Port, and as there has never been any one before in this place that professed or could rightly perform these branches of trade, he desires to inform all persons of quality and others that he makes all sorts of gold or silver chains for watches, and twezers and neck chains, waistcoat chains, Sissor chains, etc.   That he mends old ones very neatly and cleans gold chains, watch cases, and any gilded plate or other work where the gilding is worn off.   He regilds at an easy rate and makes them look as well as at the first."—*Caledonian Mercury,* 22nd January 1741.

FORBES, WILLIAM.   Kintore, 1837.

FORD, WILLIAM.   Sheriff Brae, Leith, 1813-30.

    Son of Thomas Ford, Custom House, Leith ; booked apprentice to John Paterson, Leith, 1813.

FOREMAN, WILLIAM, Watchmaker, died at St Petersburg, 1830.

FORREST, DANIEL. Opposite Tron Church, Edinburgh, 1820-38.

> 5th May 1823.—"Compeared and presented a petition for admission by purchase, which was received."
>
> 2nd February 1824.—"Compeared and presented his essay, being a clock timepiece, James Gray, landlord, John Calder, and J. Bain, essay masters. He paid fifty pounds, and was therefore admitted a freeman clock and watch maker of this Incorporation."—E. H. Records.

FORREST, DAVID. Edinburgh, 1823.

FORREST, JAMES. Edinburgh, 1763.

> 21st July 1763.—"Son of James Forrest, postmaster, of Douglas; booked apprentice to Robert Clidsdale, watchmaker."—E. H. Records.

FORREST, SIMON. Kirkfieldbank, Lanark, 1800-37.

FORREST, WILLIAM. 49 New Buildings, North Bridge, Edinburgh, 1825-35.

> "William Forrest & Co. having dissolved copartnery, the business will now be carried on as hitherto in the various departments peculiar to this establishment by John Mackay (q.v.), late partner of the above firm, in connection with Robert Chisholm who has had many years' experience in a like manner."—Edinburgh Evening Courant, 4th April 1835.

FORRESTER, PETER, & Co. Edinburgh, 1783-96.

> "Lost a new gold engraved watch, maker's name, Peter Forrester & Co., Edinburgh, No. 755. Any person who may have found it and will return it to the said Peter Forrester & Co. will receive Three Guineas reward. And it is requested that any watchmaker or others to whom it may be offered for sale will immediately give information as above."—Edinburgh Evening Courant, 30th April 1783.
>
> "CLOCKS AND WATCHES.—Peter Forrester & Co., having formed a connection with Mr Andrew Maclean (q.v.), who has been regularly bred to the business of watch and clock making, and on whose abilities and

attention the public can depend, are by this means enabled to warrant and keep in order all clocks and watches made or sold by this company."—*Ibid.*, 27th February 1792.

This business came to an end in the year 1796, and, as the advertisement which follows explains, failed to find a purchaser for the whole as a going concern. The then usual practice of a lottery was proposed and carried out. The details of the prizes as regards values, etc., are so minute, that we are induced to give them in full for the purpose of comparison with the prices realised nowadays for such articles when they come into the auction market.

"LOTTERY OF GOLD, SILVER, AND GILT WATCHES, SILVER PLATE, ETC.—"The public are respectfully informed that as no person has come forward to purchase the stock of goods formerly belonging to Peter Forrester & Co. of Edinburgh, they will now be disposed of by way of Lottery. As a very great part of that stock has been purchased within these last eighteen months, most of the goods are fashionable. This manner of disposal not being meant as a branch of business but as the only practicable method of winding up the affairs, and circumstances not permitting that business to be any longer continued than 25th May next, the terms are extremely advantageous to the Public.

"Tickets being at the very low price of 7s. each, and not two blanks to a prize, the drawing will commence on Monday the 23rd May next. As every circumstance will be conducted the same as in State Lotteries, the strictest honour may be depended on and the time of drawing will be duly adhered to :—

No. of Prizes.		Value of Prizes.		
		£	S.	D.
1	An elegant enamelled gold watch set round with pearls, with lady's gold enamelled chain, plain gold seal, and key	52	10	0
1	An elegant engraved gold watch with gold chain, gold seal, and key	31	10	0
3	Three elegant enamelled gold watches at £26, 5s. each	78	15	0
2	Two plain gold watches at £16, 16s. each	33	12	0
3	Three second-hand gold watches at £11, 11s. each	34	13	0
1	One gilt enamelled watch with gold medallion	12	12	0

No. of Prizes.		Value of Prizes.		
10	Ten elegant engraved gilt watches with ladies' chains at £5, 5s. each . . .	52	10	0
4	Four gilt enamelled watches with ladies' chains at £7, 7s.	29	8	0
10	Ten plain gilt watches with gentlemen's chains at £4, 14s. 6d. each	47	5	0
10	Ten plain silver watches with gentlemen's chains at £4, 14s. 6d. each . . .	47	5	0
10	Ten silver and gilt watches with gentlemen's chains at £3, 13s. 6d. each . .	36	15	0
1	One set of silver plate, viz., Tea Pot, Flat Sugar Basin, and Milk Pail . . .	24	0	0
1	silver porter cup, large size, with handles richly engraved	13	13	0
1	One dozen silver tablespoons, 1 tureen ladle, and 2 sauce spoons . . .	15	15	0
1	One dozen cut silver tablespoons . .	8	6	0
2	Two handsome table clocks at £10, 10s. each .	21	0	0
2	Two eight-day clocks with mahogany cases at £7, 7s. each	14	14	0
1	One plated Epergne, nine basins . .	10	10	0
1	One plated Epergne, five basins . .	8	8	0
2	Two plated tea vases at £7, 7s. . .	14	14	0
4	Four plated sauce tureens at £6, 16s. 6d. each	27	6	0
1	One fine gold diamond ring . .	7	10	0
2	Two fine gold diamond rings at £5, 15s. 6d. each	11	11	0
6	Six fine gold diamond rings at £5, 5s. each .	31	10	0
7	Consisting of Gold Faux Montres and snuff boxes with gold mounting at £4, 4s. each .	29	8	0
6	Six plated candlesticks branches at £2, 18s. each	17	8	0
23	Twenty-three pairs of plated candlesticks at £2, 5s. a pair	51	15	0
100	prizes at £1, 1s.	105	0	0
150	prizes at 18s.	135	0	0
356	prizes at 15s.. . . .	262	10	0
600	prizes at 10s.. . . .	300	0	0
800	prizes at 8s. each	280	0	0
	First drawn ticket—Gold necklace and earrings .	8	8	0
	Last drawn ticket—Gold necklace and earrings .	8	8	0

2370 prizes, 4702 blanks (not two to a prize) = 7072 tickets at 7s. each, £2475, 4s."

"The lottery of goods formerly belonging to P. Forrester & Co. is just finished. It was once intended the whole numbers should be inserted in the papers, but find it would take up the greater part of the papers. The books containing the tickets will be found at the warehouse lately occupied by Messrs Anderson, Leslie, & Co., front stair above the shop. The prizes will be ready for delivery by Monday. Those holding tickets in the country please forward them to their friends in town as no prizes will be delivered unless the tickets are given up.

"*N.B.*—All letters upon this business must be post paid, otherwise they will not be answered."—*Edinburgh Evening Courant,* 5th March and 12th May 1796.

Further details about this lottery are awanting; the only information that has been traced occurs in a short paragraph in the *Courant,* which informs us that No. 1804 in Forrester's Lottery drew a prize of the value of £52, 10s., and was understood to have been bought by a lady in Paisley. That the venture was a success is proved by the number of imitators of the scheme which followed shortly afterwards in Edinburgh.

FORSYTH, T. MORRICE or MORRISON.   Turriff, 1835.

FOSTER, ISAIAH & CO.   184 Argyll Street, Glasgow, 1836.

FOWLDS OR FOULDS, ALLAN.   Kilmarnock; died 28th March 1799, aged 80 years.

FOWLDS, JAMES.   Market Lane, Kilmarnock, 1820.

FRANCIS, THOMAS.   High Street, Dumbarton, 1837.

FRANK, ANDRO and JAMES.   Peebles, 1564-70.

FRANKLIN BROTHERS.   58 New Buildings, North Bridge, Edinburgh, 1820-35.

FRASER, HUGH.   Lamington Street, Tain, 1836.

FRASER, JAMES.   Perth, 1795.
   Apprenticed to Charles Young, Perth.

FRASER, JOHN.   30 South Methven Street, Perth, 1843.

FRASER, JOHN.   166 Union Street, Aberdeen, 1846.

FRASER, NICHOLAS.   Haddington, 1636.

FREEMAN, WALTER.   Hawick, 1780.

FRIGG, ALEXANDER.   Canongate, Edinburgh, 1759.
   Booked apprentice to George Monro, Canongate, 27th December 1759.

FRUGARD, JOHN.   Edinburgh, 1701.
   Booked journeyman to Paul Romieu, jun., 25th September 1701.

FUBISTER, JOHN.   7 Richmond Place, Edinburgh, 1836.

FULTON, JOHN. Fenwick, Ayrshire, 1834.

GALLOWAY, WALTER. Kilbirnie, 1776.

A peculiarity of this maker's clocks is that the brass dial has two round apertures below the hands, one giving the month and the other the day of the month.

GALLOWAY, WILLIAM. Dalry, Ayrshire, 1776.

A relative of Walter Galloway, Kilbirnie. His clocks have the same peculiarity.

GAMMACK, JAMES. Aberchirder, Banff, 1846.

GARDEN, PETER. Longside, Aberdeenshire, 1837.

GARDINER, JAMES. Perth, 1825-42.

GARDINER & KYNOCK. 239 High Street, Edinburgh, 1846.

GARDINER, PATRICK. Perth, 1779-1800.

Apprenticed to James Young, Perth, 1779 ; admitted freeman of Perth Hammermen Incorporation, 1790. Was in business in Perth up to 1800.

GARDINER, PATRICK. Edinburgh, 1812.

Whether this maker is the same as above we have been unable to discover, but it is just possible that it is the same individual. He compeared 11th September 1812 before the Edinburgh Hammermen's Incorporation, and presented a petition craving to be admitted a freeman watchmaker in right of his wife, Matilda, daughter of the late James Aberdour, freeman member of the Incorporation. The petition was granted, and he paid six pounds to the Treasurer.

30th October 1812.—"Compeared and presented his essay, being a watch movement, begun, made, and finished in the shop of Robert Green, in his presence as landlord, and that of James Howden and Alexander Wilson, essay masters, etc."—*E. H. Records.*

GARDINER, PETER. Perth, 1833.

GARDINER, W. & J. 39 High Street, Perth, 1837.

GARDNER, PETER. High Street, Perth, 1820.

GARRICK, FERGUS. Stranraer, 1836-50.

GARRICK, JOHN. Castle Street, Stranraer, 1836.

GARTLY, JOHN. Aberdeen, 1799.

GARVAN & WRIGHT. Main Street, Irvine, 1820.

GEDDES, JAMES. Edinburgh, 1728-55.

21st *September* 1728.—"Son to Andrew Geddes, writer in Edinburgh; booked apprentice to Patrick Gordon, clock and watch maker."

12th *November* 1743.—"The which day James Geddes, son to Andrew Geddes, writer and burgess of Edinburgh, late apprentice to Patrick Gordon, watchmaker, presented his bill for being admitted a freeman watch and clock maker, which was received accordingly, and ane essay and essay masters were appointed."

5th *May* 1744.—"Compeared James Geddes and presented his essay, a white movement of a watch, which was found a well wrought essay, etc. His essay masters were John Wilson, Archibald Straiton, and James Drysdale. His essay was made in Patrick Gordon's shop, his landlord."—*E. H. Records.*

"Lost on the afternoon of Wednesday, the 9th October, on the high road betwixt Howgate mouth and Kingside Edge, a small-sized silver watch with an enamelled dial plate, maker's name, James Geddes, Edinburgh, No. 160, and had when lost a black silk string very much worn, and in the outer case an equation table, on the back of which is wrote the owner's name and designation. Whoever has found the said watch and will return it to James Geddes, watchmaker, Back of the Guard, Edinburgh, shall have two guineas reward."—*Caledonian Mercury*, 12th October 1749.

"That on Wednesday 28th February 1750 last, there was dropt or stolen in the New Church of Edinburgh, from a lady's side, a gold watch, maker's name, Quare, London, having a pinchbeck chain with a cornelian seal of a man's head set in gold. Whoever has found and will return the same to James Geddes, watchmaker, at the back of the main Guard, Edinburgh, shall be handsomely rewarded."—*Edinburgh Evening Courant*, 1st March 1750.

"To be sold by public voluntary roup upon Wednesday the 4th of February next, at the house lately possest by the deceast James Geddes, watchmaker, and now by his relict, at the back of the Guard, great choice of Gold, Silver, and Pinchbeck watches, eight-day clocks, a repeating table clock, Barometers, and sundry pieces of the movements of watches, together with the whole instruments and utensils necessary for a watchmaker. The particulars are to be seen at any time between and the day of roup, which is to begin at 10 o'clock and to continue till all is sold off. It is hoped that those who are debtors to the said James Geddes will without delay make payment to his relict, who is entitled to discharge them, which will prevent the disagreeable necessity of a prosecution. And it is expected that those who have got watches out upon trial will either return them or the value before the day of roup."—*Caledonian Mercury*, 17th January 1755.

"Charles Geddes, watchmaker, Halifax, served Heir of Line and Provision General to his father, James Geddes, watchmaker in Edinburgh, dated 18th November 1784. Recorded 23rd November 1784."—*Services of Heirs*.

"Died at Halifax, Nova Scotia, on the 27th September 1810, Mr Charles Geddes, watchmaker, aged 61 years, native of Edinburgh."—*Edinburgh Evening Courant*, 1811.

GEORGE, WILLIAM.   70 Mill Street, Perth, 1848.

GERRARD, WILLIAM.   Turriff, 1812 ; died 1872.

Apprenticed to James Dalziel, Fraserburgh, about 1812.

GIBB, JAMES.   Trongate, Glasgow, 1846.

GIBB, JAMES.   Stirling, 1770.

Entered freeman of the Incorporation of Hammermen, Stirling, for his life only, December 1770.

GIBB, WILLIAM.   Whithorn, 1836.

GIBSON, ADAM.   Dunse, 1777.

GIBSON, HENRY.   Berwick-on-Tweed, 1848.

GIBSON, JAMES.   40 Trongate, Glasgow, 1809-25.

"Lost last night a silver watch, capped and jewelled, maker's name, James Gibson, Glasgow, No. 21, with a gold chain and seal. Whoever brings the same to James Gibson, watchmaker, 40 Trongate, Glasgow, will be handsomely rewarded." — *Glasgow Courier*, 1st September 1812.

"James Gibson, watch and clock maker, Glasgow, served Heir in General to his grandfather, Daniel Gibson, smith in Edinburgh, dated 16th February 1824. Recorded 30th March 1824."—*Services of Heirs.*

GIBSON, JOHN. Edinburgh, 1758-80.

29th December 1758.—"John Gibson, son of James Gibson, stabler, in the Grassmarket, Edinburgh, bound apprentice to Daniel Binny."

26th July 1766.—"Presented a bill for being admitted a freeman clock and watch maker, which was received."

31st January 1767.—"Compeared and presented his essay, being a watch movement, begun, made, and finished in his own shop in the presence of Samuel Brown, landlord, James Duff, Peter Taylor, and Alexander Farquharson, essay masters, which being a well wrought essay, etc., was accordingly admitted."— *E. H. Records.*

"VALUABLE MUSICAL CLOCK FOR SALE.—This capital piece of Mechanism is now exposed in Thomson's Sale Room, No. 56 South Bridge Street, Edinburgh. It was made by John Gibson, an eminent maker in this city, and is mounted in an elegant mahogany case, which as well as the movement is in complete repair. The motion is regulated by a royal pendulum with a dead escapement, and the music, consisting of eleven of our best old Scots tunes and a hymn tune, one of which it plays every hour, is performed by one barrel on a set of very sweet toned bells; it also plays any of the tunes at pleasure. This clock would be a great acquisition to the hall of a mansion house."—*Edinburgh Evening Courant,* 1st October 1808.

GIBSON, JOHN, jun. Edinburgh, 1780.

Nephew of above; booked apprentice to John Gibson, 1st November 1780.

27th January 1781.—"On the petition of John Gibson and his mother, order the officer to call at the different watchmakers, and shew them the indentures, and ascertain if none of them shall agree to take the apprentice on the same terms he had from his late uncle and master. The incorporation, in terms of the petition, allow John Gibson to learn his craft with any master he can find and agree upon his service. He shall be entitled to the freedom in virtue of his indentures."

3rd May 1781.—"It being reported that all and each of the watchmakers had declined to take John Gibson on the terms of his indenture with John Gibson his uncle, the incorporation do therefore allow the said John Gibson to learn his trade with any master he can find, and to have the benefits of his indenture." —*E. II. Records.*

GIBSON, JOHN. Bradshaw Street, Saltcoats, 1820-37.

GIBSON, JOHN. Kelso.

The particulars of this maker have been kindly supplied by Mr Thomas Craig, Kelso, as follows :— "Towards the close of the eighteenth century we had in this town a man who seemed to be a great mechanical genius, not only making clocks with ingenious features, but also being a proficient optician, having made a telescope for the British Ambassador to Russia, and another for the Duke of Roxburghe, for which he is said to have got one hundred guineas each. His gifts as a musician, linguist, etc., were also notable, so out of the common that many reputed him to be rather uncanny."

This gentleman has taken the trouble to inquire at all the local clock and watch makers, asking them to keep a lookout for any of this maker's productions, but without success. To any who own them this short note about a man of undoubted talent may be of interest.

GIBSON, JOHN. New Street, Beith, 1837.

GIBSON, JOHN. Glasgow, 1809.

GIBSON, JOHN. Glasgow, 1841.

GIBSON, ROBERT. 17 Academy Street, Dumfries, 1820.

GIBSON, THOMAS. 26 Hyde Hill, Berwick-on-Tweed, 1837.

GIBSON, ——. Ayr, 1844.

GIBSON AND CLELLAND.   Edinburgh, 1767-72.

If the reader will turn to the notes on John Gibson and John Clelland it will be seen that they were both fellow apprentices with Daniel Binny; Clelland was a transferred apprentice.   Although both finished their indentures in the same year, John Gibson was the first of the two to become a freeman of the incorporation, Clelland being admitted five years later.   As the latter could not commence business on his own account until he was also made freeman he traded with his fellow apprentice, the firm being known as Gibson and Clelland.   Whether this was done openly is a matter of uncertainty, as the copartnery name never appears in the *Hammermen's Records*, but, as can be seen by the advertisement issued by Clelland, page 82, this came to an end in 1773. John Gibson not unlikely carrying on the business at the established premises at the West End of the Luckenbooths, while John Clelland commenced on the north side of the Lawnmarket.

GIFFEN, ROBERT & SON.   Church Street, Campbeltown, 1837.

GIFFORD—The Town Clock of (Haddingtonshire).

"The first village improvement undertaken by the managers of which we have notice is the provision of a town clock in 1775.   Subscriptions to the extent of £5, 3s. were received, and the balance of £14, 19s. was paid out of the town funds, which were so low at the time that of that amount one of the managers had to advance £2, 10s.

"The clock was purchased for £20, and was erected under the supervision of Mr Hay of Hopes,[1] the factor of the Marquess of Tweeddale.   The carriage of the clock and bell from Edinburgh cost 6s.; painting the case and boards of the clock steeple meant a further expenditure of 8s.; 'pottie,' and the expense of laying it on the bottom of the spire cost 1s. 6d.   The clock steeple

---

[1] It is interesting to note that this Mr Hay of Hopes is buried in the tomb of George Heriot, senior, in the Greyfriars Churchyard, Edinburgh.

was exactly where it now is, but, as some living still may
remember, it was different in form. The tower itself
was square, with Louvre windows just underneath the
steeple. The steeple could hardly be called a steeple,
being simply a comparatively flat roof, the whole being
what would now be called a lantern roofed tower; while
the clock face was a large square board with painted
lettering. There was no glass, and during a snowstorm
the hands could be seen steadily pursuing their course
long after the figures had been covered by the snow.
The keeping of the clock formed an item of annual
expenditure. Robert Bathgate received 3s. 4d. per half
year for winding it, and by 1790 this sum had
been increased to 5s. For supervising Robert and
attending to the oiling of the clock, James Craise was
paid 5s. per annum, a fee that was later raised to 10s. 6d.
In 1779 the clock was cleaned in Edinburgh at a cost of
10s. 6d., John Gibson being paid the large sum of 2d.
for taking it to Edinburgh. To do this cleaning work
a Haddington man, James Cunningham, was afterwards
employed, and was paid at the Edinburgh rate, 10s. 6d.,
but apparently he had in addition little perquisites for
his trouble, for in February 1784 there is an item of
expenditure entered thus: 'By expense of a dinner to
Mr Cunningham at cleaning of clock 5s. 10d.'; and in
1794 there is another entry: 'By an entertainment in
John M'Connel's to Mr Cunningham and assistants at
cleaning the clock, 8s. 11d.'

"By the beginning of the century the clock winding
had been handed over to a woman, and first Nanny
Stewart and then Agnes Dixon officiated still under the
supervision of Mr Craise, whose annual account for oil,
etc., had a tendency to increase. In 1800 it was £1, 1s.
By and by in 1802 he received for keeping and winding,
£1, 5s., and his son George, in the following year, received
£1, 6s. for performing the same duties. His successor
in 1805 was Peter Begbie. This was the same Peter
who was declared unfit to be clerk to the managers, and
who apparently had almost abnormally developed the
faculty of looking after himself. In 1815 he received

a quarterly payment of 7s. 6d. In 1838 the clock passed into the care of a new custodian, James Hogg (q.v.), whose remuneration was 17s. 6d. half yearly, this being a still further advance. This old clock acted as village time-keeper for 80 years, and was displaced by a more modern article in 1856. The latter only retained its place for about 30 years when the reconstructed tower and steeple were adorned by the present time-keeper, which was presented by the late Mr P. B. Swinton, and which under its watchful winder always makes it possible for Gifford folks to catch the train."[1]

GILCHRIST, JOHN.   Kilsyth, 1820.

GILFILLAN, JAMES.   Lesmahagow, 1834.

GILGOUR, THOMAS.   Admitted a watchmaker of Hammermen Incorporation, Elgin, 1697.

GILL, DAVID.   Aberdeen; died 1877, aged 88 years.

"Purchased in 1857 the lands of Blair Ythan and Gavock in the parish of Foveran. On his death, in 1877, at the age of 88, Mr Gill was succeeded in the former property by his eldest son, David, a distinguished Fellow of the Royal Astronomical Society, and in the latter by his third son Andrew."—JERVISE'S *Epitaphs and Inscriptions*.

GILL, PETER & SON.   80 Union Street, Aberdeen, 1846.

GILLAN, JOHN.   Keithhall, Inverury, 1837.

GILLIES, ROBERT.   Beith, 1790.

GILLIES, WILLIAM.   St Ninians, 1775.

GILMOT, HARIE or HENRY.   Canongate, Edinburgh, 1711.

Admitted a freeman clockmaker, Canongate Hammermen, 11th April 1711, his essay being ane balance of a watch and ane spring pendulum. This is the earliest clockmaker's name appearing in the records of this incorporation of this date, previous ones having disappeared.

[1] I am indebted to the Rev. John Muir, B.D., minister of Gifford, for the above, which appeared in the columns of the *Haddington Advertiser*, 1913.

GIN, WILLIAM. Perth, 1778.

GLADSTONE, JOHN. Biggar.

Born 22nd August 1772; died 8th July 1851. The above particulars are noted on a tombstone in Biggar Churchyard erected to the family of Gladstone, to which the late Rt. Hon. Wm. E. Gladstone was allied.

GLASGOW—Notices regarding the Town Clocks of, from 1576 to 1657.

30th June 1576.—"Item, to Dauid Kaye[1] in Carraill (Crail) for his expenssis in remanyng about the knok, he being send for   iij lib. vjs. viijd."

12th July 1576.—"Item, Geivin to William Herury to ryn to Carraill anent the knok   xvjs."

24th July 1576.—"Item, Geivin to Dauid Kaye for the price of the knok, and upsetting of hir in the tolbuyth, quhilk wes borrowit fra Thomas Garne

jc lib. (£100 Scots)."

17th October 1576.—"In presens of Johne Wilsoun, ane of the bailies of Glasgow, comperit Dauid Kay in Carrill, and of his awin consent and confessioun renuncead all uther jurisdictiounes and submittand (him) to the jurisdictioun of the prouest (and) bailies of Glasgu, in this cais, to cum to the towne of Glasgu how sone he be requeyrit be the prouest, bailies, and counsalle thairof, upone the expenssis of the said touneship of Glasgu, and thair to set up and repair or mend the twa knokkes, the ane maid be himself and the uther auld knok mendit be him, how oft he beis requirit thairto be thame or ony in thair name, and that upone the tounes rationable expenssis to be payit and done to him thairfor."

"Item, to Dauid Kaye in Carrill for the rest of the auld knok mendyng and for his bunteth of the new knok   vj lib. xiijs. iiijd."

18th May 1583.—"Steine Dikkie, tailyeour, is maid burges and freman of this guid toune, and hes geiffin his ayth of fidelttie to the toune and his fiencs, is assignit and grantit to Sir Archibald Dikkie for rowlling and

[1] See page 124 for further reference to David Kay.

gyding of the knok, and for lying nychtlie in the tolbuith to rewll and keip the samyne, and for helping and support of him to his bed clais."

" *Item*, To Sir Archibald Dicky for keiping of the knok iiijs. iiijd."

27th January 1610.—"George Smyth, rewler of the Tolbuith knok, hes bund him to the toun to rewll the said knok for all the dayis of his lyfetyme for the sowme of tuentie pundis money yeirlie, and siklike oblisses him to rewll the Hie Kirk knok and keep the same in gang and grath, and visie hir twa seurall dayis in the wik, the sessioun payand him ten merkis yeirlie."

31st March 1627.—"The bailyeis and counsell aggreit with Johne Neill to mak ane new knok and haill furnitour of irne wark, als sufficient fyne and worthie as the great knok in the laich stepill of the Metrapolitan Kirk vpoun his awin expenssis for sax hundrethe merk to be payit be the toun to him, and ane contract to be drawin vp betuix thame and him thairanent."

17th November 1627.—"*Item*, ordanes the thesaurer to gif to Johne Neill for chainging the knok and bywark ten pundis money."

23rd August 1628.—"The prouest, bailyies, and counsill hes condescendit and aggreit to gif to Johne Neill thrie hundrethe merkis money, and that by and attour sax hundrethe merkis quilk the toun wes bund to pay him for the great new knok of the Tolbuithe maid be him to the toun vpoun his awin chairges, becaus they fand that he was ane loser and the said knok was worthe the foresaid haill sowme."

30th August 1628.—"The treasurer to have a warrant for 50 markis given to Johne Jaffray forder nor (more than) Johne Neill gave him for forging of the knok, becaus it was lang in working and sindrie pairtis thairof wrocht ouer agane, and also a warrant for 390 markis to be gevin to Vallentyn Ginking, paintour, for gilting of the horologe brodis, palmes, mones, the Kingis armes, an all paintrie and cullouring thairof, and of the justice hous."

L

162   OLD SCOTTISH CLOCKMAKERS

21st February 1657.—"Appoints the haill horologes to be mendit in letters for the better knowing of the hours, and that with all convenience, and Bailie Hall to speak James Colquherine thairanent, and to report."

28th February 1657.—"Appoint the provest and Johne Walkingschaw to deall with James Colquhone anent the coulcuring of the horologe in the Tolbooth."

14th March 1657.—"It is concluded upon that Androu Purdoune have the knokis in rewling, and is to have ane cair of the haill three knokis for payment of the old yeirlie fie that was payit to umquhill Johne Neill."

13th June 1657.—"It is condescendit and agreed to pay to James Colquhone three hundret and fifty merks for to coller and dress again the horologis and gilting of the letters."

20th June 1657.—"Walter Neilsoune made report that, conform to the council's order, he had agreed with Patrick Wilsoune for drawing of the High Kirk knok pais quhilk the town is to pay hereafter and is to be remembered."

8th August 1657.—"It is concluded and agreed upon by the said magistrates and council that James Colquhoun paint and fix the toun's armes and year of God on every horologe brod, and that being done, grants warrant to James Bornis to pay to the said James Colquhoun, for the painting and coulouring of the four horologe brods of the tolbooth and gilding the letters thereof as they now stand, the sum of four hundret merks out of the money collected for the buckatis, and what the said James does furthur to the globes he is to be satisfied thairfore be sight of John Walkingshaw."
—-Extracts from *Glasgow Burgh Records*, published by the Burgh Record Society.

GLASS, JAMES. Bannatyne, Alexandria, Dumbartonshire, 1837.

GLASS, JOHN. Edinburgh, 1692.

GOLDER, John.   Alloa, 1830-45.

"John Golder, Watch & Clock Maker, Mill Street, Alloa, begs to inform the inhabitants of the town and vicinity that he continues to keep on hand a good assortment of Lever and Vertical watches, eight-day clocks, etc.   Clocks in the country cleaned and repaired " —*Alloa Monthly Advertiser*, 7th May 1842.

"To be disposed of, the stock and goodwill of that old-established business carried on here by J. Golder, who is retiring from business.   To any person possessed of a small capital a more eligible opportunity seldom occurs.   The shop, the rent of which is moderate, is situated in the principal street ; application to be made to J. Golder here."—*Ibid.*, 7th February 1845.

GOODAL, Adam.   Canongate, Edinburgh, 1744.

Booked apprentice to James Nicoll.

GOODFELLOW, John.   Stirling, 1765.

Admitted a freeman of the Incorporation of Hammermen, Stirling, 13th April 1765 ; had to make for an essay a lanteret wheel for a watch and to redeem it by paying the sum of fifteen shillings sterling.

"Stolen this day from Whitehouse, a silver watch with a china dial plate and a silver seal and a ribbon for a string ; maker's name, Fra Haines, London, No. 12290.

"The man who is suspected of the theft had on a blue bonnet, a loose wide coat of a drab colour, and a bundle in his hand, pock-pitted a little, reddish hair, and spoke Earse, and said he was going to Inverness. Whoever can give information to the publisher of this paper, or to Mr Goodfellow, watchmaker in Stirling, shall have half a guinea reward."—*Caledonian Mercury*, 23rd October 1765.

GOODOUNE, John.   Edinburgh, 1680.

Booked apprentice to Richard Milne.

GORDON, Adam.   Abbey of Holyrood, Edinburgh, 1797.

GORDON, Alexander.   Dundee, 1729.

Maker of the first clock in Brechin Town Hall.

GORDON, George.   Perth, 1795-1810.

Apprenticed to Charles Young, Perth, 1795.

"George Gordon, served Heir General to his father, James Gordon, watchmaker in Perth, 28th April 1807. Recorded 13th May 1807."—*Services of Heirs.*

GORDON, Hugh.   Aberdeen, 1748-90.

"That Hugh Gordon, who has for some time followed the business of clock and watch maker at Edinburgh, London, etc., having now settled in this place, hereby acquaints the public that all gentlemen and others may be furnished with new clocks and watches made by himself, and have old ones repaired to the best advantage at reasonable rates.   And if any boys of a suitable genius incline to follow this business he will, upon having a trial of their capacity, agree with them upon reasonable terms.   He lives at Craigie Forbes's house, in the Broadgate, Aberdeen."— *Aberdeen Journal*, 8th November 1748.

"Hugh Gordon, watchmaker, begs leave to acquaint the gentlemen and ladies who are so kind as to employ him, that since his settlement in Aberdeen (from Edinburgh and London) he has lost a much greater sum than can be easily believed, by people neglecting to pay for the cleaning and repairing of their clocks and watches, which at last forced him, much against his inclination, to acquaint his employers in this public manner that for the future he is to clean and mend for ready money only, as every one must be sensible with what trouble the recovery of trifles is attended."—*Ibid.*, 6th November 1753.

"Whereas upon Saturday, the 11th of July instant, there was lost about eight o'clock in the evening upon the road betwixt Didhope and Dundee, a watch, the case a pebble mounted with gold, maker's name, Vigne, No. 1432, the outer case black shagreen with a pinchbeck chain and two seals thereat set in gold, the one a Socrates head, the other the Duke of Cumberland. Also a small gold locket in the form of a heart set with hair.   Any person who has found the same and will return it to the Town Clerk's office in Dundee, or to Mr Charles Malcolm, at the General Post Office in Edinburgh, or Mr Hugh Gordon, watchmaker in Aberdeen, shall be very handsomely rewarded.

"*N.B.*—The town of Dundee hereby offers a reward of Five guineas to the finder of the above watch, over and above what is given by the proprietor."—*Caledonian Mercury*, 18th July 1761.

GORDON, James.   Gallowgate, Aberdeen, 1820.

GORDON, JAMES. Perth, 1771-96.

Granted liberty by the Perth Hammermen's Incorporation to exercise his trade as clock and watch maker in that city on 1st July 1771.

GORDON, JAMES. Beith, 1790.

GORDON, JAMES. Canongate, Edinburgh, 1734.

"James Gordon, son of James Gordon, watchmaker in Canongate, served Heir General to his cousin, Roger Gordon of Dendeuch, dated 26th November 1736. Recorded 14th March 1737."—*Services of Heirs.*

GORDON, JOHN. Canongate, Edinburgh, 1747-99.

Booked apprentice to George Miln, Canongate, 1747. Admitted a freeman clock and watch maker, Canongate Hammermen, 1st November 1762, his essay being a watch verge finished. Entered into partnership with Daniel Binny at the Netherbow, Edinburgh, in 1773.

GORDON, PATRICK. Edinburgh, 1699-1749.

15*th September* 1699.—"Son to the deceast Alexander Gordon of Briggs; booked apprentice to Richard Mills, clockmaker."

15*th March* 1715.—"Compeared and presented his essay, viz., an eight-day pendulum clock, and a lock to the door with a key, which was found a well wrought essay, etc. His essay masters were William Sutor and John Dalgleish. His essay was made in Thomas Gordon's shop."—*E. H. Records.*

"Lost on Saturday, April the 21st, betwixt the Gray's Close and Miln's Square, betwixt 8 and 9 o'clock at night, a large gold watch with Andrew Dunlop's name, with two gold cases and a green silk string with a small seal and an inscription on it, Love for Love. If any one can give notice of the said watch to Patrick Gordon, watchmaker in Miln's Square, opposite to the Tron Church, shall be sufficiently rewarded for the same."—*Caledonian Mercury*, 26th April 1744.

"On Saturday last died Mr Patrick Gordon, watchmaker in this city. We are told he has left several donations and mortifications, but the extent is not known, in regard his executor, Mr Gordon at Garmouth, lives at a considerable distance."—*Edinburgh Evening Courant*, 19th June 1749.

30th November 1749.—"The house being informed that their late respected fellow freeman, Patrick Gordon, watchmaker, deceased, by his deed of legacy the 13th and registered in the Court Books of this burgh the 28th day of June last, had among many other mortifications, charities, and donations, legated and bequeathed to the Deacon and Masters of this Incorporation for the use and behoof of the same the sum of Twenty pounds sterling, and that James Gordon, merchant in Garmouth, to whom he had disponed his whole effects, was ready to pay the said legacy upon a proper discharge. Therefore the Incorporation, in grateful remembrance of such donation, do appoint the name of the said Patrick Gordon to be put up in Gold Letters in their chapel among the names of their other pious benefactors.

"And hereby depute and empower James Yorston, cutler in Edinburgh, their treasurer, for and in name of their said Incorporation, and as their Act and Deed to receive and discharge the said legacy of Twenty pounds sterling, and everything concerning the same, to grant which the said Incorporation could do themselves, all which they oblige them and their successors to hold firm and ratify whereupon this act is made."—*E. H. Records.*

GORDON, ROBERT. High Street, Edinburgh, 1750.
"Robert Gordon at his shop, south side of the Cross, Edinburgh, acquaints the public that he has now ready for sale a large collection of second-hand plate. Gold watches, chased and plain, exceeding cheap."—*Edinburgh Evening Courant*, 15th March 1750.

GORDON, THOMAS. Edinburgh, 1688-1743.
3rd November 1688.—"Brother German to Alexander Gordon of Briggs; booked apprentice to Andrew Brown."
18th September 1703.—"Compeared and presented his essay, viz., a pendulum clock with alarum and short swing and a lock to the door with a key, which was found a well wrought essay, etc., and therefore they admit him to be a freeman among them in the clock-

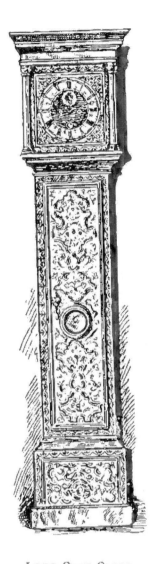

LONG CASE CLOCK,

In marquetry case. By Thomas
Gordon, Edinburgh, 1688 - 1743.
(See p. 166.)

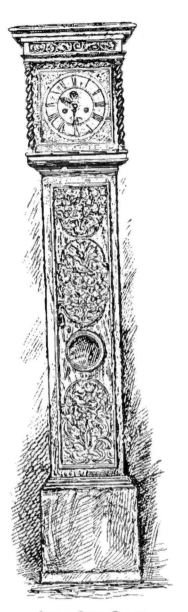

LONG CASE CLOCK,

In coloured marquetry case. By
Paul Roumier, jun., Edinburgh,
1682-1712. The property of J.
Paterson, Esq., Biggar, Lanarkshire.
(See p. 328.)

[To face page 166.

maker's art.   His essay masters were Deacon Letham
and Paul Romieu; his essay was made in Andrew
Brown's shop.   He paid the boxmaster one hundred
and six pounds thirteen shillings and four pennies (Scots)
and the other dues."—*E. H. Records.*

12*th April* 1712.—" In presence of the Incorporation
of the Hammermen of Edinburgh, Thomas Gordon,
clockmaker, payed this day thirteen shillings sterling
to the boxmaster for being twenty-six times absent,
before he could get William Murray his apprentice
discharged.   And the Incorporation declare they will
free none hereafter of what absents they shall be, before
they get their apprentices discharged."—*E. H. Records.*

" Lost near the Causeyside last week, a new gold
watch, made by Thomas Gordon.   Whoever has found
the said watch and returns it to Thomas Gordon, watchmaker in Edinburgh, shall have five guineas reward."—
Caledonian Mercury, 14th October 1728.

Thomas Gordon died in the beginning of the year
1743, having been in business for a period of forty
years.   If the reader will turn to the notes on Robert
Fairholm it will be seen that the minute quoted gives
Patrick Gordon as his brother.   This is probably correct,
although the first minutes dealing with both these men
respectively show that they were uncle and nephew.
Possibly this last is a mistake of the writer of the
original records, but that undoubtedly they were brothers
is afforded by the fact that Patrick Gordon was served
Heir to his brother Thomas Gordon, 20th April 1749.
Specimens of the two brothers' art are exceeding rare :
two of Thomas Gordon's having come under my notice,
one in a marquetry case formerly the property of
Messrs T. Smith & Sons, watchmakers, George Street,
Edinburgh, but now, we believe, in London; the other
still located in the Head Office of the Bank of Scotland.
One by Patrick Gordon was seen in an antiquarian
dealer's shop in Edinburgh.   All three show, in a
marked degree, not only the characteristics of the period
in which these men lived, but also remain as examples
of the careful handiwork of capable men.

GORDON, THOMAS.   Edinburgh and New York, 1748.

6th February 1748.—" Son of James Gordon, merchant in Gartmouth ; booked apprentice to Patrick Gordon."

19th December 1749.—" Anent the petition offered by Thomas Gordon, late apprentice to Patrick Gordon, watchmaker, deceased, craving to be transferred to another master for the remaining space of his indentures, and in terms thereof. And the said Thomas Gordon being called in, and having pitched upon William Nicol, watchmaker, to be his master, and William Nicol accepted thereof, the house transfers the said Thomas Gordon to be apprentice to the said William Nicol for the space yet to run in the said indentures on the conditions and the terms thereof."—*E. H. Records.*

The opening minute in above shows that this was a son of the "executor" of Patrick Gordon's will, and although the designation of his location is slightly spelt different, it is clear that it is the same individual.   What relation he was to the two clockmakers is uncertain, but all information seems to point that he was another brother, which surmise, if correct, made this Thomas Gordon a nephew.   The choice of William Nicol as his master was no doubt due to the fact that William Nicol had served his apprenticeship with Patrick Gordon, and as Nicol had only been made freeman a year or so before, it was only natural that he should pitch upon one who was certain to be well known to him.   His future movements in Edinburgh after this date are unknown, but in the year 1770 he was served heir to his father, and is designated as belonging to New York. Of his career in this last city we have not the slightest information, but as it is just possible that some of his descendants are still in New York, this brief but authentic note may interest and be of value to them.

GORDON, WILLIAM.   Lauder, 1780-1805.

12th December 1780.—" Bound apprentice to Turnbull & Aitchison, Edinburgh."

21st December 1804.—" William Gordon, sometime apprentice to Turnbull & Aitchison, with which he had

personally compeared at a meeting called together for
his accommodation on the 17th curt., he being obliged to
leave town for Lauder, where he carries on business,
early next morning. He craved to have an essay and
essay masters appointed in order to his being admitted
a freeman locksmith, which in the circumstances of the
case was granted. His essay to be produced at the
next Whitsunday meeting. The treasurer received nine
pounds, being the first moiety of his entry money."

4*th May* 1805.—"Compeared and presented his
essay, a clock movement begun, made, and finished in the
shop of James Ramage, landlord, in presence of him and
William Drysdale, James Brackenrig, John Henderson,
and Robert Ancrum, essay masters, as they declared."—
E. H. Records.

It will be observed that this individual received his
training in Edinburgh and settled in Lauder. He was
in business there in 1797. It is evident that quite a
number of Edinburgh trained craftsmen settled in
country districts.

GORDON, WILLIAM.   60 Potterrow, Edinburgh, 1811.

GORDON, WILLIAM.   Convel Street, Dufftown, 1836.

GORDONE, THOMAS.   Aberdeen, 1595. *See* page 8.

GORDOUNE, JOHN.   Edinburgh, 1680.

> 7*th February* 1680.—"Son to Alexander Gordoune
> of Edencore ; booked apprentice to Richard Mylne."

GOURLAY, JAMES.   Newton-Stewart, 1836.

GOW, JAMES.   Dunblane, 1837.

GOW, WILLIAM.   Edinburgh, 1779.

GOWANS, JAMES.   East Linton, 1837-50.

GRAHAM, CHARLES.   Edinburgh, 1782-90.

> 1*st November* 1782.—"Son of the deceased John
> Graham, bookbinder ; bound apprentice to Laurence
> Dalgleish."
> 1*st November* 1788.—"Discharged of his indentures."
> 9*th April* 1790.—Married Elizabeth Stewart.

GRAHAM, J.   Kirkintilloch, 1735.

GRAHAM, JAMES. Whitburn, 1833.

"Elizabeth Graham in Whitburn served Heir Portion General to her father, James Graham, clockmaker there, dated 19th August 1833. Recorded 4th October 1833."—*Services of Heirs.*

GRAHAM, JAMES. Glasgow, 1793.

GRAHAM, JAMES. High Street, Girvan, 1837.

GRAHAM, JOHN. Church Wynd, Langholm, 1837.

GRAHAM, JOHN. Moffat, 1837.

GRAHAM, JOHN. Stirling Street, Airdrie, 1836.

GRAHAM, JOSEPH. 71 Trongate, Glasgow, 1837.

GRAHAM, THOMAS. Buccleuch Street, Hawick, 1837.

GRAIG, WILLIAM. Stewartfield, Aberdeenshire, 1836.

GRANT, ALEXANDER. Newburgh, Fife, 1834.

GRANT, ALEXANDER. 10 Bow, Stirling, 1825; died 1875.

GRANT, GEORGE. Edinburgh, 1776-83.

Booked apprentice to Joseph Durward, 1776; discharged of his indentures 28th April 1783.

GRANT, JOHN. 23 Main Street, Anderston, Glasgow, 1818-41.

GRANT, JOHN. 1 Bishop Street, Glasgow, 1828-41.

GRANT, JOHN. Fyvie, Aberdeenshire, 1846.

GRANT, JOSEPH. Sinclair Street, Helensburgh, 1837.

GRANT, WILLIAM. Edinburgh, 1750-55.

28th *July* 1750.—"Son of Thomas Grant, Bower; booked apprentice to John Stiell."

24th *July* 1755.—"The meeting authorised their Deacon, Treasurer, and Masters of the Locksmith's Art to transfer William Grant, apprentice to John Stiell, watch and clock maker, deceasit, to Robert Clidsdale, for the space to run of his indentures."

7th *February* 1756.—"William Grant having applied to the Incorporation to be transferred to a new master, they remitted to their present Deacon and Treasurer to inquire how William Grant has spent his time since John Stiell's death, and according how he has behaved, to transfer him not to Robert Clidsdale, and in general with full powers to them to do therein as they shall cause."—*E. H. Records.*

GRANT, WILLIAM. Edinburgh, 1821.

> 30*th July* 1821.—"Apprenticed to William Drysdale."

GRANT, WILLIAM. High Street, Perth, 1820.

GRAY, ALEXANDER. Elgin, 1754-74. *See* Elgin Common Clocks, page 137.

GRAY, ——. Elgin, subsequent to 1820.

GRAY, HENRY. Inverkeithing, 1834.

GRAY, JAMES. Elgin, 1772.

> "James Gray, Clock and Watch Maker in Elgin, at the sign of the gold watch, who has regularly been bred to and practised the said business in all its different branches, in some of the most noted shops in London, makes, mends, and sells all sorts of musical, repeating, and plain clocks, spring dials, and timepieces. Also, all sorts of repeating, horizontal, and plain watches, with gold or silver, plain shagreen, nuriskine or chased cases, all at very reasonable rates, and after the latest methods. As the communication with Elgin is frequent and very extensive, watches and clocks that need repair may be easily sent from a considerable distance, and those who do may depend on having them well done and speedily returned. As there have been many gentlemen bit, or deceived by imposters who call themselves watchmakers, such as runaway apprentices and the like, that have not the least pretensions to that name, but any gentleman that is doubtful of me can see a specimen of my work and also have good security for what they entrust me with. Any young man of a good genius who has a mind to learn watchmaking, may be properly instructed by applying to the advertiser. If any incline to clock-making only he will be instructed on very reasonable terms.
>
> "*N.B.*—Ready money for old gold and silver lace."— *Edinburgh Evening Courant,* 18th September 1772.

GRAY, JAMES. Edinburgh, 1765-1806.

12th February 1765.—" Apprenticed to Daniel Binny, and discharged of his indentures, 27th February 1771. Presented a bill craving to be admitted a freeman watchmaker, 26th July 1771. Compeared on 2nd May 1772, and produced his essay, being a watch movement made and finished in the shop of John Murdoch, in presence of John Murdoch, landlord, William Nicol, Normand Macpherson, and John Sibbald, essay masters, as they declared, etc."—*E. H. Records.*

" James Gray, Watch and Clock Maker, west end of Luckenbooths, has now, after great labour and at much expense, finished a most elegant musical clock, which is allowed by the nobility and others who have seen it to be the most complete of its kind, and containing the greatest variety of curiosities of any ever shown in this city.

" It is proposed to dispose of the said clock by way of a lottery at half a guinea each ticket, and so soon as he procures a sufficient number of subscribers the time and place of drawing will be advertised. The drawing will be conducted with the greatest care and attention under the direction of persons of skill and fidelity.

" The clock goes eight days, and plays a tune of itself three times over every three hours in the day. It plays ten different tunes, which may be shifted at pleasure by turning a hand on the dial plate. While the music plays, two figures dance, and a musician plays on the violin, all of them keeping accurate time to the music. There is likewise represented a landscape and rural scene, with a windmill going, and a number of figures of various character walking along in regular procession. As also a distant view of an encampment, with a soldier on duty constantly walking backward and forward, and may be seen at No. 19 Princes Street, New Town, any lawful day from ten o'clock forenoon till six in the evening.

" Subscriptions are taken in by Andrew Ramsay, at the Exchange Coffee House, and if a sufficient number of subscribers cannot be obtained in six weeks from this date, Mr Ramsay will return the gentlemen subscribers their money.

" *N.B.*—The clock is valued at eighty guineas."— *Edinburgh Evening Courant*, 27th July 1785.

"MUSICAL CLOCK.—James Gray, watchmaker, having now sold off (to a few) the tickets for the lottery of his musical clock, respectfully informs the Nobility, Gentry, and others who have so liberally patronised him that the drawing of the said lottery is to be held in Magdalen Chapel, Cowgate, on Monday, 12th December next, at 12 o'clock noon. He therefore expects those who have subscribed will send their tickets to the Exchange Coffee House, or to his shop, immediately above the entry to the Tolbooth, where those who choose yet to favour him may be served with tickets previous to the drawing.

"*N.B.*—He continues to make, sell, and repair all sorts of watches and clocks on the most reasonable terms. Variety of watch chains, seals, etc."—*Ibid.*, 23rd November 1785.

An account of the drawing of the clock, and the name of the successful subscriber, is given below :—

"On Monday last the lottery for the ingenious musical clock invented by Mr Gray, clock and watch maker here, was drawn in Magdalen Chapel before Mr Ferguson of Craigdarroch, and Mr Charles Mitchell, writer in Edinburgh, judges to oversee it, when No. 157, the property of Mr Archibald Maxwell, writer, was found entitled to the prize. There were 160 tickets in the wheel, which sold at 10s. 6d. each."—*Caledonian Mercury*, 24th December 1786.

Its further career is shown by the following advertisement, which appeared in the *Caledonian Mercury*, 11th February 1788 :—

"LOTTERY OF A MUSICAL CLOCK.—The musical clock made by James Gray, and disposed of by him by lottery some time ago, is now again to be disposed of in the same manner by the representative of the gainer. One hundred and sixty tickets will be given out, and the gainer will be burdened with the payment of five guineas, to be divided equally among the holders of ten other tickets.

"The clock goes eight days, and plays a tune of itself three times over, every three hours. It plays twelve different tunes, which may be shifted at pleasure by turning a hand on the dial plate. The clock is at William Bruce's, upholsterer and auctioneer, above the

North Bridge, High Street, Edinburgh, and may be seen gratis every Monday, Wednesday, and Saturday, from 12 to 3 o'clock, where tickets, 10s. 6d. each, may be had, and of Andrew Ramsay, Exchange Coffee House. Notice of the time and place of drawing will be given so soon as the tickets are disposed, and the price of the tickets will be returned if the drawing does not take place within three months from the 15th of February 1788."

The above was made at a period when the construction of such like mechanical movements occupied the attention of a number of capable men, and would no doubt come in for a close inspection by his fellow craftsmen. Further proofs of his skill are shown by the accurate performance of the numerous examples of his workmanship that remain. Some of these · he dated, and one made in 1782 is now located in the post office, Coldingham, Berwickshire, and does duty as official timekeeper. He was also, at his death, which took place in 1806, His Majesty's Clock and Watch Maker in Scotland.

GRAY, JAMES, jun.   Edinburgh, 1805-36.

26th January 1805.—"Son of above; presented a petition craving to be admitted to an essay and essay masters."

2nd August 1806.—"Compeared and produced his essay, a watch movement, begun, made, and finished in his own shop, in presence of Robert Green, landlord, and Robert Hinmers, Thomas Morgan, and Thomas Sibbald, essay masters, as they declared, etc."—*E. H. Records.*

"James Gray, 12 Parliament Square, respectfully informs the nobility and gentry of Scotland and the public in general that His Majesty has appointed him his watch and clock maker and keeper and repairer of clocks and watches in his houses and palaces of Scotland. J. G., having served a regular apprenticeship with his father, late watchmaker to the King, and having been several years in England, particularly with one of the most eminent watchmakers in London, he therefore humbly solicits the patronage of the nobility and gentry and the public of Edinburgh, and feels quite confident that by strict attention on his part and by able assistants, he will execute the work entrusted to him in such a manner as to give the fullest satisfaction to his employers. Clocks and Watches made on the most improved principles. Chronometers, Repeaters, Musical Watches, and boxes carefully repaired."—*Edinburgh Evening Courant*, 17th May 1823.

In 1825 he removed to 13 High Street, and about 1836 appears to have removed to 59 South Bridge.

GRAY, JAMES. 38 Shore Street, Macduff, 1846.

GRAY, PETER & CO. 18 Bank Street, Edinburgh, 1850.

GRAY, ROBERT. Edinburgh, 1844.

"Robert Gray, clockmaker in Edinburgh, served Heir of Provision General to his mother, Helen Meek, wife of W. Gray, joiner there, dated 24th June 1844. Recorded 1st July 1844."—*Services of Heirs*.

GRAY, ROBERT & SON. 78 Argyle Street, Glasgow, 1837.

GRAY, WILLIAM. Huntly; died 1799.

GREEN, ROBERT. Edinburgh, 1781-1834.

3rd November 1781.—"Bound apprentice to James Howden."

17th January 1789.—"Discharged of his indentures."

4th May 1793.—"Compeared and presented his essay, being a watch movement, begun, made, and finished in presence of James Howden, landlord, Geo. Skelton, David Murray, and John Sibbald, essay masters as they declared, etc."—*E. H. Records*.

"WATCH LOST.—Left in the Black Bull Inn on Tuesday evening, the 25th inst., a silver watch, maker's name, Scott and Coutts, London, with a cairngorm seal set in gold, having the letters P.S. engraved thereon, suspended to the watch by a yellow and black silk ribbon. Whoever has found the said watch, by returning it to Mr Green, watchmaker, Parliament Square, Edinburgh, will be handsomely rewarded." — *Edinburgh Evening Courant*, 31st July 1806.

21*st May* 1809.—"Married at Edinburgh, Mr Robert Green, watchmaker, to Miss Deuchar, only daughter of the late David Deuchar, Esq., of Morningside."

"Retiring from business. Sale of superior watches and clocks at reduced prices. Robert Green, watch and clock maker, Edinburgh, returns most sincere thanks to his friends and the public for the liberal share of the patronage which he has so long enjoyed, and respectfully informs them that he is retiring from business, and will, at greatly reduced prices, dispose of the whole of his valuable stock, consisting of a great variety of Repeating Chronometers, Duplex Detached Levers, Horizontal and Vertical Watches, new and second-hand, in Gold, Silver, and Metal Cases. A good choice of eight-day clocks, regulators, spring clocks, with quarter and alarm and musical clocks, gold chains, seals, and keys. Silver, steel, and gilt guard chains, with every other article connected with the trade. 200 High Street, Edinburgh."—*Ibid.*, 14th May 1832.

He repeated the above advertisement on 22nd May 1834, where he announces he is removed to 7 Buccleuch Place.

GREENHILL, WILLIAM, of London ; died at Leslie, Fife, 9th August 1830.

GREIG, DAVID. Perth, 1810-37. 99 High Street and 30 St John Street, Perth.

GREIG, DAVID. Stonehaven, 1835.

GREIG, JAMES GIBSON. 20 Princes Street, Edinburgh, 1819.

GREIG, JAMES. Perth, 1765-1800.

Apprenticed to David Bisset, Perth, 1765. Admitted freeman of the Incorporation of Hammermen, Perth, 28th March 1769, on payment of £6, 3s. 4d. sterling, as he had not served the full seven years of his indentures. Appointed Deacon of his Incorporation 1774-75.

GREIG, JOHN. Perth, 1801-9.

"Lost on Friday last, the 25th of July, on the road betwixt Perth and Glasgow, a box containing a single case jewelled watch, engine turned, Nos. on the cases. Also a small silver glass hunting watch, engine turned, No. on the case. The above box was regularly entered at the coach office at Perth to be forwarded from thence by the light post coach to Glasgow, and it is supposed it has either dropped from the coach or been abstracted therefrom. The watches are made on so peculiar a construction that they will be easily discovered by the manufacture at any distance or period. A reward of five guineas will be given to any person who will give information to Messrs A. M'Donald & Co., Jewellers, 120 Trongate, Glasgow, or Mr Greig, watchmaker, Perth, which may lead to where the watches may be found. The names of informers will be concealed."—*Glasgow Courier*, 2nd August 1806.

"Wanted a steady, sober watchmaker, who can repair well. His salary will be £50 per annum. Apply to John Greig, watchmaker, Perth."—*Edinburgh Evening Courant*, 20th February 1809.

GREY, ERNEST. Aberdeen, 1848.

"DR DUFF'S LIBRARY AND APPARATUS FUND FOR CALCUTTA.—Many of our friends are aware that for more than a year past an astronomical clock has been preparing under the gratuitous superintendence of Mr Ernest Grey, late of Calcutta, and now of Aberdeen, for the Missionary Institution. The clock has been for some time completed, and on trial proves a first-rate instrument. Under Mr Grey's superintendence, and partly constructed by himself, it has cost about £80, while if ordered from a London maker it would not have been procured for more than double that sum. When ready for shipment it was entrusted to the care of Mr George Smith & Sons, who have not only forwarded it, but paid the whole shipping charges and insurance from Aberdeen to Calcutta."—*The Witness*, 16th February 1848.

GREY, JAMES. Perth, 1777-1801.

GRIGOR, GEORGE. Elgin; admitted a Hammerman of Elgin, 1805.

GRIMALDE, SAMUEL. Edinburgh, 33 Princes Street, 1819; 51 North Bridge, 1822.

We have been unable to trace this individual before or after the above dates, but his name comes into an amusing skit dealing with the Calton Hill Observatory,

Edinburgh, published in the *Scotsman*, 30th September
1820. The introduction of his name is to his credit,
while the sequel shows that the *Scotsman* appears to
have been cleverly hoaxed :

"CALTON HILL OBSERVATORY.

" To the Editor of *The Scotsman :*—

"SIR,—It is utterly impossible that any stranger
should visit your city without being impressed with
emotions of delight, whilst those improvements which
were pointed out to me as of a more recent date
impress every visitor with admiration and astonishment.

" I am a seafaring man, Captain of the *Dirk Van
Heering* of Schiedam, and for the first time, about a
month ago after a very long voyage, moored myself in
your capital. Having found it necessary on my arrival
to compare my chronometer with the best timepiece in
Edinburgh, I applied to a merchant there to whom I
had letters of introduction, and who was so kind as
procure for me admission to the Observatory on the
Calton Hill, where I was informed the clock was placed
by which all the others in the city are regulated.

"My first inquiry on reaching the outside of the
small apartment (for no person, I am told, is admitted
to a nearer inspection) where the timepiece is deposited
was to know the rate of the clock's going. To this
question the keeper, to my surprise, answered he could
not tell. I next enquired what was the difference
between mean and apparent time, but to this and to
every other question necessary for my purpose I was
mortified in the extreme to find the most profound
ignorance.

"To a nautical man this is a subject of vital
importance, and before I proceeded on my voyage it was
imperative for me to ascertain this point, both for the
safety of myself and crew as well as for protecting the
interests of my owner.

"My next resource was to discover some intelligent
clockmaker, and by advice of my cousin, who has charge
of the Albyn Club House, I called for one Grimalde in
Princes Street, whom I found to be exactly the character
I was in pursuit of. He has a very good transit
instrument of his own making, and, to my delight, I also
perceived in his shop the nautical almanac for the year.

Thus provided, and with his assistance, I soon got extricated from my dilemma, lifted up my voice, and gave thanks to the obliging artisan, and I have just reached the port in safety from which I date my present communication to you.

" Now, Mr Editor, as the difficulties and vexations which I unhappily experienced may be the lot of others, and in order to avert similar evils in future, I (with submission) would recommend that a register or journal of the rate of the going of the clock in the Observatory should be weekly exhibited at the window of the room, and at the same time a note of the difference between mean and apparent time, when any clockmaker in your city could at once furnish to seamen or travellers the desideratum of true time.

" The Observatory clock, I was actually informed, is frequently set at random, and when I was there it was no less than five minutes fast. Had I gone to sea with such an error in my chronometer I should have been thrown no less than seventy-five miles out of my reckoning, or equal to one degree and a quarter of longitude, a circumstance which might involve the most disastrous consequences.

" May I beg the insertion of this letter in your valuable paper, and sure I am others will thank you as well as yours,   TOM BOWLING.

" STRALSUNDT, 18*th August* 1820."

" CALTON HILL OBSERVATORY.

" We insert with great pleasure the letter which follows on the subject of our title, regretting at the same time, as we heartily do, that the communication to which it is an answer ever appeared in the *Scotsman*.

" That it did so at all was owing to an accident, which we need not explain, but by which we were prevented from seeing in time to prevent its publication. To its author we readily concede that we have been occasionally indebted, but we disapprove entirely of the spirit and manner in which his letter was written. A greater mistake cannot be committed than to suppose we would on any occasion lend ourselves to querulous and unnecessary complaints or be willing to publish what is obviously calculated to give pain to individuals without being more obviously calculated to accomplish some public good.

"It has been uniformly with pain to ourselves that we have inserted any stricture on individual conduct, and we have never done so consciously without believing that we were answering the call of public weal, and those who persist in a public course after the danger to which it leads and the evils which it produced have been exposed, deserve the severest reprehension, but so far as regards the Observatory we are not yet able to see that any thing has been wrong, and although there had, a milder and more delicate proceeding should in the first instance have been resorted to."

GRINLAW, ALEXANDER. Market Place, Dunse, 1837.

GROOM, JOHN. Edinburgh, 1703.

Booked journeyman to Andrew Brown, 13th May 1703.

GROUNDWATER, ROBERT PATERSON. Kirkwall, Orkney; died July 1850.

GUTHRIE, NICOL. Gorbals, Glasgow, 1764.

GUVANE, PATRIK. Edinburgh, 1552. *See* page 133.

HADDINGTON—Notices regarding the Common Clock of the burgh of, from 1539 to 1831.

14*th November* 1539.—"The which day the council think it expedient to complete the Knok house and the slating of the Tolbooth this year."

12*th October* 1540.—"The council ordained the treasurer to make dilligens to set up the Knok at Candlemas."

7*th April* 1687.—"John Elliot, surgeon apothecary, deponded 800 merks for buying a clock for the use of the burgh to be set up in the Tolbooth. (It cost £25 sterling.)"

4*th October* 1732.—"Owing to the ruinous condition of the Tolbooth the meeting of the council was held in the town library, and on the 17th of the same month the steeple clock and great bell was ordered to be taken down as a measure of safety. It took over ten years to erect a new steeple, etc., and on 10th June 1745 the council agreed that a new clock should be provided for the town house to cost £30 sterling. This clock was made by Roger Parkinson, Edinburgh. It required winding up every twenty-four hours, which was performed by the bellman."

"The present excellent clock (1831) with chime quarters (see below), which goes eight days, was made in the year above mentioned· by the celebrated Mr James Clark, Edinburgh (q.v.), and cost with the fitting up in the new steeple £300 (?) The clock still strikes on the fine old bell."—"Records of the Burgh of Haddington" given in Miller's *Lamp of Lothian.*

"We have had pleasure in observing great improvements of late years in the burgh town of Haddington. The public spirit of the Magistrates is nowise abated, and they have at a very considerable expense nearly finished an exceedingly handsome spire designed by our townsman, Mr Gillespie Graham, for the Town Hall. We have been informed that the inhabitants are desirous that a clock made upon the most improved principles should be placed in it, and actuated by the spirit in which they have supported the Magistracy in improvements in the town, they have opened a subscription to raise £200 towards the sum required to procure a clock of that description, the town council having agreed to put it up in the spire agreeably to their wish. Above two-thirds of the sum was very soon made up in the town, but it being suggested that the heritors and resident landward parishioners would contribute towards the attaining of so desirable an object, application was made to the Earl of Wemyss and March, the chief heritor, when his lordship most handsomely directed his name to be put down for ten guineas in aid of this subscription."— *Edinburgh Advertiser*, 6th September 1831.

HALBERT, WILLIAM. 99 Glassford Street, Glasgow, 1800-18.

HALDANE, CHARLES. 12 South St Andrew Street, Edinburgh, 1825.

HALDANE, JAMES. 6 Princes Street, Edinburgh, 1811.
"Married on the 29th April 1811, Mr James Haldane, watchmaker, Princes Street, to Miss Janet Thomson, daughter of Mr Andrew Thomson, Kennetpans, Clackmannanshire."

HALL, JOHN. Kirkcudbright, 1576. *See* page 214.

HALL, THOMAS. Canongate, Edinburgh, 1729-83.
Admitted freeman clockmaker, Canongate Hammermen, 22nd July 1729.

"T. Hall, Watch and Clock Maker, Edinburgh, makes and sells all sorts of watches and clocks made upon the best principles. Having studied in London under the ablest masters, and likewise in Paris where he resided some time and was under the inspection of the most eminent Geneva watchmaker there, he hopes to give satisfaction to those who please to favour him with their employment. He has at present for sale a horizontal stop seconds watch, caped, jewelled, and in silver cases, made by the most ingenious George Graham, London, who finished only a few to oblige his intimate friends, so are rarely to be met with."— *Edinburgh Evening Courant*, July 1774.

"Houses in Canongate and Portsburgh.— To be sold by public voluntary roup within John's Coffee-house, Edinburgh, upon Saturday the 31st of January 1784, betwixt the hours of five and six in the afternoon, the following subjects which belonged to the deceased Thomas Hall, late watchmaker in Canongate, in several lots following :—

"Lot 1. That lodging or dwelling house in the Head of the Canongate, lately possessed by Mr Hall, thereafter by his widow, being the second story from the ground of that tenement of land lying on the north side of the Head of the Canongate, above the close called the Uppermost Common Close, consisting of three rooms and a kitchen, with closets and other conveniences, and a workshop formerly used as a watchmaker's shop.

"The lodging is well situated for trade, being in the most public place of the Canongate Head, is of very easy access, and particularly adapted for a Watch or Clock Maker, the front of the house being fitted up as a watchmaker's shop, with a Bow window and other conveniences, having been used in that way for many years."—*Caledonian Mercury*, 7th January 1784.

HALL, WILLIAM. Eyemouth, 1837.

HALLIDAY, PETER. Wigton, 1837.

HALLIDAY, ROBERT. Union Street, Kirkcudbright, 1832.

HALLIE, THOMAS. Glasgow, 1721.

HAMILTON, JAMES. New Sneddon, Paisley, 1820.

HAMILTON, JOHN. Gallowgate, Glasgow, 1783.

MUSICAL CLOCK,

In mahogany case. By John Hamilton, Glasgow, 1750-83.
Shown at the Glasgow Historical Exhibition, 1911. The property
of William B. Smith, Esq., Glasgow.

[To face page 182.

HANNAY, WILLIAM. Above the Cross, Paisley, 1805.

HANNINGTON, WILLIAM. Argyle Street, Glasgow,
1796; died 22nd February 1812.

"Watch lost on Tuesday afternoon, a single cased
Pinchbeck watch, maker's name, Kentish, junr., London,
on the dial; was left in the Black Bull Inn. It is desired
that the finder will bring the said watch to Mr Hannington,
watchmaker, Argyle Street, and they will receive a genteel
reward."—*Glasgow Courier*, 18th July 1799.

HARDIE, JAMES. Woodside, Aberdeen, 1846.

HARDIE, WALTER M. Edinburgh. *See* page 25.

HARDY, JOHN. 17 Huxter Row, Aberdeen, 1837.

HARPER, SAMUEL. Ayr, 1799.

"Allan Stewart, weaver, Cunninghamhead, served
Heir General to his sister, Margaret Stewart, wife of
Samuel Harper, watchmaker, Ayr, dated 7th December
1799. Recorded 1st January 1800."—*Services of Heirs*.

HARRIS, ALEXANDER. Paisley, 1834.

"Joanna Harris or Thomson, wife of A. Harris,
watchmaker, Paisley, served Co-heir of Provision
General to her aunt, Elizabeth Henry, dated 1st
February 1841. Recorded 8th February 1841."—
Services of Heirs.

HARRIS, ROBERT. 63 High Street, Paisley, 1820.

HARRISON, JOHN DAVID. Edinburgh, 1821.

Discharged of his indentures by George Skelton,
11th May 1821.

HARRISON, JOHN. 16 Salisbury Street, Edinburgh, 1822.

Possibly the same individual as above.

HARRISON, ROBERT. Edinburgh, 1776.

Bound apprentice to John Skirving, 28th March 1776.

HART, JOHN & ROBERT. Glasgow, 1821.

HARVEY, ALEXANDER. Sanquhar, 1811.

"GOLD WATCH STOLEN.—There was stolen from
the shop of Alexander Harvey, watchmaker, Sanquhar,
on Tuesday the 24th curt., a French Horizontal Gold
Watch, maker's name, Godemars, No. 2105. Whoever
will bring the said watch to the said A. Harvey, or give
such information as may lead to its recovery, shall
receive a reward of Five pounds Sterling."—*Dumfries
and Galloway Courier*, 1st October 1811.

HARVEY, GEORGE. St Ninians, 1805; 80 Baker's Street, Stirling, 1834.

Father of Sir George Harvey, President of the Royal Scottish Academy.

"Lost on the night of Thursday, the 13th curt., between the Bridge of Allan and Port of Stirling, a silver watch with a steel chain, maker's name, George Monro, B.A., Edinburgh. Whoever has found the same, on bringing it to George Harvey, watchmaker, Stirling, will be handsomely rewarded."—*Stirling Journal*, 17th February 1823.

George Harvey was the maker of an eight-day clock that in his time, and even down to the present day, links his name with a most romantic story. Notices of this story are to be found in the pages of *Chambers's Journal*, dating more than half a century ago, and even in papers of a much more recent date. It has also been made the subject of a historical ballad entitled "The Russian Emperor and the Sailor's Mother." Briefly, the story rests on the adventures of a sailor lad named John Duncan, who was apprenticed to Robert Spittal, master of a sailing-vessel called the *Ann Spittal*, of Alloa. He was, along with his master, taken prisoner at St Petersburg, where he remained till he was set at liberty in the year 1804. His liberation was procured by the loving exertions of his mother, who, conceiving the idea of knitting three pairs of silken stockings for presentation to the Russian Emperor, travelled from Stirling to Paisley to buy the materials for her presentation. As this was a distance of 30 miles, and was travelled on foot, the sacrifice of time and trouble makes the incident more pathetic. Having finished the articles, and enclosing a petition praying for her son's release, she contrived to interest the master of a vessel sailing from Dysart to convey the parcel to the Emperor. Arriving at St Petersburg he succeeded in getting the Emperor's physician, Sir David Wylie, who was a native of Kincardine-on-Forth, to make the presentation. Sir David read the letter and translated its purport to the Emperor, and this, coupled with the extraordinary nature of the gift, had the desired effect. The sailor lad was immediately released, and in recognition of his mother's gift, was given a purse of gold to take to her from the Emperor. Reunited to her son and proud of the success of her efforts, she resolved to have in her lowly home some memorial to mark the happy event. She gave George Harvey, who was at this date in St Ninian's—the village where she resided—an order for an eight-day clock, stipulating that on the dial scenes should be depicted giving the principal events of the story. It afterwards became located in the village of Dunning in Perthshire, but how long it remained there has not transpired. Eventually it was brought to Edinburgh, where it was disposed of by auction at least twice this century, the last time being at the sale of the late Mr Allan's effects at his house, Belleville Lodge, Blacket Place, on 21st November 1917, when it brought £46, 4s.

HARVEY, WILLIAM. Stirling, 1834; died 1883. Son of above.

"Late on the night of Monday last, or early on the morning of Tuesday, the shop of Mr William Harvey, watchmaker, Baker Street, Stirling, was entered at the back part of the premises, by breaking through some brickwork below a window looking into the back shop, and a great deal of valuable property carried away. It would appear that the thieves, before attacking the brickwork, had first attempted the window by breaking two panes, but finding the shutter on the inside strongly bound with iron, they abandoned this mode of effecting an entrance. It would also appear that on entering the shop they had, by means of an iron chisel, endeavoured to force the lock of an iron safe, where the greater part of Mr Harvey's valuable stock was deposited, and that, having failed in effecting their purpose, they broke the lid by means of a hammer or some such powerful instrument, and abstracted from the safe five new gold watches, twenty-two new silver watches, about ten second-hand ones, two silver snuff-boxes, nine pounds in money, and a few other valuable articles. This extensive robbery appears to have been committed with no small degree of deliberation, for, on the shop being entered in the morning, they appear to have very

carefully selected their booty from a number of less
valuable articles, which were found strewed on the floor.
A candle, nearly burned, was also found, and was no
doubt used for the purpose of carrying their intentions
more completely into effect.   Such a clue to the thieves
has been discovered as leaves no doubt of their being
very speedily brought to justice."—*Edinburgh Evening
Courant*, 7th May 1836.

HAUGHTON, JOHN. New Castleton, 1836.

HAY, ANDREW. Edinburgh, 1777.

Bound apprentice to Alexander Dickie, 9th August
1777.

HAY, JAMES. East Street, Inverness, 1793.

"SHOP-BREAKING AND THEFT.—On the night of
Wednesday the 8th of January curt., some evil-disposed
person or persons broke into the shop of James Hay,
watchmaker, on the East Street of the burgh of
Inverness, and carried off from thence the following
watches :—

				No.
A silver watch, maker's name,	H. Butt,	London .	.	8229
One ,, ,,	B. Hosken	,, .	.	14389
One ,, ,,	T. Parsons	,, .	.	1701
One ,, ,,	Geo. Clarke	,, .	.	1815
One ,, ,,	T. Grafton	,, .	.	4588
One ,, ,,	J. Thomson	,, .	.	15305
One ,, ,,	K. M'Lennan	,, .	.	129
One ,, ,,	Geo. Clarke	,, .	.	12744
One ,, ,,	Thos. Sykes	,, .	.	9006

One large watch of the old kind, Michl. Johnson, no value.
One silver watch cap'd, Benj. Taylor, London .   .   .   1109
One silver watch in pieces that lay in a spale box with
    the verge broke, as also the cases and steel chain
    belonging to the said watch.   And a small gold watch,
    box and case in one, with a small cord and key and
    no number thereon.   Besides a variety of tools used
    in making and repairing of watches.

"It is entreated that if any of the above articles are
exposed to sale that the same will be stopped and
information sent to Simon Fraser, procurator-fiscal of
the Sheriff Court of Inverness, who hereby engages to
pay ten guineas to any one that apprehends the person
or persons concerned in said shop-breaking and theft
upon their conviction."- *Edinburgh Evening Courant*,
28th January 1793.

HAY, JOHN. Waterloo.Buildings, Leith, 1822.

"Begs respectfully to intimate to his numerous friends and the public that his stock of watches is at present very complete and extensive, comprehending Duplex Improved Lever, horizontal and plain movements, upon the most approved principles, in gold and silver cases."—*Edinburgh Observer*, 22nd June 1822.

HAY, PETER. 39 Leith Street, Edinburgh, 1850.

HAY, THOMAS. Kelso, 1814.

"WATCH LOST.—There was lost in College Wynd, Edinburgh, on Wednesday, a silver hunting watch, small glass, maker's name, Thomas Hay, Kelso, No. 40, with an orange ribbon, gold ring, and brass key. Information has been lodged with all the watchmakers should it be presented for sale. Whoever will bring it to the *Courant* office will be liberally rewarded."—*Edinburgh Evening Courant*, 29th January 1814.

HEARNE, E. Chalmers Close, Edinburgh, 1850.

HEITZMAN, JOHN. Links, Kirkcaldy, 1837.

HENCHER, THOMAS. Musselburgh, 1776.

HENDERSON, EBENEZER, LL.D. Dunfermline, 1826.

This gentleman perhaps is best known by his writings, his book, *Annals of Dunfermline*, being the standard history of that town. He was, in addition, a clever mechanic and constructor of astronomical and other forms of time-keepers. The following description of two of his productions are extracted from his book :—

"The ORREY was a small machine, contained in a box of twelve sides corresponding to the twelve signs of the Ecliptic, which supported a brass ring on which were engraven the signs and degrees of the Ecliptic, days of month, etc. It exhibited the rotation of the sun on its inclined axis on 25 days 6 hours, the solar and sidereal rotation of the earth, on its inclined axis, and its revolution round the sun in 365 days, 5 hours, 48 minutes, 57 seconds, of the synodic revolution of the moon in 29 days, 12 hours, 45 minutes, and of the Nodes of her Orbit in 18 years, 224 days, and consequently all the eclipses of the sun and moon. The Orrey contained 21 wheels and 5 pinions and was 12 inches in diameter and 7 inches deep.

"ASTRONOMICAL CLOCK, was constructed of brass wheels and steel pinions, mounted in a mahogany case of about seven feet in height, and exhibited the following astronomical particulars, viz., the seconds, the minutes, the hours, day of the month, day of the sun entering the sign of the Zodiac, the time of the rising and setting of the sun throughout the year, with the different length of the days and nights, the age and phases of the Moon; the apparent diurnal revolution of the Sun and Moon, the ebb and flow of the tides and times of their occurrence, solar and sidereal time.

"The ring on which the latter was shown had the necessary motion of a revolution on its axis, in 25·920 solar or 25·868 sidereal years, and hence supposing the clock to keep in motion for, say, 200 years, the sidereal and solar motions would be indicated on the dial plate with great precision. The clock contained 32 wheels and 7 pinions, and is now in Liverpool."

HENDERSON, FRANCIS. Musselburgh, 1790.

"Stolen on Tuesday, June 29, from the house of Alexander Clark in Tranent, a silver watch, maker's name, David Allan, London, No. 5232. Whoever will bring the same to Francis Henderson, watchmaker, Musselburgh, shall be handsomely rewarded and no questions asked. It is entreated that said watch may be stopt if offered for sale and notice given as above."— *Edinburgh Evening Courant*, 15th July 1790.

HENDERSON, FRANCIS. West Port, Edinburgh, 1794.

HENDERSON, GEORGE. Canongate, Edinburgh, 1762.

Booked apprentice to James Panton, Canongate, 6th April 1762.

HENDERSON, JOHN. Kirk Gate, Dunfermline, 1820.

HENDERSON, JOHN. Edinburgh, 1795-1808.

"Bound apprentice to David Murray, 16th May 1795. Compeared on 29th October, and presented his essay, being a watch movement, begun, made, and finished in the shop of James Ramage, in presence of him and Robert Green, essay masters, as they declared, etc. And in respect of the absence of Andrew Wilson, one of the essay masters, he was fined six shillings and eightpence."—*E. H. Records*.

"His Majesty has been pleased to appoint Mr John Henderson, watchmaker in Edinburgh, to be his clock and watch maker in Scotland, in room of James Gray, deceased."—*Edinburgh Evening Courant*, 12th March 1808.

HENDERSON, ROBERT. Edinburgh, 1750.

HENDERSON, WILLIAM. Edinburgh, 1760.

Booked apprentice to William Nicol, 1st May 1760.

HENDERSON, WILLIAM. 32 Nethergate, Dundee, 1850.

HENRY, JAMES. Keith, 1837.

HEPBURN, JOHN. Perth, 1769.

Apprenticed to James Greig.

HERBERT, WILLIAM. Edinburgh, 1785-91.

Bound apprentice to Brown & Skelton, 20th September 1785. Discharged of his indentures by George Skelton, October 1791.

HERON, ERSKINE. Edinburgh, 1752.

Booked apprentice to George Monro, Canongate, 20th September 1752.

HERON, JAMES. William Street, Greenock, 1836.

HERON, JOHN. 1 Square, Greenock, 1797-1822.

"ONE GUINEA REWARD.—There was stolen out of a house in Port Glasgow, a watch with a tortoise-shell outer case, having the figure of Hope leaning on an anchor and pointing to a ship, painted on the back. The inner case was silver, and the maker's name, Churchill, London, No. 7730. Whoever can give any information of the said watch will please apply to Mr John Heron, watchmaker, Greenock."—*Glasgow Courier*, 13th May 1797.

HERON & SON. 1 William Street, Greenock, 1836.

HEWIT, JAMES. Edinburgh, 1816.

Apprenticed to Charles Clark, 10th August 1816.

HILL, DAVID.   Edinburgh, 1761-79.

"Booked apprentice to Andrew Dickie, 7th February 1761.   On 1st May 1779 a petition was read from David Hill setting forth that his indentures were lost, but that he had served his time with Andrew Dickie, with whom he was bound in the year 1761, afterwards with Daniel Binny, and therefore craving that the Incorporation would authorise the said Daniel Binny to discharge him, so as to entitle him to the freedom. Which was refused in respect of several of the members declaring that it consisted with their knowledge that he ran off from his master and did not implement the indentures."

24th July 1779.—"Anent the petition of the watch-makers against David Hill, an unfreeman, for carrying on the trade of watchmaking within their priviledges, the Deacon, Robert Clidsdale, and Treasurer were authorized to bring a complaint against him before the Magistrates."—*E. H. Records.*

HILL, GEORGE.   Bo'ness, 1844.

HILL, GEORGE.   Whitburn or Whiteburn, 1836.

HILL, THOMAS.   Kilbride, 1836.

HIND, GEORGE.   Edinburgh, 1823.
Apprenticed to Robert Bryson, 5th May 1823.

HINMERS, ROBERT.   Edinburgh, 1779-1809.

"Bound apprentice to John Cleland, 22nd June 1779. Discharged of his indentures by Mrs Cleland, 15th June 1786.   Compeared on 28th January 1797 and presented his essay, being a watch movement begun, made, and finished in his own shop in presence of Robert Cairnton, landlord, Ebenezer Annan, George Skelton, and James Howden, as they declared, etc."—*E. H. Records.*

"CLOCK AND WATCH MAKING.—Robert Hinmers, late superintendent to the business of Mrs Cleland (q.v.), watchmaker, High Street, Edinburgh, most respectfully begs to inform the public that he has commenced business in the watch and clock making line on his own account, in that shop lately possessed by Mr Laing, saddler, being No. 39 South Bridge, nearly opposite Adams Square, where he has laid in a neat assortment of Clocks, Watches, Chains, Seals, etc.

" R. H. flatters himself that from his long experience in the profession, and having given satisfaction to those whose work he had under his inspection when with Mrs Cleland, he will obtain a share of public favour which it will be his constant study to merit." — *Edinburgh Evening Courant*, 6th June 1796.

Admitted a member of Lodge St David, Edinburgh, 1st December 1800.

HISLOP, ADAM. Biggar; died 7th June 1827, aged 74 years.

HISLOP, ALEXANDER. 77 Cathcart Street, Greenock, 1821.

HISLOP, ALEXANDER. Glasgow, 1823.

HISLOP, JOHN. Peebles, 1836; died 12th June 1856, aged 76 years.

" Clock and Watch Maker, has on hand an extensive stock of new and second-hand Lever, Horizontal, and Vertical Watches, in silver cases of the finest quality and newest fashion. All of which will be sold considerably below the usual prices, and at the same time warranted to give the best satisfaction in their performance. The greatest attention paid to clock and watch repairs. Orders from the country punctually attended to."—*Peeblesshire Monthly Advertiser*, 1845.

HODGE, CHARLES. Edinburgh, 1752-59.

Son to John Hodge, wright, in New Town of Sauchie; booked apprentice to Andrew Dickie, 18th November 1752; discharged of his indentures, 17th November 1759.

HODGSON, JOHN. High Street, Annan, 1837.

HODGSON, ROBERT & SON. High Street, Annan, 1820.

HOG, CHARLES. Prestonpans, 1788.

" A silver watch lost betwixt Edinburgh and Prestonpans, maker's name, Saml. Bayley, No. 1371. Any person finding the same and returning it to Mr Charles Hog, watchmaker, Prestonpans, or Mr Daniel Douglas, spirit dealer, Potterrow, Edinburgh, will be handsomely rewarded. If a watch of the above description be offered for sale to watchmakers or others it is entreated they will stop it and give information as above."— *Edinburgh Evening Courant*, 11th July 1788.

HOG, THOMAS. Edinburgh, 1698.

· Son to James Hog, late bailie in Dalkeith ; booked apprentice to Andrew Brown, 17th September 1698.

HOGARTH, THOMAS. Church Street, Berwick-on-Tweed, 1806-22.

HOGG, ALEXANDER. Haddington, 1790.

HOGG, JAMES. Gifford, 1837.

HOME, ROBERT. Edinburgh, 1766.

"Robert Home at his shop in the Parliament Close, Edinburgh, sells the late invented Lunar and Calendar Watch Key, and the Ass skin memorandum books, both made by patent. The former ingenious and useful, the latter preferable to any ivory or any thing formerly used in that way, as the writing either by ink or pencil is easily rubbed off and a dry cloth restores the leaves to the same gloss as before. He continues to sell a variety of Sheffield, Birmingham, and London hardware goods, and makes all sorts of turnery work in ivory or wood at the most reasonable rates."—*Edinburgh Evening Courant*, 17th February 1766.

HONDERWOOD, JAMES. Main Street, Ayr, 1820.

HOOD, GEORGE. Colinsburgh, Fife, 1840-55.

HOOD, JOHN. Cupar-Fife, 1840-88.

For many years one of the magistrates of Cupar. He died in 1888 at the age of 72 years.

"John Hood, Clock and Watch Maker, Bonnygate, Cupar-Fife, begs to acquaint the inhabitants of Cupar and the surrounding towns and country, that he has taken that shop in the Bonnygate belonging to Mrs Boyd, where he will carry on the above business in all its departments, and hopes from the intimate knowledge he has acquired of the Trade (having been for the last three years under the immediate instruction of that eminent workman, Mr R. S. Rentzsch, watchmaker to the Queen and Royal Family, London), to merit a share of public patronage. J. H. also begs to intimate that he intends beginning a watch and clock club as soon as a sufficient number of subscribers comes forward.

"*N.B.*—Watches and clocks of every description made and repaired."—*Fifeshire Journal*, 12th November 1840.

HOOD, WILLIAM. Tarbolton, 1843.

"William Hood, Tarbolton, watchmaker, served Heir of Line and Conquest General to his father, William Hood, labourer there, dated 29th September 1843. Recorded 3rd October 1843."—*Services of Heirs*.

HOPE, HUGH. Dumfries, 1758-1828.

Son of Charles Hope, late barber in Edinburgh; bound apprentice to Daniel Binny, 29th December 1758; believed to have commenced business in Dumfries about 1770, which he continued until 1828, when he died, aged 83 years.

"Hugh Hope, watchmaker in Dumfries, served Co-heir of Provision General to his grandfather, Alexander Hope, Tailor in Edinburgh, dated 6th November 1801. Recorded 14th November 1801."—*Services of Heirs*.

HOPTON, ANTHONY and MATTHEW. Edinburgh, 1799-1817.

Were wooden clockmakers and evidently brothers, though occupying different premises, Anthony being located at the back of the Fountain Well, while Matthew was in the Lawnmarket. They were in business from 1799 up to 1817 or thereabout, and along with another maker they enjoyed a monopoly of the manufacture of these humble though useful articles here. Probably they were of German descent, as a James Knie Hopton succeeds to the business of a Baltshazar Knie (q.v.), who was one of the first barometer makers in Edinburgh, and a German. He is described as a grandson of this man, and as the business was in the Lawnmarket, we surmise that they were closely related. A son of Anthony, named John, carried on the business at 329 Lawnmarket up to 1850.

N

HOPTON, JAMES.   Edinburgh, 1826-50.

"German Wooden Clock Warehouse, 22 Greenside Street, Edinburgh.—James Hopton respectfully informs his friends and the public that he has just received by the Frankfort Packet a new and elegant assortment of German clocks, in great variety, which he will warrant to go well. As his present stock comprises upwards of 400 clocks, he will dispose of them on moderate terms. German clocks of all kinds cleaned and repaired.

"*N.B.*—The old establishment at 46 West Bow continued as formerly."—*Edinburgh Evening Courant*, 23rd November 1826.

HORN, ALEXANDER.   Fyvie, about 1825.

A self-taught clockmaker who made several fine clocks.

HOURSTON, WILLIAM.   Albert Street, Kirkwall, Orkney, 1845.

HOUSTON, JAMES.   59 High Street, Johnstone, 1836.

HOW, ANDREW.   Kilbarchan, 1700.

6th April 1700.—" Andrew How of Kilbarchan undertakes to provide a new pendulum clock for the Tolbooth and paint the dial of the same for £12."—*Burgh Records of Dumbarton.*

HOWDEN, JAMES, sen.   Edinburgh, 1764-1809.

4th August 1764.—" Booked apprentice to Alexander Farquharson."

30th January 1768.—" The Incorporation, with consent of Alexander Farquharson, agreed that James Howden should serve out the remainder of his indenture with James Cowan."

2nd November 1771.—" Discharged of his indenture by James Cowan."

4th November 1775.—" Compeared and presented his essay, being a watch movement, begun, made, and finished in his own shop, in presence of James Cowan, landlord, Samuel Brown and Thomas Letham, essay masters, as they declared, etc."—*E. H. Records.*

This maker, by the excellence of his production. soon formed a large and lucrative connection, which he handed on to his sons on his retirement in 1809.

Probably there was not a better known business in
Edinburgh at the beginning of the nineteenth century
than that of James Howden, Hunter Square, and the
following advertisements are only a few of the many
that appeared in the local newspapers,[1] but they convey
the popularity of the firm and the changes that occurred
during his business career :—

"Lost betwixt the foot of Canongate and the Old
Playhouse Close the 20th of last month, a plain gold
watch, maker's name, Jos. Soley, London, No. 129.
Any person who will bring the same to James Howden,
Parliament Square, shall be handsomely rewarded."—
Edinburgh Evening Courant, 1st December 1781.

"Lost a gold watch on the 9th curt., maker's name,
William Clarke, Greenock, No. 150. If offered to any
watchmaker it is begged it will be retained, or if
delivered to Mr James Howden, Hunter Square, a
handsome reward will be given and no questions asked."
—*Ibid.*, 15th August 1805.

"James Howden, watch and clock maker, Hunter
Square, begs leave to acquaint his numerous customers
that besides his former accommodation he now occupies
that part of his present shop lately possessed by his
brother, and that he is assisted in the operative
departments of his business by his son, who has been
bred under one of the most eminent watchmakers in
London, and flatters himself by having added also
largely to his former stock he will have it in his power
to give complete satisfaction to his employers."—
Edinburgh Advertiser, 11th June 1805.

"James Howden, 3 Hunter Square, Edinburgh, in
returning his warmest thanks to the numerous class of
friends and customers who have so steadily patronised
him in business for a long series of years, begs leave to
intimate to them and the public that he retired from
business in December last (1808), and that the shop
occupied by him since that time has been possessed by
his sons James and William Howden, the former as
watchmaker, the latter as jeweller and silversmith.
They have been bred to their several professions under
the first masters in London, and being fully confident
of their strictest attention and assiduity he presumes to

[1] Especially those relating to articles lost.

solicit on their behalf a continuation of that patronage with which he has so liberally been favoured."

" James Howden, Watchmaker, and William Howden, Jeweller and Silversmith, respectfully beg leave to announce that their stock of watches and jewellery, etc., is complete, and will be found at all times various and extensive and of the best quality. They hope by an unremitting superintendence to every particular of their concerns to merit a share of the public favour."— *Edinburgh Evening Courant*, 22nd April 1809.

Died on 18th January 1810 at his house, Borough-muirhead, Edinburgh.

HOWDEN, JAMES, jun., F.R.S.E.   Edinburgh, 1781-1842.

"Son of James Howden, sen.; compeared on 29th October 1808, and presented a petition craving to be admitted a freeman clock and watch maker in right of his father if found qualified, the prayer of which was granted, and his essay, a watch movement, to be produced at next quarter.   He paid six pounds as the first moiety of his entry money."

28th January 1809.—" James Howden, jun., being unwell, and this day being the day on which he was to produce his essay, it was accordingly produced by James Howden, sen., his father, being a watch movement begun and finished in his father's shop, in presence of the said James Howden, landlord, and Robert Green, Thomas Chalmers, and William Auld, essay masters, as they declared, etc.   Owing to his non-appearance he was not formally admitted a freeman of the Incorporation of Hammermen until 24th April 1809."—*E. H. Records.*

As noted before, he and his brother succeeded to the business of the father at the end of the year 1808. Large and flourishing as the connection was when taken over, they soon made it even more so, and two changes in the location of their shop—the last being to the New Buildings, North Bridge—finally made their establishment one of the foremost in the city.   A selection of advertisements dealing with these changes are now given, and as affording a glimpse of the select and high-class nature of their business, no mention is to be found of the stock phrases of a number of their contemporaries, such as "moderate prices," "cheap," or "below cost price," etc., showing that the quality of their goods combined with their reputation was enough.

"James Howden, watchmaker, and William Howden, jeweller and silversmith, 3 Hunter Square, respectfully beg leave to announce that their stock of watches and jewellery and silver plate, cutlery, etc., is now complete ; and as their stock of the above and every article connected with the line of business will be found at all times various and extensive and of the best quality, they hope by an unremitting superintendence to every particular of their concerns to merit a share of the public favour."—*Edinburgh Evening Courant*, 18th March 1809.

"J. and W. Howden & Co. beg leave to intimate their removal from Hunter Square to No. 9 South Bridge, nearly opposite their former shop, which they have this day opened with a new and elegant stock of goods in watches, jewellery, and silver plate, and where they solicit the inspection and patronage of their friends and the public.

"*N.B.*—The watchmaking part of the business will be conducted as formerly, part of the premises having been fitted up for the accommodation of the workmen."
—*Ibid.*, 23rd July 1814.

"James Howden, surviving partner of the late firm of J. & W. Howden, takes the liberty of informing his friends and the public that he has now removed from 9 South Bridge to that large and elegant shop, No. 56 New Buildings, North Bridge Street, where he continues to carry on the business as formerly in all its branches. J. H. has also the opportunity by the extent of his premises, and it will be found by the arrangements which he has made that the watch making and watch repairing department of the business will be so conducted as to render this one of the best establishments in town. J. H. begs to return his most sincere thanks for the patronage he has hitherto enjoyed, and trusts that the same support will be continued to him which was experienced by the late copartnery."—
Ibid., 24th June 1824.

"James Howden, Jeweller and Watchmaker, 56 New Buildings, North Bridge Street, begs respectfully to intimate to his friends and the public that he has assumed as partner Mr William Brown, who has for several years been his assistant in the business, which will in future be carried on under the firm of James Howden & Company. In announcing this arrangement, James Howden would at the same time acknowledge most gratefully the liberal patronage with which he has hitherto been honoured, and humbly solicits a continuance of it under the new firm."—*Ibid.*, 5th January 1828.

HOWDEN, John. Edinburgh, 1824-32.

Probably a cousin of above. Advertises on 12th August 1824: "he respectfully intimates the completion of extensive alterations on his shop, No. 9 Waterloo Place, and his daily receiving the newest patterns of silver and plated goods and watches from the best makers, which, having been purchased with ready money, he is enabled to sell at the lowest price."

HOWIE or HOW, Allan. Irvine, 1774.

HOWIESON, George. Crosscauseway, Edinburgh, 1794.

HOWIESON, John. George Street, Perth, 1808-22.

"There was stolen from the waiting-room, George Inn, Perth, a silver watch, maker's name, John Howieson, Perth, No. 101. Should the watch be offered for sale it is hoped that it will be stopped and notice given to Mr Howieson, watchmaker, Perth."—*Edinburgh Evening Courant*, 11th May 1809.

HOY, Thomas. Kesso (? Kelso), about 1778.

HUDSON, William. Edinburgh, 1746.

Where this individual belonged to we have not been able to discover—probably he hailed from London— but his appearance in Edinburgh so early after the episode of "Prince Charlie's" rising shows the comparative quiet that prevailed throughout the country. He seems to have been one of a class of clever mechanics and craftsmen whom no difficulty could daunt, and so we find during all the eighteenth century and part of the nineteenth men such as he visiting all the busy centres, with examples of their own work, with the purpose of earning a livelihood by their exhibition. Hudson's announcement of his exhibits is a strange mixture of fact and fancy, but was well calculated to draw the attention of our worthy citizens, who delighted in viewing such productions.

"It is too common a mistake that persons even of a superior rank are made bubbles of and cheated of their money by impostors. Among the many bad effects that are consequential to this, it is not the least that Arts are discouraged and the ingenious ranked with those pests of Society. Instances of this kind are fresh in every one's mind, nor need they be repeated. But in justice to the public, as well as to endeavour to correct the false taste which prevails, advertisement is hereby made that there is arrived in Edinburgh one of the greatest curiosities that perhaps human art has produced.

"It is a musical clock of surpassing magnificence, but still to be more admired for its various movements. It plays finely on the Organ, German Flute, and imitates the notes of a variety of singing birds; it represents the Ptolemaick as well as the true solar system. There are paintings of an elegance not to be expressed; but what strikes the spectator most by the movements of the clock—they all move to and play on different musical instruments and beat exact time. You see Apollo and the nine muses in a concert; Orpheus charming the wild beasts in a forest—all moving in a manner extraordinar to describe. You see a carpenter's yard, the sawyers at work, coal engines, etc.; and, to conclude this little sketch of such an admirable piece of art, you see the ocean at a distance, ships sailing and diminishing by degrees, porpoises tumbling in the sea; a fresh-water pond, swans feathering themselves and fishing, the sport of the dog and duck; a landscape where you view wheel-carriages passing and repassing, with other curiosities too tedious to mention. As all these many performances are the effect of art alone, the public will imagine the vast expense in finishing such a machine. The maker and proprietor, William Hudson, will show it to the curious at one shilling the front seats, and sixpence those backwards, any time through the day. He lives in Niddry's Wynd, opposite to Mary's Chapel. He has likewise an Orrery, the first ever finished in England, complete and large, which he proposes to dispose of. A description would be needless, as the ' Literari ' are only judges. He will show it any time when desired."—*Caledonian Mercury*, 20th March 1746.

HUE, JAMES, jun. Edinburgh, 1741.

The advertisement that follows is interesting, for it has been a somewhat disputed point as to whether there were any one in Edinburgh able to execute the lacquering of clock cases, etc., or not. Generally put down as being the production of the Chinese or Japanese, although there were a large number which must have been decorated in London, James Hue's announcement makes it pretty certain that there was at least one (who lived at the best period of this class of work) qualified to carry it out in Scotland.

"James Hue, jun., Gilder, at the sign of the Eagle, immediately within the Netherbow Port, Edinburgh, gilds and japans after the newest form and genteelest fashion all sorts of joiner's work, such as clock cases, corner cupboards, dressing boxes, tea-tables, all at very easy rates."—*Caledonian Mercury*, 31st March 1741.

HUME, JOHN. Horse Market, Kelso, 1836.

HUNTER, ALEXANDER. New Cumnock, 1837.

HUNTER, GEORGE WILLIAM. Perth, 1789.

Apprenticed to Alexander M'Farlane, Perth.

HUNTER, JOHN. Dunfermline, 1790-1812.

Tailor by trade ; made an Astronomical Clock, which is described in Henderson's *Annals of Dunfermline* :—

" The frame and axles of the wheels were made of wood, and also the dial, on which were 24 hours, and a number of indexes or hands. It showed the minutes and hours of the day and night, the rising and setting of the sun, the daily motion of the moon, the rise and fall of the tides at Limekilns, and the day of the month. From 1790 being scratched on the works, it would seem to have been made this year. He also made a hand machine to show the tides and predict them, and like the clock, most of the wheels were made of very large coat buttons of the period. He also used such buttons to make the wheels of clocks in his clockmaking operations, of which he made several. He died at an advanced age in 1812."

HUNTER, JOHN. Edinburgh, 1824.

Apprenticed to Lawson & Millar, 17th May 1824.

HUNTER, NATHAN. Dock Head, Port Glasgow, 1820-36 (also Postmaster).

HUNTER, PETER. Edinburgh, 1794-1822.

"Found a gold watch case. Whoever can prove it their property will please apply to Mr Peter Hunter, watchmaker, Crichton Street, Edinburgh."—*Edinburgh Evening Courant*, 21st July 1806.

HUNTER, PETER. Alloa, 1786.

HUNTER, PETER. 13 Frederick Street, Edinburgh, 1846.

HUNTER, ROBERT. Newtown, Girvan, 1820.

HUNTER, WILLIAM. Campbeltown, 1803-34.

Began business in 1803, and was succeeded in 1834 by his son, also named William, whose son Thomas still continues the business.

HUNTER, WILLIAM. Bridge Street, Dunfermline, 1820-46.

"William Hunter, watchmaker in Dunfermline, served Co-heir of Provision General to Catherine Bevridge, grocer there, dated 14th January 1846. Recorded 20th March 1846."—*Services of Heirs*.

HUNTER, WILLIAM. Stirling, 1807.

HUSBAND, D. High Street, Kirkcaldy, 1820-37.

HUTCHISON, GEORGE. Edinburgh, 1770-76.

Booked apprentice to Turnbull & Aitchison, 26th June 1770. Discharged of his indentures 26th June 1776.

HUTCHISON, GEORGE. Stirling, 1782.

"That on Thursday, the 10th of October curt., there came to Stirling a young man who called himself William Colquhoun, and said he was a youth of landed property near Greenock, but a minor, and that a gentleman in the west country whom he named was one of his tutors, and that when at home he lived with the said gentleman.

He bought a new watch from George Hutchison, watchmaker, Stirling, the maker's name, Robt. Innes, London, No. 6972, a bar movement with a sham repeating pendant, with a common steel chain and key, but the young man made his elopement without paying the watch or tavern bill. He was dressed in a drab duffle big coat, a blue undercoat and vest with yellow metal buttons, black breeches, and boots. He is dark complexioned, black hair, a large cocked hat. He rides on a small brown horse or mare inclining to a switch tail. It is entreated that all watchmakers, jewellers, or others who may see the said watch may stop the same and inform the Publishers or the said George Hutchison, watchmaker in Stirling.

"*N.B.*—It has been since found out that he goes by different names, particularly that of William Gairdner." —*Caledonian Mercury*, 12th October 1782.

HUTCHISON, ROBERT. Douglas, Lanarkshire, 1836.

HUTTON, GEORGE. Perth, 1780-1800.

Apprenticed to Joseph Taylor, Perth, 1780. Admitted freeman of Perth Hammermen, 1798.

HUTTON, JAMES. Edinburgh, 1685.

Son to Henry Hutton in Burntisland; booked apprentice to Richard Mills, 17th December 1685.

Idem Die.—"The house having read and considered ane act against those that does not timeously book their apprentices, they ordain Richard Mills to pay to the boxmaster twenty pound Scots for not booking of his apprentice, James Hutton, in the incorporation's books in due time, and the boxmaster to be comptable for the same, and in the meantime appoint his apprentice to be booked."—*E. H. Records.*

HUTTON, JAMES. Portsburgh, Edinburgh, 1764-79.

5th March 1764.—"James Hutton, clock and watch maker in Portsburgh, compeared and presented a bill to be admitted a clock and watch maker burgess of Portsburgh, which was received and he admitted to an essay, and essay masters were appointed to him."

3rd November 1764.—"Compeared and presented his essay, being a watch movement without the striking part, made in his own shop. William Colville, his landlord, Normand Macpherson and Robert White his essay-masters, as they declared, etc."—*E. H. Records.*

"Stolen out of a shop in the West Port, Edinburgh, on Friday, 11th October, a silver watch with a china dial plate. The man who stole the watch goes under the name of —— Clerkson, but his real name is James Heddie. He is a young man, middle-sized sturdy lad, with a bluish coloured short coat, with a large blue bonnet, short black hair with coloured stockings drawn above his breeches, in appearance like a drover. Who-ever can apprehend the above person may acquaint or write to James Hutton, watchmaker in Portsburgh of Edinburgh, and shall be sufficiently rewarded."—*Caledonian Mercury*, 14th October 1765.

HUTTON, WILLIAM. Edinburgh, 1768-74.

Bound apprentice to James Cowan, 5th March 1768. Discharged of his indentures 22nd April 1774.

IBACH, ALEXANDER. 14 St David Street, Edinburgh, 1831 Watchmaker from Geneva.

"To those ladies or gentlemen in Edinburgh or its vicinity who are in possession of French watches, clocks and musical boxes, A. Ibach begs most respectfully to give notice that he has arrived from Paris to undertake the repairing of these articles. A. I. has also an assort-ment of Lepine Watches and Musical Boxes imported by himself and warranted to go well. Reference in Edinburgh to Mr Wilson, 21 George Street, corre-spondent of Messrs Vieyres and Aubert in London, and Messrs Molinier and Bautte from Geneva."—*Edinburgh Evening Courant*, 15th October 1831.

"A. Ibach, watchmaker from Geneva, in returning his most sincere thanks to the nobility and gentry for their liberal support since his arrival in Edinburgh, begs leave to mention that he has removed from St David Street, to that more commodious shop, 24 South Hanover Street, where he will continue the repairing watches of every description, also Musical Boxes."—*Ibid.*, 2nd June 1832.

INGLIS, WALTER. Glasgow, 1813.

INGLIS, WILLIAM. Hope's Land, Canongate, Edinburgh, 1811.

INGRAM, RICHARD.   156 High Street, Dumfries, 1820-37.

INGRAM, WILLIAM.   8 New Market Street, Ayr, 1836.

INGRAM & SON.   106 High Street, Ayr, 1850.

INGRAM, WILLIAM.   St Germain Street, Catrine, 1850.

INKSTER, HENRY.   Stromness, Orkney, 1836.

INNES, ALEXANDER.   Dalkeith, 1783-1824.

"Lost betwixt Dalkeith and Gilmerton on Monday the 21st of April current, a small-sized silver watch with an enamelled dial, steel chain, and silver seal with a pebble stone, maker's name, Thomas Winter, London, No. 775.   If the same is offered to be sold or repaired, it is expected that watchmakers or others into whose hands it may come will stop it and acquaint John Murdoch, watchmaker, Edinburgh, or Mr Innes, watchmaker, Dalkeith, who will give a suitable reward."— *Edinburgh Evening Courant*, 23rd April 1783.

"Died at Dalkeith on the 13th September 1824, Mr Alexander Innes, watchmaker, aged 67 years."—Obituary notice in *Edinburgh Evening Courant*, 18th September 1824.

INNES, DAVID.   Edinburgh, 1785.

Bound apprentice to Thomas Morgan, 30th July 1785.

INNES, GEORGE.   58 Argyll Street, Glasgow, 1828-41.

INNES, GEORGE.   Aberdeen, 1820; died 22nd May 1842. Well known for his attainments as an astronomer and a man of general science.

INNES, WILLIAM.   Glasgow, 1825.

IRVINE, ALEXANDER.   Canongate, Edinburgh, 1710-17.

Admitted freeman clockmaker for his life, Canongate Hammermen, 1710.   His is the first name occurring in the records to receive this freedom.   (See below.)

IRVINE, ALEXANDER.   Edinburgh, 1717.

Son to the deceast Alexander Irvine, clockmaker in Canongate; booked apprentice to Thomas Gordon 11th April 1717.

IRVINE, JOHN.   Edinburgh, 1799.

IVORY, JAMES. Dundee, 1762-95.

22nd September 1767.—"Which day James Ivory, watchmaker in Dundee, was admitted burgess for having paid 50 merks Scots to James Dick, sometime treasurer, and having just now paid other 50 merks to Henry Geekie, present acting treasurer, in full of his freedom."

"The terms of this entry show that James Ivory had no previous claim to admission as a burgess through his ancestors, and it distinctly proves that he was the first of a family of eminent men who have reflected considerable lustre upon Dundee. The name seems to be a corrupt form of the Gaelic cognomen Iverach, and the family had probably a Highland origin, though the locality from whence they sprang is merely a matter of conjecture. James Ivory rose to considerable eminence as a watchmaker in Dundee, and was entrusted with the making of the clock for the steeple of St Andrew's Church in the Cowgate. He served frequently as a Town Councillor from 1768 till 1789, and it was whilst acting in this capacity that his son James, the famous mathematician, afterward Sir James Ivory, was appointed one of the teachers in the Dundee Academy. James Ivory, sen., died previous to 1795."—*Roll of Eminent Burgesses of Dundee.*

IVORY, THOMAS. Dundee, 1795-1825.

"Thomas Ivory, watchmaker, Dundee, was admitted burgess 6th July 1795, by the privilege of the deceased James Ivory, his father."

"Thomas Ivory was the third son of James Ivory, watchmaker, and for a considerable time followed the same occupation as his father. His talent as a draughts-man led him to abandon this calling early in the nineteenth century, and to take up the art of engraving, and he is believed to have been the first native engraver in Dundee. He executed illustrations for an edition of Rollin's *Ancient History*, published in Dundee by Francis Ray in 1800. His best known work was a set of copy-lines prepared for teaching handwriting published in 1811, and long used as a model in the

Dundee schools. He made the education of the youth of Dundee his special study, and it was largely owing to his trenchant letters signed ' Parens' in the newspapers of the period that important reforms were accomplished in the scholastic system with the burgh. He died (*circa*) 1825. His son, Lord Ivory of Session, was admitted burgess on the 21st November 1816, and another son, William Ivory, writer, Dundee, was enrolled, 6th April 1818."—*Roll of Eminent Burgesses of Dundee.*

JACKSON, ALLAN. Argyle Street, Lochgilphead, 1836.

JACKSON, JAMES H. Perth, 1828-36.

JAFFRAY, JOHN. Stirling, 1790.

"John Jaffray, late watchmaker in Glasgow, now in Stirling, to whom certain creditors of James Campbell endorsed for behoof of their claims, having now received a dividend from the price of the unentailed lands of the said James Campbell, those creditors or their representatives will call on John Wilson, one of the town clerks of Glasgow, to receive their dividend and sign a discharge, etc."—*Glasgow Mercury*, 28th September 1790.

JAFFRAY, WILLIAM. 329 Argyll Street, Glasgow, 1841.

JAMES, JOHN. Union Place, Edinburgh, 1846.

JAMESON, GEORGE. Hamilton, 1729.

"To be sold, several curious sundials engraven on brass plates, each plate 20 inches square, containing : 1st, an horizontal dial 9 inches diameter, having each tenth minute with the Meridians and differences of longitude of several remarkable places of the world, showing the hour of the day in those places ; 2nd, the curved lines for showing the length of the day, the 11th and 25th of each month, with the Babylonish, Jewish, and Roman hours, also the day of the month the sun enters into each sign of the Zodiac; 3rd, a dial for showing the hour of the night by the moon, with the epacts for 19 years placed by it, beginning at 1728. Lastly, there is an equation table for each 5th day of the year. They are calculated for the latitude of 56 degrees, and will serve 60 miles further south or north with little variation. All done according to astronomical rigour by George Jameson at Hamilton.

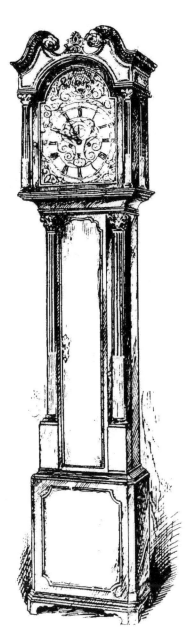

MUSICAL CLOCK.

In elm root case. By Anthony
Jeeves, Edinburgh, 1774. The pro-
perty of the Merchant Company,
Edinburgh. (See p. 207.)

LONG CASE CLOCK,

In oak case. By James Cowan,
Edinburgh 1744-81. The property of the Society of Writers to
the Signet, Edinburgh. (See p. 89.)

" They are to be seen at Mr Butchers in the Abbey-Hill, or at Bailie Jameson, Candlemaker in Canongate-Head, his house on the north side of the street."—*Caledonian Mercury*, 28th August 1729.

JAMESON, JAMES. Castle Street, Stranraer, 1836.

JAMIESON, JAMES. Main Street, Newton Stewart, 1820.

JAMIESON, JOHN. Ayr, 1798.

"John Jamieson, Clock and Watch Maker, Ayr, served Heir General to his brother, William Jamieson, writer, Edinburgh, dated 3rd October 1798. Recorded, 11th October 1798."—*Services of Heirs*.

JAMIESON, ROBERT. Glasgow, 1838.

JAMIESON, THOMAS. 79 High Street, Ayr, 1836-50.

JARDINE, JOHN. Glasgow, 1765-1801.

" Died at London on Sunday sennight, after a short illness, deeply and justly regretted by his numerous friends and acquaintances, Mr John Jardine, watchmaker, a native of Glasgow, not more distinguished through life by great skill and ingenuity in his art than by amiable and cheerful disposition and the most obliging manner." — Obituary notice in *Edinburgh Evening Courant*, 23rd November 1801.

JARDINE, ROBERT. Hopetoun Street, Bathgate, 1836.

JEEVES, ANTHONY. Edinburgh, 1744.

No mention of this maker's name is to be found in any of the records of the Hammermen of Edinburgh. The only known example of his skill that can so far be ascertained has been preserved in or near Edinburgh : it is a magnificent chiming clock which plays twelve tunes. This really fine clock bears upon the dial that it was made by Anthony Jeeves, Musical Clockmaker from Oxford, Edinburgh, and likewise a coat of arms, and the name Daniel Davidson, for whom in all probability it was made. The date 1774 is to be found on the end of the barrel that acts on the bells, the whole movement and case affording conclusive proof of the high constructive ability of this artist. It may not be out of place to note that when described in the first edition of this volume it was located in the outer lobby of James Gillespie's Schools, but attention having been drawn to the danger and incongruity of such a situation, the Merchant Company, who were governors of the schools, removed it to their own meeting place, namely, the Merchant's Hall, Hanover Street, Edinburgh, where it occupies a prominent position in the main staircase of that building.

JERDAN, ——. Glasgow, 1754.

Maker of clock in Greenock Bell House.

JOHNSON, JOHN. Main Street, Ayr, 1819.

JOHNSON, ROBERT. High Street, Linlithgow, 1835.

JOHNSTON, DAVID. Boyd's Close, Canongate, Edinburgh, 1800.

JOHNSTON, HUGH. Barrhead, 1836.

JOHNSTON, JAMES. Portsoy, about 1825-37.

JOHNSTON, JAMES. Edinburgh, 1785.

Booked apprentice to Alexander Dickie, 20th October 1785.

JOHNSTON, JOHN. West Port, Linlithgow, 1820.

JOHNSTON, JOHN. Peterhead, 1837.

JOHNSTON, JOHN. Edinburgh, 1757.

Son of Laurence Johnston in Bankhead of Saline; booked apprentice to John Dalgleish, 7th May 1757.

JOHNSTON, JOHN. Edinburgh, 1812.

Booked apprentice to Reid & Auld, 1st August 1812.

JOHNSTON, JOHN. Ayr, 1789; died 1st November 1829, aged 74 years.

"Stolen out of the shop of John Johnston, watchmaker in Ayr, on Thursday the 21st or Friday the 22nd May 1789, the following silver watches:—

					No.
1 new silver watch,	Matthew Prior,	London	.	.	5946
1 ,, ,,	,,	,,	.	.	5948
1 old ,,	James Warne,	,,	.	.	18596
1 ,, ,,	James Reid,	,,	.	.	2454

2 new silver watches by James Johnston, Liverpool. The numbers of the two last were unfortunately not taken down, only new come to hand.

" If any of the above watches are offered to sale it is hoped they will be stopped and notice sent to John Johnston, Ayr, who will give as a reward a guinea for each of the above watches. There is every reason to believe that they were stolen by a lad who wrought some time in the shop as a clockmaker, who made his elopement the day after they were stolen. He called himself James Brown and said he belonged to Wolverhampton. He was traced as far as Sanquhar, and was offering the watches for sale all that road. As he had very little money and supposed to be gone to London by the way of Moffat and Carlisle, it is earnestly requested that all dealers, particularly on that road, will be upon their guard what watches are offered to sale, and give information as above, as he must very soon have disposed of some of them. Not to be repeated."— *Edinburgh Advertiser*, 19th June 1798.

JOHNSTON, MATTHEW. 2 Davie Street, Edinburgh, 1820.

JOHNSTON, SAMUEL. Langholm, 1837.

JOHNSTON, WILLIAM. Trongate, Glasgow, 1847.

JOHNSTONE, JAMES. Linlithgow, 1830.

JOHNSTOUN, ALEXANDER. Edinburgh, 1688.

Son to the deceast Alexander Johnstoun, lister, burgess of Edinburgh; booked apprentice to Andrew Brown, 3rd May 1688.

JOHNSTOUN, JOHN. Edinburgh, 1671.

Booked apprentice to Robert Smith, 1671.

JOHNSTOUNE, DAVID. Edinburgh, 1679.

Son to Robert Johnstoune, merchant burgess of Stirling; booked apprentice to Andrew Brown, 27th May 1679.

JUNOR, DANIEL. Canongate, Edinburgh, 1797.

JUST, GEORGE. Kirkcaldy, 1761.

KAY, DAVID. Dundee, 1553-76. *See* Common Clocks of Dundee, page 124.

KAY, JOHN. Aberdeen, 1582. *See* page 3.

KEELLER, JOHN. Musselburgh, 1814.

KEIR, DUNCAN. Stirling, 1706.

O

KEIR, PETER. Falkirk, 1823.

KEITH, DAVID. Inverness, 1850.

KEITH, GEORGE. Strathaven; died 1812.

KEITH, ROBERT. Forfar, 1819-37.

KEITH, WILLIAM. 50 High Street, Inverness, 1837.

KELLY, ANDREW. Glasgow, 1835.

KELLY, PETER. Edinburgh, 1770.

  Booked apprentice to John Gibson, 9th June 1770.

KEMPIE, ANDREW. Carr's Croft, Perth, 1837.

KENNEDY, ALEXANDER. Canongate, Edinburgh, 1753.

  Booked apprentice to James Nicoll, 27th February 1753.

KENNEDY, JOHN. Maybole, 1820-37.

KENNEDY, JOHN, jun. High Street, Maybole, 1837.

KENNEDY, JOHN. Dalmellington, 1793.

KENNEDY, THOMAS. 1 Portland Street, Kilmarnock, 1837.

KERR, ALEXANDER. Scotch Street, Annan, 1820.

KERR, HENRY. Dundee, 1863. *See* page 24.

KERR, HENRY. Loanhead, 1850.

KERR, HENRY. 10 South St James Street, Edinburgh, 1857. *See* page 24.

KERR, JOHN. Saltmarket, Glasgow, 1783.

KETCHING, WILLIAM. Edinburgh, 1850.

KETTLE, WILLIAM. Edinburgh, 1758-1804.

  Son of John Kettle, merchant in Leith; booked apprentice to James Duff, 29th December 1758. Discharged of his indentures 14th December 1764. Admitted a freeman clockmaker, Canongate Hammermen, 31st October 1774. Died 1804.

KILGOUR, PATRICK. Aberdeen, 1672-92. *See* Common Clocks of Aberdeen, page 7.

KILGOUR, PATRICK. Canongate, Edinburgh, 1702.

KILGOUR, WILLIAM. Glithnow, 1775-1837.

In the churchyard of Cowie, in the parish of Fetters, is a tombstone, an account of which is given in Jervise's *Epitaphs and Inscriptions*:—" The inscription (from the headstone) relates to a person whose genius lay in constructing eight-day clocks, which he made from beginning to end, and in being a superior weaver of bedcovers and tablecloths.

" To the memory of William Kilgour, an original genius, who exercised the craft of weaver at Glithnow for the long period of sixty-two years in the same house. He departed this life on the 12th day of March 1837 at the advanced age of 86 years.

BY HIS FRIENDS.

' Here lyes the man for aught we know
That lived and died without a foe ;
Now mould'ring here beneath that clod,
An honest man th' noblest work of God.' "

KILPATRICK, GILBERT. Edinburgh, 1767.

Bound apprentice to Normond Macpherson, 15th October 1767.

KING, ALEXANDER. Peterhead, 1826.

KING, BENJAMIN. Rose Street, Peterhead, 1846.

KING, DAVID. Castle Street, Montrose, 1821-51.

" David King, shoemaker, Montrose, served Heir General to his father, David King, watchmaker there, dated 5th February 1851. Recorded 18th February 1851."—*Services of Heirs*.

KING, DUNCAN. Fore Street, Port Glasgow, 1820.

KING, JOHN. Aberdeen, 1784.

KING, JOHN. Montrose, 1840.

KINNEAR, C. D. Portobello, 1836.

KINNEAR, CONRAD, Father and Son. Glasgow, 1836.

" Conrad Kinnear, clock merchant in Glasgow, served Heir General to his father, Conrad Kinnear, clock merchant there, dated 10th October 1840. Recorded 14th October 1840."—*Services of Heirs*.

KINNEAR, J. 475 Lawnmarket, Edinburgh, 1850.

KINNEIR, JAMES. Edinburgh, 1774.

Bound apprentice to John Skirving, 14th September 1774.

KIRK, JAMES. Edinburgh, 1648.

Though this individual never got any further than an apprentice and that only for a year, yet his name deserves to be remembered not only for his being the first indentured to the art after the admission of the clockmakers as a branch of the locksmith craft in the Incorporation of Hammermen, Edinburgh, but also for the extraordinary dispute that cancelled his indentures.

25th March 1648.—"James Kirk, sone laufull to Robert Kirk, merchand burgess of Edinburgh, buikit prentise to Robert Smith, knokmaker, freeman and burgess of the said burgh of Edinburgh, conforme to ye indentures past betwixt thame, he payit to the boxmaister xxs. with the clerk and officer thair dewis (duties)."

6th December 1648. — "The qlk day anent the supplication given be Helen Fergusonne, spous to Robert Kirk, merchand burgess of Edinburgh, upoun Robert Smith, knokmaker and freeman burgess of Edinburgh, making mention that quhair the said Robert Smith did take James Kirk thair sone to be his prentice and servant for certane zeiris conforme to the indentures past betwixt thame, quharin the said Robert Smith band and obligit him to ken, teach, learne, and instruct the said James Kirk in the haill poyntis, practices, and ingoyings of his airt of knok smithis craft, and sould maintane his said prentice during the space of his prenticeschip honestlie in meat, bed, and board as the said indentures in them selffis at mair length beiris. Notwithstanding thairof the said Robert Smith hes keipit the said James Kirk his prentice the space of ane zeir preceding the date heirof in his service, and hes gotten no insight nor learning of his calling, and could not have sufficient maintenance for preserving of his lyfe qlkar against all reasone, equity, and conscience, and against the heidis of the indentures past betwixt them as the said supplication in itself at mair length beiris.

"Quilk being heard, read, seen, and considderit be the Deacone, Maisteris, and haill hous, and they being ryplie advisit yairwith, they all in a voice statut and ordaine lykas be thir prests. statutis, and ordaines that the said Robert Smith sall teach and learne the said James Kirk in the haill poyntis, practices, and inganes of his said airt of knokmaker craft, and sall furnische and sustane him honestlie in meat, bed, and boord during the space of his prenteischip, and George Smith the said Robert his brother is become cautioner for him fulfilling of his pairt of the indentures to his said apprenteis, lykwyes the Deacone and haill hous statutis and ordaines in cais it sall happine the said James Kirk complaine upoun Robert Smith, his maister, the said James haveond just reasone and caus yairfoir at ony tyme heirefter, then and in that cais the Deacone and hous ordaines and be thir prestes ordaines the said James Kirk to be liberat and frie fra his said maister service, the fault being noter and trouble to the Deacone and hous, injuring the Deacone and Maisteris their pleisyre (pleasure)."

As James Kirk's name does not appear again in the *Hammermen's Records* it is not unlikely that he took advantage of the last part of the above minute and turned his attention to some other craft.

KIRK, JOHN. Dalkeith, 1800.

KIRKCUDBRIGHT — Notices regarding the Common Clock of the burgh of, from 1576 to 1897.

"In regard to the history of the old town clock of Kirkcudbright, which is undoubtedly one of the oldest in the kingdom and which is about to be superseded, tradition, avowedly founded on documentary evidence, has it that the clock came from Holland. The first authentic notice of the town clock, or, as it was then quaintly styled, the knok, is to be found in the earliest existing records of the Town Council, and is dated

1576, wherein, after a narrative of the election of magistrates and office-bearers, it is set forth that one John Hall is appointed keeper of the knok, and subsequently he and others continue to be made custodiers of the old timepiece from year to year.

"The following excerpt from the Council minutes shows the existence of a curious regulation, namely, that every burgh was bound to maintain and uphold a town clock, and from the same excerpt it will be seen that in 1642 the question was not one of erecting a new clock, but of transferring the old one to a new steeple :—

"'Kirkcudbryt, the first day of January the year of God jm vjc fourtie twa, the quilk day the Provest, Bailies, and Counsell of the burgh of Kirkcudbryt, with advice and consent of the remanent burgess and committee of the said burgh, having taken to their serious consideration the loss and want of their knok through the fault of ane steple and bellhouse, to put their knok and bells in (the old Tolbooth quilk of before keipit thair knok and bell being ruinous and decayit), and having taken into their consideration the necessity of ane steple and bellhouse to keep their knok and bell qlk is a special ornament belonging to every burgh, and qlk they are bound by the ancient laws of this kingdom to maintain and uphold, and likewise they taking to their serious consideration the decay of their common good, and that it is superspendit upon the common affairs of this burgh. Therefore the said Provest, bailies, and counsell of said burgh, with advice and consent of the remanent burgess and committee of the said burgh, have all in a voice cheerfully and voluntarily offered themselves to be stentit in their goods for buying of a piece of ground quhair it may be most and best convenient for building of the said bellhouse and steeple, and for furnishing of the materials and paying of workmen to build the same.'

"The steeple was shortly afterwards built and the knok and bells placed therein, and there the veteran timepiece continued to fulfil its destiny under the oversight of a regularly appointed caretaker till 1723, in which year a serious fire occurred in the steeple, by which much damage was done to the clock and bells and many old burgh records were destroyed.

" In those days there was no watch or clock maker resident in Kirkcudbright, and the clock was sent to Ringford, where there lived a cunning blacksmith named Law, who enjoyed locally the reputation of being well versed in the art of cleaning clocks and watches. This Law, by the way, became the progenitor of a celebrated race of clock and watch makers of the same name, his nearest living relative being Mr Thomas Law, watchmaker, Castle-Douglas. In the Ringford smithy the old clock lay for six months before being thoroughly overhauled. It was then restored to its old quarters and kept jogging on doggedly under the charge of several tradesmen, among others Bailie Martin, Mr Walker, and Archie Miller, watchmakers, and Bailie Law, the artificer of the church clock.

" Some fifty years ago the old clock, as if it felt that having passed the allotted span of horological life it was entitled to its *otium*, became irritable and irregular, sometimes chapping the whole twelve hours twice over without a pause, as if to exhibit its proficiency in the art, and then remaining sullenly silent for hours till at last it stopped. The Law family were again appealed to in the person of Bailie Law, who, observing that the pivot holes were worn out, filled them with hard type-metal, and re-bored them. Since then, until recently, the clock continued to 'ring out the old, ring in the new' with wonderful regularity, under the doctoring of Bailie Law's son, William Law, and his successor, Bailie M'Skimming. Latterly, however, various eccentricities, indicating extreme old age and debility, were noticed, fits of absolute coma alternating with sudden accessions of unnatural activity, and it had at last to be admitted that this great grandfather's clock must now be treated as a 'guid auld hes been.' Provost Cowan, much to his honour, has commissioned Mr M'Skimming to replace it with a splendid new illuminated dial clock, with which, let us hope, the genial provost's name will be associated for another 500 years. The auld knok finds a fit resting-place in the Stewartry Museum.

"To the foregoing account Mr W. W. M'Skimming adds: 'The old clock was made wholly of malleable iron, but a good few years back a new brass wheel had been put in. It is placed in an old steeple called the Old Tolbooth, at the end of the town, and has two dials. The clock has no dial work, and the hour is shown by a single hand. It only went twenty-four hours, and was formerly driven by granite weights. The papers do not give it credit for good timekeeping, but my father says that since April 1859, when he first took charge of it, its performance has been wonderfully correct. It was my duty as apprentice to wind it up every morning at ten o'clock, but latterly it would not go, for the pinions were cut so much that you could put your thumb in the holes made by the wheel teeth.'"—*The Horological Journal,* January 1897.

KIRKLAND, JAMES. Glasgow, 1775.

KIRKLAND, RICHARD. Port Glasgow, 1783.

KIRKWOOD, ALEXANDER. 215 High Street Paisley, 1820.

"Agnes Allan or Kirkwood in Galston, served Co-heir of Provision General to her mother, Elizabeth M'Kechnie, wife of A. Kirkwood, watchmaker, Paisley, dated 18th May 1824. Recorded 29th May 1824."— *Services of Heirs.*

KIRKWOOD, JAMES. Perth, 1771.

Granted liberty to exercise his trade as clock and watch maker in Perth, 1771. Admitted a freeman Perth Hammermen, 1772.

KIRKWOOD, JOHN. Lauder, 1734. *See* Common Clock of Lauder, page 219.

KIRKWOOD, JOHN. Redpath, near Melrose, 1798.

KNIE, BALTHAZAR. Edinburgh, 1774-1817.

Among the many crafts which were carried on in Edinburgh during the eighteenth century, one of the most unique was the manufacture of barometers or weather-glasses, as they were then named. Though closely allied and partaking somewhat of the trade of clockmaking, it never seems, at that period, to have had the attention given to it as the latter craft had. Probably this was owing to the fact that the principles of the barometer and thermometer were unknown, or not sufficiently studied, and the introduction of its manufacture here is due to foreigners. Although nearer the end of the century Scotsmen were beginning to turn out barometers of the highest class—to name one, John Russell (q.v.) of Falkirk—yet the introduction and use of these useful articles, at least in Edinburgh, was due to Balthazar Knie, who settled here in 1774. A German by birth, he apparently opened a shop for the purpose of exhibiting the marvels of glass-blowing and bending. This would infer that this process was something of a novelty, which is further increased by an announcement in the *Courant :*—" Friday next being the Equinox, Mr Knie desires you to take notice of the barometer. If the mercury be marked fair it will be fair for some time, but if it is marked rain or changeable it will be rain or changeable for some time," and a note adds, "that it is worth while for the curious in those matters to take notice of it."

In 1793 a card informs us that his shop is situated opposite the well, north side of Lawnmarket, and he returns his sincere thanks for the patronage he has received for the nineteen years he has been in Edinburgh. It is rather surprising to find he was still living and in business as late as the year 1815. In that year he gives out that from the growing infirmities of old age, he finds it necessary to dispose of his elegant and valuable stock of barometers and thermometers, valued at £309, 14s. He disposed of it by lottery, and his death, occurring on 28th March 1817, removed one who was in his day a credit and benefactor to the city. His business was carried on for a few years later by his grandson, James Knie Hopton, who was related to the Hoptons (q.v.), the wooden clockmakers in the

Lawnmarket. The only specimen of Balthazar Knie's weather-glass, of which particulars have reached us, is now located in the treasurer's room in the Royal Infirmary. Mr Caw states that it is still in complete working order, and he has for many years kept a record of its performance.

KNOX, ALEXANDER. Berwick-on-Tweed, 1770.

KNOX, JAMES. 80 High Street, Paisley, 1820-36.

KNOX, ROBERT. 141 High Street, Paisley, 1820-37.

KNOX, ROBERT. Beith, 1766.

He appears to have been the chief of the little band of clockmakers who flourished in Beith during the latter part of the eighteenth century. Several of his clocks are still in existence, all of good workmanship and still keeping excellent time. As a rule the case and hood are of dark mahogany with the scrolled or Chippendale pediment, the dial of brass with engraved centre and corner pieces, silvered hour circle and seconds dial, day of month in square aperture below the hand, and the phases of the moon in the arch of the dial.

One of these clocks has been in the family of Hugh Broun of Broadstone for 150 years. In an inventory of 1809 it is valued at £2, 10s., and in another of 1817 at £3.

In 1912 at a sale in Lochwinnoch Parish a Robert Knox clock brought £13.

KNOX, WILLIAM. Paisley, 1780.

KNOX, WILLIAM. Beith, 1785.

KULLBERG, VICTOR. 12 Cloudesly Terrace, Islington, London. *See* page 24.

LAIDLAW, ALEXANDER. Edinburgh, 1799.

Bound apprentice to James Howden, 1st July 1799.

LAING, DAVID. Perth, 1767.

"PERTH COUNCIL HOUSE, *5th March* 1767.—The calling considering that David Laing, an unfreeman Clock and Watch Maker, has proposed to the calling to exercise his trade in the place, without being admitted freeman, and that he has offered to pay twenty shillings sterling yearly, yet there are three freemen of the calling of that science (in Perth at the date). They by a great majority refuse to accept of his offer and appoint it to be notified to him that if he exercises his trade in the place without the calling's consent they will proceed against him as law directs."—*Perth Hammermen Records.*

LAING, GEORGE. Aberfeldie, 1837.

See also note on Patrick Robertson, Perth, page 319.

LAING, JAMES. Mid Street, Keith, 1837.

LAING, WILLIAM. Fort William, 1837.

LAIRD, DAVID WHITE. Bridge Street, Leith, 1836-50.

LAIRD, JAMES. Kilmacolm, 1770.

LAIRD, JOHN & ANDREW. Delftfield Lane, Glasgow, 1837.

LAMBERT, PETER. Hyde Hill, Berwick-on-Tweed, 1837.

LAMOND, J. & Co. 9 Kirkgate, Leith, 1850.

LAUDER — Notices regarding Common Clock of, 1734-1859.

"LAUDER, 13*th November* 1734.—The bailies and council having taken into their consideration that the clock of the burgh is in great disrepair and very insufficient, the same having been visited by John Kirkwood, clocksmith at Hardgatehead, have resolved that a new clock shall be made by him with the greatest expedition and settup in the steiple of the Tolbooth of the said burgh. Orfore they hereby empower and authorise John Moffat and Richard Allan, present bailies, to contract with the said John Kirkwood for making of a sufficient new clock at a price not exceeding four hundred merks, for which this shall be their warrant, and appoints this to be subscribed by the Clerk of Court in their name and presence."

The following is a copy of the inscription engraved on a brass plate attached to the above clock :—

"John Moffat, Bailie, MDCCXXXV., William Lauder, Treasurer, John Kirkwood, Fecit. This clock was removed to Mellerstoun, 1859. New one made by R. & R. Murray."—A. THOMSON, *Lauder and Lauderdale*.

LAUDER, JAMES. Prestonpans, 1796.

LAUDER, JOHN. Prestonpans, about 1790.

LAULE, T. 4 North Bridge, Edinburgh, 1850.

LAUSSINE, ESAIUS. Edinburgh, 1595.

LAW, DAVID. 1 Croft Street, Kilmarnock, 1837.

LAW, GEORGE. Peebles, 1808.

LAW, JAMES. Aberdeen, 1782.

LAW, JAMES. King Street, Castle-Douglas, 1836.

LAW, JAMES, son of Robert Law. Castle-Douglas, after 1830.

LAW, JOHN. High Street, Kirkcaldy, 1821.

LAW, JOHN. Beith, 1784.

LAW, JOHN. Edinburgh, 1795-1842.

2nd November 1811.—"Compeared and presented a petition to be admitted a freeman in right of his wife, daughter of the late John Morton, smith, member of the incorporation. The prayer thereof was granted He payed the Treasurer six pounds as the first moiety of his entry money."

1st February 1812.—"Compeared and produced his essay, a clock movement, begun, made, and finished in the shop of James Paterson, landlord, and James Howden, Robert Green, and William Thomson, essay masters, as they declared, etc. He paid the treasurer six pounds, being the second moiety of his entry money."—*E. H. Records.*

He died on the 5th December 1842, at the age of seventy-two years, his remains being interred in the Old Calton Burying Ground, Edinburgh.

LAW, ROBERT. Castle-Douglas, 1818-30.

LAW, —— Ringford, Kirkcudbright, 1723. *See* page 215.

LAW, SOLOMON. Lantonside, 1748.

"That there is ready to be published after a long and tedious inquiry of eighteen years the discovery of the longitude, which may be made plain to any capacity in less than half an hour, and taken at the same time with the latitude, and with the same or greater certainty by Solomon Law, Lantonside, near Dumfries, in Scotland. Mr Law, in expectation of the reward provided by Act of Parliament and other ways, is now ready to make such discovery." — *Edinburgh Evening Courant*, 1st September 1748.

LAW, THOMAS. Castle-Douglas. *See* page 215.

LAW, WILLIAM. High Street, Kirkcudbright, 1820.

LAW, WILLIAM. High Street, Kirkcudbright, 1836.

LAW, WILLIAM. High Street, Linlithgow, 1820-37.

LAWRENCE, GEORGE. Keith, 1837.

LAWRIE, ARCHIBALD. Portsburgh, Edinburgh, 1720.

LAWRIE, ARCHIBALD.

Son of above ; booked apprentice to William Bowie, Canongate, 1731.

LAWS, MICHAEL GRAHAM. Berwick-on-Tweed, 1845.

LAWSON, CHRISTOPHER. 19 North Bridge, Edinburgh 1820-37.

4th *February* 1822.—" Compeared and presented a petition craving to be admitted a freeman clock and watch maker by purchase, and the meeting having consented, granted the prayer, and appointed as an essay a watch with the movements to be produced at next quarter. He paid fifty pounds as the first moiety of his entry money. James Paterson, landlord, John Bain, and James Clark, essaymaster. Admitted freeman in terms as above, 5th May 1823."—*E. H. Records*.

He died on 22nd April 1837, at 25 St James Square, which by a coincidence is the present residence of the writer of these notes. *See* Lawson & Millar.

LAWSON & MILLAR. 19 North Bridge, Edinburgh, 1822-25.

"NOTICE.—That business carried on here by the subscriber as clock and watch maker, under the firm of Lawson & Millar, was this day dissolved by mutual consent. The subscriber, C. Lawson, is authorised to receive and discharge the debts due to the concern. 18th June 1825—Christopher Lawson, Richard Millar (q.v.)."—*Edinburgh Evening Courant*, 23rd June 1825.

"INTIMATION.—C. Lawson, Clock and Watch Manufacturer, respectfully begs leave to return his sincere thanks to his numerous friends and the public for the liberal patronage he has enjoyed during the period he has been in business, both on his own account and as a partner of the late firm of Lawson and Millar,[1] and at the same time takes the liberty of intimating that he now carries on business on his own account in the premises formerly occupied by L. and M., where he hopes to meet a continuance of that support which he has hitherto enjoyed, and which shall at all times be his study to merit. 19 North Bridge, 21st June 1825." —*Edinburgh Evening Courant*, 23rd June 1825.

LEADBETTER, ANDREW. Canongate, Edinburgh, 1764.

Apprenticed to Andrew Clark, Canongate, 29th May 1764.

LECK, ROBERT. High Street, Jedburgh, 1837.

LECK, ROBERT. Mauchline Tower, 1850.

LECK, WILLIAM. Market Place, Jedburgh, 1837.

LECKIE, DAVID. Annan, 1800-20.

LEES ——. Lecturer on Natural Philosophy in Edinburgh, 1837.

"Mr Lees' Duiranian, as we believe it is called, consists of two discs, the one eight inches in diameter representing the earth, the three feet representing the heavens. From the centre or pole of the former are drawn diverging lines at every 15th as the projections of meridians, while on the latter are drawn sketches of the sun, moon, and starry spheres. By a very simple combination of wheels and pulleys connected with cords, one of these discs is made to revolve on the other, thus showing either the real motion of the heavens from east to west. The earth is made to carry an index by traversing a dial, points out the hours corresponding to its own place, while the horizon exhibits the rising,

---

[1] Richard Millar (q.v.).

culminating, and setting of the heavenly bodies with the greatest accuracy and distinctness. The great value of this instrument, however, consists in its giving at one glance the most simple and correct ideas of the relation of longitude and time, a subject of fundamental importance in the study of astronomy."—*Edinburgh Evening Courant*, 27th April 1837.

LEGGET, JOHN. Dunse, 1720.

LEIGHTON, WALTER. Montrose, 1830.

LEITCH, DANIEL. Chapel Street, Kincardine-on-Forth, 1836.

LEITHEAD, JAMES. Moffat, 1835.

"James Leithead, watchmaker, Moffat, served Heir General to his father, William Leithead, carter there, dated 30th January 1841. Recorded 10th February 1841."
—*Services of Heirs*.

LEITHHEAD, JAMES. Channel, Galashiels, 1836.

LENNOX, EDWARD. Perth, 1783.

Apprenticed to Joseph Taylor, Perth, 1783.

LESLIE, J. & P. Kirkcaldy, 1815.

LESLIE, JOHN. High Street, Kirkcaldy, 1821.

LESLIE, PETER. High Street, Burntisland, 1837.

LESLIE, THOMAS. Edinburgh, 1775-90.

"Booked apprentice to Normond Macpherson, 1775."

4th February 1786.—"Compeared and presented a petition craving to be admitted a freeman."

27th January 1787.—"Compeared and presented his essay, being a plain watch movement, begun and finished in his own shop in presence of Robert Aitchison, landlord, James Gray, Charles Mollison, and Robert Cairnton, essay masters, as they declared, etc.—*E. H. Records*.

"Lost or stolen from a gentleman within these few days, betwixt the Theatre Royal and George Square, a very handsome plain gold watch, jewelled, maker's name, Normand Macpherson, No. 342. Whoever is in possession of the above watch upon delivery to Mr Leslie, watchmaker, at Macpherson & Co. (q.v.)

here, shall receive five guineas reward and no questions asked. Whoever will give such information as shall lead to a discovery of the above watch, upon conviction of the offender shall receive from Mr Leslie ten guineas. The informer's name concealed if desired."—*Edinburgh Evening Courant*, 8th August 1785.

LESLIE, THOMAS. Borrowstouness ; died 1788.

LIDDELL, JAMES. Bathgate, 1825.

LIDDELL, WILLIAM. Portobello, 1839.

LIDDELL, WILLIAM. Edinburgh, 449 High Street, 1819; 5 Bank Street, 1822.

LIDDLE OR LIDDALL & SONS. 5 Bank Street, Edinburgh, 1830-50.

"REMOVAL AND SALE OF WATCHES AND CLOCKS.— Liddall & Sons, watchmakers, 5 Bank Street, respectfully intimate that they remove at Whitsunday to No. 24 South Bridge, and will at reduced prices dispose of their present extensive stock of watches, clocks, etc."— *Edinburgh Evening Courant*, 22nd March 1834.

"Liddall & Sons, watchmakers, 5 Bank Street, return their sincere thanks for the liberal share of patronage which they have so long received, and respectfully intimate that at Whitsunday last they opened additional premises, 24 South Bridge, at both of which places they will have always on hand a select assortment of gold and silver watches, new and second-hand. A few eight-day clocks in mahogany cases, £6 each, spring timekeepers for shops, counting-houses, etc., five guineas and upward.

"*N.B.*—Watches of every description repaired and cleaned equal to any house in London on very moderate terms."—*Scotsman*, 17th September 1834.

LIGHTBODY, JAMES. West Port, Lanark, 1820-37.

LIGHTBODY, JOHN. High Street, Lanark, 1799-1837.

LINDSAY, LUKE. 46 Hamilton Street, Greenock, 1823-38.

LINDSAY, WILLIAM. 239 Canongate, Edinburgh, 1825.

LINLITHGOW—Notices regarding Town Clocks of, 1710-1857.

2nd December 1710.—"The council for the future agree that George Brown, last Deacon, shall keep the two clocks for 18 lib. yearly, and a quart of oil, during the council's pleasure."

13th September 1760.—"The council having considered the estimate by Deacon Davie for repairing the town clock, also a report by Robert Thomson, clock and watch maker in Bo'ness, concerning the necessary repairs to be made on the said clock, the council appoints Deacon Davie immediately to set about the said repairs and to finish the same in terms of Mr Thomson's report sufficiently, for which the Deacon is to have the sum of six pounds sterling in full, of all he can ask or claim for making the said repairs, and the Deacon submits himself to the council as to the sufficiency of the said work when it is finished, and the estimate lodged with the clock."

21st November 1761.—"The which day the council considering the report from John Davie, that he wanted the town clock to be taken off his hands at this term of Martinmas, and desired a visation thereof, therefore the council do hereby nominate and appoint Mr Robert Alexander, clockmaker in Bathgate, and John Johnstoun, smith, in Swine Alley (to give a report)."

By the kindness of James Russell, Esq., Town Clerk of Linlithgow, these minutes from the Council Records are now given for the first time. Our application to him for inspection of these records was cordially granted, and it is a pleasure to announce that nowhere have we seen, excepting Edinburgh or Glasgow, and one or two large towns in Scotland, such an immense number of finely bound manuscript volumes and records as those contained in the safe of the Council Chambers of Linlithgow.

" The above clock appears to have done duty till 1847, when it was destroyed by fire, and not till 1857 was a new one erected, which was made by Mr Mackenzie, Glasgow, and is believed to be the first turret clock constructed in Scotland on the same principles as the celebrated Westminster Palace clock, the works being principally of cast iron and the escapement the new gravity one."—WALDIE'S *History of Linlithgow*, page 16.

LION, Robert. Carnwath, 1836.

LITTLE, James. High Street, Annan, 1820.

LITTLE, James. Annan; died 1831, aged 56 years.

LITTLE, John. High Street, Annan, 1836.

LITTLEJOHN, Wilson. Peterhead, 1846.

LIVINGSTONE, Edward. Dundee, 1790.

LIVINGSTONE, George. Edinburgh, 1769.

    Booked apprentice to John Murdoch 7th January 1769.

LOCHART, William. Canongate, Edinburgh, 1813-22.

LOCK, Robert. 4 West Arthur Place, Edinburgh, 1825.

LOCKE & HUTTON. Dunfermline, 1825.

LOGAN, Thomas. Maybole, 1820-37.

LOGAN, William. Ballater, 1846.

LOGIE, Robert. Richmond Street, Edinburgh, 1784-1827.

    26th November 1784.—"Bound apprentice to John Cleland."

    3rd May 1806.—"Compeared and produced his essay, a watch movement begun, made, and finished in his own shop in presence of Robert Green, landlord, and Robert Hinmers, Thomas Morgan, and Thomas Sibbald, essay masters, as they declared, etc."—*E. H. Records.*

    "Lost or stolen on Wednesday night last a silver caped and jewelled day of the month watch, maker's name, David Craig, Ford, Pathhead, No. 765. Whoever will bring the same to Robert Logie, watchmaker, Richmond Street, Edinburgh, shall have forty shillings of reward."—*Edinburgh Evening Courant,* 9th June 1804.

LOUDON, David. Kilwinning, 1843.

LOUDON, John. Irvine, 1820.

LOVE, James. Edinburgh, 1774.

LOVE, James. Elgin, 1712.

LOVE, John. Edinburgh, 1779.

LOVE, John. 48 King Street, Glasgow, 1828.

LOVE, Neilson. Port Glasgow about 1770.

LOW, ALEXANDER. Edinburgh, 1799.

LOW, ALEXANDER. Errol, 1815-37.

" Alexander Low, watchmaker in Errol, served Heir General to his father, John Low, smith in Cupar-Angus, dated 17th November 1815. Recorded 1st December 1815."—*Services of Heirs.*

LOW, JAMES. Edinburgh, 1755-61.

"Son of George Low, staymaker in Canongate; booked apprentice to Robert Clidsdale 3rd February 1755. Discharged of his indentures 19th December 1761."—*E. H. Records.*

LOW, JOHN. St Malcolm's Lane, Kirriemuir, 1837.

LOW, THOMAS. Bridgend, Perth, 1843.

LOW, THOMAS. 204 Overgate, Dundee, 1828.

LOW, THOMAS. Murray Street, Perth, 1843.

LOWE, ——. Arbroath, 1784.

LOWE, ——. Errol, Perthshire, 1836.

LUCAS, ALEXANDER. Argyll Arcade, Glasgow, 1849.

LUMSDANE, WALTER. Cupar-Fife, 1740-92.

" James Bell, smith in Edinburgh, served Heir Portioner General to his grandfather, Walter Lumsdane, watchmaker in Cupar, dated 28th December 1792. Recorded 2nd January 1793."—*Services of Heirs.*

LUMSDANE, WALTER. Cupar-Fife, 1792.

" Watchmaker in Cupar; served Heir General to his father, Walter Lumsdane, watchmaker there, dated 6th October 1792. Recorded October 1792."—*Services of Heirs.*

LUMSDEN, DAVID. Anstruther, 1850-1909.

Born 1827; was nephew of George Lumsden, sen., of Pittenweem, with whom he served his apprenticeship. Subsequently a magistrate and member of the School Board of Anstruther. Retired from business in 1896.

LUMSDEN, GEORGE, sen. Pittenweem, 1818-49.

This maker was an apprentice of his celebrated townsman, John Smith (q.v.), and commenced business for himself about 1818. He carried on an extensive trade, and his productions are to be found all along the coast fishing towns and villages in the East Neuk of Fife. Suiting the designs of his clock dials to the tastes of his customers, many of them have painted on them ships, fishing-boats, and the like, which were in a large number of cases the production of the pencil of James Brown, joiner, Pittenweem. George Lumsden died 28th March 1849, aged 55 years.

LUMSDEN, GEORGE, jun. Pittenweem, 1849-99.

Succeeded to his father's business about 1849; died 27th December 1899, aged 67 years.

LUMSDEN, JOHN. Aberdeen, 1735-57.

LUNAN, CHARLES, sen. Aberdeen, 1760-1816.

"Died at Aberdeen on the 10th January 1816 Mr Charles Lunan, clock and watch maker. He was a man of uncommon shrewdness, intelligence, and native strength of mind, and from his inventive genius in mechanics much might have been expected had his powers received a more early culture, a circumstance which he often regretted during the latter part of his life. He has, however, left behind him many specimens of his ingenuity and of the accuracy with which he could execute the finest pieces of mechanism."—*Edinburgh Evening Courant*, 20th January 1816.

"Ann Aiken or Hewit, served Co-heir of Provision General to her grand father and mother, Charles Lunan, watchmaker, and Mary Thomson, spouse, Aberdeen, dated 8th March 1855. Recorded 19th March 1855."— *Services of Heirs*.

LUNDIE, JOHN. High Street, Dundee, 1809-37.

LUNDIE, JOHN. Elgin; apprentice to John Brown, Elgin, 1743.

LUNDIE, WILLIAM. Inverurie; died 1816, aged 73 years. Was the first postmaster of that town.

LUNN, CHARLES. Edinburgh, 1799-1806.

Bound apprentice to James Howden, 31st October 1799. Discharged of his indentures, 24th November 1806.

LYNDSAY, ALEXANDER. Aberdeen, 1537. *See* page 2.

LYON —— Bathgate, 1810.

LYON, ANDREW. Port Glasgow, 1783-99.

LYON, CHARLES. Castlegate, Lanark, 1820.

LYON, JAMES WALTER & Co. 80 George Street, Edinburgh, 1842.

MACADAM, WALTER. Glasgow, 1800.

MACADAM, WALTER. Bathgate, 1840-50.

MACARA, ROBERT. High Street, Dunfermline, 1796-1820.

MacCLYMONT, JAMES. Ayr, 1761.

MACFARLAN, DUNCAN. 159 Trongate, Glasgow, 1818; and Son, 1828.

MACFARLANE, A. P. 76 Trongate, Glasgow, 1841.

MACFARLANE, D. 3 Nelson Street, Glasgow, 1841.

MACFARLANE, PATRICK. Gallowgate, Glasgow, 1781.

MACFARLANE, PETER. 10 Arcade, Glasgow, 1841.

MACGREGOR, DUNCAN. Comrie, 1837.

 Model, description, and drawing of an inside pendulum escapement by Mr Duncan Macgregor, smith, Comrie, shown at a meeting of the Royal Scottish Society of Arts held on 10th May 1837.

MACIVER, MURDO. High Street, Dingwall, 1836.

MACKAY, ALEXANDER. Peterhead, 1798-1807.

 "John Mackay, farmer in old town of Coynach, served Heir General to his brother, Alexander Mackay, watchmaker, Peterhead, dated 7th February 1807. Recorded 14th February 1807."—*Services of Heirs.*

MACKAY, ALEXANDER. Banff, 1774.

MACKAY, JOHN. Edinburgh. *See* page 148.

MACKAY & CHISHOLM. Edinburgh, 1835 to present day. *See* note on Wm. Forrest & Co., Edinburgh, page 148, for the origin of this firm.

 "Mackay & Chisholm, 49 New Buildings, North Bridge, Edinburgh, respectfully invite the continued continuance of their Friends and the Public to this warehouse for all kinds of Antique and Modern Plate, Jewellery, Watches, as from M. & C.'s practical knowledge in every branch of the business they feel assured that superior advantage in some departments at least may be obtained by patrons of this establishment.

"A set of medals of the Kings of England in bronze, from William the Conqueror to George III., also sets of Napoleon medals in bronze and silver. M. & C. being authorized to collect and discharge the debts of the late copartnery, those due are respectfully requested to order payment as soon as possible."—*Edinburgh Evening Courant*, 4th April 1837.

This well-known firm removed to 57 Princes Street in 1879, and to No. 59 in 1908, where the business is still carried on.

MACKENZIE, COLIN. Inverness, 1800.

MACKENZIE, —— Glasgow. *See* page 225.

MACKERSON, DAVID. Edinburgh, 1704-12.

"Son to the deceased George Mackerson, maltman in Wester Weems; booked apprentice to Paul Romieu, jun., watchmaker, 5th February 1704."

17th May 1711.—"There being a petition given in by David Mackerson, late apprentice to Paul Romieu, clockmaker, craving that although the eight years contained in his indentures will not be expired until the 2nd of December next, that the Incorporation may grant warrant to discharge his indentures in regard that both his master and mistress are dead and that he cannot get work among the freemen of the Incorporation. The house do unanimously grant warrant to the present Deacon and Boxmaster to discharge the said David Mackerson his indenture, to the effect he may get his freedom thereby in regard there is but a short time of the eight years to run, and that his art have consented to his being admitted freeman, especially considering there are few watchmakers in this city at present to serve Her Majesties lieges. But they do declare that this is not to be a precedent for the time to come but only granted to the petitioner upon the special considerations above given."

9th February 1712.—"Compeared and presented his essay, viz., the movements of a watch, which was found a well wrought essay, etc. His essay masters were George Mitchell and Richard Alcorne. The essay was made in

Robert Alexander's shop (rest of minute same as given in admission of Robert Alexander)."—*E. H. Records.*

MACKIE, ANDREW. Fraserburgh, 1837.

MACKIE, JOHN. Ellon, 1837.

MACKIE, WILLIAM. 73 George Street, Aberdeen, 1837.

MACLEAN, ANDREW. Edinburgh, 1783-1812. *See* note on Peter Forrester & Co., Edinburgh, page 148.

Apprenticed to Robert Aitchison, 8th May 1784.

"Andrew Maclean, watchmaker, Edinburgh, served Heir General to his father, Robert Maclean, Accountant of Excise, dated 27th December 1811. Recorded 2nd January 1812."—*Services of Heirs.*

MACLEAN, GEORGE. Bristo, Edinburgh, 1776.

20th February 1776.—" Presented a petition offering Forty pounds for the freedom, which was remitted to the watchmakers, who were ordered to make their report against next meeting."

4th May 1776.—" The clock and watch makers reported that they had agreed to refuse George Maclean's petition."

26th June 1776.—" The Incorporation appointed the deacon and treasurer to prosecute the process of advocation against George Maclean, late clock and watch maker in Bristo, and authorised them to advise with the best lawyers thereanent."—*E. H. Records.*

MACLENNAN, JOHN. Born at Dingwall ; died in London, 1886, aged 72 years.

MACNAB, JOHN. Perth, 1824-42.

MACNAB, ROBERT. Perth, 1800.

MACNEE, WILLIAM. 153 High Street, Edinburgh, 1850.

MACPHERSON, JOHN. Edinburgh, 1773-85.

23rd September 1773.—" Booked apprentice to his father, Normond Macpherson."

19th July 1783.—" Presented a petition craving to be admitted freeman."

19th August 1783.—" Compeared and presented his essay, being a plain watch movement begun, made, and finished in presence of the essay master as they declared, etc."—*E. H. Records.*

"Mrs Macpherson, relict of the deceased Normond Macpherson, late clock and watch maker in Edinburgh, and John Macpherson, his son, are to continue and carry on the business of clock and watch making in all its branches. John Macpherson, for some time previous to his father's decease, managed and conducted the business, and he hopes his unremitted attention and assiduity will secure him the favour and continuance of his father's employers."—*Caledonian Mercury*, 16th June 1783.

"The copartnership of Macpherson & Co., clock and watch makers, Edinburgh, being now dissolved by the death of John Macpherson, the business is to be carried on as formerly for the behoof of the widows of Normond and John Macpherson by a well-known experienced workman, Thomas Leslie (q.v.), who has been for these ten years past in the shop and bore a very active hand in the management. It is therefore humbly hoped that those who were pleased to employ Normond Macpherson (see below), or the company since his decease, will continue their favours, as every effort shall be used and the greatest attention paid to merit the approbation of the public."—*Ibid.*, 1st January 1785.

MACPHERSON, NORMOND. Edinburgh, 1749-83.

"Son to William Macpherson, Excise Officer; booked to Andrew Dickie 5th August 1749. Discharged of his indentures 17th November 1759. Presented a bill to be admitted freeman, and an essay and essay masters were appointed to him on 23rd July 1763.

"Compeared on 4th February 1764, and presented his essay, being a watch movement made in his own house, as Samuel Brown, Daniel Binny, and William Auld, his essay masters, declared, which was found a well wrought essay, etc., and the said Normond Macpherson was admitted a freeman clock and watch maker of this Incorporation."—*E. H. Records*.

"Macpherson, Watchmaker, Edinburgh, gives his most grateful acknowledgments to his friends and customers, and acquaints them that he has moved from the back of the City Guard to a well frequented shop at the upper or west end of the Luckenbooths, fronting the Lawnmarket, where he carries on the clock and watch

EIGHT DAY CLOCK

In mahogany case, with Seconds Hand from centre, by
Normond Macpherson, Edinburgh, 1743-83. The property
of the British Linen Bank, Edinburgh. (See p. 284.)

[To face page 232.

making business in all its branches, and has at all times a good assortment of `clocks and watches which he sells on the most reasonable terms, also repairs clocks and watches of all kinds. An apprentice wanted."— *Caledonian Mercury*, 8th September 1781.

"To be sold by public roup on Wednesday, the 30th January, betwixt the hours of five and six afternoon, the dwelling-house and shop lying at the back of the City Guard as previously possessed by Mr Macpherson, watchmaker, at the yearly rent of £18 sterling."—*Ibid.*, 12th January 1782.

"Macpherson, Clock and Watch Maker, formerly at the back of the City Guard, now in the Lawnmarket, near the head of Forrester's Wynd, has at present on hand a very valuable assortment of the following goods, all warranted, which he is determined to sell on the most moderate terms :—Gold and silver cap'd, jewelled, and horizontal watches; gold and silver repeating watches; gold, pinchbeck, and silver stop watches with seconds from the centre or from the cantrate axis; gold and pinchbeck graved and chessed watches; gold cap'd and jewelled or with plain movements; gold and pinchbeck enamelled watches; pinchbeck watches of all kinds with plain, graved, chessed, Nourse skin and tortoise-shell cases; the much approved of and fashionable large-sized silver watches, with seconds from the cantrate axis; eight-day spring or table clocks for striking the hours and chiming the quarters; eight-day plain spring or table clocks, with a variety of eight-day long clocks and timepieces in mahogany or wainscot cases; timepieces for chapels or gentlemen's kitchens, with large or small dials. Clocks and watches lent out by the month or year. Clocks wound up, regulated, and kept by the year at a moderate rate.

"*N.B.*—At said shop and no where else may be had equation tables, without which no gentleman or watch-maker can set clocks or watches with the sundial. Commissions from the country carefully attended to."— *Ibid.*, 2nd January 1783.

To Normond Macpherson has been given the honour of having his name and pedigree duly recorded in Douglas's *Baronage of Scotland.* His father was the fourth son of William Macpherson of Nuid. In 1722 the eldest son of this latter, named Lauchlin, succeeded to the chieftainship and was ever afterwards designated by the title of Cluny. It thus followed that Normond was the nephew of this chieftain, and it is interesting to note that all Normond's brothers, five in number, were engaged in industrial or commercial pursuits, such as a hosier, merchant tailor, schoolmaster, another captain of a privateer, who, having made a handsome fortune, settled in Philadelphia, while the fifth was bred a writer and invented some new machine of great use in the dressing of flax and hemp. There can be no doubt that this aristocratic family connection was a considerable factor in Normond Macpherson's career. He died in 1783, after carrying on an extensive business for over twenty years, when it was continued by his son, who died two years later (*see* page 232). The business was next carried on under the title of Macpherson & Co., or Macpherson and Leslie. A characteristic example of Normond Macpherson's handiwork is now located in the board room of the British Linen Bank, St Andrew Square, Edinburgh (*see* illustration, page 232), and there is a capital example of a bracket clock in ebony case, the property of —— Mackay, Esq., W.S., Edinburgh.

MACPHERSON & Co.   Edinburgh, 1783-85.

"Lost yesterday, betwixt the bottle work in Leith and the Friggate Whins or thereabouts, a silver watch, maker's name, John Gibsted, London, No. 74. Whoever has found the same by applying to Macpherson & Co., watchmakers, Edinburgh, shall be handsomely rewarded." —*Edinburgh Evening Courant*, 4th July 1785.

MACPHERSON & LESLIE.   Edinburgh, 1785-88.

"Lost or stolen at Dunfermline on the 25th curt., a gold watch made by Charleson, London, No. 4572, with a gold dial plate. Whoever is in possession of the same, upon delivering it to Macpherson and Leslie, watchmakers here, shall be handsomely rewarded. It is entreated that if the above watch is offered for sale or otherwise, it may be stopped, and information sent as above."—*Edinburgh Evening Courant*, 31st December 1785.

MACRAE, ALEXANDER. 13 Bridge Street, Inverness, 1837.

MACRAE, JOHN. 11 High Street, Inverness, 1837.

MACVICAR, ARCHIBALD. Lundie Mill, Fife, 1830-42.

MAGDALEN CHAPEL, Cowgate, Edinburgh—Notices regarding Bell and Clock of,

This old pre-Reformation building was the meeting-place of the Incorporation of Hammermen of Edinburgh. Although the place was in their keeping from 1560, it was not until well into the seventeenth century that the erection of a public clock was accomplished. The steeple or spire where the clock was put is of a later date than the chapel itself. It took the place of a wooden belfry, which was erected about 1580, and owing to the expense the upkeep of it caused, and the danger of fire, it was resolved to build a new stone spire in 1618. Not till 1628 was it finished, and the "minutes" during those ten years are of great interest, but, as these lie outside the purposes of this book, we confine ourselves to the earliest mention of the erection of the fine bell which still hangs in this same steeple, making it undoubtedly the only one in Edinburgh still to the fore which has never been disturbed by the hand of the restorer or moved from the position for which it was originally made, making its survival unique in the annals of old bells in the city of Edinburgh. The acquisition of the bell paved the way for a clock, and the following notices, entirely from the MSS. records of the Incorporation of Hammermen, and now made available for the first time, give in language sometimes quaint and pathetic the history of what turned out to be a serious matter for the finances of the craft. As noted elsewhere every clock and watch-maker had to become a member of the Hammermen craft, therefore it is reasonable to assume that the official clock and bell would receive due attention from these members during their erection and installation.

25th October 1631.—"The same day ye Deakene, Maisteris, and haill bretherene of ye Hammermen ordenis ye Chapell and Clerkis hous to be beitit (probably harled) and ye bell hung in ye new stepill, and ye chairges yairof sall be allowit to ye boxmaister."

(This refers to the old bell which had hung in the wooden belfry, and, as will be seen further on, was quite inadequate for such a powerful incorporation.)

25th February 1632.—"The qlk day ye Deakin Maisteris, and haill breitherene of ye Hammermen of Edinburt being convenit wtin yair chaipell callit ye Magdalene Chaipell, and yair efter rype deliberatioun maid and ressouning amongst yame selvis, considering yat they have ane fair steipill bot ane small bell ye sound yrof is not far hard, and for ye credeit of yair craft, decoirment and honour of ye guid toune, and yat yair bell may be hard throw ye haill toune at all occasiounis, and to move utheris to gif to so guid ane work, they all in ane voice have thocht guid yat every airt convene be yame selvis and contribuit and gather amongst yame selvis, that thing yat it sall pleis God to move every ane of yair hertis to gif to buy ane new bell of gritter wecht, and ane knok gif it can be ateinit to, and this collectioun to be collectit, gatherit, and given in to ye Deakin and Maisteris betwixt and paische next to cum. And for yat effect hes appoyuntit ye persounis of every airt underwritten to be collectoris yairof fra yair awin airtis. To wit :—Thomas Baxter, for ye blaksmythis ; Alexander Thomsone, for ye cuitleris; Richard Maxwell, for ye saidleris ; Thomas Broun, elder, for ye loksmythis ; Johne Callender, for ye lorimeris ; Thomas Quhyt, for ye armoraris ; Thomas Inglis, for ye peudereris ; Johne Ormestoun, for ye scheirsmythis."

21st June 1632.—"The same day ye Deacin and haill Maisteris all in ane voice appoyntis ye bell to be maid to yair steipill to be castin in Flanderis and to be stokit yair. And appoyntis Thomas Quhyt, pret. Deakin, Thomas Weir, Thomas Broun, elder, and James Smyth, Thomas Inglis, to be doeris for ye same."

31st October 1632.—"The qlk day ye Deakin and haill maisteris ordenis ye bell to be hung in ye steipill, and

MAGDALEN CHAPEL, COWGATE, EDINBURGH.
Founded 1542. (See p. 255.)

appoyntis Thomas Quhyt, prest. Deakin, Thomas Weir, Thomas Broun, elder, Thomas Inglis, Johne Ormestoun, and James Smyth, to be docris for ye same, and to sic ye samyn weill done, and orderis yame wt Thomas Baxter, Andro Haliburtoun, Alexander Thomsone, Johne West, Richard Maxwell, Dauid Broun, Thomas Broun, William Baxter, and Johne Kello, to be collectouris and gathereris of ye moneyis alreddie collectit, and to do yair seact dilligence to collect mair, and qtever they do yairintill sall be allowit.

"The same day Thomas Quhyt, prest. Deakin of ye Hammermen, declairit to ye craft yat he had ressaunt fra Williame Carnegie, lait Deakin Convenour, ye sowme of nyne scoir merkis qlk ye said Williame Carnegie had collectit and gatherit amongst ye Deakinis following to help to pay for ye bell in ye Magdalene Chaipell in maner following, viz., given in be ye said—

"Williame Carnegie as Deakin of ye Skinneris

Tuentie merkis.
" Ye Deakin of ye Chirurgianes   Tuentie merkis.
" Thomas Quhyt, Deakin of ye Hammermen

Tuentie merkis.
" Deakin of ye Tailzeris   Tuentie merkis.
" Deakin of ye Cordineris   Tuentie merkis.
" Deakin of ye Maesounis and Wrichtis

Tuentie merkis.
" Deakin of ye Baxteris   Tuentie merkis.
" Deakin of ye Fleschouris   Tuentie merkis.
" Deakin of ye Wobsteris   Ten merkis.
" Deakin of ye Walkeris   Fyve merkis.
" Deakin of ye Bonatmakeris   Fyve merkis.

" Qlk sowme of nyne scoir merkis the said Thomas Quhyt, Deakin, promicit to mak furt comand to ye craft qnevir they pleisit, qlk ye said craft was content wt and ordainit yat ye extract of this prest. act under yair clarkis hand sould be ane sufficient chairg to ye said Williame Carnegie qrupoun this act is maid."

22nd day of December 1632. — "The qlk day ye maisteris and greatest pairt of ye haill craft ordenis ane band (bond) to be maid to Thomas Weir and to be subscribit be ye Deakin and boxmaister of ye sowme of sevin hundreth pundis, and thretie fyve pundis for ye anuell yairof to be payit at witsounday next to cum qlk is zit restand awand (owing) of ye pryce of ye bell, and ye saidis maisteris and breitherene prest. bindis and obleiss yame to releive yame yairof."

1st *day of August* 1633.—"The Deakin and haill maisteris all in ane voice ordanis ye meikill bell to be rung fra Sunday next to cum at fyve houris in ye morning, and aucht houris at nicht; and ye littell bell to be rung at sevin houris in ye morning and sevin houris at nicht.

"The same day ye Deakin and breitherene ordenis Johne Ormestoun to deburse and gif furt. to Thomas Weir ye sowme of fourtie thrie pundis ane schilling of ye foir end of his intromissiounes, with ye moneyis yat is collectit to pay for ye bell qrof yair is thretie fyve pundis allowit to ye said Thomas Weir for his witsunday termes anuell last by past of ye sowme of sevin hundreth pundis addetit to him be ye craft. And yt was lost out of his band sextene schillingis. And yat he payit out of chairgis in helping of ye bell in wricht work and yrone work sevin pundis fyve schillingis."

24th *day of September* 1633.—"The qlk day ye Deakin and haill maisteris appoyntis Thomas Quhyt, Thomas Weir, Thomas Baxter, Johne Wast, Thomas Wilsoun, Thomas Broun, younger, Dauid Clark, and Johne Ormestoun to go throw (through) ye nytbouris (neighbours) and collect ane collectioune to help to pay ye bell."

21st *day of November* 1633.—"The qlk day ye haill craft ordenis Richard Maxwell, yair prest. Deakin, and Andro Haliburtoune, yair prest. boxmaister, to gif ane band (bond) to Thomas Weir in name of Mr James Wallace, his brother in law, of ye sowme of Thrie hundret pundis as zit restand awand (owing) of yair bell siluer."

7th *day of Appryll* 1640.—"The qlk day ye Deakin and maisteris ordenis ye great bell to be taikin doune (taken down) out of ye steipill for preventing of danger, and appoyntis James Monteith, prest. boxmaister, Andro Haliburtone, Robert Kennedie, James Smythe, Thomas Broun, elder, maister smyth, Thomas Inglis, and Johne Scharpe, to have ane kair (care) of ye doun taking yairof and to put ye same in sume saiff place."

In the boxmasters' accounts for the year 1640 occurs the following items dealing with the removal of the bell:—

"*Item*, for careying of ane great cabell tow (rope) from ye parliament hous to ye chapell   iiijs.

"*Item*, for len (loan) of towis to tak doune ye bell

xxxs.

"*Item*, given to ye workmen for taking doune ye bell
liijs. iiijd.

"*Item*, to Alexander Baxter, wricht, for taking doune of ye bell   v lib. viijs."

23rd day of February 1641.—"The qlk day ye Deakin and haill maisteris considdering yat they have ane stepill and ane bell and wantit ane knok qlk is verie necessyre wt thrie brodis and handis, and ye glob for ye chainge of ye moone. Thairfoir thay appoyntit Andro Haliburtoun, blaksmyt, Johne Wast, cutler, Dauid Broun, saidler, Thomas Broune, younger, and Robert Kennedie, loksmyts, Samuell Burrell, lorimer, Thomas Weir, and Thomas Inglis, peutereris, to meitt wt James Smythe or any utheris knokmakeris and to try what all will be and what will mainten hir and yairefter to try at nytbouris (neighbours) qt they will gif for advancing yairof."

In the accounts for the year 1641 occur the following disbursements for the re-erecting of the bell and the fitting up of the knok:—

"*Item*, to Robt. Kennedie for naillis to ye bell   xxs.

"*Item*, to him for eiking of ye stirop bandis to ye stok of ye bell   viijs.

"*Item*, for a farlok and wadges to it   vs.

"*Item*, to ye wricht for workmanschip in hinging ye bell   vj lib.

"*Item*, for towis for binding of blokis and tyeing to of ye great towis to ye stok of ye bell xxs.

"*Item*, for ane new tow for drawing up of ye bell

vj lib. viijs.

"*Item*, for careying of ye great cabill to and fra ye chapell viijs.

"*Item*, to James Clark for taking ye roust of ye yrone (iron) work of ye bell xvjs.

"*Item*, to Robt. Kennedie for ane new band to ye stok of ye bell xls.

"*Item*, for ane quarter hundreth naillis to put on yt band wt xs.

"*Item*, for towis to ye paiss of ye litill knok yat was giftit be ye Lady Kilbabertoune xs."

This gift appears to have been in their possession for at least two years, as mention is made of a sum of nine shillings being paid for "bringing up of ane knok out of ye abay," which we take to be Holyrood, and as its arrival came at a time when they were busy redecorating and refurnishing the chapel, a new pulpit and panels bearing the ten commandments, the creed, etc., being then put in, the probability is that the rehanging of the bell and the wish for a large knok, induced them to put up this knok, when, as the accounts show, the knokmaker was in the town for the purpose of advising them in the manufacture and erection of this steeple clock :—

"*Item*, for naillis to naill up the same ijs.

"*Item*, to James Alisone (q.v.), knokmaker in Cowper (Cupar), in pairt payment of ye pryce of ye knok to ye new bell xxxiij lib. vijs. viijd.

"*Item*, mair to him for his chairges in ower cuming to agrie wt us v lib. viijs."

15*th day of May* 1641.—"The qlk day ye Deacone reportit yat ye Gray Freir Kirk desyrit yat ye great bell mycht be rung to ye preiching of ye Grey Freir Kirk, and yat they wald gif fourtie pundis zeirlie for ringing yairof. Quhilk report being considderit be ye Deacone and haill maisteris and they being ryplie and weill advysit yairwith, assentit to ye bell ringing upoun conditioun yat they suld not be astrictit yairto, bot duiring yair pleasur, and with all yat ye Deacone suld stryve to get als meikill for ye ringing yairof as he could."

16*th day of July* 1641.—"The qlk day ye Deacone and haill maisteris appoyntis Androw Haliburtoune and James Mairtene for ye blaksmythis, Johne Robesoune and Thomas Wast for ye cutleris, James Hadden and Johne Douglas for ye saidleris, Johne Hislope and Thomas Softlaw for ye armoureris, Samuell and Willm. Burrell for ye lorimeris, Robert Kennedie and Johne Tweidie for ye loksmythis, Thomas Inglis and Andrew Borthwik for ye peudereris, and Andro Fnilasoune for ye scheirsmythis. To go throw ye toune and collect money fra goode people to help to pay for ye knok and maintenance yairof."

18*th day of September* 1641—

"*Item*, debursit of chairges quhand I went ower to Cowper to sie (see) ye knok for hors and man   viij lib

"*Item*, for ane hundreth and twa pund wecht of copper to be orladge brodis to ye steipill at xvjs. vjd. ye pund is   iiij^{xx}iiij lib. iijs.

(four score and four pounds, three shillings).

"*Item*, for ane hundreth bookis of gold at xvjs. ye peice is   iiij^{xx} lib. (four score pounds)."

9*th day of October* 1641.—"The qlk day ye Deacone and Maisteris appoyntis Thomas Inglis, Dauid Broun, James Monteith, wt ye prest. boxmaister to meitt (meet) wt Robert Tailzefoir, painter, and agrie wt him for painting of ye orladge brodis."

15*th day of October* 1641.—"The qlk day ye Deacone, Maisteris, and haill craft, being convenit, the Deacone spak and said to Robert Tailzefeir, painter, yat they mycht have yair orladge brodis, handis, and glob all done for fourscoir pundis, and gif he wald (would) not doe yame weill, and upoun yat prycc they wald tak ane uther. To ye qlkis was ansrit be ye said Robert Tailzefeir yat yat offer was maid to yame upoun invy (envy), zit (yet) notwtstanding he wald do yame him selff for ye said fourscoir pundis, bot gif they fand

Q

him mor worth efter yat he had done his turne he desyrit yat he mycht have libertie to gif in his bill to ye craft to scik from yame anything yat they wald bestow upoun him more for his paines, gif they fand yair turne weill done. And yane ye Deacone replyit yat they wald be no farther obligat to him bot in fourscoir pundis, and qrof he had ressaint (received) fyve merkis in hand."

18*th* *day of December* 1641. — " The qlk day ye Deacone and Maisteris ordenis Samuell Burrell yair boxmaister to sell yair hous knok for quhat he caud get." [1]

3*rd day of Februar* 1642.—" The qlk day ye Deacone and haill Maisteris ordenis Samuell Burrell, yair prest. boxmaister, to advance to Johne Scott, wricht, ye sowme of ane hundreth merkis in pairt of payment of his work in ye steipill for furneisching and building up of ye trie turnpyk yairin and brodis to ye orladges."

15*th day of Merche* 1642.—" The qlk day ye Deacone and haill Maisteris all in ane voice ordenit Samuell Burrell, yair boxmaister, to pay ye knokmaker and haill chairges yat is debursit yair upoun, and to agrie wt Johne Scot, wricht, and utheris quha hes wrocht to ye knok, and qt ever they do sall be allowit and payit."

In the boxmaster's accounts for this year (1642) occur the details referred to in the preceding minutes, and as they are of special interest we give extracts of these items, as showing the care taken in giving full accounts of how the money was disbursed :—

" *Item*, to ye knokmaker in pairt of payment of ye pryce of ye knok   iij^{xx}vj lib. xiijs. iiijd.

" *Item*, to him for his mertimes fie and ringing of the bell   ix lib. xs.

" *Item*, to ye wrichtis of drinksilver at ye up-putting of ye trap and orladge brodis in ye steipill at several tymes   iiij lib. xvs.

" *Item*, for careyeing of ye thrie orladge brodis from

---

[1] This is the knok that was gifted by Lady Kilbabertoun in 1638.

Johne Scotis to ye painteris, and from ye painteris to ye chapell xijs.

"*Item*, for careyeing of ye paiss and wechtis to and frome ye Deacones xijs.

"*Item*, spent wt James Alisone and Johne Scot, wricht xxvijs.

"*Item*, for towis to ye knok xiijs. iiijd.

"*Item*, unto ye maissounis of drinksilver for drawing and making up of dyellis xxiijs.

"*Item*, to ye knokmaker in compleit payment of ye knok j^{c}xxxiij lib. vjs. (£133, 6s. Scots).

"*Item*, mair to him at directioun of ye Deacone and maisteris quhen he was appoyntit be ye haill craft for his attendance heir, and for his sones drinksilver

xiiij lib. xvijs.

"*Item*, to Johne Scot, wricht, for making of ye trapis and orladge brodis

j^{c}iiii^{xx}xiiij lib. 13s. 4d. (£194, 13s. 4d. Scots).

"*Item*, to Wm. Scharpe for copper naillis to ye thrie brodis xiiij lib.

"*Item*, for oyll to ye knok and bell, and for ane glas to put ye samyne in xxvjs. viijd.

"*Item*, to ye painter for painting and gilting of ye thrie orladge brodis wt ye handis and glob

iiij^{xx} lib. (four score pounds the contract price).

2nd day of September 1642.—"*Item*, to ye knokmaker at directioun of ye Deacone for his painis in cumeing ower ye watter to visit ye knok, and helping of hir

iij lib."

23rd of August 1644.—" The Deacone, Maisteris, and breitherine, havand considderit the supplicatoun gevin in be Johne Carmichell, officer, makand mentioun that quhair he had keipit, ordourit, and attendit the knok, and had nather feis (fee) nor gottin any thing thairfoir, thir thrie (three) quarteris of ane zeir last bygane. And off the extraordinar paines, and travellis this tyme past quhrin he might have made benefit be his craft giff his chairge as officer and utherwayes had sufferit him to attend upoun the samen. And thairfoir craving modificatioun and consideratioun for byganes, and to

have a certane fie modefit to him in tyme cuming for
keiping and ordouring the said knok as the samen
supplicatioun at length beiris. The Deacone, Maisteris,
and breitherine ordenit thair prest. boxmaister to give
and delyver to the said Johne Carmichell for his bygane
paines and travellis for keiping and ordouring and
attending the said knok, the sowme of twentie pundis
Scottis. And als hes appoyntit and ordeanit the said
Johne ane fie of twentie pundis zeirlie heirefter for
keiping, ordouring, and attending the knok and ringing
of the bell. And that fra Allhallowis next to cum qlk
sall be ye said Johne his entrie."

8th day of Septembris 1647.—"The qlk day the auld
Deacones, Maisteris, and haill hous ordeanis James
Monteith, thir prest. Deacone, to tak doune the knok
in the steipill and send hir away to Londoune, and
change hir with ane new one or qr (whatever) he sall
think expedient."

This, however, was not done, the knok being next
taken in hand by John Milne (q.v.), whose name appears
for the first time at this date. He attended to the
keeping of the clock for at least two years later, and
on the 23rd of September 1648 the following minute
is given :—

"The qlk day, Johne Milne, keiper of the knok,
desyrit some suplic yairfoir, and seeing he had this
lang tyme bygane keipit the said knok they wald be
plasit (pleased) to suplic his present necessatie, as the
bill in its self at mair length beiris the saidis tradis
being ryplie advisit they ordeain thir prest. boxmaister,
Thomas Haliburtoun, braiser, to give to him the sowme
of ten pundis at aince (once), the other ten pundis at
Witsonday next to cum, with this provisioun, that he
wait and attend upoun the said knok faithfullie and
treaulie to the next terme of Witsonday 1649."

It is evident that John Milne was not able to keep
the clock in going order, and his name, along with any
disbursements on the same, disappears from the minutes
and accounts. The clock apparently had got into a
very bad state, and it was not till the year 1661 that we

have any further mention of it. It was then taken in hand by Humphrey Milne (q.v.), who was possibly the most practical craftsman in Edinburgh at this date.

2nd of November 1661.—"It is aggreid be the Deakone and haill Maisteris of the hous, with Vmphra Mylne, clokmaker, that he mak the clok of the Magdallen Chappell to be perfyte and rycht confourme to the toune clok for sevin zeiris to cum, for the sowme of sevin pund sterling, and to be in reddines against the first day of May next to cum."

4th of May 1672.—"The qlk day it is statute and ordained be the Deakone, Maisters, and haill remenant breitherin of the Hammermen of Edinburgh, that thair bell sall not be rung heirefter for ony deceisit persoune quhat somevir, except they legat (bequeath) and leave somewhat to the house for the use of the poore."

14th of November 1681.—"The hous recommends to the Deacon and Boxmaster to agree with any person that desires the ringing of the bell to any burial and to take as much as they can get therefor."

11th August 1688.—"Andrew Brown, clockmaker, delivered to the Boxmaster four[1] rix dollars for ringing the bell when Mr Edmund Appley, watchmaker in London, was buried."

23rd February 1695.—"The whilk day, in presence of the haill house, the committee appointed for visiting of the clock, and to speak with the clockmakers and with William Weir, or any other person, for making of a new clock, gave in yr report that there was an necessity for a new clock, and that they had been speaking with the freemen clockmakers and with William Weir yranent, but had not made any agreement yr anent. The house do yairfor nominate the Deacon, Boxmaster, George Dalgleish, Patrick Drysdaill, William Brown, John Lethom, and Andrew Dunlop, to be a committee to treat and agree with any of the freemen clockmakers for making a new clock to the Magdalene Chapel at as reasonable a rate as they can, and to settle and determine yairin as they think fit. And in case they agree, impower them to set the person they agree with presently to work. And appoint the boxmaster to pay the price of the clock in the way and manner as the said committee shall ordain. The person whom they employ always finding sufficient caution for the suffeincie of the clock."

29th October 1696.—"The house having heard read in their presence a petition given in by Andrew Brown, clockmaker, craving an addition to the price he is to get for making the pendulum clock, they remit the consideration thereof, and the contract betwixt the Incorporation and him, to the committee to be appointed upon the tradesmen's accompts, and to report their opinion thereof to the haill house at the next meeting."

15th December 1696.—"The meeting appoints the boxmaster to give Andrew Brown's servants ten shillings sterling of drink money for their pains with the new clock."

6th February 1697.—"The house by plurality of votes appoints Andrew Brown to get from the boxmaster £5 sterling for making up the loss which he alleges he has sustained in making the new clock, and appoints him to use his judgment to make the new clock strike louder."

22nd February 1698.—"It is the committee's opinion that the boxmaster should presently employ a wright for laying of some joists beneath the paics (weights) of ye clock for securing of the house in case the paies should happen to fall back."

11th September 1698.—"Paid Andrew Brown for ye new clock to ye Incorporation as per contract and discharge £360 Scots (£30 sterling)."

This contract and discharge is still in existence.

13th February 1705.—"The house having heard the petition given in by Andrew Brown read in their presence, craving payment for keeping of the clock these five years bygane conform to the contract betwixt the Incorporation and him, they do remit the consideration thereof to the committee to be appointed: the box-master to pay unto the said Andrew Brown what they

The Belfry and Clock Dial,
Magdalen Chapel, Edinburgh.

think fit for his said five years' service, and to get his discharge of the same which shall be allowed to the boxmaster in his accompts. As also impowers the said committee to commune with the said Andrew Brown anent the keeping of the said clock in time coming or not as they think fit."

7th April 1705.—"The committee having considered the reference made to them anent Andrew Brown, they conform to the said power, appoint the boxmaster to pay to the said Andrew Brown four pounds sterling in satisfaction of his bygone keeping of the clock for the space of five years preceding, and to get his discharge for the same. And they appoint the boxmaster and his successors to pay the said Andrew Brown nine pounds Scots for keeping of the clock, commencing from the said term of Candlemas 1705, provided he keep her well."

24th May 1712.—"There being an accompt given in by Robert Alexander for dressing and mending the clock of the Magdalen Chapel extending to £31, 4s., by and attour his keeping the clock and helping it three times, being a year and a half which he does not state in his accompt. It was put to the vote whether or not he should be payed £30 in full of the said accompt of all that he could ask of the Incorporation. And it was carried without a contrair vote that he should be payed £30 as above."

28th August 1730.—"The committee are of opinion that the easter and wester dial plates of the steeple should be immediately taken down and timber set upon their place."

26th September 1730.—"It being represented that the bell in the steeple is in danger of coming down, being loose in the stock, therefore they ordain the Boxmaster to cause rehang the bell and get it fixed fast in the stock as soon as possible—and names James Wilson, James Edgar, David Hodge, Robert Maxwell, and the boxmaster to see it right done."

From this date onwards various minutes are recorded of repairs to the clock, which did duty till well on into the nineteenth century; but change of ownership of the building, combined with neglect, soon caused it to stop, and its remains lie to-day up in this old steeple, a mass of rusty wheels and pinions silent for ever. In the minutes dealing with the ordering of the bell no mention is made of the maker's name, simply that it was to be "castin in Flanderis." The Committee entrusted with this commission appears to have had in their eye one whose work was well known in Scotland, namely, Michael Burgurhuys of Flanders, and the following fragmentary list of bells yet remaining in Scotland made by this man and his son is not without interest :—

"1. Lundie, inscribed, 'Michael Bvrgerhvys Me Fecit 1617.'

"2. Kinnell, inscribed, 'Michael Bvrgerhvys Me Fecit 1624. Soli Deo Gloria.'

"3. Benvie, inscribed, 'Michael Bvrgerhvys M. F. 1631. M. Henrie, Fithie.'

"4. Lintrathen, inscribed, 'Michael Bvrgerhvys Me Fecit 1632.'

"5. Magdalene Chapel, Edinburgh, two inscriptions, 'Soli Dea Gloria. Michael Bvrgerhvys Me Fecit 1632.' 'God blis the Hammermen of Edinburgh,' with their crest, the crown and hammer on a shield, on both sides of the bell.

"6. Leslie, Aberdeen, inscribed,' Michael Bvrgerhvys Me Fecit 1642.'

"7. Maryton, inscribed, 'Michael Bvrgerhvys M. F. 1642. Soli Deo Gloria.'

"8. Cramond Parish Church, inscribed, 'Michael Bvrgerhvys Me Fecit 1619. Soli Deo Gloria.'

"9. Farnell, Aberdeenshire, inscribed, 'Johannes Bvrgerhvys Me Fecit 1662.'

"10. Panbridge, which at one time belonged to the Parish Church of Arbroath, inscribed, 'Soli Deo Gloria. Johannes Bvrgerhvys Me Fecit 1664. Timor Domine Est Principivm Sapientiæ—Proverbs i. 7.'

"11. Liff, Aberdeenshire, inscribed, 'Jan Bvrgerhvys, Hecft. My. Gegoten 1696.'

"12. South Queensferry, 'Soli Deo Gloria. Michael

Bvrgerhvys Me Fecit. David Jonking, Maerchant of Edenbvrge, gifted this to the Kirk of the Queen's Ferrie. Cursed be they that takes it frae. Anno Domino, 1635.'

" 13. Aberdeen, St Nicholas Church, known as Auld Lowrie. This bell was broken by falling to the ground when the lead-covered steeple was burnt in 1874. Fragments of it were shown at the Glasgow Exhibition in 1911, and the following are parts of the inscriptions that remain decipherable :—Me Fecit Anno Dom. 1634. Soli Deo Gloria, Michael Bvrgerhvys. Depello— Timorem—Defunct—Nensis—Hanc Campana Donavit n. Ego — Campana Sonitu no—Ecce — Vccor — Anti Cum—Vsdemove Campanæ Rima Tissa.'

" In Craigiebuckler Parish Church is the following inscription on a brass plate inside chancel of church which refers to the bell of that church :—' Old Lowrie hung in St Nicholas Steeple 1351, and destroyed by fire A.D. 1874. Young Lowrie recast from metal of Old Lowrie, A.D. 1882.'

" 14. Fyvie, inscribed, ' Michael Bvrgerhvys, 1609.'

" 15. Lundie, 1617.

" 16. Smailholm, 1647.

" 17. Peterhead Old Parish Church inscribed, ' Soli Deo Gloria, Michael Bvrgerhvys Me Fecit 1647.' "

Doubtless there are a good few more, but the point brought out by this list is that the Hammermen were determined to have the best that at that period was made, and this choice of Michael Bvrgerhvys, probably the most renowned in Flanders, was a costly business for them. This can easily be seen by the pathetic appeal for subscriptions, and after all their beating up they were obliged to grant a bond to one of their own number to make up the deficit. The self-denial of these old craftsmen does away with the absurd story that this bell contains a large quantity of silver in the composition of its metal, an assertion that has been of late frequently made.

Having been at the trouble to mount up to the belfry of this old steeple to inspect the bell, we were surprised at its large size and weight (approximately it weighs about 12 or 14 cwt.), and splendid preservation. The inscriptions are as above, and, barring a little mark where the clapper strikes the inside of it, is as fit to perform its useful duty as when first made. On looking at this authentic relic, thoughts arise of the many occasions on which it has been rung. It has tolled not only for funerals, but for nearly every pageant that has crossed the stage in those stirring days. Among the many entries about it, we were startled by seeing in the accounts for 1661 the item, "To William Campbell, for ringing of ye bell the tyme of Montrose's buryal, £1, 4s. Scots [2s. sterling]," showing the interest this solemn funeral caused, and from the sum paid for horse hire, we learn that the incorporation attended it in an official manner. Again in 1680, "For ringing ye bell that day the Prince of Orange was proclaimed King, £2, 16s. Scots [about 4s. 6d. sterling]." In fact, the times this bell is mentioned are innumerable. The Hammermen derived a considerable revenue from it, and as the demand was steady, they made the following minute on 18th July 1684 :—

"The house remands to the deacon and boxmaster to agree with any person that desires the ringing of the bell to any burial, and to take as much as they can get therefor."

That they acted up to this rule is pretty clear from the difference of the sums charged, the payments ranging from £4 Scots up to £12, showing that the fee depended very much on the status of the person wanting its use. They fined one of their own number £2 Scots for taking the liberty of tolling the bell during a deacon's funeral, and this because he had no warrant from the boxmaster to do so. Other examples could be given all dealing more or less with the care they exercised over its preservation, and it is probably to this cause that the Magdalen Chapel Bell is the only one in Edinburgh, as before mentioned, that still does duty in the location it was originally made for now nearly three centuries ago.

MAILING, ROBERT. Aberdeen, 1630. *See page 4.*

MAITLAND, JAMES. Neilston, 1830.

MAITLAND, JOHN. Cross Loan Street, Calton, Glasgow, 1818.

MAITLAND, JOHN. Church Street, Lochwinnoch, 1836.

MALCOLM, WILLIAM. Callander, 1827-37.

MALLOCH, WILLIAM. Leith Walk, Edinburgh, 1806. Clock case maker.

MANNERS, JAMES. Church Street, Berwick-upon-Tweed, 1820.

MANSON, ALEXANDER Duke Street, Thurso, 1837.

MANSON, DAVID. Dundee, 1806.

MARSHALL, FRANCIS & SON. Edinburgh, 1816.

"Francis Marshall & Son, Jewellers, No. 30 North Bridge Street, Edinburgh, next door to the Post Office, beg to inform the public that they continue their business in all its various branches. A new establishment in the jewellery line having been formed next door to them under the firm of James and Walter Marshall (q.v.), they think it proper to inform their friends and customers and the public that they have no connection with that establishment."—*Edinburgh Evening Courant*, 9th April 1816.

MARSHALL, JAMES. Wishaw, 1815-53.

Succeeded by his son William, who died in 1884. James M'Culloch, his apprentice, has now the business on the site where it was first carried on in a thatched house.

MARSHALL, JAMES & WALTER. Edinburgh, 1816.

"Beg leave respectfully to intimate that they have this day commenced business as jewellers, etc., in that shop, No. 30 North Bridge Street, formerly occupied by the late Mr Richard Bannatine. J. M. is just returned from England, where he has secured an extensive and elegant stock of jewellery, watches, plated goods, etc., by makers of the first production."—*Edinburgh Evening Courant*, 14th October 1816.

MARSHALL, P. South Queensferry, 1830-52.

"Among the tradesmen of the Queensferry there is one peculiarly distinguished as 'The Genius.' He is appropriately enough a watchmaker. Trained to

ingenuity by his avocation, Mr Marshall has certainly
attempted several extraordinary things, most of which he
has brought from time to time before the Royal Scottish
Society of Arts, but a prophet has no honour in his own
country. One of these projects was broached in 1831.
It consisted in a proposal for transporting ships by
a railway across the Isthmus of Suez. Mr Marshall
followed this up with his grand device, 'Suggestions
for preventing Collisions of Steamships at Sea, etc.'
For fuller account of this celebrated man, see the
delightful book, *Summer Life on Land and Water at
South Queensferry*, by W. W. Fyfe, published in 1852."

MARSHALL, WILLIAM. Bellie, Morayshire; died 29th
May 1833 in his 85th year.

" From a humble station in life he rose to distinction
by the industrious cultivation of a natural talent,
eventually becoming factor on the estate of Alexander,
Duke of Gordon, an office he held for many years.
Although self-taught, he made considerable progress
in mechanics, to which his leisure hours were frequently
devoted. Not only did he excel as a first-rate fiddler
but also as a composer of national airs and beautiful
Strathspeys. His music to the song, ' O a' the airts the
wind can blaw,' drew forth from Burns a complimentary
letter. He was also an ingenious clockmaker, and a
specimen of his work is preserved in Gordon Castle."—
The History of the Province of Moray, by L. Shaw
and J. F. S. Gordon, 1882.

MARTIN, JOHN. Regent Street, Kincardine-on-Forth,
1836.

MARTIN, JOSEPH. Kippen, 1798.

MARTIN, PETER. 3 Govan Street, Glasgow, 1840-50.

"Peter Martin, watchmaker and jeweller, Glasgow,
served Heir General and Heir Special to his father,
Peter Martin, Hutchesontown, who died 4th June 1846,
in a tenement and yard, etc., in the High Street,
Gorbals, dated 23rd November 1849. Recorded 7th
December 1849."—*Services of Heirs*.

MARTIN, ROBERT. Glasgow and Grahamston, 1782-99.

" Lost on Monday evening last, betwixt the head of
Stockwell and the head of Jamaica Street, a silver
watch, maker's name, Robert Martin, No. 184. Whoever

will bring the said watch to the *Courier* Office will receive one guinea reward and no questions asked." —*Glasgow Courier*, 18th April 1799.

MARTIN, ROBERT. Perth, 1745.

Robert Martin, watchmaker from Glasgow, admitted a freeman clock and watch maker in Perth Hammermen Incorporation for payment of £15 sterling on 1st January 1745.

This is, in all probability, the same individual as below. He would possibly find Perth in the year 1745 anything but a suitable town to commence business in as a stranger. A careful search of the Records of the Perth Hammermen fails to unearth his name again, and the surmise is that he returned to Glasgow.

MARTIN, ROBERT. Glasgow, 1764.

MARTIN, WILLIAM. Glasgow, 1739.

"That William Martin, Watch and Clock Maker, is now settled at the Clock and Moving Ball, next door to the Gallowgate Bridge, Glasgow, where gentlemen and ladies may be furnished with gold and silver watches, chime and spring clocks, and speaking clocks, with the best London cases at the lowest rates."— *Caledonian Mercury*, 10th September 1739.

MARTIN, ——. Castle-Douglas. *See* page 215.

MASON, JOHN. Kelso, 1809.

MATHERS, GEORGE. Errol Street, Peterhead, 1837.

MATHESON, JOHN S. Leith, 1880. *See* page 25.

MATHEWSON, ANDREW. Kilconquhar, Fife, 1795-1830.

MATHEWSON, JAMES. Kilconquhar, Fife. Son of above; died 1882, aged 69 years.

MATHEWSON, WILLIAM. Kilconquhar, Fife. Brother of Andrew; went to America about 1830.

MATHIESON, JOHN. Edinburgh, 1774.
Bound apprentice to James Gray, 12th November 1774.

MATHIESON, ROBERT. Canongate, Edinburgh, 1736.
Booked apprentice to James Nicholl, 1738.

MATTHEWSON, JOHN. Anstruther, 1755.

Among the Old Charters belonging to the Burgh of Crail given in *Fifeani*, occur the following :—

" 1st. Discharge by John Matthewson, clocksmith in Anstruther, to John Oliphant, Treasurer of the Burgh of Crail, of the sum of £5, 10s. (Scots), as a year's salary for keeping the town clock of Crail, 7th April 1755.

" 2nd. Discharge by John Matthewson to the above John Oliphant of the sum of £2 (Scots) for the striking work of the Town Clock, Crail."

Though the surname of this last maker is given with two tt's, it is not unlikely that the Mathewsons of Kilconquhar are of the same family.

MAULE, WILLIAM. Coldstream, 1837.

MAVER, FRANCIS. High Street, Fochabers, 1837.

MAVINE, DANIEL. Edinburgh, 1681.

Residenter in Edinburgh; booked apprentice to Paul Romieu, 26th August 1681.

MAXWELL, HENRY. Edinburgh, 1822.

Apprenticed to Robert Bryson, 6th May 1822.

MAXWELL, ROBERT. Wigtown, 1770.

MAXWELL, WILLIAM. Edinburgh, 1748.

Son to Robert Maxwell, late writer in Edinburgh; booked apprentice to John Dalgleish, 28th July 1748.

M'ADAM,[1] ROBERT, sen. Dumfries, 1820-45.

M'ADAM, ROBERT, jun. Dumfries, 1840-67.

M'ALPIN, GEORGE. Edinburgh, 1836-46.

257 High Street, 1836; 1 South St Andrew Street, 1846.

M'BEAN, JAMES. 89 Castle Street, Inverness, 1837.

M'BEATH, ALEXANDER. Fraserburgh, 1837.

M'BETH, DANIEL. 69 Kirk Street, Calton, Glasgow, 1818-46.

" On Sunday night the shop of Mr M'Beth, watch-maker, Kirk Street, Calton, Glasgow, was entered by

---

[1] All the names which follow under this prefix M' may, in a number of examples of their work, be found spelt Mac. It is a matter of some difficulty to give them correctly.

thieves, and all the watches on the windows, amounting to between thirty-five and forty, carried away. The dwelling-house is situated behind the shop, and the thieves had effected an entrance by wrenching off the kitchen window shutter and passing into the premises. As yet there has not been any trace of the thieves."—*Edinburgh Evening Courant*, 1st January 1846.

M'CALL, JOHN. Dalkeith, 1829.

M'CALL, JOHN. 20 Lothian Street, Edinburgh, 1836.

M'CRACKEN, WILLIAM. 22 Nelson Street, Glasgow, 1841.

M'CREDIE, THOMAS. George Street, Stranraer, 1836.

M'DONALD, DAVID. Edinburgh, 1822-35.

4 Dalrymple Place, 1822 ; 3 East Arthur Place, 1835.

M'DONALD, DAVID. 134 Trongate, Glasgow, 1836.

M'DONALD, DONALD. Inverness, 1801.

"Donald M'Donald, son and successor of Mr Peter M'Donald, many years clock and watch maker in Inverness, takes this opportunity of returning his most grateful thanks to his friends and the public for the patronage experienced by him in conjunction with his father for some time previous to his death, and begs leave to inform them that he continues to carry on the clock and watch making business as usual in the shop formerly occupied by his father and himself opposite to the Hall of the Northern Meeting. D. M'D. having been regularly bred to the profession with his father, and having also been employed in some of the best shops in London, he flatters himself that his knowledge and experience of the business will enable him to give at least some degree of satisfaction to his employers." —*Edinburgh Evening Courant*, 12th November 1801.

M'DONALD, DUNCAN. Edinburgh, 1787.

Booked apprentice to Thomas Leslie.

M'DONALD, JAMES. 28 Broad Street, Aberdeen, 1846.

M'DONALD, JOHN. Inverness, 1779-90.

"A CLOCK AND WATCH MAKER WANTED.—Mr John M'Donald, lately deceased, followed this profession here with the highest credit and reputation, and has left a very complete stock of tools and a variety of articles of value in the way of his business, which his heirs would give credit to any person of good character that would set up here on finding security. The best recommendation that can be given for this being a most excellent station for such a business here is the very favourable circumstances in which he left his family which arose from his trade alone. No person need expect the countenance of the Magistrates and Gentle‑ men of the town and county who cannot be amply recommended for integrity and knowledge of their profession."—*Edinburgh Evening Courant*, April 1790.

"Died at Inverness, on the 7th curt., Mr John M'Donald, watchmaker, convener of the six incor‑ porated trades of Inverness." — Obituary notice in *Edinburgh Herald*, 17th March 1790.

M'DONALD, PETER. Inverness, 1780-1801. *See* Donald M'Donald, Inverness.

M'DONALD, WILLIAM. Main Street, Invergordon, 1836.

M'DONALD, WILLIAM. 20 Carnegie Street, Edinburgh, 1819.

M'DONALD, WILLIAM. High Street, Nairn, 1836.

M'DUFF, J. Maybole, Ayrshire, 1830.

M'EWAN, JAMES. Crieff, 1846.

"Prize of Two Guineas awarded to James M'Ewan, Crieff, for his model of a pendulum with regulating index for common house clock."—*Royal Scottish Society of Arts.*

"The bob of the pendulum is made in two halves, being hollowed in the centre so as to admit a wheel of teeth carrying on its arbour an index hand, which points on a dial plate in front of the bob to the words 'fast' or 'slow.' The nut at the bottom of the pendulum being turned, it acts on the wheel by a pinion, and thus any person who has occasion to regulate the beat of the pendulum can see by the index hand how far he raises or lowers the bob. Of course, Mr M'Ewan intends this merely for common domestic clocks and not for fine timekeepers, whose rate would be effected by the mere motion of the index hand round the dial plate of the bob."—*Transaction of the Royal Scottish Society of Arts*, 1846.

CHAMBER CLOCK.

By Humphrey Mills, Edinburgh, 1661-1710.   The property of the
Society of Antiquaries of Scotland.   (See p. 267.)

FACSIMILE OF BRASS FRET ON CHAMBER CLOCK,
Made by Humphrey Mills, Edinburgh.
(See p. 268.)

[To face page 256.

M'EWAN, JOHN. High Street, Crieff, 1837.

M'EWAN, WILLIAM. Auchterarder, 1840-55.

"William M'Ewan, watchmaker, Auchterarder, served Heir Special to his father, William M'Ewan, merchant there, in a tenement of land in south side of the street of Auchterarder, dated 1st January 1855. Recorded 15th January 1855."—*Services of Heirs.*

M'EWEN, WILLIAM. Leith Street, Edinburgh, 1849.

M'FARLANE, ALEXANDER. Perth, 1789-1808.

M'FARLANE, D. & SON. 80 Trongate, Glasgow, 1837.

M'FARLANE, JAMES. 41 George Street, Perth, 1842.

M'FARLANE, PATRICK. Glasgow, 1781.

M'FARLANE, PATRICK. Perth, 1790.
Apprenticed to Alexander M'Farlane.

M'FARLANE, ROBERT. Perth, 1833.

M'FIE, BRICE. Sugar House Lane, Greenock, 1820.

M'GEORGE, DAVID. St Andrew Street, Castle Douglas, 1837.

M'GEORGE, JOHN. High Street, Kirkcudbright, 1836.

M'GEORGE, ——. Dumfries, 1755.

M'GILCHRIST, J. Kirkintilloch, 1818.

M'GILCHRIST, JOHN. Barrhead, 1830.

M'GILL, G. & W. 7 St Mirren's Street, Paisley, 1820.

M'GREGOR, ALEXANDER. Dunse. *See* page 107.

M'GREGOR, D. W. Glasgow, 1848.

M'GREGOR, FORREST. St Ninians, 1830-80.
Successor to David Somerville.

M'GREGOR, JAMES. Edinburgh, 1825-36. 5 Register Street, 1825; 29 West Register Street, 1836.

M'GREGOR, JAMES & SON. Edinburgh, 1836. 29 West Register Street, 1850.

M'GREGOR, JOHN. Francis Street, Stornoway, 1836.

M'GREGOR, JOHN. Bridge Street, Wick, 1837.

M'GREGOR, JOHN. 9 Calton Street, Edinburgh, 1811.

M'GREGOR, Peter. 55 South Street, Perth, 1840.

M'GREGOR, Thomas. Ayton, 1837.

M'INNES, Neal. Lochnell Street, Lochgilphead, 1837.

M'INNES, William. 10 London Street, Glasgow, 1834-41.

M'INTYRE, Joseph. High Street, Crieff, 1837.

M'KAY, Alexander. Banff, 1775.

M'KAY, David. Braick's Wynd, Arbroath, 1837.

M'KAY, James Thomson. 32 Green, Aberdeen, 1836.

M'KENZIE, Alexander. Edinburgh, 1787.
>   Bound apprentice to Robert Aitchison, 17th February
> 1787.

M'KENZIE, Francis. Edinburgh, 1753.
>   Son of Robert M'Kenzie, shipmaster in Leith;
> booked apprentice to John Dalgleish, 5th May 1753.

M'KENZIE, Kenneth. Edinburgh, 1737.
>   Brother to John M'Kenzie of Anlecross; booked
> apprentice to Thomas Gordon, 6th August 1737.

M'KENZIE, Lewis. Edinburgh, 1797.
>   Bound apprentice to James Gray, 22nd July 1797.

M'KENZIE, Murdoch. Edinburgh, 1787-94.
>   Bound apprentice to Brown & Skelton, 7th March
> 1787. Discharged of his indentures, 1st November 1794.

M'KENZIE, William. Aberchirder, about 1840.

M'KERROA, James. Ford, Pathhead, Dalkeith, 1836-50.

M'KINLAY, Peter. 11 Leith Street, Edinburgh, 1836.

M'KIRDIE, John. 28 Woolmanhill, Aberdeen, 1846.

M'KIRDY, Hugh. 3 Nelson Street, Glasgow, 1836.

M'LACHLAN, John. 5 New Bridge Street, Dumfries, 1820.

M'LAREN, James. Glasgow, 1779.

M'LAREN, L. 6 Duncan Street, Edinburgh, 1850.

M'LEAN, George. 9 Argyle Street, Glasgow, 1837.

M'LENNAN, William. 83 Church Street, Inverness, 1835.

M'LEOD, J. & Co. 11 Schoolhill, Aberdeen, 1846.

M'MASTER, William. 35 Cathcart Street, Greenock, 1820.

M'MILLAN, ANDREW. 5 Arcade, Glasgow, 1832-43.

M'MILLAN, JAMES. Glasgow Street, Ardrossan, 1850.

M'MILLAN, PETER. 45 Regent Quay, Aberdeen, 1836.

M'NAB, JOHN. Leonard Street, Perth, 1820.

M'NAB, J. & A. 35 George Street, Perth, 1837-49.

M'NAUGHTAN, ALEXANDER. 2 Catherine Street, Edinburgh, 1814.

 "Alexander M'Naughtan, watch and clock maker, respectfully intimates that he has commenced business on his own account at 2 Catherine Street, second shop below the Black Bull, with a neat choice of Watches and Clocks, all warranted to give satisfaction. The greatest attention paid to watch and clock repairs."—*Edinburgh Evening Courant*, 11th June 1814.

M'NAUGHTON, DONALD. Perth, 1768.

 Apprenticed to James Young, 30th May 1768.

M'NIESH, JOHN. Falkirk, 1805.

M'PHERSON, JOHN. High Street, Nairn, 1836.

M'QUEEN, ALEXANDER. 18 Bank Street, Edinburgh, 1788-1834.

 Bound apprentice to Thomas Morgan, 9th December 1788.

 "Alexander M'Queen, watch and clock maker, 18 Bank Street, Edinburgh, late foreman to Mr Green, begs to intimate to his friends and the public that he has commenced business on his own account in the above line. Having been for many years in the employment of Mr Green, where he acquired great experience in every department of his profession, he trusts to merit and to receive a share of public patronage."—*Edinburgh Evening Courant*, 5th June 1834.

M'ROBERT, THOMAS. Charlotte Street, Stranraer, 1820.

M'SKIMMING, ——. Castle-Douglas. *See* page 215.

M'WALTER, JAMES. Paisley, 1784.

 "A few days ago an acquaintance carried me to see a curious machine intended for the discovery of the longitude at sea, invented by James M'Walter, watchmaker, Paisley. He very readily satisfied our curiosity, and indeed the machine exceeded all the description

I had heard of it, and it is entirely upon a new construction. I was really surprised to see with what regularity and exactness it performed its various operations; the manner in which it showed the enlightened part of the earth and the length of day and night in all latitudes, and also the declination of the sun through the whole year. The manner in which it pointed out the longitude seemed to me very clear and beyond dispute. Mr M'Walter showed me also how this machine finds out the true distance of any place lying east or west the one from the other exactly, not by computation but by time. He showed me also the way that this machine can find out the number of miles a ship will sail east or west in one day if the sun can be seen rise and set the same day. Upon the whole I think it is a complete machine and one of the greatest curiousities I ever saw, and I believe every person that hath seen or may hereafter see it will say the same.— Extract from a letter from Paisley, 12th January 1784, *Caledonian Mercury*, 19th January 1784.

M'WALTER, Moses. Balfron, 1836.

M'WATERS, George. 30 Duke Street, Glasgow, 1836.

M'WHINNIE, Robert. Main Street, Ayr, 1820-38.

MEARNS, Ernest. Banff, 1749.

MEARNS, John. Steps of Gilcomiston, Aberdeen, 1792-1846.

MELLIS, John. Edinburgh, 1749.

Son of John Mellis, burgess in Edinburgh, booked apprentice to William Nicoll, 14th September 1749.

MELROSE, James. 208 Canongate, Edinburgh, 1826.

MELROSE, ——. Nicolson Street, Edinburgh, 1827.

MELVIL or MELVILL, Robert. Stirling, 1736-67.

MELVILL, Robert. Aberdeen, 1645. *See* page 5.

MEMES, James. Church Street, Berwick-on-Tweed, 1806.

MEMESS, James Garnock, 1730 (?).

MEMESS, John. Johnshaven, 1730 (?).

MEMIS, William. Aberdeen, 1787.

MENZIES, Robert. Coupar Angus, 1801.

MENZIES, ROBERT. Perth, 1804.

MENZIES, ROBERT. Crieff, 1827.

MENZIES, ROBERT. Alloa, 1830.

MERCER, HAY. 27 West North Street, Aberdeen, 1837.

MERRYLIES OR MERRYLEES, CHARLES. Watergate, Edinburgh, 1806; 39 Leith Street, 1825.

MERSON, JAMES. Huntly, 1837.

METHVEN, DAVID. St Andrews, 1768-73.

ST ANDREWS, *6th April* 1768.—"Which day Joshua Scott, present Deacon, and remnant members of trade being convened, David Methven, Watch and Clock Maker in the city, was admitted and received into the liberty and privileges and immunities of the smith trade as a watch maker and clock smith during his life allanerlie, who satisfied the trade for his dues of admission to show said freedom as above. He made faith as use is."

Elected Boxmaster of the Incorporation of Hammermen, St Andrews, 1771-72.

28th September 1773.—"Which day William Fuller, present Deacon, and remnant members of trade being met, the Deacon informed the trade that although David Methven, one of their members, was on the tenth current elected Convener of the Seven Trades for this current year, by a considerable number of legal votes, yet it appears from the conduct of the Town Council that they intend to oppose the admission of the said David Methven, legally elected Convener, and to receive Andrew Finlay who had but a few votes, and who never so much as claimed the election to himself.

"Therefore the Deacon proposed to the trade that as the said David Methven was the legally elected Convener, and in case the Council should take it upon them to reject him and receive another man, that the smith trade, as having voted the said David Methven to be Convener, were bound in duty and in defence of their rights of election, to support from their funds the said David Methven's election in pursuing or carrying on the action before the Court of Session against such members of the Town Council as shall oppose the said David Methven's admission into the Town Council as Convener, and also against the said Andrew Finlay, in case he should be either proposed or defended in any such process. All which being considered by the said trade, and considering that every attempt of the Town Council to reject any Convener or Deacon is a gross infringment upon the priviledges of the Trades and their right of election."— Extracted from the MSS. *Records of St Andrews Hammermen Incorporation*, now deposited and preserved in St Mary's College, St Andrews.

MICHIE, JAMES.   High Street, Brechin, 1837.

MILLAR, ALEXANDER.   Edinburgh, 1766-82.

"Son of John Millar, turner in Edinburgh; bound apprentice to James Duff, 25th March 1766. Discharged of his indentures 2nd May 1772. Compeared and presented a petition, craving to be admitted a freeman 23rd November 1781. Compeared on 14th June 1782, and presented his essay, being a spring clock, begun, made, and finished in his own shop in presence of Alexander Dickie, landlord, Samuel Brown, George Aitken, John Sibbald, jun., essay masters as they declared, etc."—*E. H. Records.*

MILLAR, DAVID.   Bathgate, 1790.

MILLAR, GEORGE.   Stewart Street, Carluke, 1836.

MILLAR, JOHN.   Edinburgh, 1771-84.

Bound apprentice to Turnbull & Aitchison, 19th July 1777. Discharged of his indentures by Robert Aitchison, 8th May 1784.

MILLAR, JOHN.   Edinburgh, 1790.

"An Orrery to be sold at John Millar's, optician, Parliament Close, of a very elegant construction, wherein the planets perform their periodical revolutions and the earth her diurnal motion, all moving within a glass celestial sphere wherein the constellations are neatly delineated. The Orrery is kept in motion by a time-keeper which goes a month."—*Edinburgh Herald*, 1st January 1790.

MILLAR, PETER. Alloa, 1798.

MILLAR, RICHARD. Edinburgh, 1814-60.

"Compeared on 31st August 1814, and presented a petition craving to be admitted a freeman watchmaker in right of his wife, Helen, lawful daughter of the late James Clark, clockmaker in Edinburgh, which was granted. He paid six pounds as the first moiety of his entry money. Compeared 29th July 1815 and produced his essay, a clock movement begun, made, and finished in the presence of James Clark, as landlord, and John Bean, James Paterson, and John Picken, essay masters, as they declared. He was accordingly admitted, and paid six pounds as the second moiety of his entry money.—*E. H. Records.*

In partnership with Christopher Lawson (q.v.) 1825, and on dissolution of the firm of Lawson & Millar, issued the following :—

"NOTICE.—Richard Millar, Watch and Clock Manufacturer, begs leave to intimate to his numerous friends and to the public in general, that in consequence of a dissolution of that trade carried on by him and his late partner[1] he has opened that shop No. 5 North Bridge near head of east side, with an extensive assortment of the finest description of Gold and Silver Horizontal, Duplex, Lever, and plain watches, and where every exertion in his power shall be evinced to secure a continuance of that approbation and favour so largely bestowed on him, both as a partner in that concern and also for years previous, when in business on his own account.—Orders from the country punctually attended to. Good Clock Makers will meet with constant employment and the best encouragement."—*Edinburgh Evening Courant,* 23rd June 1825.

"TEN GUINEAS REWARD.—Lost on Tuesday night the 7th instant, a Gold repeating musical watch, gold face with a figure of a car drawn by a lion, with the initials P.M. on back, maker's name, Hry. Capt, a Geneve, Number on case bottom 483, with gold chain, two gold seals, with arms and initials. Any person returning the same to Mr Millar, watchmaker, No. 5 or at No. 14 North

---

[1] C. Lawson (q.v.)

Bridge, shall receive the above reward of ten guineas."—
Ibid., 4th March 1826.

"ATTEMPT AT HOUSEBREAKING.—About three
o'clock yesterday morning the watchman on the
North Bridge heard a strange noise below the shop
of Mr Millar, watchmaker, and going down the adjoining common stair, he discovered that a strong double
panelled door leading into a cellar below the shop had
been forced open. The watchman pursuing his search
entered into the cellar, and came upon a stout young
fellow attempting with a crowbar to force up the hatch
communicating between the cellar and the shop. He
was immediately taken into custody, and his case being
remitted to the Magistrates. It appears that he had
broken open the door of the cellar with the crowbar, and
there can be no doubt that but for the timely discovery
by the watchman the fellow would have eventually
succeeded in forcing up the hatch and gaining an
entrance into the shop. We understand that he is
quite a stranger to the police, and describes himself
to have come from Lanark."—*Ibid.*, 11th June 1833.

Richard Millar died 31st March 1860, aged 69 years.

MILLAR, ROBERT. 14 North Bridge, Edinburgh, 1826-38.

MILLAR, R. & SON. 44 North Bridge, Edinburgh, 1850.

MILLER, ALEXANDER. Methven Street, Perth, 1820.

MILLER, ALEXANDER. Montrose, 1798; died 26th
September 1808.

MILLER, ARCHIBALD. Castle-Douglas. *See* page 215.

MILLER, ARCHIBALD. Glasgow, 1781.

MILLER, ARCHIBALD. High Street, Kirkcudbright,
1820.

MILLER, ARCHIBALD & WILLIAM. 99 Graham Street,
Airdrie, 1835.

MILLER, ANDREW. 5 West Nicolson Street, Edinburgh, 1827.

Acquired Robert Logie's (q.v.) business at above
address about 1827. He was succeeded by his son, who
carried it on till his death in 1903. The business was
then carried on by another watchmaker, thus continuing
one of the oldest establishments in Edinburgh.

MILLER, GEORGE. Perth, 1811.

"On the 3rd January curt., the shop of Mr George Miller, George Street, Perth, was broke into and jewellery, watches, snuffboxes, and gold seals to the amount of £200 were stolen therefrom. The maker's name on two of the watches is George Miller, Perth, Nos. 171 and 80."—*Edinburgh Evening Courant*, 7th January 1811.

MILLER, JAMES. West Quay, Port Glasgow, 1820-38.

"Christian Buchanan or Miller, wife of J. Miller, watchmaker, Port Glasgow, served Heir Portr. General to her grandfather, Andrew Young, Cooper, Falkirk, dated 18th October 1825. Recorded 25th October 1825."—*Services of Heirs*.

MILLER, JAMES. Stormont Street, Perth, 1848.

MILLER, JAMES. Alloa, 1768.

Maker of the clock in the old steeple in Alloa Churchyard.

MILLER, JAMES. 41 George Street, Perth, 1845.

"At a meeting of the Society of Arts held in Edinburgh, 23rd January 1845, there were read descriptions of the following inventions by Mr James Miller:—1st. A telegraph; 2nd. An atmospheric railway; 3rd. A conical pivot for locomotive carriage axles in two parts; 4th. A substitute for bells and bell wires and cranks when laid under ground; 5th. On a substitute for railway bridges.

Mr Miller submits, that in small bridges for railways there is too great a rigidity when built of stone or brick, and that they are liable to be destroyed by their want of elasticity and their not yielding to the vibration of the train, and he suggests that they should be made of strong rings of iron upon which longitudinal iron bars should be riveted, somewhat in the form of a cooper's chaffer. They could be made at a distance in pieces and carried to the spot and then bolted together. Thanks voted by the meeting for the paper."

"Silver medal, value £3, awarded by the Society of Arts to Mr James Miller, Perth, for his model and description of a new self-acting method of throwing the shuttle in the common hand loom, 23rd February 1846. In this model an improvement is introduced, calculated in Mr Miller's opinion to prevent the recoil of the shuttle, viz., by interposing a driver as in the common loom. He has also made simple arrangements, by which the strength of the driving springs may be tempered or increased at pleasure."

MILLER, JOHN. Kirk Wynd, Selkirk, 1836.

MILLER, ROBERT. New Row, Perth, 1841.

MILLER, WILLIAM. 178 St Nicholas Street, Aberdeen, 1846.

MILLIGAN, ANDREW. Ayr, 1801.

"Ann Adamson or Milligan, wife of Andrew Milligan, watchmaker in Ayr, served Heir General to her father, Thomas Adamson, feuar in Creetown, dated 24th April 1801. Recorded 2nd May 1801."— *Services of Heirs.*

MILLIGAN, ANDREW, Watch Case Maker. Edinburgh, 1781-1810.

Married Susan Richardson, daughter of the deceased John Richardson, smith in Edinburgh, 2nd September 1781.

23rd November 1781.—"Compeared and presented a petition to be admitted freeman in right of his wife."

4th May 1782.—"Compeared and presented his essay, being a watch case, begun, made, and finished in his own shop, in presence of Robert Clidsdale, landlord, Normond Macpherson, James Howden, and Thomas Sibbald, essay masters, as they declared, which was found a well wrought essay, etc., and was accordingly admitted."—*E. H. Records.*

"A silver watch lost on Friday, 23rd curt., between Edinburgh and Dalkeith, maker's name Jaspar Tayler, Holborn, London, No. 573. Whoever has found it will be handsomely rewarded on delivering it to Mr John Rule, watchmaker, Kelso, or Andrew Milligan, watch case maker, Parliament Close, Edinburgh."—*Edinburgh Evening Courant*, 29th September 1791.

MILLIGAN, ANDREW, jun. Watch Case Maker, Milne's Court, Edinburgh, 1811.

"Andrew Milligan, son of the late Mr A. Milligan, watch case maker, returns sincere thanks to the friends of his father, and the public in general, for the liberal support he met with in that line during a period of more than forty years; respectfully informs them that he intends to carry on the business on his own account, and hopes by unremitting attention to merit a continuance of their favour."—*Edinburgh Evening Courant*, 5th October 1811.

MILNE, ALEXANDER. North Street, Aberdeen, 1820-37.

MILNE, GEORGE. Canongate, Edinburgh, 1725-54.

Married Margaret Sibbald, relict of William Burgess, gunsmith in Bristo, 6th February 1725.

"Lost betwixt Linlithgow and Falkirk on Wednesday, the 3rd inst., a silver watch, maker's name Jackson, London, No. 282. Whoever gives notice thereof to George Milne, watchmaker in Canongate, shall be sufficiently rewarded. *N.B.*—There is a scratch on the Bissel betwixt the place where the pendant comes through and the joint."—*Caledonian Mercury*, 8th October 1750.

MILNE, GEORGE. 29 Mealmarket Lane, Aberdeen, 1846.

MILNE, GIDEON. Edinburgh, 1676.

Apprenticed to Humphrey Milne, 12th January 1676.

MILNE, HUMPHREY, or UMPHRA MILLS. Edinburgh, 1660-92.

Supposed to have been admitted a freeman of the Edinburgh Hammermen in the year 1660—the leaf in records of that date having either been lost or stolen. An Act was passed in his favour in the year 1687, declaring the want of this leaf and their restoring to him all the priviledges of the Incorporation. To which part of the country he belonged we cannot definitely state but in all probability he was an Englishman. This surmise is strengthened by the unusual name, Humphrey and the fact that Richard Mills (q.v.), who succeeded him, was of that nationality. Be that as it may, what has come down of his handiwork bears testimony that he was master of his craft. We have only succeeded in locating where four of his clocks are to be found. One a fine specimen in the Museum of the Society of Antiquaries, Queen Street, Edinburgh; the other the property of Quintain Galbraith, Esq., Helensburgh, who kindly supplies the following information :—

"I have an old brass clock having four brass pillars forming a square, or rather an oblong, surmounted by a dome formed by the bell, the brass-engraved dial on one of the squares forms the front, and it has a saw-pierced ornament above the dial. The corresponding ornaments on the two sides are evidently castings taken from the front one, apparently of a later date and coarsely finished. The pinions of the driving wheels are just four pins cut out of the end of the spindle, the rack on the pulleys of the driving wheels being primitive, just a semi-circular spring that catches on to the four spokes of the driving-wheel. The fly of the fly-wheel is solid brass, about three-thirty seconds of an inch thick. The bell is $5\frac{1}{2}$ inches in diameter, domed $2\frac{3}{4}$ inches. The head of the hammer weighs $1\frac{1}{2}$ ounces, and is a nice bit of forging. Some of the small screw nails have square heads and are hand-made. The whole clock is about 12 inches high by $6\frac{1}{2}$ inches square, goes eight days, has ropes and weights, and a 39-inch pendulum. It has only the hour hand, there being no provision for two, the iron hand forged, parts incised, and ornamental in shape. The name, Humphry Mills, being engraved on the plain part of the fretted brass ornament above the dial."[1]

A third example, now the property of the Rev. Alex. T. Bell, Dundee, was discovered there in 1910, and, strange to say, in going order. The fourth and most unique is now in the possession of William B. Smith, Esq., 118 Queen Street, Glasgow, which was shown at the Glasgow Exhibition of 1911. A reference to the illustration facing page 268 shows its uniqueness, as the case (which is of oak) into which it is fixed has probably no equal in Scotland. Although there are plenty of long case clocks made by English makers contemporary

[1] A facsimile of this fret is given opposite page 256, and it is worth noting that, in all the four specimens mentioned, the frets are of the same design, which would imply that this was his favourite pattern.

LANTERN OR CHAMBER CLOCK

In unique oak case, by Humphrey Milne or Mills, Edinburgh
1600-02. Shown at Glasgow Memorial Exhibition, 1911.
The property of William B. Smith, Esq., Glasgow.

To face page.

with Humphrey Mills, few have the decorative treatment displayed in such a characteristic manner as this one has. It must be regarded as one of the first attempts in Scotland to break away from the orthodox make. We understand that this clock case is of the same design as a carved oak pulpit in the Parish Church of Fenwick, near Kilmarnock, which was erected between 1736 and 1760. This suggests that the clock was highly valued by its owner, who, long after Mills died, thought so much of it that he provided this beautiful case for it.

Further information about this maker will be found in the notes on the Magdalen Chapel Clock and Bell, page 235, and, supplementing what is given there, it would appear from an inspection of the MSS. Records of the Hammermen of Edinburgh that he was a wealthy man, as there are several entries relating to sums of money being borrowed from him, which shows his willingness to help them. They, in return for his kindness, elected him to the highest honour they could give him, namely, Deacon of the Incorporation. He died about the year 1622, having been over thirty years in business. An interesting sidelight is given in that valuable work, *Services of Heirs*, where we are informed that "Ester Ross or King, in Kirkcaldie, is served Co-Heir of Provision General to her grandmother, Jean Mathie, widow of Humphry Mills, watchmaker, Craig-wells, dated 18th June 1725."

MILNE, JAMES. St Ninian's, 1761-84.

MILNE, JOHN. Edinburgh, 1647-50. *See* note on Magdalen Chapel Clock and Bell, page 235.

MILNE, JOHN. Edinburgh, 1753.

MILNE, JOSEPH. Huntly, 1797.

MILNE, RICHARD, or MILLS. Edinburgh, 1661-1710.

AT THE MAGDALEN CHAPEL, *22nd July* 1661.— "The quilk day Richard Mylne, son lawful to Thomas Mylne, in the county of Stafford, is booked apprentice to Umphra Mylne, clockmaker, burgess of Edinburgh, conforme to the indenture passed between them."

5th September 1678.—" Compeared and presented his essay, viz., ane clock watch and luminary, and ane lock and key. His essay masters were John Alexander and James Foulis, his essay was made in his own shop, which was found a well-wrought essay, etc.

2nd May 1696.—" The House unanimously quits Richard Mylls his two shillings and sixpence sterling, that he is resting for being absent from meetings preceding this date, for certain good and onerous causes known to 'yair selvis.' "

11th September 1703. — " Elected boxmaster or Treasurer to the Incorporation of Hammermen of Edinburgh."

25th September 1703.—" The 'whilk' day, in presence of the haill house, Richard Mills, who was lately chosen boxmaster, having appeared before the Incorporation, declares he was very sorry that he was not able to officiate as boxmaster by reason of his old age, weakness, and inability of body, and therefor entreated the Incorporation to excuse him, and he should be very willing to give Fifty pounds presently to the succeeding boxmaster for the use of the poor.

" Which representation and desire of Richard Mills being taken into consideration by the haill house, they do thereby excuse the said Richard Mills from being boxmaster because of his inability and weakness as said is. And declare him free of the foresaid Act whereby he was chosen boxmaster ; he paying in the foresaid Fifty pounds to the succeeding boxmaster so soon as he shall call for the same. But the Incorporation do hereby declare that whatsomever freeman of the house who shall hereafter refuse to accept thereof shall be liable in the sum of one hundred pounds Scots without defalcation."

13th February 1705.—" The house, for certain considerations moving them, do quit and free Richard Mills, ten pound of the Fifty pound Scots that he was appointed to pay for refusing to be boxmaster, notwithstanding of the former Act against him for Fifty pounds."—*E. H. Records.*

The only other contemporary notice of Richard Mills which we have been enabled to glean occurs in a number of one of our earliest Scots newspapers, viz., *The Edinburgh Gazette* for the year 1699:—

"Stolen out of a house near the West Port on the 19th, a gold watch with a steel chain and a shagreen case. Whoever can bring the said watch to Richard Mills, watchmaker in Edinburgh, shall have two guineas reward."

Richard Mills died about the close of the year 1710, which is brought out in the minute dealing with his last booked apprentice, John Wilson (q.v.), but, strange to say, no particulars of any clock bearing his name has reached us. A correspondent in the *Weekly Scotsman* supplies the following information:—"I have a recollection of seeing a clock bearing his name and the date 1710. In any case he had in 1698 a charter from the town of a tenement in the Canongate on the east side of Leith Wynd. The writ confirmed to him as Richard Mills, clockmaker, burgess of Edinburgh, and to Esther Mills (perhaps his sister), spouse of Robert Carstairs, W.S., the tenement in question, which had been granted to Richard and Esther in 1693 by Humphrey Mills, clockmaker at the Craigwell, etc."

This interesting note, read in conjunction with the last given in the notes on Humphrey Mills, reveals the close relationship of these two men, namely, uncle and nephew.

MILNE, ROBERT. Queen Street, Aberdeen, 1821.

MILNE, ROBERT. 50 High Street, Montrose, 1837.

MILNE, THOMAS. Huntly, 1780.

MILNE, WILLIAM. Dunfermline, 1842.

MITCHELL, ALEXANDER. Gorbals, Glasgow, 1798.

"Stolen from a house in the neighbourhood of Pollokshaws, a capt. silver watch, name Alexander Mitchell & Son, Glasgow, No. 257. Any person bringing the same to Alexander Mitchell, Gorbals, will receive one guinea reward."—*Glasgow Chronicle*, 21st June 1798.

MITCHELL, ALEXANDER. Glasgow, 1822-47. *See* Alexander Mitchell & Son, Gorbals.

MITCHELL, ALEXANDER & SON.   Gorbals, and 10
   Gallowgate Street, Glasgow, 1798-1837.

   "Alexander Mitchell & Son, sensible of the very
liberal share of employment they have long received
from their friends and public, beg leave to return them
their sincere thanks, and to inform them in addition to
the shop in Gorbals where the business is still carried
on, William Mitchell has opened the shop, No. 10
Gallowgate Street, Glasgow, where he has laid in an
assortment of Gold, Silver, and Metal Horizontal seconds,
day, month, hunting cap'd, jewelled, and plain watches.
Clocks and Cases, Time Pieces, Gold, Silver, Gilt and
Steel Chains, Seals and Keys, Silk Strings, Pebble Seals,
Gold Rings, Silver Plate, etc.   W. M. most respectfully
informs the trade that he has a stock of Watch and
Clock Tools and Materials consisting of Clock brass and
steel work, Dials, Weights, Bells, Hands, etc., Watch
springs, Dials to suit, with or without brass edges,
finished wheels and pinions, fine oil, best Lancashire and
Sheffield files, with most of the articles necessary in the
business, which have all been purchased from the best
makers, and will be sold on the most moderate terms.
No exertion will be wanting to render the assortment
still more complete.   Orders carefully and expeditiously
answered."—*Glasgow Courier*, 12th July 1798.

   "GOLD WATCH LOST.—There was dropped in
Glasgow on Tuesday last, a gold watch, caped and
jewelled, horizontal watch, No. 1791, with gold chain
and seal.   Whoever will bring it to William Mitchell,
watchmaker, Gallowgate, shall receive two guineas
reward."—*Ibid.*, 22nd January 1801.

   "Patent granted unto William Mitchell of Glasgow,
watchmaker, and John Lawton, King Street, Snowhill,
London, manufacturer, for their improved lock and key
applicable to various purposes, 7th March 1815.

   "Alexander Mitchell, Clockmaker and Jeweller,
served Heir General to his father, William Mitchell,
Clockmaker and Jeweller, dated 13th December 1837.
Recorded 5th January 1838."—*Services of Heirs.*

MITCHELL, JAMES.   Saltcoats, 1810.

MITCHELL, JOHN & WILLIAM.   80 Argyle Street,
   Glasgow, 1836.

MITCHELL, WALTER. Edinburgh, 1749.

Son of John Mitchell, mariner; booked apprentice to James Geddes, 13th November 1749.

MITCHELL, WILLIAM. St Nicholas Street, Aberdeen, 1820.

MITCHELL, WILLIAM. Gallowgate, Glasgow, 1798-1838. *See* A. Mitchell & Son, Gorbals.

MITCHELL, BISHOP, of Aberdeen, who was deposed of office in 1638, but afterwards reinstated, during his exile in Holland made a livelihood as a clock and watch maker. Was a native of Garvock.

MITCHELL & RUSSELL. Glasgow, 1803-41.

"A gold watch lost on Wednesday afternoon on the road from Kilwinning to Glasgow, by Irvine and Stewarton, double-cased, with a figured dial, to which was suspended, by a black and yellow ribbon, a gold seal with a Shakespeare head on it, and a gold key. Those who will bring the said watch to Mitchell and Russell, watchmakers, Glasgow, will receive two guineas reward."—*Glasgow Courier*, 24th January 1803.

"Lost, a jewelled cased gold watch, with a gold chain and gilt key, no name or number. If found, apply to Mitchell & Russell, watchmakers, who, upon receiving it, will give a reward of one guinea."—*Ibid.*, 26th March 1805.

"TURRET OR STEEPLE CLOCKS.—Mitchell & Russell, Clockmakers, etc., have just now for sale two second-hand steeple clocks, of the largest size, which, being thoroughly repaired, are little inferior to new ones, and at prices less than half their original cost.

"M. & R. manufacture every variety of clocks for church and other towers. They have also a superior method of illuminating the dials of public clocks, which, considering the advantage obtained, can be done at a comparatively small expense, 2 Argyll Street, Glasgow."—*The Witness*, 20th May 1840.

MITCHELSON, ALEXANDER. Edinburgh, 1752-61.

"Son of James Mitchelson of Garcropper, in the Shire of Galloway; booked apprentice to William Nicol, 8th February 1752. Discharged of his indentures 14th November 1761."—*E. H. Records.*

MITCHELSON, JAMES. Edinburgh ; died 1755.

MITCHELSON, JOHN. Edinburgh, 1749-56.

"Late apprentice to James Geddes, clock and watch maker, deceased ; transferred by the Incorporation to Robert Clidsdale, for the space yet to run of his indentures, 11th May 1756. Discharged of his indentures 20th December 1756."—*E. H. Records.*

MOFFAT, ALEXANDER. Musselburgh, 1790-1831.

MOFFAT, JAMES. Son of above. 7 High Street, Fisherrow, Musselburgh, 1831.

"James Moffat in Musselburgh, served Heir in General to his father, Alexander Moffat, watchmaker there, dated 1st March 1831. Recorded 9th March 1831."—*Services of Heirs.*

MOLLISON, CHARLES. Edinburgh, 1770-87.

"Bound apprentice to Turnbull & Aitchison, 6th April 1770. Discharged of his indentures, 3rd May 1777. Presented a petition craving to be admitted freeman 29th January 1785. Compeared on 12th November 1785, and produced his essay, being a plain watch movement made in his own shop in presence of Robert Aitchison, landlord, Laurence Dalgleish, and William White, essay masters, as they declared, etc."—*E. H. Records.*

"A WATCH LOST.—That about the beginning of November last, there was lost upon the Gallawater Road a silver watch, maker, as far as the owner remembers, John Martin, London, No. 804 or 408. The watch had an inner case and a shagreen outer case, very much worn. Whoever will deliver the said watch to Mr Charles Mollison, watchmaker in the Lawnmarket, shall receive one guinea of a reward."—*Caledonian Mercury,* 11th January 1787.

MONRO, GEORGE. Canongate, Edinburgh, 1743-1804.

Married Mary Alexander, daughter to the deceased James Alexander, distiller in Stirling, 15th December 1757.

Was admitted a freeman clock and watch maker in Canongate Hammermen 28th November 1750. Not only was he a most capable craftsman, but also one of the most enterprising tradesmen in Edinburgh. This will be best seen by the following selection of advertisements which he issued in the local newspapers, and will show the methods he adopted to build up one of the most extensive businesses in Edinburgh. Probably there was not a craftsman in the city during the latter half of the eighteenth century who advertised so largely, the result being that the name of George Monro and his productions were known all over the country, especially north of the Forth.

His success, however, did not please the members of the Incorporation of Edinburgh Hammermen, which the following minute, dated 1755, brings out:—

"George Monro, watchmaker, having applied to this house by his missive letter dated 8th February 1755, directed to Deacon Armstrong, setting forth that he had spoke to him last year, concerning his inclination to remove from the north side to the south side of the Canongate, where he apprehended he could have a house somewhat more convenient than he had at present on the north side. That he proposed to do so in hopes that this Incorporation would allow it upon a small yearly payment to them. That last year, having found it necessary to continue a year longer in his present possession, there was no further use insisting on it, but now craving that it would please the Incorporation to allow the aforesaid favour which could be no hurt to them."

"Which letter being read and considered by the house, they refused the desire thereof."—*E. H. Records.*

"To be sold by George Monro, watchmaker in the head of Canongate, Edinburgh, a large assortment of new watches, viz., enamelled, set in gold, chased do., plain do., pinchbeck do., of the most fashionable kinds for ladies and gentlemen, the work being as good as if they were in gold cases; variety of silver do. As the above watches are all manufactured by his own hands, their goodness and soundness may be depended upon.

"*N.B.*—He has also a shop at Inverness, and keeps

a person there well qualified for repairing clocks and watches in the best manner, where gentlemen may be served in new clocks and watches of all kinds, and at the same prices as at Edinburgh or London. Commissions given in there or at his shop in Canongate will be faithfully answered."—*Edinburgh Evening Courant*, 31st January 1758.

"Wanted a journeyman Clockmaker of a good character that can make a good clock; he shall have good wages, and after working some time at clock-making may be taught watchmaking upon reasonable terms if he pleases. Wanted also one or two apprentices to be taught watchmaking. Inquire at George Monro, watchmaker in Canongate, Edinburgh."—*Ibid.*, 16th September 1761.

"George Monro, watchmaker in the Canongate, has made ready for sale a parcel of exceeding sound Scots Watches. Some of them are for Doctors, having the seconds from the centre, made after a plain and simple method, which must go very well and can be sold at very moderate prices.

"*N.B.*—He intends to begin a clock and watch club about the end of the month. Those that want a clock or watch in that way may send their names betwixt and that time."—*Caledonian Mercury*, 14th January 1764.

"On the 27th April 1769, George Monro, clockmaker, Edinburgh, advises the Magistrates of Nairn that he has shipped, by Colonel Hector Monro's order (their member of Parliament), a new steeple clock for the town. He assures them he has proved the clock and it goes well, and he believes it to be as good a clock as in Scotland for its size."—L. SHAW'S *History of the Province of Moray*.

"New silver watch, London, made to be sold by George Monro, watchmaker in Canongate, good and strong, at a low price for ready money, being the stock of one gone wrong, so that a great pennyworth may be had on calling soon before the completion of said sale; also a few of the best Edinburgh shade watches, which he can warrant to be very strong and cheap at different prices."—*Caledonian Mercury*, 6th May 1769.

"To be sold by George Monro, watchmaker in Canongate Head, Edinburgh, an exceedingly good clock dial or regulator showing the hours and minutes, two opposite airths, on the outside of the house where it is placed. Its dial boards are 26 inches in diameter, and its projection from the wall to the centre of the dial boards are 4 feet 2 inches. The clock within the house which turns the hands of the outside dials goes eight days, and has a white dial plate 12 inches square, showing the hours and minutes within the house as well as without, so that the hands without are set by turning them within.

" It is no more trouble or expense to keep it agoing than a plain eight-day clock, and it is so made that the weather cannot hurt it. It was made by the late George Scott (q.v.), who was known to excel in the art of making that kind of clock. It goes with great exactness, is preserved in good order, the woodwork is lately renewed ; it will answer for a country town, street, or manufactory. Also a handsome new eight-day clock in mahogany case resembling tortoise-shell, mounted with Corinthian capitals.

" *N.B.*—As the above George Monro has been at greater expense and labour than any in his way in this country to bring his clock and watch engines to the greatest degree of perfection, by which he can make it appear he can serve those who please to favour him with their employment, with goods equal if not superior in quality to any hitherto manufactured in this country."—*Ibid.*, 7th September 1771.

" IMPROVEMENT UPON HORIZONTAL AND PLAIN WATCHES.—The virtue and utility of watch jewelling is obvious to all watchmakers, and has been practised by the most eminent of them since discovery, but they never extended this valuable improvement any further than in jewelling the last and swiftest moving wheel commonly called the balance.

" George Monro, watchmaker in Canongate Head, Edinburgh, has found out a method of extending this invention of watch jewelling to three more of the swiftest wheels of the watch, by which the watch will go three degrees better, last three times longer, and will go without cleaning to better purpose for six years than the best watch, made without this improvement, can go two. The advantages of this additional jewelling are as follows :—The pivots that move in those jewels or hard bushes are never galled nor impaired by the motion of the one into the other, and go with much less friction and greater velocity than a wheel moving in brass, for brass corrupts and putrifics the oil, and turns it sometimes in half a year to a thick substance which clogs the wheels and roughens the pivots, making them stand in need of repairs, commonly in one year, or two at the most. So soon as this alteration is made by the oil and the motion of the watch, it becomes very variable, although made of the finest workmanship.

"As a demonstration of what is here advanced, George Monro has made, and has now for sale, a silver horizontal watch, caped and jewelled as above described, with some other curious and necessary improvements; one of them is a diamond hand resembling three moving stars or planets revolving every minute. This is the best construction of a second or stop watch, as it consists of not one wheel more than the plainest watch; besides, it is in other respects better qualified for measuring time than any other invented.

"*N.B.*—Good old watches made by noted watchmakers, if in good condition, can have this new improvement applied to them as well as new watches, by which they will be made to measure time with much more exactness than they did at first. Noblemen and gentlemen that please to favour George Monro with their employment may depend upon being served with the greatest care and despatch. The expense of jewelling is one guinea a wheel."—*Edinburgh Evening Courant*, 25th January 1774.

"A GOLD WATCH CLUB.—George Monro, watch maker and watch jeweller in Canongate Head, Edinburgh, proposes to take in subscribers' names for a gold watch club; at which club gentlemen shall be served in the best gold watches, of any fashion they choose, horizontal or plain, chased or engraved, from eighteen guineas to thirty guineas, they paying monthly in proportion to the value of the watch they choose.

"A specimen of the said watches is to be seen at his shop. Those who live in town or country may be served in this manner without being put to the trouble to attend the club, by sending their monthly payment the day before the club meets, or appointing a friend to act in their place. They will be as carefully drawn for as if they were present.

"*N.B.*—New gold, silver, and pinchbeck watches of

the best kind and of different qualities, very fine spring clocks and spring alarms. House clocks, in mahogany and wainscot cases, ready to be sold at the lowest prices. Continues to jewel old gold and silver watches, which greatly improves their going, and is a great preservation to them. He gives the highest price for old gold and silver watches in exchange for new ones."
—*Caledonian Mercury*, 2nd August 1777.

" A SALE OF GOLD, SILVER, AND PINCHBECK WATCHES AND SPRING CLOCKS. — George Monro, watch maker and watch jeweller, has now opened a laigh shop opposite to the White Horse Inn, Canongate Head, Edinburgh ; has now ready for sale the following kinds of Clocks and Watches :—The first parcel consists of a Gold Horizontal Watch with seconds. This watch is of the greatest value to gentlemen going long voyages, as it measures time with much more exactness than other watches. It will also go four or five years without cleaning ; and, if they should go six or seven years without cleaning, it will be without damage to the watch. Besides, of all other watches they are the soonest brought to time after cleaning, and must continue much longer regular going than any hitherto invented."—*Ibid.*, 14th August 1779.

" To be sold, two houses in Maitland's Lane, Canongate, one of six rooms, kitchen, garret, and cellar, as lately possessed by Major Melvill of Cairney ; the other, of three rooms, kitchen, and cellar, as lately possessed by George Monro, watchmaker, now by Mr Schetky ; both free of vermin and smoke." — *Edinburgh Evening Courant*, 29th November 1779.

"George Monro, watchmaker, inventor of the extension of watch jewelling by liquid steel bushes, is now moved from the Canongate Head to the East End of Rose Street, New Edinburgh, where he carries on his business of Watch and Clock Making in all their branches, and has ready one of these fine watches with the jewelling extended in gold, which goes with much more exactness than any watch made upon the common principle of brass bushes. Noblemen, Gentlemen, or Ladies that have good old watches of their ancestors that they may 'chuse' to improve in going by applying this new invention, they will go more regular than when first made."—*Edinburgh Advertiser*, 15th July 1788.

Admitted a member of Lodge St David, Edinburgh, 16th January 1754.

"Died at his house in Canongate, at the advanced age of 80, Mr George Monro, sometime watchmaker in Edinburgh."—Obituary notice in *Edinburgh Evening Courant*, 18th October 1804.

MONRO, HECTOR. 40 Bridge Street, Leith, 1836; died at Couper Street, Leith, 22nd March 1847.

MONRO, HUGH. 7 West Bow, Edinburgh, 1825.

MONRO, HUNTER. Edinburgh, 1804. Bound apprentice to James Howden, 13th September 1804.

MONTEITH, JAMES. Edinburgh, 1781.

MOORE, GEORGE. Cumnock, Ayrshire, 1837-50.

MORGAN, DONALD. Bridge Street, Kirkwall, Orkney, 1845.

MORGAN, THOMAS. Edinburgh, 1767-1803.
Married Elizabeth Bayne, 18th April 1788.

"Booked apprentice to William Nicoll, 20th November 1767. Thomas Morgan, sometime apprentice to the deceased William Nicoll, presented his bill craving to be admitted a freeman on 4th May 1776. Compeared on 18th November 1776, and produced his essay, being a plain watch movement begun, made, and finished in his own shop in presence of Samuel Brown, landlord, Laurence Dalgleish, James Gray, and Thomas Sibbald, essay masters as they declared, etc."—*E. H. Records*.

"On Tuesday the 1st January, between the hours of ten and twelve o'clock forenoon, was dropped between St John Street and the meeting-house in Carrubber's Close the gold chased case of a lady's watch. Any person who has found it is desired to return it to Thomas Morgan, watchmaker, who is empowered to give a handsome reward.

"*N.B.*—If offered to sale, it is entreated to be stopped, and information given as above mentioned."—*Caledonian Mercury*, 4th January 1779.

"Lost on the 3rd day of October current, on the road either between Lauder and Greenlaw and Dunse, a large silver repeating watch, maker's name John May, London, with a steel chain. Whoever has found the same, upon informing or delivering it to Thomas Morgan, watchmaker, Edinburgh, or to Mrs Buchan, innkeeper, Greenlaw, or George Purves, innkeeper at Dunse, shall be handsomely rewarded. All watchmakers, jewellers, etc., are requested to stop the watch if offered for sale."—*Ibid.*, 14th October 1780.

"T. Morgan respectfully acquaints his friends and the public that he has moved from his late shop in the Clam Shell, Turnpike, High Street, to No. 30, east side of South Bridge, where he will continue to carry on the watch and clock making in all its branches. He has at present an elegant variety of plain and ornamented Gold, Silver, and Pinchbeck Watches, also elegant spring quarter clocks of all sorts. Barometers and Thermometers made and repaired upon the shortest notice."— *Edinburgh Advertiser*, 3rd March 1789.

"T. Morgan embraces the opportunity to return his grateful acknowledgments to his friends and the public for their very liberal countenance towards him hitherto in the way of his profession, and begs leave to acquaint them that he has removed from his former shop on South Bridge to a more commodious shop, No. 1 Infirmary Street, where he intends to carry on the clock and watch making business in all its branches and on the lowest terms. J. M. at present is provided with an excellent stock of clocks and watches and timepieces of all descriptions, particularly spring or table clocks, together with a variety of articles in the jewellery line, all well deserving the notice of purchasers. Clocks and Watches repaired and mended as usual with care and attention."—*Caledonian Mercury*, 21st May 1803.

MORISON, WILLIAM. Drysdale Street, Alloa, 1841.

"Takes this opportunity of returning his sincere thanks to those who have favoured him with their liberal support in the above line. With a continued attention to business, he humbly hopes to merit a share of public favour. W. M. has always on hand for sale a quantity of jewellery and watches which he is determined to sell on reasonable terms."—*Alloa Monthly Advertiser*, 2nd January 1841.

MORRISON, ALEXANDER. 252 Argyle Street, Glasgow, 1837.

MORRISON, GEORGE. Aberdeen, 1792.

MORRISON, George. Auchtermuchty, 1795.

MORRISON, John. Edinburgh, 1787-94.
Bound apprentice to David Murray, 10th April 1787.
Discharged of his indentures 1st November 1794.

MORRISON, Theodore. Bridge of Dee, Aberdeen, 1846.

MORRISON, William. King Street, Glasgow, 1820.

MORRISON & M'EWEN. Leith Street, Edinburgh, 1849.

MORTIMER, William. Lower Castle Street, Cullen, 1837.

MORTIMER, William. Portsoy, 1837.

MORTON, James. Dunbar; died 12th December 1836.

MORTON, Robert S. Dunbar, 1837.

MOSELY, M. King Street, Glasgow, 1825.

MOSSMAN & SON. 12 North Bridge and Princes Street, Edinburgh, 1813-1906.

MUIR, James. Glasgow, 1792.

MUIR, Robert. Drakemyr, Dalry, Ayrshire, 1850.

MUIRHEAD, ——. 33 Nelson Street, Glasgow, 1838.

MUIRHEAD, Henry. Montague Street, Rothesay, 1836.

MUIRHEAD, Henry. Royal Exchange Place, Glasgow, 1839.

MUIRHEAD, James. Glasgow, 1823.

MUIRHEAD, James. 90 Buchanan Street, Glasgow, 1817-41.

MUNRO, Dugald. Aberfeldie, 1837.

MUNRO, Hugh. Dollar, 1837.

MUNRO, John. Edinburgh, 1783.

MURDOCH, Andrew. 20 St Andrew Square, Glasgow, 1828.

MURDOCH, James. Bridge Street, Ayr, 1837.

MURDOCH, James. Tarbolton, 1850.

MURDOCH, James & Son. Main Street, Ayr, 1820-50.

MURDOCH, John. Edinburgh, 1752-75.

"Bound apprentice to Andrew Dickie, 30th October 1752; discharged of his indentures, 17th November 1759. John Murdoch, late apprentice to the deceased Andrew Dickie; compeared on 31st July 1767 and produced his essay, being a finished watch movement begun, made, and finished in his own shop in the presence of Daniel Binny, landlord, Robert Clidsdale, Normand Macpherson, and James Auchterlony, essay masters as they declared, etc."—*E. H. Records.*

MURDOCH, John. Son of above; booked apprentice to his father, 13th April 1767.

MURRAY, David. Edinburgh, 1769-1832.

"Born 17th October 1755; died 3rd January 1832; buried in the Greyfriars Churchyard, Edinburgh; booked apprentice to James Cowan, 16th January 1769. Compeared and presented a bill craving to be admitted a freeman, 22nd February 1779. Compeared and presented his essay, being a plain watch movement, made and finished in presence of James Howden, landlord; James Cowan, Samuel Brown, and Thomas Sibbald, essay masters as they declared, etc., on 14th July 1779."—*E. H. Records.*

"Lost on the 13th of June, between Crossford and Gateside near Dunfermline, a silver watch, out case engraved marked J. D. S., maker's name D. Edmonds, Liverpool, No. 161. Whoever has found her may apply to David Murray, watchmaker, Lawnmarket, Edinburgh, who will give a handsome reward."—*Edinburgh Evening Courant,* 12th July 1787.

MURRAY, George. Lochnell Street, Lochgilphead, 1837.

MURRAY, George. Doune, 1798.

MURRAY, James. Perth, 1790.

Apprenticed to James Young, Perth, 1790.

MURRAY, James. Moffat and London, 1823.

"The Lords Commissioners of the Admiralty having advertised a premium of £300 for the best Chronometer which should be kept at Greenwich for one year, thirty-six were sent thither by the principal chronometer

maker in London, and were kept in 1823. It was
announced that if any chronometer varied six seconds
it could not obtain a prize. At the end of the year the
prize was decided to be gained by Mr James Murray, of
Cornhill, whose instrument on no one month varied
more than one second and eleven hundred parts of a
second. This distinguished artist, who had the honour
of producing the best instrument ever known, is a
native of Moffat in Dumfries. The Chronometer is
now sent out with Captain Parry."—*Glasgow Mechanics'
Magazine*, 1825, vol. ii., page 145.

MURRAY, John. Lanark, 1790.

MURRAY, John. Aberdeen, 1843.

MURRAY, Robert. Lauder, 1837.

MURRAY, R. & R. Lauder. *See* page 220.

MURRAY, William. Edinburgh, 1706.

Son to William Murray, merchant, Edinburgh;
booked apprentice to Thomas Gordon, 9th February 1706.

MYLES, George. Edinburgh, 1676.

Son lawful to John Myles; booked apprentice to
Humphrey Milne or Mills, 12th January 1676.

MYLNE, J. A. Montrose, 1740.

MYLNE, James. Windmill Street, Edinburgh, 1793.

MYLNE, James. West Register Street, Edinburgh, 1793.

NAPIER, Thomas. Glasgow, 1789-1803.

"Lost on Monday, 12th December, a silver watch,
maker's name Thomas Napier, Glasgow, No. 1688. A
cornelian seal set in gold affixed to it by a black silk
ribbon. Whoever will bring it to the *Courier* office
will be handsomely rewarded."—*Glasgow Courier*, 14th
December 1803.

NAPIER & DUNN. Head of Stockwell, Glasgow, 1783.

NEALL, James. Edinburgh, 1775.

Bound apprentice to Turnbull & Aitchison, 28th
January 1775.

NEILL, John. Glasgow, 1627-49. *See* page 161.

NEILSON, George. 50 Friars Vennel, Dumfries, 1820.

NEILSON, JOHN. Glasgow, 1810-17.

"On the 7th of March a boy came into the shop of John Neilson, watchmaker, and said he wished to purchase a watch. The boy appearing to be only 12 or 13 years of age, the watchmaker asked at him how much money he had; he said he did not know. He then asked leave to count it, which the boy allowed him to do. On asking some further questions anent the money, he said he got it from an uncle in Tollcross. The watchmaker then told him to bring his uncle and he would either get his money or a watch. The boy ran off and has never yet appeared. Any person who can give information concerning this boy or the money will be satisfied by applying at 94 Gallowgate, Glasgow."
—*Glasgow Courier*, 31st March 1812.

"Early on Wednesday morning the shop of Mr John Neilson, watchmaker, Gallowgate, Glasgow, near the foot of Campbell Street, was broken into, and about 100 watches, besides seals, chains, etc., amounting in value to £500 carried away. The thieves entered by cutting the window above a back door, and made their escape by the front door, which was bolted in the inside. A person with a screw-driver in his possession was secured about two o'clock near the spot by the watchman after considerable resistance, and is now in custody. He, we understand, is an old offender, and the marks on the window which was broken open exactly fit the screw-driver. It is strongly suspected that a considerable party had been engaged in the robbery. About the time it happened a disturbance, no doubt intentional, took place in Kent Street, which drew the attention of the watchmen from their respective stations on the spot; the consequence was the villains were enabled to commit their depredations with less chance of it being detected."
—*Edinburgh Advertiser*, 6th June 1817.

NEVAY, WILLIAM. Castle Street, Forfar, 1837.

NEWLANDS, L. F. 130 Trongate, Glasgow, 1816.

NEWLANDS, JAMES & LUKE. Glasgow, 1823.

NICHOLSON, JOHN. 52 Bridge Street, Berwick-on-Tweed, 1837.

NICHOLSON, RICHARD. Bridge Street, Berwick-on-Tweed, 1806-22.

NICOL, James. Mill Lane, Kilmarnock, 1850.

NICOL, Joseph. Coupar Angus, 1801-37.

"Mary or May Edward or Nicoll, wife of Joseph Nicoll, watchmaker in Coupar Angus, served Heir General to her father, John Edward, Flesher there, dated 10th July 1801. Recorded 7th August 1801."— *Services of Heirs.*

NICOLL, James, or NICCOLL. Canongate, Edinburgh, 1721-60.

Apprenticed to Alexander Brand, 1721. Admitted freeman clock and watch maker, Canongate Hammermen, 2nd July 1729.

This individual was present at the execution of Andrew Wilson, when the spectators were fired on by command of Captain Porteous. The story is most graphically described in Sir Walter Scott's *Heart of Midlothian.* We give Nicoll's evidence as it is reported in the volume of *State Trials,* for the year 1736 when the occurrence took place :—

"James Nicoll, watchmaker in Canongate, aged 36 years or thereby, married,[1] solemnly sworn, purged of malice, partial council examined and interrogated, deponed, that he was present, time and place libelled, at the execution of Andrew Wilson, and that he did observe panel, fire his gun, holding it straight before him amongst the multitude there assembled ; and as he heard the report of the gun, so he observed the smoke of the powder coming from the gun, and this shot was the first he heard upon that occasion, and the panel when thus fired was standing betwixt the gibbet and one Mr Cunninghame's shop on the north side of the street, near the north-east end of the scaffold ' Causa Scientie Patet.' And this is the truth as he shall answer to God.—*Sic Subscribitur,* JAMES NICOLL and DAVID ERSKINE."

A capital example of this maker's handiwork is now

[1] He apparently was married twice, for according to the *Edinburgh Register of Marriages,* his name appears as having married Charlotta Bachelor, residenter in Edinburgh, 19th March 1748. Of course, it might be a son of his that this last date refers to, but no evidence is available as to relationship.

LONG CASE CLOCK,

In mahogany case. By James
Nicol, Edinburgh, 1721-62. The
property of the Royal Bank of
Scotland, Edinburgh. (See p. 286.)

LONG CASE CLOCK,

In oak case. By Thomas Gordon,
Edinburgh, 1688-1743. The property
of John Whimster, Esq., St Mary's,
Ontario, Canada. (See p. 168.)

located in one of the rooms of the Royal Bank of Scotland, St Andrew Square, Edinburgh, and it is worth noting that although the surname on this particular clock is spelt " Niccoll " instead of " Nicoll," this difference may be due rather to the vagary of the engraver than to any attempt of the maker to spell his surname with the two c's.

NICOLL, WILLIAM. Edinburgh, 1740-75.

Married 28th April 1745.

" Booked apprentice to Patrick Gordon, 1740. Compeared 4th June 1748, and presented a bill craving to be admitted a freeman clock and watch maker. Compeared on 16th Sept. 1748, and presented his essay, viz., a plain eight-day clock, which was found to be a well wrought essay, etc. His essay masters were John Brown, Alexander Brand, and William Richardson. His essay was made in his own shop, and Patrick Gordon, landlord."— *E. H. Records.*

" Lost on Thursday night, the 27th April 1750, betwixt Todrick's Wynd and the Fish Market Close, a fashionable silver watch, maker's name William Liptrot, London, No. 205. If any can give account of it let them call at William Nicoll, watchmaker, first turnpike above Bell's Wynd, Edinburgh, where they will be rewarded for their trouble."—*Caledonian Mercury*, 7th May 1750.

" Sarah Nicoll or Ramage, wife of William Nicoll, watchmaker, Edinburgh, served Heir Portioner General to her uncle, George Ramsay, Shipmaster, Linktown of Arnot, dated 3rd July 1753."—*Services of Heirs.*

" Lost on Saturday, the 7th instant, betwixt the Abbey Hill and Jock's Lodge, a large silver watch, maker's name Deschurines, London, without a number, with a gold rim round the glass, and with a shagreen case studded with Pinchbeck ; a black leather string with a small padlock key and the watch key hanging to it. Whoever will bring the same to Mr William Nicoll, watchmaker, Back of the Guard, Edinburgh, shall receive a handsome reward."—*Ibid.*, 10th June 1755.

" There was lost on Wednesday last betwixt the east corner of the Meadows and the Cage, a silver watch, maker's name William Nicoll, Edinburgh, No. 70.

Whoever returns the same to Mr William Nicoll, watchmaker, at the Back of the Guard, Edinburgh, shall have half a guinea reward and no questions asked."—*Edinburgh Evening Courant*, 25th May 1767.

"Lost by a Lady on Wednesday the 6th instant, at Mr Strange's ball or going home in the chair, the 'outwart' case of a watch 'chassed' in gold, and whoever has found the same and will bring it to William Nicoll, watchmaker, at the Back of the Guard, shall have one guinea reward and no questions asked."—*Caledonian Mercury*, 9th March 1771.

NIMMO, ALEXANDER. High Street, Kirkcaldy, 1820.

NIMMO, ALEXANDER. Leith, 1819.

NIMMO, J. New Quay, Leith, 1806.

NISBET, JAMES. Edinburgh, 1760.

Booked apprentice to Daniel Binny, 8th Nov. 1760.

NOBLE, JOHN. Perth, 1791.

Apprenticed to James Greig, 1791.

NORRIE, DAVID. Leith, 1787-1811.

Admitted freeman clock and watch maker, Canongate Hammermen, 16th November 1787; was in business New Quay, Leith, up to 1801; continued by his widow in North Leith up to 1811.

OGG, HENDRIE. High Street, Dunfermline, 1820.

OGG & M'MILLAN. 30 Regent Quay, Aberdeen, 1846.

OLIPHANT, ALEXANDER. Anstruther Easter.

Nephew of John Smith, Pittenweem; born on 18th June 1784, at Pittenweem; served his apprenticeship with his uncle; started business in Anstruther Easter about 1818. Clock made by him in possession of his grandson Mr Oliphant, Stenton House, Elie, Fife.

OLIPHANT, ALEXANDER. Shore, Anstruther, 1837.

OLIPHANT, ALEXANDER. Pittenweem, 1815-40.

ORR, JAMES. East Breast, Greenock, 1817.

ORR, WILLIAM. Bradshaw Street, Saltcoats, 1850.

OTT, WILLIAM. 48 Leith Street, Edinburgh, 1850.

PAISLEY—Notices regarding the Common Clock of, 1603.

22nd November 1603.—" The quhilk day it is aggreit betwix the Baillies and Counsell of this burgh of Paisley on the ane pairt, John Wallace, Smythe, and Thomas Quytfurd, cautioner for him, on the other pairt, that the said John Wallace sall not onlie keip and oyill the knock, and gif onie pairt thairof breckis that scho [so] neids mending, he sall mak and mend the samin upon his awin expensis, and als sall ring and knell the samin ilk nicht at ten houris at even, for the space of ane yeir next efter the dait heirof, for the quhilk causis and for the said John Wallace making of ane quheel quhilk wes broken of the said knock, mending and graithing of hir, and keeping of the samin in order for the said space of ane yeir, and for making of ane iron band or clasp to the Brig Port, the Baillies and Counsell actet and obleist thame to caus thar Treasurer pay to the said John Wallace the sowme of ten merkis fyve schilling usuall money of this realm for his wark, expensis, travell, and painis in mending and keeping of the said knock."— Extracted from the *Burgh Records of Paisley*, 1902. Edited with an introduction by W. M. Metcalfe, D.D., F.S.A. Scot.

PANTON, JAMES. Canongate, Edinburgh, 1750-65.

Apprenticed to James Nicoll, 9th November 1750. Admitted freeman clock and watch maker, Canongate Hammermen, 22nd November 1760.

PANTON, ROBERT. 79 Princes Street, Edinburgh, 1825.

PARK, GEORGE. Fishcross Street, Fraserburgh, 1836.

PARK, JAMES. Kilmacolm, 1802.

" There was found in the parish of Kilmacolm some time ago, a gold watch. Any person producing the maker's name and number or any sufficient proof of the watch being theirs, may have it on paying necessary charges, by applying to James Park, clockmaker, Kilmacolm."—*Glasgow Courier*, 4th May 1802.

PARK, JOHN. Inverurie, 1837.

T

PARKER, MATTHEW. Dunfermline, 1786-1830.

We have been unable to trace where this maker belonged to, but he occupies the unique position of being one of the three men, born or resident in Fife, who did so much for the art and craft of clockmaking during the closing years of the eighteenth century. We have John Smith in the East Neuk, Thomas Reid born in Dysart, and Matthew Parker in the west part of the "Kingdom," each of whom excelled in their vocation. Their gifts of execution were of course unequal; John Smith perhaps excelling in what may be termed great mechanical skill, but this, when pitted against the attainments of the other two, made a poor show. Thomas Reid was far and away the master of the trio, but in the description of the clock which follows, made by Matthew Parker, it will be seen that he· had some claims to be recognised as a craftsman of no mean skill, combining great mechanical execution with a masterly grasp of the intricate calculations necessary for its construction. Its location, if in existence, is unknown to us, but it and the fact that he made a new clock for Dunfermline Town House in 1796, and was also responsible for the introduction of the Jacquard Loom into Dunfermline 1820-30, is the only information that can be gleaned about this capable man.

" To the Curious and Ingenious.—To be seen at Launie's Auction Room, Clam-Shell, Turnpike, High Street, Edinburgh, on Monday, the 24th of July, and every lawful day from ten till six o'clock, a Planetary and Musical Clock of exquisite workmanship in an elegant mahogany case made by Matthew Parker, Dunfermline, and performs the following motions, viz., points out the rising and falling of the horizon to show the sun's and moon's rising and setting every day through the year, shows the annual and diurnal motion of the earth when the sun is in the equinox and on the meridian, the revolving of the moon round the compass with its changes, and quarters, her lunation, viz., 29 days, 12 hours, 45 minutes, High water at any port in Britain by a motion convertible, the golden number epact, Dominical letter, the perpetual day of the month and year with numbers and notes for the same. Plays a variety of tunes, with curious figures in the arch, and goes one year without winding up.

"It is proposed to dispose of said clock by way of a lottery at 10s. 6d. each ticket, and as soon as a sufficient number of subscribers are procured, the time and place of drawing will be advertised in all the Edinburgh newspapers. Tickets to be had at the auction room, Messrs William Roy, watchmaker, Dunfermline, James Christie, Vinter, Kirkcaldy, and Alexander Lumsden, merchant, Borrowstounness. Admission to see the clock, 6d. each, subscribers gratis."—*Caledonian Mercury*, 22nd July 1786.

A careful search for the results of this lottery has been made without success, and the probability is that the clock is still located in the county where it was originally made.

PARKINSON, ROGER. Edinburgh, 1745-61.

Maker of new clock in Haddington Town House, 1745.

PATEN, ARCHIBALD. Edinburgh, 1722.

"Son to ye decesit Archd. Paten, miller at ye Water of Leith; booked apprentice to John Brown, 10th November 1722."—*E. H. Records.*

PATERSON, ALEXANDER. Leith, 1814.

Was in business before this date, but being prosecuted for working as an unfreeman, joined the Canongate Hammermen in 1814.

PATERSON, GEORGE & CO. Cotton, Aberdeen, 1836.

PATERSON, JAMES. Banff, 1779 to about 1829.

"Admitted and received Burgess and Guild Brother of the Burgh of Banff on account of the singular regard the said magistrates bear to him."—Burgess Act in favour of James Paterson, watchmaker, Banff, dated 14th June 1779, on parchment.

Baptised at Mill of Durn, Fordyce, 21st April 1757. Buried at Banff, 15th October 1829.

PATERSON, JAMES. Edinburgh, 1789-1825.

"Bound apprentice to James Howden, 20th July 1789; compeared 1st February 1806 and presented his essay, a watch movement begun, made, and finished in his own shop, in presence of James Howden, landlord, Robert Green, John Sibbald, and Laurence Dalgleish, essay masters as they declared."—*E. H. Records.*

"James Paterson acquaints his friends and the public that having been near fifteen years with Mr James Howden learning and practising the art of watch and clock making, he has now opened shop for himself at the foot of Lawnmarket, north side, where, by attention to business, he hopes to attain a share of public favour. A variety of fashionable clocks and watches always on hand. Watches and clocks cleaned and repaired upon moderate terms. Orders from the country carefully attended to."—*Edinburgh Evening Courant*, 2nd June 1804.

"PATERSON, JAMES, Watch and Clock Maker, at the sign of the Gilded Watch, foot of the Lawnmarket, north side, opposite the City Guard, grateful for past favours, informs his friends and the public that he has always on hand a good stock of eight-day clocks in mahogany and wainscot cases; also a great variety of watches in gold, silver, and gilt cases, which he can recommend as good and useful articles. As it is acknowledged by every one that no person can be a proper judge of a watch but those who have been bred to and are workmen and understand the business, J. P., being himself a workman, and having a proper knowledge of the trade, flatters himself that a discerning public will see the advantage of and security that they have in purchasing from such as are judges of what they recommend. Clocks and Watches of every description cleaned and repaired in the best manner and on moderate terms."—*Edinburgh Evening Courant*, 9th April 1809.

PATERSON, JOHN. North Leith, 1807.

Admitted a freeman clock and watch maker, Canongate Hammermen, 11th August 1807.

"Lost a few days ago a silver watch, maker's name Thos. Martin, London, No. 9090. Any person who may have found the same, on restoring it to John Paterson, watchmaker, North Leith, shall receive a reward. Watchmakers and others are requested to be on their guard if it is offered for sale."—*Edinburgh Evening Courant*, 11th May 1809.

PATERSON, PATRICK. Edinburgh, 1728.

Son to George Paterson of Dunmore; booked apprentice to Thomas Gordon, 21st September 1728.

PATERSON, WALTER. Edinburgh, 1744.

"Stolen out of Pierre Lamotia, dancing master, his garden at Lillyporhall, about half a mile west of Newhaven, a black marble horizontal dial of an octagon figure, with each second, minute, or the distance of each hour divided into thirty parts with a fleur de luce at the half hours. It has also the Equation Table and eight points of the compass on it and a brass stile made for the latitude of 56 degrees. The maker's name, Walter Paterson. Any person who can inform the author of this paper about the said dial so as it can be got back shall be handsomely rewarded."—*Caledonian Mercury*, 12th January 1744.

PATERSON, WILLIAM. Edinburgh, 1768-74.

"Booked apprentice to James Duff, 9th July 1768. Transferred from James Duff to James Gray, 29th January 1774. William Paterson, sometime apprentice to James Duff and afterwards transferred to James Gray, on account of some difference between him and James Gray, is allowed by the Incorporation's consent to serve out the remainder of his time with any master he can find."—*E. H. Records*.

PATERSON, ———. Carbarns, 1700.

Made brass dial clocks as a hobby.

PATERSON, ———. Glasgow, 1824.

"MR PATERSON'S IMPROVED CLOCK.—A clock which shows the hours, minutes, and seconds on a more improved plan than either Franklin's or Ferguson's."— Described and illustrated in *Glasgow Mechanics' Magazine*, 17th May 1824.

PATON, DAVID. Dunfermline, 1824.

"PLANETARIUM AND LUNARIUM.— These two machines were made in the year 1824 by David Paton, Dunfermline. The Planetarium, a very fine one, was made of wood, wooden wheels, wooden pinions, tin tubes, etc. It showed with great accuracy the mean motion of all the planets round the sun. The Lunarium showed the apparent diurnal revolutions of the sun and moon, as also the time of high water and low water at Limekilns."—HENDERSON'S *Annals of Dunfermline.*

PATON, JAMES. Niddry's Wynd, Edinburgh, 1773.

PATTISON, JAMES. Glasgow, 1824.

PAUL, THOMAS. 45 Sauchiehall Street, Glasgow, 1837.

PAXTON, JOHN. Bridge Street, Kelso, 1837.

PEARSON, THOMAS. Western Lane, Berwick-on-Tweed, 1820.

PEARSON, WILLIAM. Berwick-on-Tweed, 1843.

PEAT, JOHN. Crieff, 1782.

1782 is the date of the clock in the tower of Kenmore Church. Peat was paid in 1781 £40 for the clock, less £2 allowed for the old one, which he then removed.

PEAT, THOMAS. Stirling, 1818.

PEAT, THOMAS. Crieff, 1784.

PEATT, DAVID. Crieff, 1844.

"John Peatt, merchant in Glasgow, served Heir General to his father, David Peatt, watchmaker in Crieff, dated 20th December 1844; recorded 24th December 1844."—*Services of Heirs.*

PEDDIE, ANDREW. 20 Broad Street, Stirling, 1806-32.

"Houses in Stirling for sale which belonged to the deceased Robert Sconce, writer, etc. All and whole that tenement in Broad Street as presently occupied by Andrew Peddie, clockmaker."—*Stirling Journal,* 5th May 1825.

PEDDIE, JAMES. Stirling, 1786.

"There was lost or stolen in Stirling a silver watch, carved on the outer case, the maker's name, engraved in the inside and on the dial plate, Rose & Son, London, with no number. Any watchmaker who will stop her and give information of the same shall have one pound sterling by delivering her to James Peddie, watchmaker, Stirling."—*Edinburgh Evening Courant*, February 1786.

PEDDIE, JAMES. Stirling, 1801-50.

PEEBLES, JAMES. Town Head, Selkirk, 1836.

PEEBLES—Notices regarding the Common Clock of the burgh of, from 1462 to 1632.

23rd October 1462.—"*Item*, that ilk the gude men of the quest statuted and ordained that whoever break the price of bread or ale shall be fined xiijd. (which is to be given) to the buying of a knok."

14th November 1494.—"*Item*, the burgh mails are assigned to Sir Thomas of Craufurde for his clerk's fee and to Sir Patrik of Stanhous for his fee for keeping of the knok."

2nd March 1497. — "George of Myrra for ten schillinges payed for oil to the knok."

1509.—"The quilk day was made burgess William Tuedall (and the fees) given to Sir Patrik for oil and cords to the knok."

18th January 1556.—"The inquiest ordains to cause make an new door to the steeple and ordains James Frank to fulfil all points of his promise and contract betwixt him and the town anent the steeple and knok."

4th March 1556.—"And likemanner finds that the baillies has failed that causit nocht James Frank reform the points of his contract anent the knok and steeple as the said contract proportis, and ordains them to cause the said James to have all things that pertains to the town in his keeping in readiness to be delivered to the council, and to warn him instantly to remove from keeping of their common house and knok at Beltane next to come quhill [until] he and the town agree."

2nd December 1564.—" The council gave the keeping of their knok and common house in the steeple to Thomas Dikesoun, son to William Dikesoun off Winkstoun, and the said Thomas fand [found or got] William Dikesoun, his father, and John Dikesoun, his aperand, and their heir's surety and caution, that the bell and knok sauld keip na skayth in the keeping of the said Thomas nor others quilk he should appoint under him, but in any skayth [damage] was sustained by their fault the said sureties obliges thair gudes and lands for recompence of the samin."

6th December 1570.—" Siclyke ordains the steeple and knok to be orderly and sufficiently kept (use and wont) and to ring xij houris, vj houris, and courfyre nychtlie, and to pay Andro Frank his fee therefore byganes as to come always quhill he be dischargit."

5th March 1632.—" Compeared personally Johnne Robene, burgess of Peblis, and being received, sworn, and admitted Javellour and keeper of the steeple and keeper guyder and rewlar of the knok, and to ring the bells at the ordinary tyme accustomed and appointed."

22nd January 1650.—" Alexander Williamsone being appointed Javellour and keeper of the steeple of Peblis and keeper guyder and rewlar of the knok theirof and to ring the bells of the same."—*Records of the Burgh of Peebles.*

In 1797,[1] the year of the tax on clocks and watches, there was made the following returns to the assessors :—

---

[1] In connection with this short-lived tax, repealed 1798, the following was announced in the *Edinburgh Evening Courant* :—

" *Edinburgh,* 15*th July* 1797.—At a meeting held of the watch and clock makers in and about Edinburgh to consider the effects likely to be produced by the Bill before Parliament proposing an annual duty on the wearers of watches, it was resolved unanimously that the intended tax on watches and clocks was partial and oppressive and would be the means of annihilating the trade, and depriving many thousands of manufacturers of employ ; besides the object of it would be entirely defeated by its lessening the number of clocks and watches manu. factured, and would consequently diminish the annual duty on gold and silver cases. The watchmakers in and about Edinburgh do therefore agree to join in all legal and constitutional measures to prevent the Act passing into law and appointed a committee to correspond with the manufacturers of London and other cities in England."

"In the town of Peebles 15 clocks, 19 silver, and 2 gold watches. In the country part of the parish, 4 clocks, 5 silver and no gold watches. In the whole county, town, and parish of Peebles included, 106 clocks 112 silver, and 35 gold watches.—CHAMBERS'S *History of Peeblesshire*.

PEET, THOMAS. Bow, Stirling, 1820.

PEN, WILLIAM. Edinburgh, 1696.

Booked journeyman to Andrew Brown, 12th November 1696.

PENMAN, ROBERT. High Street, Dunfermline, 1820.

PENNECUIK, JAMES. Glasgow, 1791.

PETERKIN, J. Mint, Edinburgh, 1825.

Clock Dial Maker.

PETERS, DAVID. 84 High Street, Arbroath, 1837.

PETRIE, JOHN & WILLIAM. New Deer, Aberdeenshire, 1846.

PETTIGREW, JOHN, or PETTYGREW. Portsburgh, Edinburgh, 1780-1804.

"Stolen from James Anderson's house, West Pans, near Musselburgh, a silver watch, maker's name John Pettygrew, Edinburgh, No. 1. Whoever will restore the said watch to John Pettygrew, watchmaker, Portsburgh, Edinburgh, or to James Anderson, West Pans, shall receive one guinea reward."—*Caledonian Mercury*, 6th June 1780.

"Rachel Pettigrew or Reid, wife of John Reid Glasgow, served Heir of Provision and General to her brother, John Pettigrew, watchmaker, Edinburgh, dated 24th February 1804. Recorded 4th March 1804."—*Services of Heirs*.

PHILLIP, ALEXANDER. Glasgow, 1803.

PHILLIP, ALEXANDER. 60B Princes Street, Edinburgh, 1814-37.

"Lost on Saturday last, betwixt Edinburgh and Kirkliston, a Cairngorm Seal set in gold and engraved D.C., also a small pebble seal and gold key. Whoever may have found the same, and will return it to Mr

Mackenzie, Red Lion Inn, Linlithgow, or Mr Phillip, watchmaker, Greenside Street, Edinburgh, shall be handsomely rewarded."—*Edinburgh Evening Courant*, 21st April 1814.

PHILLIP, WILLIAM.   Edinburgh, 1796-1846.

Bound apprentice to Robert Green, 11th March 1796. Discharged of his indentures 13th May 1803.

"William Phillip, Clock and Watch Maker, 27 Thistle Street, respectfully intimates to his friends and the public that he has removed from 35 Thistle Street, where he has been for the last six years, to a larger and more commodious shop in the same street, three doors further east, in which he continues to carry on the business of clock and watch making in all its branches and will endeavour to merit a share of the public favour by unremitting attention and moderate charges. William Phillip was for 12 years previous to the death of the late Mr George Watson, watchmaker and jeweller, High Street, the sole person employed by him in his clock and watch making department.   On this ground he presumes to solicit the patronage of Mr Watson's former customers.   W. P. continues to repair musical boxes, and has at present for sale a Musical Box, Geneva made, superior to any that are usually brought to this country, the keys have a range of seven octaves, and the chime barrel is adapted for the four following tunes:—'Kinloch, Tirohorme Ditanti, Palpiti, and Chant du Crone.'   To be sold at a greatly reduced price."— *Edinburgh Evening Courant*, 7th August 1824.

"William Phillip begs to intimate to his numerous employers and the public in general that he has just removed from his premises in Thistle Street, in which he has been for many years, to that large corner shop, No. 50 Hanover Street (corner of Thistle Street), which he has opened with a complete assortment of everything connected with that line of business.   Having thus procured the most ample accommodation for carrying on his business, W. P. hopes to secure by steadiness and attention a continuance of the patronage he has hitherto so largely experienced and for which he takes this opportunity of expressing his thanks.   W. P. can at present recommend with confidence his stock of Gold and Silver watches, particularly those with the detached lever escapement, which from experience he can warrant to give the most complete satisfaction. The greatest attention given as formerly to the repairing and cleaning of Clocks and Watches and Musical Boxes of every description."—*Ibid.*, 22nd July 1826.

"William Phillip begs to inform his friends and the public that he intends removing to No. 48 Hanover Street, only two doors south from his present shop, same side, and to make room for an entire new assortment of goods which he purposes to open his new shop with, he will this day commence a sale of his present stock of clocks and watches at greatly reduced prices. The Clocks and Watches are in a variety of escapements and warranted of the very best workmanship."—*Ibid.*, 14th February 1831.

"Some days ago a robbery was committed in the shop of Mr Phillip, watchmaker, Hanover Street, under the following circumstances. Mr Phillip had, while at his dinner, left his shop in the charge of his apprentice, a lad between 15 and 16 years of age. One of the workmen sent out the boy upon a pretended message, and during his absence abstracted four gold watches and a silver one from a glass case. On the boy returning he discovered what had taken place and accused the man of the theft. This the latter denied for some time, until finding the boy resolute in his statement he decamped the shop, followed by his accuser, who, however, lost sight of him at the corner of St David St. Information of the circumstances was immediately communicated to the police and every effort has been made to discover the delinquent but hitherto without success."—*Ibid.*, 25th June 1846.

PHINN, THOMAS. Edinburgh, 1761.

Engraver of clock dials; was in business east wing of New Exchange, High Street, Edinburgh.

PICKEN, CHARLES. Edinburgh, 1784-1800.

"Bound apprentice to William Thomson, 15th June 1784. The incorporation gave their consent that Charles Picken, apprentice to the deceased William Thomson, serving out the remainder of his indentures with James Howden, 7th May 1785. Discharged of his indentures 23rd July 1791."—*E. H. Records.*

"Janet Picken or Smellie, widow of Charles Picken,

watchmaker, Edinburgh, served Co-heir of Provision General to Allan Boyd, Maltster in Lanark, dated 25th December 1800. Recorded 2nd January 1801."— *Services of Heirs.*

PICKEN, JOHN. Leith, 1822-30.

PICKEN, JOHN. 8 Gilmour Street, Edinburgh, 1796-1850.

"Bound apprentice to James Howden, 29th March 1796. Compeared on 30th April 1808, and produced his essay, a clock movement, begun, made, and finished in his own shop, in presence of James Howden, landlord, Robert Green, James Paterson and John Sibbald, essay masters, as they declared, etc."—*E. H. Records.*

PICKEN, THOMAS. 114 West Bow, Edinburgh, 1813-1850.

Bound apprentice to John Picken, 18th June 1813. Discharged of his indentures 31st July 1820.

PINCHBECK, EDWARD. Edinburgh, 1745.

No apology is needed in introducing the man's name among the lists of Scottish Clockmakers, seeing the metal or alloy called Pinchbeck gold was well known and used all over Scotland. The fact that the above individual, son of Christopher Pinchbeck, the inventor of the metal, was resident for some little time in Edinburgh, has hitherto escaped notice. We give his own words in the advertisements which follow, and may mention that the year he was in Edinburgh was a time of great anxiety to all business men, owing to the rumours in the city of the approach of Prince Charles Stuart and his army. No doubt that this factor must have occasioned Edward Pinchbeck some anxiety, which is easily seen in his determination to quit Edinburgh.

"Pinchbeck, Toyman, from the Musical Clock in Cheapside, London. To prevent the great impositions that have a long while been carried on by persons who deal to and in this city and pretend to have and sell the true Pinchbeck metal, though they have not one grain, Mr Pinchbeck has himself taken a shop at the Head of the Canongate, the corner of Leith Wynd, where Gentlemen, Ladies, and Merchants may be accommodated with any sorts of toys in his curious metal (the particular properties of which are such that where the same care is taken with it in the wear as with gold, it answers the same end in every respect, and so nearly resembles it in all its most beautiful capabilities that it has often deceived the best judges even on the touchstone).

"Chased and Plain Watches, Snuff Boxes, Tweezer Cases, Pocket Cases, Toothpick Cases, Canes and Cane-Heads, Swords and Sword Hilts, Buckles, Coat and Sleeve Buttons, Seals, Thimbles, Stay Hooks, Rings, Earrings, Trinkets for ladies' watches, such as Hearts, Buckles, Eggs, Globes, Acorns, Tuns, Bottles, and, in short, anything in his metal that is made either in Gold or Silver by the best workmen and in the neatest manner.

"*N.B.*—He allows half-a-crown an ounce for his metal as usual and buys old gold and silver or any curious stones."—*Caledonian Mercury*, 14th January 1745.

"This is to acquaint the public that Mr Pinchbeck, at the Head of the Canongate, the corner of Leith Wynd, being sent for home with all expedition on very urgent business, and as there are no ships immediately bound from this place for London with a proper convoy, so that he cannot at present have an opportunity of sending his goods to London, and as the leaving of them here will be of great loss to him, he begs leave to give this public notice to all gentlemen, ladies, and merchants, that he will dispose of what goods he has remaining under prime cost.

"*N.B.*—He will have no longer time to dispose of them than till the 16th of next month, he being obliged to set out next day for London."—*Ibid.*, 8th March 1745.

"That as Mr Pinchbeck, at the Head of the Canongate, having formerly advertised of his departure from this place to London some time last week, yet as he had been imposed upon in bargaining about a certain particular, and in seeking redress for such an imposition, he being a stranger has been used in a very harsh and arbitrary manner. He therefore is advised to stay longer here in order to have justice done him agreeably to the laws of the country, and it is upon this account only he acquaints the publick of his former advertisement at the usual place where Gentlemen, Ladies, and others will be attended as usual."—*Ibid.*, 25th March 1745.

PINKERTON, JOHN. Haddington, 1804-50.

PIRRIE, JOHN. 1 King Street, Perth, 1820; appointed
    receiving postmaster 1848; died 6th February 1857.

PIRRIE, J. Cullen, 1830-50; died about 1870.
    Made the town clock in Cullen, and the turret clock
of the Home Farm, Cullen House.

PITCAIRN & ROBERTSON. 9 Wellmeadows Street,
    Paisley, 1836.

POARSON, EMMANUEL. Edinburgh, 1700.
    Booked journeyman to Paul Romieu, 1700.

POLWARTH, WILLIAM. Dunse, 1825.
    "William Polwarth, watchmaker in Dunse, served
Heir in General to his brother, John Polwarth, Purser,
R.N., dated 9th June 1825. Recorded 17th June 1825."
—*Services of Heirs.*

PORTER, ROBERT. Polwarth Street, Galston, 1850.

POTTS, JAMES. Western Lane, Berwick-on-Tweed, 1806.

POURIE, HENRY. Bridgend, Perth, 1820.

POWRIE, HENRY. Edinburgh and Glasgow, 1822-37.
    "Henry Powrie, Glasgow, once watchmaker, Edin-
burgh, served Heir of Provision General to his wife,
G. Richardson, widow of Alexander Skae, Edinburgh,
dated 6th December 1837. Recorded 18th December
1837."—*Services of Heirs.*

POZZIE, JOSEPH (POZZIE & STEWART). Elgin, sub-
    sequent to 1820.

PRINGLE, ADAM. Bristo Street, Edinburgh, 1794-1820.
    "Lost on Wednesday last betwixt Dicksons' Nursery
and the foot of Leith Walk, a metal watch, outer case
covered with tortoise-shell, maker's name Jno. Rayley,
No. 3681. If the same is offered for sale to watchmakers or others, please acquaint Mr Pringle, watchmaker, Bristo Street, or give notice thereof at the
Printing Office."—*Edinburgh Evening Courant*, 23rd
May 1801.

    "There was lost upon the 9th of October current,
near the Grange Toll, a gold watch, indented outer case,
caped and jewelled, maker's name James Howden,
Edinburgh, No. 731, with two gold seals and a steel chain.
Whoever has found the said watch shall receive Three

Guineas of reward and no questions asked. Apply to Mr Pringle, watchmaker, Bristo Street, Edinburgh. It is requested that any person to whom the said watch may be offered will detain her."—*Ibid.*, 13th October 1808.

PRINGLE, GEORGE. Edinburgh, 1793-1822.

Bound apprentice to Thomas Reid, 10th January 1793.

PRINGLE, GEORGE & SON. High Street, Edinburgh, 1822.

"EDINBURGH WOODEN AND MUSICAL CLOCK MANUFACTORY, 227 High Street, Edinburgh.—George Pringle and Son respectfully intimate that they have now on sale at moderate charges an excellent assortment of wooden clocks both foreign and of their own manufacture. G. P. and Son have at present for sale an elegant musical clock just finished, which plays a variety of the most favourite Scots Airs. From the superiority of the workmanship they flatter themselves that upon inspection, both as to the music and mechanism, this article will give the utmost satisfaction. Clocks of all kinds made and repaired on reasonable terms. Orders from the country punctually attended to."—*Scotsman*, 21st May 1825.

"George Pringle and Son respectfully intimate to their friends and the public that they carry on the above business in all its branches—Kitchen and Alarm Clocks, Musical and Fancy do., in great variety. Musical Clocks and Barrel Organs repaired and set to new music. G. P. and Son have at present for sale a superior musical clock having an eight-day movement elegantly fitted up in a mahogany case of the Gothic order, which performs a variety of Scots Airs. As a prejudice exists that such articles cannot be made nor repaired by others than foreigners, G. P. and Son, to obviate such, have only to invite an inspection of their stock."—*Edinburgh Evening Courant*, 5th November 1825.

PRINGLE, JAMES. Dalkeith, 1763.

PRINGLE, THOMAS. Edinburgh; died at 54 Bristo Street, 4th June 1825. We have been unable to ascertain to which family of Edinburgh clockmakers he belonged.

PRINGLE, THOMAS. Dalkeith, 1830-36. Business continued by his widow.

PRINGLE, WILLIAM. 99 Nicolson Street, Edinburgh, 1825-36.

PROCTER, ALEXANDER. Tarland, 1837.

PROCTER, ROBERT. Edinburgh, 1749.

"Seal Cutter and Lapidary near the Palace of Holyrood House, first close within the Strand, north side of the street. Cuts stones of all sorts for Watch Cases, Snuff Boxes, Rings and Ear-rings, Coat, Vest, and Sleeve Buttons, according to his employers' fancies. Daily customers served pretty quickly by his having plenty of hands at work and a good collection always by him ready to cut."—*Caledonian Mercury*, 22nd August 1749.

PURDOUNE, ANDREW. Glasgow, 1657. *See* page 162.

PURVES, WILLIAM. Edinburgh, 1539.

This individual is one of the first Scottish clock-makers we have authentic history about. For the notes on the Common Clocks of the burghs of Aberdeen, Dundee, and Stirling, his name occurs there as either making or repairing the public clocks of these respective towns. That this is the same craftsman mentioned in each is without doubt, and it is singular that his name should turn up in the records of these places. Where he was a native of we have been unable to trace, but all the evidence available points to him as being a native and burgess of Edinburgh. This latter fact is brought out in the contract regarding the Dundee clock, but it may be noted that the burgess-ship con-ferred there was invariably bestowed at that period on craftsmen who were brought to any particular town on special work, so as to bring them into line, so to speak, with the incorporations already established there. From an inspection of the *Edinburgh Hammermen's Records* we find that a William Purves was appointed to a responsible post in the management of that craft in 1541-42. This accords with his movements as recorded in the Aberdeen notes, and although his name does not turn up again in the Edinburgh records, this can be accounted for by his travels over all the country, ful-filling the contracts which he executed. He probably died before 1560, as in the notes on the Town Clocks of Edinburgh it will be observed that the magistrates entered into a contract with a craftsman in Leith to perform the work, the surmise being that Purves was dead and no other capable man was available in the city to carry out the repairs.

Be this as it may, there is no question that William Purves was a man of great ingenuity and skill, as may be seen in the specification of the clock made for Dundee in 1547, and his name must be held in respect as one who, so far as can be gleaned, did his part in the furtherance of the welfare and convenience of his country and fellow-citizens by his useful labours.

PYOT, JAMES. West Bow, Edinburgh, 1796; afterwards removed to Shore, Leith; at St Bernard's Street, 1829.

RAE, REV. PETER. Kirkconnel, 1703-48.

Made the astronomical chime clock in Drumlanrig Castle.

RAIT, D. C. 16 Argyll Street, Glasgow, 1841.

RAMAGE, JAMES. Edinburgh, 1780-1820.

"Bound apprentice to James Gray, 17th August 1780. Discharged of his indentures 15th September 1787. Admitted freeman of the Incorporation of Edinburgh Hammermen 1797."—*E. H. Records.*

"Lost on the night of Wednesday the 25th current, between the Canongate head and the Grassmarket, a silver watch, maker's name Gregory Dublin, No. 1772. Whoever has found the same will, upon delivering it up to Mr Ramage, watchmaker, Lawnmarket, Edinburgh, receive a handsome reward."—*Edinburgh Evening Courant,* 30th October 1809.

"Lost or stolen a small gold watch, with a gold engine, turned case, capped and jewelled, maker's name Samuel Brown, Edinburgh, No. 583; had a gold crib chain and a cairngorm, with a crest and motto. Any person who has found the same and will return it to James Ramage, No. 61 Cowgate, will be handsomely rewarded, and any person to whom it may be offered to sale or pawn is requested to stop it and inform the above."— *Edinburgh Evening Courant,* 3rd March 1817.

U

RAMSAY, DAVID.   Dundee and London, 1600-50.

This maker, celebrated in his day as being clock-maker to his Majesty King James VI. of Scotland and I. of England, also has the further honour of being introduced by Sir Walter Scott as a character in *The Fortunes of Nigel.*

Considerable licence has been taken by Sir Walter in his treatment of David Ramsay, as will be seen by the extracts following from the *Calendar of State Papers,* which does not warrant the somewhat lowly position he is made to fill.   His picture of him as being an old man with a tall, thin, lathy skeleton, extending his lean jaws into an alarming grin, hardly portrays the kind of man who was promoted to be a Page of the Royal Bed-chamber.   One naturally associates such appointments as being occupied by men who were suited in every respect to the honourable post they were called to *fill,* and not to men whose peculiarities, as quoted by Sir Walter, would make it an impossibility for any in such a position to carry out.

Where he learned the craft has not been recorded, but Dundee is credited as being the town from which he came.   In the notes on Dundee Public Clocks mention is made of a family of the name of Ramsay, who for a long period had the contract and care of the town clocks, and it is believed that David Ramsay was either a member of this family or closely related to them. [1]

In all probability he learned the art in France, as the specimens of his work, which are now preserved in the British and South Kensington Museums, bear out. One significant fact, warranting the assumption that he worked abroad, is afforded by the watch preserved in the South Kensington Museum, which has engraved on the hinged covers of the front and back the Annunciation and the Nativity.   This, it is needless to say, would not have been the case if it had been made in Scotland, as

[1] Sir Walter Scott, however, gives Dalkeith as his native place, but this, of course, is to make it fit in with the Ramsays of Dalhousie, of which family the King (see chapter xxxvii.) was determined to make David Ramsay a member.

the reaction against everything savouring of Popery would have made it a difficult matter to dispose of at that period. The watch in the British Museum has the period 1600-10 assigned as the date of its manufacture, while this one, and another supposed to have belonged to James I., have each inscribed on them "David Ramsay, Scotus, me fecit," a designation which would have been otherwise if he had made them in a particular town in Scotland.

We assume that he returned from his foreign sojourn and making his way to London direct, had specimens of his handiwork submitted for inspection by the King, who, no doubt, glad to have such a capable craftsman near him, took him under his patronage. The following extracts from the *Calendar of State Papers* show his progress :—

25th November 1613.—"Grant to David Ramsay, Clockmaker Extraordinary, of a pension of £50 per annum."

1616.—"Warrant to pay David Ramsay, Clockmaker, £234, 10s., due to him for purchase and repair of clocks and watches for the King."

1618.—"Grant to David Ramsay of the office of Chief Clockmaker to the King, with fees and allowances for workmanship."

27th July 1619.—"Grant to David Ramsay, the King's Clockmaker, born in Scotland of denization" (in Latin).

30th March 1622.—"Warrant to pay David Ramsay, Clockmaker, £113 for work for the late Prince Henry and for watches and clocks for the King."

30th September 1622.—"Warrant to pay £232, 15s., to David Ramsay, the King's clockmaker, for repairing clocks at Theobalds, Oatlands, and Westminster, and for making a chime of bells adjoining to the clock at Theobalds."

25th January 1626.—"Warrant to pay to David Ramsay, for coins to be given by the King at the close of his coronation."

17*th March* 1627.—"Warrant to pay to David Ramsay, Page of the Bedchamber and clockmaker, £441, 3s. 4d. for work done for his late Majesty, and £358, 16s. 8d., in lieu of diet and bouche of court."

10*th July* 1628.—"Warrant to pay to David Ramsay, £415 for clocks and other necessaries delivered for the King's service."

1632.—"Warrant to pay David Ramsay, clockmaker, on his bills for one year £219."

These authentic notices give in a marked degree the esteem and patronage bestowed on him by his royal patrons, and these, along with the specimens of his skill that are in existence yet, show him to have been not only a capable craftsman but a good business man as well. This is emphasised by the fact that on the foundation of the Clockmakers' Company of London by Royal Charter, 22nd August 1631, David Ramsay was appointed by this charter the first master to hold office. He died about 1650, but his age has not been recorded.

RAMSAY, MARK. Watch-case maker, Canongate, Edinburgh, 1795.

RAMSAY, PATRICK, JOHN, AND SILVESTER. Dundee, 1599-1646.
See notes on Dundee Town Clocks, page 125.

RAMSAY, ROBERT. 67 High Street, Dumfries, 1816-23.

RANKEN, JAMES. Edinburgh, 1791.
Bound apprentice to George Skelton, 26th January 1791.

RANKIN, ALEXANDER. 10 William Street, Greenock, 1836.

RANKIN, JOHN. Old Cumnock, 1789.

RANKINE, JOHN. Canongate, Edinburgh, 1761.
Apprenticed to Andrew Clark, 6th June 1761.

RANKINE, J. & W. Sorn, 1798.

RANNIE, ALEXANDER. Turriff, 1836.

REED, ANDREW. Sanquhar, 1798.

REED, WILLIAM. Native of Montrose; died at White-haven, 1815.

REED, WILLIAM. Watch-glass maker, 92 High Street, Edinburgh, 1837.

REDPATH, ——. Kelso, 1835.

REDPATH, HENRY. 1 Bow, Stirling, 1787-1820.

REID, ALEXANDER. Edinburgh, 1790.

Bound apprentice to Thomas Reid, 24th July 1790.

REID, ANDREW. Biggar; died 2nd August 1860, in the 93rd year of his age.

REID, DAVID. 95 Hutcheson Street, Glasgow, 1805-18.

REID, FRANCIS. Saltmarket, Glasgow, 1789-1806.

"Lost on Friday, at Paisley, betwixt the Cross and the Race Ground, a silver watch, with a steel chain and steel seal, with the initials cut J. D. on it, the chain is a little rusted, maker's name Peter Le Roy, London, No. 2720. Whoever will return the said watch to Francis Reid, watchmaker, Saltmarket, Glasgow, will receive half a guinea of reward."—*Glasgow Courier*, 19th August 1800.

"Lost in the Trongate, on Thursday the 17th, a silver watch, maker's name Joseph Denton, Hull, No. 827. Whoever will bring the same to Francis Reid, watch-maker, No. 142 Saltmarket, will receive a reward of one guinea."—*Glasgow Courier*, 25th April 1806.

REID, FRANCIS & SONS. 142 Saltmarket, Glasgow, 1812-23.

"A reward of Five Guineas is hereby offered to any person who will return the gold watch, maker's name Bracebridge, London, No. 14,598, with its appendages, lost by a gentleman in Bell Street, about ten o'clock on Sunday evening last. Apply to F. Reid & Sons, watch-makers, 142 Saltmarket, Glasgow."—*Glasgow Courier*, 12th July 1816.

REID & HALBERT. 11 Gallowgate, Glasgow, 1823.

REID & TOD. 1 Trongate, Glasgow, 1828.

REID, JAMES. Canongate, Edinburgh, 1798.

REID, JAMES. High School Yards, Edinburgh, 1804.

REID, JOHN. Glasgow, 1814.

REID, JOHN. Bull's Close, Canongate, Edinburgh, 1798-1806.

REID, JOHN. 13 Frederick Street, Edinburgh, 1819-36.

REID, JOHN. Banff, 1721. *See* page 38.

REID, JOHN. Sanquhar, 1837.

REID, ROBERT. Glasgow, 1806.

REID, THOMAS. Montrose, 1788.

REID, THOMAS. Auchtermuchty, 1837.

REID, THOMAS. Watch-case maker, Canongate, Edinburgh, 1788.

REID, THOMAS. Edinburgh, 1762-1823.

"Bound apprentice to James Cowan, 9th October 1762. Presented a petition craving to be admitted a freeman on 14th December 1781. Compeared on 14th June 1782, and presented his essay, being a plain watch movement, begun, made and finished in his own shop, in presence of Samuel Brown, landlord, Robert Aitchison, James Howden, and Thomas Sibbald, essay masters as they declared, etc."—*E. H. Records.*

The above is all the official information that is to be gleaned about him from the *Hammermen's Records*, but, fortunately, as will be seen further on, we learn that he was a native of Dysart. By his birthplace he thus must be classed as being one of the three men who had close connection with Fife, and who distinguished themselves in the science and art of Horology. We refer to John Smith, Pittenweem, and Matthew Parker, Dunfermline, but of the trio Thomas Reid was the most eminent of them all. Apprenticed at the age of sixteen years, his choice of James Cowan as his master had a good deal to do with the moulding and training of a mind singularly adapted for the profession. As James Cowan was also his cousin, this may account for the interest he took in his apprentice, which resulted in the apprentice succeeding to the business of the master, when the latter died in 1781. Doubtless this succession was a powerful factor in determining Thomas Reid's career, as not unlikely the thought of possessing a business so prosperous as Cowan's nerved him to acquire all the experience and training he could during his eleven years' residence in London.

When James Cowan, who had been over thirty years in business, died, Thomas Reid's opportunity arrived, and he issued the following advertisement in the *Edinburgh Evening Courant*, of the date 28th November 1781 :—

"Thomas Reid, Clock and Watch Maker, from London, takes this method of informing the friends and customers of the deceased Mr James Cowan, Clock and Watch Maker, in Edinburgh, that he continues the business[1] in the same shop as formerly. As T. Reid was cousin and apprentice to Mr Cowan, and has for eleven years resided in London, where, after having received the instructions of the first masters in that profession, did carry on business and was employed in the execution of the first-rate work there, he makes no doubt of giving entire satisfaction to his employers."

This modest announcement is remarkable as showing the confidence he had in himself of being a worthy successor to a person who had carried on one of the best known businesses in Edinburgh. That this confidence was not misjudged, speedily brought him into public favour. How rapidly his reputation rose, is seen by his selection by his fellow-citizens to construct the first clock for the spire of St Andrew's Parish Church, George Street, Edinburgh, in 1788, and this having given great satisfaction, he was commissioned to carry out the extensive alterations and repairs of the clock of St Giles' Kirk (q.v.) in 1797. He took special pains with these two clocks, the result being that in a retrospect forty years after, he expresses satisfaction at their perform-

---

[1] It is interesting to note that it is his shop that is represented in the left-hand corner of the well-known picture of "The Parliament Close in the Olden Time" now hanging in the Lord Provost's room, City Chambers, Edinburgh.

ance. He erected clocks not only in Edinburgh but all over the country. Two which he made for the Town Hall, Annan, are worthy of special mention, for in the making of the movements he so arranged the frames that any wheel could be separately lifted out without taking the clock to pieces or removing any of the other wheels. Other examples of his skill may be noted, but particulars will be found of some of his most famous productions under the notes on Reid and Auld (see p. 313).

Having a high ideal of his profession, his own words are well worth quoting, "that there are few who excel in this art, as in those of sculpture, painting, or engraving, which are called fine arts, a name to which watchmaking is in every sense entitled but which labours under the great misfortune in not being properly seen." Endued with such a high standard, his thoughts were embodied in a number of scientific articles dealing with the problems of his profession, culminating in the production of his treatise, *On Clock and Watch Making*, which ran into six editions. This book was written long after the allotted span of life, and although it does not, from its technical nature, appeal to the ordinary reader, yet from the large number of sources from which he quotes, both home and foreign, it is easily seen that the work is full of the observations and experiences of one who had a minute and complete acquaintance with his art Having retired in 1823, he devoted the closing years of his honourable life to the preparation of the above treatise, and, after a busy and useful life, he died on the 24th September 1831, aged eighty-five years. In the notes given under William Auld, p. 20, a full description is given of the tombstone erected in Calton Burying Ground, Edinburgh. From it we learn that Thomas Reid married the widow of William Auld, printer, who died in 1777, thus making William Auld, junior, his stepson, in addition to being his partner. The admiration and respect for Thomas Reid by the Auld family is brought out in this memorial stone. Content to record their family names on the least conspicuous part of the monument, the whole centre panel is given up to the following inscription :—" To the memory of Thomas Reid, Esq., H.M.W.C.M.C.L., distinguished in his profession as an eminent watch and clock maker. Author of a Literary and Scientific Work on Horology, etc., etc. Born at Dysart, Fife, January 1746. Died at Edinburgh, 24th September 1831."

REID & AULD. 66 Princes Street, Edinburgh, 1806-23.

This well-known firm was enabled by the skill and experience of its two partners (Thomas Reid and William Auld) to occupy a very high place in the art of horology in Edinburgh. Having more than a local fame, it is safe to say that during the early part of the nineteenth century the name of Reid & Auld was synonymous with high-class work. To what extent the capabilities of the two were devoted to their productions is difficult now to tell, both being practical men, but it is easily seen that they had complete satisfaction in their work, it being an art congenial to them. Thomas Reid adopted William Auld as partner in 1806, the business being then carried on in the quaint old shop situated under the shade of St Giles' Kirk, which they occupied till 1809, when they announced :—" Reid and Auld, having removed from Parliament Close to No. 33 Princes Street, invite attention to their eight-day weight clocks and regulators for astronomical purposes. They also intimate that a Transit instrument is kept for the obtaining of true time, without which the rate of the going of time-keepers of whatever description cannot be well ascertained, etc."

While thus mindful of the ordinary class of work, yet it is to the manufacture of the intricate and complex movements known as astronomical regulators that the firm was specially famed. At least three of these are in existence yet, and though they have performed their useful duties for nearly a century they seem likely to do so for another. A short account of two of those is now given, the one being a description of a very excellent regulator or astronomical clock made for the Right Honourable Lord Gray, in the Observatory, Kinfauns Castle :—

"It had a mercurial compensation pendulum, and its time of going without winding was forty-five days. The pivots of the great wheel, the second wheel, and the swing wheel are run on rollers, three being put to each pivot; the pivots of the centre and of the fourth wheel run in holes and are the only pivots in the clock to which oil is applied. The pivots of the said centre and fourth wheel would have been run on rollers also, but not choosing to go further, for even, with those which were made to run so, the trial was new ; besides, had these two been done, it would have required such a number of additional pieces as in the end would have been truly appalling ; even as it is about 500 individual pieces were in the clock. The clock has been going about nine years with a close and steady rate of time-keeping, during which it has not required the smallest help, even of cleaning."

The other is the clock made for the Royal Observatory, Calton Hill, Edinburgh. It has the same kind of escapement and pendulum as the foregoing, goes eight days, but has no friction rollers in any part of it. It has been going upwards of ten years [1] without requiring any help or even cleaning. In a note kindly forwarded by the late Professor Copland, Royal Observatory, Blackford Hill, referring to this last clock, he says :—" It always seems to have been rated to show mean time, and was eventually employed for many years to drop the time ball on Nelson's Monument, Calton Hill, and to transmit the signal to the time gun at Edinburgh Castle. It is provided with a dead beat escapement, quicksilver compensation pendulum, and still keeps excellent time." This clock became the property of the City of Edinburgh in 1895, and is still in use at the Observatory on Calton Hill.

These two clocks, along with another now located

---

[1] It was made in the year 1813.

in the Horological Institute, London, are sufficient testimony to the skill and enterprise of the firm of Reid & Auld.

They continued in business till 1823, when the following advertisement was issued :—

" Reid and Auld, No. 66 Princes Street, return their most grateful acknowledgments to their friends in particular, and to the public in general, for that liberal patronage which they have received for many years and beg to inform them that, intending soon to retire from business, they particularly recommend their stock consisting of Gold, Silver, and Metal watches, among which are some most excellent Repeaters, Regulators, Eight-day and Spring Clocks (some of which are fitted up in a superior manner), an eight-day weight quarter clock, a most elegant spring quarter organ clock, with different barrels, eight tunes on each. This clock, which would be a most superb drawing-room ornament, is fitted up in a beautiful rosewood case inlaid with brass ornaments, is well worth the attention of the public; indeed the whole are such that, in all probability, their like will not be met with soon again. If there are any debts outstanding against the company they may be sent in immediately, when they will be paid. R. and A. beg the favour that payment will be ordered as soon as possible of all accounts due to them."—*Edinburgh Evening Courant*, 10th February 1823.

No one appears to have directly succeeded to their business, though Thomas Watt (q.v.), who was a nephew of Thomas Reid, solicited the support of the customers of the late firm. Both partners lived for some years after their retiral from active business life, and, as can be seen in the separate notes on the two men, showed such a devotion to each other that even in death they were not divided but sleep their last sleep in the one tomb. *See* notes on William Auld, page 23, for account of the Reid and Auld Bequest.

REID, THOMAS, Watch Glassmaker. 79 High Street, Edinburgh, 1819.

REID, WILLIAM. Edinburgh, 1781-1819.
   Bound apprentice to James Cowan, 1st June 1781.

REID, WILLIAM OTTO. Biggar, 1820-49.

Born at Sanquhar 4th October 1820; died at Biggar 4th October 1849.

RENNIE, ALEXANDER DAVID. 65 High Street, Arbroath, 1837.

RENNIE, ALEXANDER. Turriff, about 1835.

RHIND, THOMAS. 78 High Street, Paisley, 1836.

RICHARDSON, GEORGE. Edinburgh, 1802.

Discharged of his indentures by Thomas Reid, 12th February 1802.

RICHARDSON, WILLIAM. Alloa, 1769-90.

"WILLIAM RICHARDSON, Clock and Watch Maker in Alloa, makes, sells, and repairs all kinds of clocks and watches. He likewise makes and sells the best kinds of fishing wheels of different sorts and sizes from one shilling and eight pence to fifteen shillings, also all kinds of swivels of different sizes. Gentlemen may be served on proper notice with any of the above articles at a reasonable rate, and a good allowance will be given to merchants who, it is hoped, will be particular in their directions as to the different sizes and prices, and they shall be answered with the utmost despatch. Apply to Alloa carrier, at Campbell in the Grassmarket of Edinburgh, who arrives on Wednesday and goes off on Thursday morning, and who will be careful to deliver any commissions to or from the above William Richardson.—*Edinburgh Evening Courant*, 2nd April 1774.

RICHARDSON, WILLIAM. Balfron, 1828.

"William Richardson, watchmaker, Balfron, served Heir in General to his brother John, son of William Richardson, watchmaker, Alloa, dated 18th June 1828. Recorded 25th June 1828."—*Services of Heirs.*

RICHARDSON, WILLIAM. Paisley, 1801.

"Married at Paisley on Monday last Mr William Richardson, watchmaker there, to Miss Margaret Craig, only daughter of the late Robert Craig, Esq., of Faulheads."—*Scots Magazine*, 30th September 1801.

BRACKET CLOCK,

In mahogany case, inlaid with brass, with seconds and calendar dials, dated 1841.
By James Ritchie & Son, Edinburgh, 1895. The property of the North British
Railway Co., Waterloo Place, Edinburgh. (See p. 517.)

RICHARDSON, WILLIAM. Charles Street, Edinburgh, 1793.

Business continued by his widow for a few years later.

RIDDEL, CHARLES. Old Meldrum, 1800-37.

RIDDEL, D. & J. 72 Broad Street, Aberdeen, 1846.

RIDDEL, JAMES. 72 Broad Street, Aberdeen, 1853.

RITCHIE, ——. Dundee, 1831.

RITCHIE, ANDREW. Edinburgh, 1822.

Bound apprentice to James Clark, 5th August 1822.

RITCHIE, GEORGE. 199 High Street, Arbroath, 1837.

RITCHIE, JAMES. Leith Street, Edinburgh, 1805.

The earliest mention of this maker's name occurs not in the *Hammermen's Records* but in the *Edinburgh Evening Courant* of the date of 7th January 1805, and is as follows :—

"Married here on the 28th ult., Mr James Ritchie, watchmaker in Edinburgh, to Miss Sally Neill, second daughter of Mr Andrew Neill, builder there."

He was then in business at No. 29 Leith Street, and on the retirement in 1819 of Joseph Durward (q.v.), who had been established at No. 2 for forty years, he succeeded to his connection also. About 1836 the name appears as James Ritchie & Son, which has been the designation of the firm down to the present day, making it the oldest watch and clock making business in the city of Edinburgh, as well as being one of world-wide repute. Their prominence in electrically controlled clocks is brought out in the list of the awards in the Reid and Auld bequest, p. 24, where one of the partners at that date took a high place. The new clock in St Giles' Cathedral and the Bracket Timepiece in Brass inlaid case (see illustrations) show the capabilities of this firm.

RITCHIE, JAMES. Muthill, 1836.

RITCHIE, JOHN. Edinburgh, 1765.

Booked apprentice to Samuel Brown, 3rd April 1765.

RITCHIE, JOHN. Coupar Angus, 1847.

RITCHIE, PETER. Canongate, Edinburgh, 1749.

RITCHIE, SAMUEL. Forfar, 1800-37.

RITCHIE, THOMAS. Cupar-Fife, 1833.

ROBOLD, ZEPRIAN (German). 19 East Quay Lane, Greenock, 1836.

ROBB, WILLIAM. Montrose, 1776.

"Found on Saturday last, the 27th July current, between Cramond Bridge and Muttonhole on the Edinburgh Road, a silver watch. It is imagined this watch has lately been repaired, as there is a clean paper in the case on which are engraved these words, Clocks and Watches by William Robb in Montrose. The watch is lodged with William Jamieson, factor on the estate of Pitfarrane, a mile west from Dunfermline, and whoever can prove the property shall be entitled to the watch on paying expenses of advertising."—*Edinburgh Evening Courant*, 31st July 1776.

ROBERTSON, CHARLES. Coupar Angus, 1814-37.

ROBERTSON, DANIEL. 18 Arcade, Glasgow, 1836.

ROBERTSON, DAVID. 109 High Street, Perth, 1837.

ROBERTSON, DAVID. Edinburgh, 1741.

Son of David Robertson, merchant in Edinburgh; booked apprentice to Alexander Brand, 15th August 1741.

ROBERTSON, DUNCAN. Blairgowrie, 1837.

ROBERTSON, EBENEZER. Glasgow, 1801.

ROBERTSON, GEORGE. Edinburgh, 1802.

Bound apprentice to James Breakenrig, 5th March 1802.

ROBERTSON, GEORGE. Dundee, 1806.

ROBERTSON, JAMES. Edinburgh, 1758.

Son of Hugh Robertson, residenter in Edinburgh; booked apprentice to Samuel Brown, 20th July 1752.

ROBERTSON, JAMES. Dundee, 1785.

ROBERTSON, JAMES. High Street, Dundee, 1811-28.

ROBERTSON, JAMES. Perth, 1770.

Booked apprentice to James Young.

ROBERTSON, JAMES. Leith, 1818-36.

Admitted freeman clock and watch maker, Canongate Hammermen, 1818; 25 Bridge Street, Leith, 1825; 4 West Nicolson Street, Edinburgh, 1836.

ROBERTSON, JAMES. Edinburgh, 1806.

Bound apprentice to Robert Hinmers, 3rd May 1806.

ROBERTSON, JOHN. Netherbow, Edinburgh, 1783-1821.

"Lost on the Glasgow Road by Calder on Wednesday last, 22nd January, a silver watch, maker's name J. Johnson, London, No. 101. If said watch is offered for sale, please acquaint John Robertson, watchmaker, Netherbow, Edinburgh, or John Smith, Glasgow, and a handsome reward will be given."—*Edinburgh Evening Courant*, 27th January 1783.

"The Rev. Alexander Robertson, minister at Burford, Oxfordshire, served Heir in General to his father, John Robertson, watch and clock maker, Edinburgh, dated 2nd January 1822. Recorded 8th January 1822"—*Services of Heirs*.

ROBERTSON, MATTHEW. Mauchline, 1837.

ROBERTSON, PATRICK. Perth, 1765.

"The calling agree to grant liberty and tolerance to the above to exercise his trade as a clock and watch maker in Perth during his lifetime for payment of one pound sterling yearly."—*Perth Hammermen Records*.

ROBERTSON, ROBERT. 17 George Street, Perth, 1825-37.

ROBERTSON, ROBERT. 86 Argyll Street, Glasgow, 1802-28.

ROBERTSON, THOMAS. 169 Argyll Street, Glasgow, 1837.

ROBERTSON, THOMAS. Rothesay, 1837.

At a meeting of the Royal Scottish Society of Arts, held on 15th November 1837, a drawing and verbal description of an improved vertical watch was exhibited by Mr Thomas Robertson, Watchmaker, Rothesay; also drawing and verbal description of an improved Lever Watch, and a drawing and description of an improved escapement for a chronometer.

ROBERTSON, WILLIAM. Edinburgh, 1749.

Son of Colin Robertson, Barber and Wigmaker in Edinburgh; booked apprentice to Archibald Straiton, 30th March 1749.

ROBERTSON, WILLIAM. Dunbar, 1803.

"A gold watch found on Friday, the 18th ult., between the town of Dunbar and village of East Linton. Any person proving it their property may have it by applying to Mr William Robertson, watchmaker, Dunbar, and paying expenses."—*Edinburgh Evening Courant*, 2nd April 1803.

ROBERTSON, WILLIAM. Falkland, Fife, 1830.

ROBERTSON, WILLIAM. Canongate, Edinburgh, 1764-80.

Admitted freeman clock and watch maker, in Canongate Hammermen, 7th November 1764.

"Lost last night, betwixt Musselburgh and Newhaven or Newhaven and Edinburgh, a pinchbeck watch in a black shagreen case and a steel chain with a silver seal and a cupid cut upon the stone of the seal, the maker's name William Robertson, Canongate. Any person that has found the same and will deliver it to the said W. R. shall be handsomely rewarded."—*Caledonian Mercury*, 16th August 1768.

"Lost on the evening of Saturday last, betwixt Newhaven and Edinburgh, a gentleman's gold watch. Any person who has found the same upon restoring it to William Robertson, watchmaker, Head of Canongate, will be handsomely rewarded."—*Edinburgh Evening Courant*, 10th August 1772.

ROBERTSON, W. Parliament Close, Edinburgh, 1791.

"Improved Pedometer or Way Wiser which, when worn in the pocket, ascertains with accuracy the distance the wearer walks. These very amusing machines are at present very much in repute in London, and are now at the shop of W. Robertson, No. 6 Parliament Close, who sells them at the same price charged by the manufacturer in London; and also an assortment of watches in gold, gold enamelled, pearl and enamelled silver, plain metal and enamelled cases, which he sells on the most reasonable terms."—*Edinburgh Herald*, 11th April 1791.

ROBSON, W. Linton, 1787.

RODGER, ALEXANDER. Harvey's Lane, Campbeltown, 1837.

ROGER, WILLIAM. Stonehaven, 1820-46.

ROSS, CHARLES. Broughty-Ferry, 1828.

ROSS, DAVID. Pathhead, Dysart, 1836.

ROSS, GEORGE. Inveraray, 1835.

ROSS, JAMES. Gallowgate, Glasgow, 1790-1800.

" Lost on the banks of the Great Canal, near Stocking-field, about the 24th January 1797, a silver watch, maker's name R. Herbert, London, No. 6850. Whoever has found the same, by returning it to Mr James Ross, watchmaker, Gallowgate, Glasgow, shall receive half a guinea reward."—*Glasgow Courier*, 30th January 1797.

" All persons who stand indebted to the deceased James Ross, watchmaker in Gallowgate, Glasgow, are desired without delay to pay their accounts to David Ross, at the shop lately possessed by the said J. Ross, who alone is empowered to discharge the same. The whole watch and clock makers' tools which belonged to the said J. Ross are to be sold by public roup within the workshop lately possessed by Mr Robert Somervell, watchmaker, fifth close east from the Gallowgate Bridge, south side, on Wednesday, the 5th day of February next, at eleven o'clock forenoon."—*Ibid.*, 25th January 1800.

ROSS, THOMAS. High Street, Tain, 1836.

ROSS, WILLIAM. High Street, Montrose, 1820.

ROSS, WILLIAM. Stonehaven, 1846.

ROSS, WILLIAM. Dingwall, 1849.

ROSS, WILLIAM. Duke Street, Huntly, 1836.

ROUGH, DAVID. Hill Town, Dundee, 1820.

ROUGH, JAMES. Links, Kirkcaldy, 1836.

ROUMIEU, PAUL, sen. Edinburgh, 1677-94.

With the exception of David Ramsay, who is the earliest watchmaker belonging to Scotland that we have authentic account of, little information is to be gleaned about any other till the latter part of the seventeenth century. As Ramsay died between 1640-50, and was resident in London for at least thirty years, there is therefore a period of nearly thirty years during which the name or even mention of a watch-maker being in Scotland is unrecorded. What remains of Ramsay's make in the British Museum is put down as having been made 1600-10, and though they were the production of a Scotsman, still it is not clear that they were manufactured in Scotland, seeing the date of his arrival in London is uncertain. As remarked above, no other name or even a single specimen of a watch made in Scotland earlier than 1677 survives, and it is to a foreigner that the honour is due of reintroducing an art into Scotland that prospered exceedingly although of slow growth. During the sixteenth and seventeenth centuries the trade con-nection between France and Scotland was, as is well known, of an extensive nature, and as France led in the manufacture of articles of luxury and artistic merit, the arrival of Paul Roumieu in Edinburgh, as a practical watchmaker, must have been hailed with satisfaction by the clockmakers of that city as an event of the greatest importance.

The first appearance of the name occurring here is found in the records of the Incorporation of Hammermen, under the date of 2nd June 1677 :—

"AT MAGDALEN CHAPEL.—The Deacon, Boxmaster and remanent bretheren of ye Hammermen being met, compeared presonally Paull Roumieu, who presented ane essay, viz., the movements of ane watch, which was found to be a weill wrought essay, able to serve his Majesties' leiges, and therefore they have received him to be ane ordinary freeman amongst them in the airt and trade of clockmaker. His essay masters were George Neill and Andrew Brown, his essay was made in his own chamber. He payed to the Boxmaster ane hundred pounds (Scots) and the clerk and officers' duties."

This minute, giving us the exact date of his admission, is of great interest, showing that the essayist was more than an ordinary craftsman. He being the first in whose favour the other part of the essay was waived, namely, the construction of a lock and key, thus making him, along with his son, the only two men (at that date) who were relieved of this part of the essay, clearly demonstrates that in Paul Roumieu they had a master in the art. One important omission requires to be noted here : no mention is to be found where he belonged to, but all the evidence available points to him as being a native of France. The late Dr Chambers, in his well-known book, *The Traditions of Edinburgh*, says, speaking of the West Bow : "The house immediately within the ancient port on the east side of the street was occupied about the beginning of the last century by Paul Roumieu, an eminent watchmaker, supposed to have been one of the French refugees driven over to this country in consequence of the revocation of the Edict of Nantes. In front of the house, upon the fourth story, there is still to be seen the remains of a curious piece of mechanism, namely, a gilt ball representing the moon which was made to revolve by means of a clock. This house was demolished in 1835." (*See* Frontispiece.)

This has been quoted by all writers on Old Edinburgh, making it the only information available up to the present time. As can be seen from the date of the minute 1677, his appearance here cannot be set down as having been caused by the Revocation of the Edict of Nantes, which occurred in 1685, eight years after, and it is certain that his settlement here was not due to that important event. We must look for another cause, and we hazard the opinion that his presence here may have been due to a royal command or invitation. The Hammermen of Edinburgh as an incorporate body must have been pretty well known to King Charles II., as his royal father, King Charles I., had in 1641 granted to them, as patrons of the Magdalen Chapel (their meeting place), a mortification or gift out of the revenues of the suppressed Bishopric of Dunkeld, of one hundred and nine pounds sterling yearly for the benefit of the poor of the craft. This bequest they enjoyed more or less (an inspection of their records reveals that some years this was a difficult matter) till 1661, when King Charles II., again establishing Episcopacy in Scotland, swept away their right and the revenue was lost. The Hammermen were greatly assisted in the acquisition of this mortification by Sir James Carmichael, the King's Advocate; and as he was a great favourite with Charles II., being created a Baron by him, it is not unreasonable to suppose that the disappointment caused by the loss of this bequest to the Hammermen would remain unknown unto the King. Sir James Carmichael had a direct interest in the matter, as the Hammermen out of gratitude for his efforts for them granted to him and his heirs in perpetuity the right to appoint one bedesman in the chapel. This right was, of course, lost also, and it may be here remarked that the Hammermen, by some strange oversight, neglected to revoke the gift, the consequence being that in 1710 they were drawn into a lawsuit with the then holder of the title for count and reckoning of this appointment. The story is too long for insertion here, but in trying to strengthen our surmise it has been necessary to bring the matter in. By a curious coincidence Sir James Carmichael, who was now Earl of Hyndford, had a son, Sir William, who was a member of the bodyguard of Louis XIV. of France, and undoubtedly in close touch with that monarch. It may have been that representation was made to the Earl by the Hammermen to influence his royal master to make amends for their loss, and that the best thing to be done was to get his majesty to negotiate with Louis XIV. to arrange for a French watchmaker to settle in Edinburgh. The matter may have been broached by this Sir William, and Louis, finding out that there was in Rouen a craftsman who was in every respect qualified to fulfil the part of instructor, arranged with Paul Roumieu to emigrate and come to Edinburgh. Of course one may say why not get one from London, but the native jealousy of their "auld enemies" precluded the idea of an Englishman coming here, and also the worthy

WATCH, WITH SILVER DIAL AND GOLD CENTRE.

By Paul Roumieu, Edinburgh, 1677-94. In the Museum of the Society of Antiquaries of Scotland. Reproduced by permission.

Scots clockmakers knew pretty well that the country that is credited as having been the first to construct a watch was the best fitted to supply a competent master.

Be that as it may, there is another point in the admission minute which may be referred to, namely, he was not a burgess—a condition which was then imperative on every aspirant for admission into the various Incorporation of Crafts in the city. Then the essay was made in his own chamber, not shop, which, however, is mentioned in the admission minute of his son, and lastly, the only known specimen of a watch bearing the name of Paul Roumieu that is to be found in Scotland has engraved on the dial the Royal Arms; all showing that this man must have had powerful influence at his back to account for his setting up business here.

He appears to have taken very little interest in the affairs of the Hammermen, as he is fined £26 Scots for being fifty-six times absent, and his name only turns up in the Records when his apprentices were booked, and on the occasion when his son was made a freeman.

Coming now to his work, it is needless to say that specimens of such are very rare and seldom turn up. We have been able to note the location of three examples, one in Edinburgh and two in London. The Edinburgh one, with silver dial and gold centre (see illustration), is to be seen in the Museum of the Society of Antiquaries in Queen Street, and has the name Roumieu, Edinburgh, engraved in italics on the face. One of the London ones we are enabled to describe more fully by extracts taken from the Catalogue of the addition to the collection of clocks and watches presented to the Worshipful Company of Clockmakers of the City of London by the late Rev. H. L. Nelthropp M.A., F.S.A., kindly forwarded by that gentleman to me.

"No. 15A. P. Roumieu, à Rouen.—A beautifully made watch with a vertical escapement. The dial white enamel, one hand only. The movement is in its original condition, having had little wear and no repair of any kind. The ornamental steel work on the top plate excessively fine and elegant. The fusee is cut for catgut and not for a chain. No spiral spring to the balance. The case is enamelled and the subject on its outside is in the style of Boucher. The movement was probably made between 1645 and 1670."

A note following after the above description informs us that great interest attaches to it in consequence of it having been made by a Roumieu, the celebrated French watchmaker of Edinburgh, a contemporary of Tompion, Quare, and Gretton, coupling his name with the most famous men that England had produced in the art of Horology.

The other London specimen is as follows :—

"The gold dial, an extremely elegant one, has a piece cut out of it for the purpose of exposing to view the balance arm made to represent a pendulum bob. The hands are the original steel ones. The top plate of the movement is extremely well engraved, and it has on a circular piece the name Paul Roumieu, Edinburgh, with the number 259. The metal box which holds the movement and the outer silver cases are decidedly not original. There is very little doubt that the cases were originally made of gold. The escapement is a vertical one. The pillars are open tulip shaped. The regulating index is on the dial as well as a cartouche bearing the name ' Roumieu.' "

A note explains that it is seldom that a watch by Roumieu can be bought in London. The above one was sold by Messrs Christie, Manson, and Woods, at their great rooms, 8 King Street, St James's Square, on Thursday, 14th February 1895, forming one of the collection of watches, the property of the Rev. W. Bentinck, L. Hawkins, deceased ; lot 856.

Doubtless there are more specimens in existence, but enough has been mentioned to show the skill and execution of this famous craftsman. He died in March 1694, and was buried in the Greyfriars' Churchyard, where in the records of that old burying-ground his interment is noted as follows : "Paul Rowmie, Watchmaker,"

ROUMIEU, PAUL, jun. Edinburgh, 1682-1717.

The existence of another maker bearing the same name has only now been satisfactorily proved, and the important testimony recording this is given in a minute from the *Hammermen's Records* under the date of 16th August 1682 :—

"At the Magdalen Chapel in the afternoon, in presence of Deacon Anderson, Deacon Coulstoun, the Boxmaster, Boxmaster Ramsay, Master Blacksmiths and Locksmith airts, compeared Paul Roumieu, son to Paul Roumieu, clockmaker, burgess of Edinburgh,[1] and presented his essay, viz., the movements of a watch which was found a weill wrought essay, able to serve his majesties leiges, and therefore they admitted him to be a freeman among them in the clockmakers' airt. His essay masters were Richard Mills and John Sympsone. The essay was made in his father's shop. He gave in a sufficient fyrelock and bandilier and paid the boxmaster ane hundreth merkis for his upset and the clerk and officers' dues."

It is curious that the son's identity should have remained so obscure. So far as can be gleaned, he appears to have inherited all the father's skill and ingenuity, and was eminently qualified to conduct the business his father's death made him master of in 1694. This he managed so successfully that it is evident it reached some dimensions, judging from the number of apprentices he booked. The father, during his career, appears never to have had more than two, John Cousteill and David Marine. The son had no less than two apprentices and two journeymen, their names being Jacques Thibou, John Frugard, Emmanuel Poarson, and David Mackerson (q.v.). These names give an idea of the French element in the city at that date.

Where his shop was situated does not appear, and as can be seen in the notes on the father, tradition makes it to have been in the Clockmaker's Land, Bow. (*See*

[1] Though careful search has been made into the Burgess Rolls preserved in the City Chambers no entry is to be found recording this statement.

Frontispiece). The only contemporary notice regarding him that we have been able to discover occurs in that rare old newspaper, the *Edinburgh Gazette*, of the date 1699, which is as follows :—

"Stolen this day in the Parliament House, out of a gentleman's pocket, a silver pendulum watch with a minute hand, in a green shagreen case. Whoever can give notice of said watch to Mr Roumieu, watchmaker, shall be thankfully rewarded."

Specimens of his work are very rare ; the only clock of which particulars have reached me is in the possession of Mr Paterson, Biggar, Lanarkshire. The case is covered with most elaborate marquetry. The dial is rather small, being 11 inches square, and has the name Paul Roumie, Edinburgh, engraved on the lower part of the chapiter, while the centre is matted, and it has the usual raised seconds disc. It goes a month without winding. By a curious coincidence, this clock is believed to have been originally the property of the Earl of Hyndford, whose estate of Carmichael is only a few miles distant from Biggar. As we have tried to show in the notes on Paul Roumieu, senior, that his arrival in Scotland was largely due to the efforts of the above nobleman, it is therefore not impossible that this clock may have been made and presented to the Earl of Hyndford as a token of gratitude for his powerful interest in the matter. The fact of its present location, and it being the only known specimen in existence by this man, warrants the surmise so largely given in the notes on the elder Roumieu.

The son, like the father, took no interest in the affairs of the Hammermen, but notwithstanding this seeming inattention the members highly valued his services to the craft, as the following minute testifies :—

20th September 1712.—"The which day, in presence of the haill Incorporation, there being a petition given in by Anne Roumieu, daughter to the deceast Paul Roumieu, watchmaker freeman in the Incorporation, craving to be presented to the Governors of the Maiden Hospital, by this Incorporation, in the room of Janet

Cowan, who is to come out of the said hospital in April next. And after reading of the said petition, and the Incorporation considering the same, and knowing she is a great object of their charity, they do by these presents condescend and agree that the said Anne Roumieu shall be presented to the Governors of the said hospital to be received in place of the foresaid Janet Cowan, who is to come out in April next, and as soon as she can go in by the acts and rules of the said hospital. This act was approven without a contrair vote."

This kindly worded minute is remarkable for two things, the first being that in the candidature of Anne Roumieu for the vacancy there was no opposition. An inspection of the Records invariably reveals the fact that there was a great competition for the appointment, but in her case none was offered. It also brings out in the second place, that the members of the Hammermen Incorporation were anxious to do justice to the memory of one who by some unexplained calamity had unfortunately left a daughter totally unprovided for. This, the last mention of the name of Roumieu, closes the honourable and useful career of two men to whom the craft in Edinburgh were deeply indebted. Paul Roumieu, jun., had three children interred in the Greyfriars Churchyard, his name in the Records being spelt as follows:—Paul Rovnie and Paul Rwmbie, watchmaker.

ROWLAND, JOHN. Western Lane, Berwick-on-Tweed, 1837.

ROWLAND, JOHN. High Street, Berwick-on-Tweed, 1780-1820.

ROWLAND, WALTER. Bridge Street, Berwick-on-Tweed, 1806-20.

ROWLAND, WALTER. Yetholm, 1833.

ROY, JAMES. Edinburgh, 1759.

Booked apprentice to John Aitken.

ROY, WILLIAM. Edinburgh, 1787.

ROY, WILLIAM. Dunfermline, 1786-1811.

"A gold watch lost or stolen on Saturday in Edinburgh, maker's name Roy, Dunfermline, and the owner's name engraved on the inside of the inner case, William Hart, 1791. Whoever will bring said watch to the *Advertiser* Office, Cross, will be rewarded, and it is hoped it will be stopt if offered for sale or cleaning by any watchmaker, and information given as above." *Edinburgh Advertiser*, 5th March 1811.

RULE, JAMES. 44 High Street, Dundee, 1837.

RULE, JOHN. Kelso, 1791-1836.

"Lost on Friday, 23rd curt., between Edinburgh and Dalkeith, a silver watch, maker's name Jasper Taylor, Holborn, London, No. 573. Whoever has found it will be handsomely rewarded on delivering it to Mr John Rule, watchmaker, Kelso, or Andrew Milligan, watchcase maker, Parliament Close, Edinburgh."—*Edinburgh Evening Courant*, 29th September 1791.

RULE, WALTER. Edinburgh, 1733.

Son of Mr William Rule, merchant in Edinburgh; booked apprentice to John Brown, 23rd January 1733.

RUSSELL, D. Leith, 1833.

"Leishman Russell, painter, Edinburgh, served Co-Heir of Provision General to his mother, Mary Maving, wife of D. Russell, watchmaker, Leith, dated 21st October 1833. Recorded 2nd November 1833."— *Services of Heirs.*

RUSSELL, HUGH. Moffat, 1837.

RUSSELL, JOHN. Falkirk, 1783-1817.

This was a craftsman of more than ordinary ability, and, as will be seen in the following notices, turned out work of the highest class :—

"TO THE CURIOUS IN MECHANICS.—To be Sold a very curious Organ Clock, being the first ever made in Scotland, which plays a tune every two hours. The barrel it has at present consists of twelve different tunes and more may be made if required.

"To be seen at any time at Mr Russel's, watchmaker, Falkirk, to whom proposals from intending purchasers may be made. He likewise makes and repairs Musical Clocks, Organs, etc.; also makes portable jacks of a new construction, Barometers, Thermometers, and every kind of machinery in the watch and clock branch.

"By a long course of study and practice, having brought his Organ Clock to the utmost perfection, Mr Russel humbly begs leave to solicit the patronage and encouragement of the public, and all favours will be thankfully and gratefully acknowledged."—*Edinburgh Evening Courant*, 12th May 1783.

"WATCHES STOLEN.—Whereas a man naming himself William Muir, an Englishman journeyman Clockmaker with Mr John Russel, Falkirk, went off on Monday, the 25th curt., carrying away eight silver watches, one of them cap'd and jewelled, with seconds from the contrate wheel figures in place of hours upon the dial plate, maker's name John Lamb, London; another cap'd with the name John Henderson upon the cape, and maker's name John Russel, Falkirk, No. 132; the other six are common watches, one of the makers' names John Russel, Falkirk, and another of them James Upjohn, London.

"He appears to be a man between 30 and 40 years of age, about five feet five inches high, short black hair, thin on the forehead, a large mark of a cut upon the right corner of his brow; had on when he went off a snuff brown coat tore at the right armpit, dark brown velveret vest with small yellow spots, plain drab-coloured breeches, round hat, blue-white stockings, and shoes tied with leather thongs. Whoever will apprehend, or cause to be apprehended, the above person shall on conviction be handsomely rewarded.

"It is entreated that all watchmakers and those dealing in the business will stop the offerer of such articles, and information being given to John Russel, or Mr George Williamson, messenger, Edinburgh, will be gratefully received and rewarded."—*Edinburgh Evening Courant*, 30th June 1792.

"LOTTERY, By John Russel, Clock and Watch Maker, Falkirk.—The prizes are a Chamber Barrel Organ with four stops, which plays 24 different select tunes at pleasure, neatly fitted up in a mahogany case, elegantly ornamented on the front with round towers and gilt pipes; a silver watch cap'd and jewelled with seconds and Prince of Wales escapement; two fine eight-day spring Clocks; a brass solar microscope;

with a number of eight-day clocks, silver watches, Barometers and Thermometers; also a number of capital prints engraved by the late Sir Robert Strange neatly framed with inside gilt mouldings.

"Tickets at five shillings each with Schemes to be had of J. Russel, Falkirk, Messrs Goldie and Robertson, merchants, opposite to the Cross, and C. Elliot, bookseller, Parliament Square, Edinburgh.   Also by J. Bannerman, Carver and Gilder, Glasgow.

"As a great number of the tickets are already sold, those who wish to become adventurers will please apply for tickets as soon as possible that the time of drawing may be fixed.   Gentlemen who please to call at J. Russel's will have an opportunity of viewing the organ, etc., and he is persuaded they will sufficiently recommend themselves.

"J. Russel returns his most grateful thanks to his friends and the public for past favours, and begs leave to inform them that he has been in London and other manufacturing towns in England purchasing a fresh stock of materials for the better carrying on of his business in the Clock and Watch line.   Also he has selected a number of capital prints engraved by the best masters, among which are a few impressions of Mary Queen of Scots with James VI., both engraved on one plate by Bartolozzi."[1]—*Edinburgh Evening Courant*, 26th July 1792.

"On Monday, Mr Russell of Falkirk, watchmaker to His Royal Highness the Prince Regent, waited on his Royal Highness at Carlton House, when he had the honour of delivering a superb gold chronometer of his making, according to his R.H. gracious order.   His Royal Highness, with his usual condescension, was pleased to declare his satisfaction with this specimen of Mr Russell's workmanship.   Mr Russell had also the honour of presenting to his Royal Highness a box made from the celebrated Wallace's Tree, in the Torwood, Stirlingshire, elegantly mounted in gold.   The box contained a quantity of wheat which was found in a vault of the Roman wall or Graham's Dyke at Castlecary, where it is supposed to have lain upwards of 1400 years. The lid of the box contained a very elegant inscription with the above particulars.   Mr Russell also presented

---

[1] This is now a scarce engraving, original impressions being difficult to procure.

to His Royal Highness a silver Crookstone dollar, being a coin of Queen Mary and her husband Lord Darnley, struck at Crookstone Castle in the year 1565, and a very ancient watch of curious workmanship. His Royal Highness conversed for some time with Mr Russell with great affability, and showed him a great many curious clocks and watches."—*Edinburgh Evening Courant*, 6th July 1812.

"Died at Falkirk on the 24th September, Mr John Russell, Watchmaker to his Royal Highness the Prince Regent. From a different line of trade to which he was originally bred ; by his ingenuity and industry he raised himself to an eminent and prominent situation in his profession."—Obituary Notice in *Edinburgh Advertiser*, 30th September 1817.

His remains were interred in the parish churchyard near to the unique memorial erected to the great Sir John Graham. On a recent visit to this old town and burying-ground we observed with satisfaction that a beautiful and chaste designed monument marked his last resting-place. As the inscription on it informed us, it was erected by a brother in loving memory of John Russell, watchmaker to H.R.H. Prince Regent, 1818.

RUSSELL, John. Falkirk, 1850.

RUSSELL, Robert. Moffat, 1774.

RUSSELL, Samuel. New Road, Selkirk, 1837.

RUSSELL, Samuel. Selkirk, 1773.

"Martha Russell or Douglas, wife of Samuel Russell, watchmaker, Selkirk, served Heir General to her father William Douglas, baker there, dated 22nd June 1773. Recorded 7th August 1773."—*Services of Heirs*.

RUSSELL, William. Glasgow, 1802 ; died 22nd April 1816.

RUSSELL, William. Glasgow, 1827 ; probably son of above.

RUSSELL, William. High Street, Falkirk, 1820.

RUTHERFORD, Walter. Jedburgh, 1836.

RUTHERFORD, William. High Street, Hawick, 1837.

SAFELY or SAFLEY, John. Portsburgh, Edinburgh, 1764-1803.

"Presented a bill craving to be admitted a freeman clock and watch maker in Portsburgh, 3rd November 1764. Compeared on 4th May 1765, and presented his essay, being a clock movement without the striking part, made in his own shop, as John Chalmers, his landlord, and James Duff and James Hutton, his essay masters, declared."—*E. H. Records.*

He died 17th October 1803.

SAFELY, John. Carluke; died 17th June 1857, aged 54 years.

SAFLY or SAIFLOY, John. Lanark, 1790.

SALMON, Colin. Dundee, 1811.

SANDERSON, Alexander. Dunblane, 1798.

SANDERSON, John. Wigtown, 1715.

It is only through the records of the Edinburgh Hammermen that any information of this maker is to be found, and the mention of his name is due to the exercising of one of their "rights," namely, the searching of the market in Edinburgh to see if any articles were exposed for sale by unfreemen. Two clocks were offered for sale by Sanderson, and this infringement was duly noted and the articles at once seized. The minutes which follow explain exactly how the matter was settled.

18th May 1715.—"The meeting appoints the two clocks taken from John Sanderson, clockmaker in Wigtoun in England, to be restored back again upon payment of twenty shillings sterling for the use of the poor of the Incorporation, and granting bond not to import into this burgh or privileges thereof any clocks or watches or any other work than that made by the members of the Incorporation in any time hereafter under the penalty of £120 Scots. *Toties quoties.*"

21st May 1715.—"The bond appointed by the last sederunt to be granted by John Sanderson, watchmaker, in the terms of the minute as specified, was accordingly granted, which the boxmaster received, and the twenty shillings for the use of the poor."

Particulars of three clocks made by this maker have reached me : one, a very fine one, now located at St Louis, Missouri, America, the others being in Edinburgh and South Queensferry. These last two have a verse of Scripture engraved on the dials, showing the religious temperament of the maker, and as we notice in the Boxmaster's accounts recording the payment of the fine, he is termed a Quaker, which may account for these pious texts.

SANDY, JAMES. Alyth, 1780-1819.

"The originality of genius and eccentricity of character which distinguished this remarkable person were perhaps never surpassed. Deprived at an early age of the use of his legs, he contrived by dint of ingenuity not only to pass his time agreeably, but to render himself a useful member of society. He soon displayed a taste for mechanical pursuits, and contrived as a workshop for his operations a sort of circular bed, the sides of which, being raised about eighteen inches above the clothes, were employed as a platform for turning lathes, table vices, and cases for tools of all kinds. His genius for practical mechanics was universal. He was skilled in all sorts of turning, and constructed several curious lathes, as well as clocks and musical instruments of every description no less admired for the sweetness of their tone than the elegance of their execution. He excelled, too, in the construction of optical instruments, and made some reflecting telescopes, the specula of which were not inferior to those finished by the most eminent London artists. He suggested some important improvements in the machinery for spinning flax, and he was the first who made the wooden jointed snuff-boxes generally called Laurencekirk boxes, some of which fabricated by this self-taught artist were purchased and sent as presents to the Royal Family.

"For upwards of 50 years he quitted his bed only three times, and on these occasions his house was either inundated with water or threatened with danger from fire. Naturally possessed with a good constitution and an active, cheerful turn of mind, his house was the

general coffee-room of the village, where the affairs both
of Church and State were discussed with the utmost
freedom. In consequence of his long confinement his
countenance had rather a sickly cast, but it was
remarkably expressive, and would have afforded a fine
subject for the pencil of Wilkie, particularly when he
was surrounded by his country friends. This singular
man had acquired by his ingenuity and industry an
honourable independence, and died possessed of considerable property. In short, his history holds out this
very instructive lesson, that no difficulties are too great
to be overcome by industry and perseverance, and that
genius, though it should sometimes miss the distinction
it deserves, will seldom fail unless by its own fault to
secure competence and respectability. He was married
only three weeks before his death, which occurred on
3rd April 1819."—*Edinburgh Advertiser*, 30th April
1819.

SANGSTER, ALEXANDER. Rose Street, Peterhead, 1837.

SCOT, JAMES. Dalkeith, 1760.

"Lost on Friday the 22nd instant, betwixt Channel-
kirk and Dalkeith, a silver watch, maker's name
J. Steel, London, No. 101. Whoever has found the said
watch and will return it to James Scot, Clockmaker in
Dalkeith, will receive half a guinea of reward."—
Edinburgh Evening Courant, 25th August 1760.

SCOTT, ANDREW. Water of Leith, Edinburgh, 1764-76.

Booked apprentice to George Monro, Canongate,
29th April 1764.

SCOTT, ANDREW. Dingwall, 1794.

SCOTT, ANDREW. Dundee, 1776.

SCOTT, DAVID. 73 High Street, Dundee, 1850.

SCOTT, DAVID. Canongate, Edinburgh, 1750.

SCOTT, FREDERICK. 3 Overgate, Dundee, 1837.

SCOTT, GEORGE. Canongate, Edinburgh, 1716-55.

Married Christian Scott, indweller in Edinburgh
18th September 1746.

Admitted freeman clock and watch maker, C. H.,
3rd October 1716. *See* notes on George Monro.

SCOTT, JAMES. Shore, Leith, 1774-91.

"Lost on Saturday last, the 30th April, betwixt the south end of Potterrow and Leith Walk, by the way of the Bridges, a small silver watch, maker's name William Creak, London, No. 9772, and marked on the outside of the inner case, D. G. It had a steel chain with a large seal set in silver, having the impression of a head. One Guinea of reward will be given to the persons who shall return the above at the Printing Office or to Mr James Scott, Clockmaker, Leith."—*Edinburgh Evening Courant*, 9th May 1791.

SCOTT, JAMES. Kirk Wynd, Selkirk, 1837.

SCOTT, JOHN. Princes Street, Edinburgh, 1779-98.

"Bound apprentice to James Gray, 13th January 1779. Discharged of his indentures 30th July 1785. Presented a petition craving to be admitted a freeman in E. H., 6th May 1786."—*E. H. Records*.

"SCOTT, Watch and Clock Maker to his Royal Highness the Prince of Wales, No. 2 East Register Street, Edinburgh, having been lately for a considerable time in London, studying under the direction of some of the best artists in England, humbly solicits the patronage of a generous public. He returns his most grateful thanks for the numerous favours he has already received, and begs leave to assure those who shall do him the honour to employ him, that his most assiduous endeavours shall ever be used to deserve their patronage. J. Scott makes, repairs, and cleans watches with detached escapements, the newest and best construction, musical, spring, quarter, plain, and all other sorts of clocks. *N.B.* Commissions will be punctually attended to."—*Edinburgh Advertiser*, 30th November 1790.

"GILDING OF WATCHES.—Scott, Watchmaker to his Royal Highness the Prince of Wales, returns his grateful thanks, and to the public in general, for the encouragement he has already met from them in the Clock and Watch trade ; hopes for a continuance of their favours, and assures those who shall honour him with their employment that his most assiduous endeavours shall always be exerted to make his work give general satisfaction. He takes this opportunity of informing the public that he has invented a new method of gilding on metal which is far superior in lustre and durability to the method formerly practised in Britain.

Y

"J. S. begs leave to inform the Lord-Lieutenants, Noblemen, and Gentlemen commanding the Militia and other Military Corps in Scotland, that he has of late manufactured and gilded swords and other military accoutrements for a number of volunteer corps, and will execute any further orders with despatch. He manufactures regulation swords as ordered by his Majesty for the army, upon more reasonable terms than has hitherto been done in England. Officers may have their swords regilded, and those who have blades only may have them fitted up after the regulation pattern.

"*N.B.*—Watchmakers may have inside works of watches or cases gilded that will have a superior richness either in the French or British style upon the shortest notice and upon reasonable terms, 13 Princes Street, Edinburgh."—*Edinburgh Evening Courant*, 21st May 1791.

"SALE OF A WATCHMAKER'S STOCK.—The whole goods in the shop occupied by the deceased John Scott, watchmaker, Princes Street, Edinburgh, with the counters and glass cases, works, tools, and possession of the shop till Whitsunday next, are to be sold by public roup for behoof of his creditors within the shop itself upon Monday the 17th day of September curt. The roup to begin at ten o'clock forenoon. The goods consist of a number of spring clocks, watch movements nearly finished, Gold, Gilded and Steel Chains in great variety, particularly a large assortment of ladies' watch chains, Gold and Metal Seals, Peeble blocks, with complete sets of working tools, a watch engine, Implements for gilding, with a complete set of burnishers. The whole will be set up in large or smaller lots as intending purchasers may incline. The stock is well worth the attention of any person wishing to enter into the clock and watch trade as it presents an opportunity of setting themselves in a fixed business at once. Inventories of the whole goods may be seen at the shop or in the hands of Thomas Stewart, solicitor-at-law, Mid Rose Street, who will treat with any person wishing to make a private bargain for the whole betwixt and the day of sale."— *Edinburgh Evening Courant*, 15th September 1798.

SCOTT, JOHN. Portsburgh, Edinburgh, 1770-1802.

Booked apprentice to James Hutton, Portsburgh, 5th May 1770.

"Lost a silver watch with a steel chain and seal between Lauriston and Grassmarket, on Monday forenoon the 13th September, maker's name Joseph Addison, London, No. 903. Whoever will return the same to John Scott, watchmaker, West Port, Edinburgh, will receive a handsome reward."—*Edinburgh Evening Courant*, 18th September 1802.

"Isabella Scott, in Edinburgh, served Co-Heir General to her father John Scott, Clock and Watch Maker there, dated 3rd December 1851. Recorded 11th December 1851."—*Services of Heirs*.

SCOTT, ROBERT. Virginia, America, 1779.

"Robert Scott, watchmaker in Virginia, served Heir General to his father George Scott in North Leith, one time baker in Edinburgh, dated 21st May 1779."— *Services of Heirs*.

SCOTT, WALTER. Lauder, 1780.

SCOTT, WILLIAM. 69 Overgate, Dundee, 1820.

SCOTT, WILLIAM. Aberdeen, 1798; sometime of London and afterwards at Falkirk and thereafter at Hardgate, Aberdeen.

"To be exposed to sale by public roup on Monday the 4th of March, in the Hall of the New Inn, Castle Street, Aberdeen, a great variety of Watchmakers' and other tools; also a very valuable pocket chronometer or longitudinal watch in Arnold's construction, in strong gold case, the whole of the holes jewelled with a going fusee, all the acting parts of the escapement jewelled, a thermometer balance, several gold, silver, and metal watches, and a table clock—all the property of the deceased William Scott, sometime of London and lately residing in the Hardgate."—*Caledonian Mercury*, 25th February 1799.

SCOTT, WILLIAM. Ferryport-on-Craig, Fife, 1837.

SCOTT & Co., Clock Dial Makers. Glasgow, 1837.

SCOTT & STEELE. 13 Princes Street, Edinburgh, 1790-99.

SCRYMGEOUR, JAMES. 90 Glassford Street, Glasgow, 1816-37.

SCRYMGEOUR, JAMES. Aberdeen, 1846.

SELLAR, JOHN. Elgin, 1820-37.

SHARP, ROBERT. Coldstream, 1825.

SHARP, ROBERT. Jedburgh, 1815-25.

SHARPE, FRANCIS. 3 Church Place, Dumfries, 1837.

SHEARER, MICHAEL. Edinburgh, 1786-1825.

"A CURIOUS ORGAN CLOCK.—Mr Shearer, wooden clock maker, middle of the West Bow, Edinburgh, returns his most grateful thanks to the ladies and gentlemen and the public in general for former favours, and acquaints them that he continues to make, sell, and repair all sorts of wooden clocks and musical clocks in the neatest taste and on the lowest terms. Mr Shearer has just finished an organ clock which plays eight principal tunes—its equal has never been produced in this country for elegance and beauty. It has two stops, a Diapason and Principal. It has an elegant carved and gilded dial and a mock organ in the arch with a man playing on the organ. If the above clock is not sold in a short time M. S. intends to dispose of it by way of lottery. The clock is to be seen at his own house (gratis). *N.B.* Commissions in town and from the country carefully attended to and expeditiously answered."—*Edinburgh Evening Courant*, 3rd March 1788.

SHEARER & WALKER. 35 Arcade, Glasgow, 1836.

SHEARER, MRS CHARLES. 38 Glassford Street, Glasgow, 1836.

SHEDDEN, CHARLES. 3 George Street, Perth, 1813-71.

"THE INCORPORATED TRADES.—In the evening the Trades dined in the various Hotels, when the usual supply of Breadalbane venison appeared on each table. At the Hammermen's dinner in the British Hotel, Ex-Bailie Shedden was presented with a handsome silver tea-set and a silver claret-jug. The presentation was made by Bailie Gray, who in a highly complimentary speech referred to the able manner in which Bailie Shedden had performed the duties devolving upon him as Deacon of the Hammermen's Incorporation during the past 25 years. The tea-pot and claret-jug bear the following inscription :—

"' Presented by the Hammermen Incorporation of Perth to Charles Shedden as a mark of respect and esteem, and in testimony of his energetic, zealous, faithful, and efficient services, as Deacon for the period of 25 years—Perth, 7th October 1863.'

"The service is £50 in value, and was furnished by Mr D. Greig, 8 John Street, Perth."—*Source unknown.*

"Our obituary of to-day contains an intimation of the death of Mr Charles Shedden, watchmaker, formerly one of the Magistrates of the City, Convener of the Trades, and Deacon of the Hammermen Incorporation, which took place on Thursday at his residence in Princes Street. Deceased, owing to failing health and the infirmities incident to old age, retired from his business several years ago, and had attained to the advanced age of 79 years. He was a native of Perth, and during upwards of half a century followed the calling of a clock and watch maker, and was a person of enterprise and activity. He was during the long period of 28 years Deacon of the Hammermen Incorporation, and devoted a great deal of his time to the promotion of its interests. He likewise for some time filled the office of Convener of the Incorporated Trades. During a number of years he was entrusted by the Town Council with the charge of keeping in order the public clock and the music bells in the tower of St John's Church. In 1835 he was appointed by the Council Inspector of Weights and Measures for the Burgh. Until incapacitated by failing health, he discharged the duties of the latter office with much satisfaction and acceptability, and, in fact, he performed all his public duties with faithfulness and integrity. About 1850, he for three years filled the office of a Magistrate of the city. He was a Liberal Conservative and a staunch supporter of the Church of Scotland, though not much of an ardent political or ecclesiastical partisan. He was of a social and genial disposition, and had many friends among his fellow-citizens, by whom his demise will be greatly regretted."—*Source unknown.*

SHEILL, JAMES. Earlston, 1730.

"Isobel Sheill or Pringle, wife of James Sheill, watchmaker in Earlston, served Heir Portr. of Line to her father George Pringle, meal dealer there. Dated 18th July 1730."—*Services of Heirs.*

SHERRIFF, WILLIAM. Edinburgh, 1727.

Son of the deceased Alex. Sherriff, painter in Edinburgh; booked apprentice to Hugh Barclay, 11th November 1727. *See* notes on Hugh Barclay.

SHIER, THOMAS. Lowe Street, Banff, 1837.

SHORT, RAMSAY. Edinburgh, 1781.

> Booked apprentice to Robert Clidsdale.

SHORT, THOMAS. Edinburgh. Keeper of the Calton Observatory, 1777.

SIM, JOHN. Longside, Aberdeenshire, 1837.

SIME, ROBERT. Edinburgh, 1768.

> Booked apprentice to Robert Clidsdale, 27th January 1768.

SIMPSON, DAVID. Portree, Isle of Skye, 1837.

SIMPSON, JOHN. Canongate, Edinburgh, 1761.

> Booked apprentice to George Monro, 1761.

SIMPSON, JOHN. Hamilton Street, Girvan, 1850.

SIMPSON, ROBERT. Edinburgh, 1761-68.

> Booked apprentice to John Brown, 1st August 1761. Discharged of his indentures 13th August 1768.

SIMS, FRANCIS. Edinburgh, 1767.

SINCLAIR, ALEXANDER. Canongate, Edinburgh, 1764.

> Booked apprentice to George Monro.

SINCLAIR, ALEXANDER. Edinburgh, 1767.

> Booked apprentice to Normond Macpherson, 6th July 1767.

SINCLAIR, JAMES. Alloa, 1835.

SINCLAIR, PETER. 67 Canning Street, Glasgow, 1837.

SKELTON, GEORGE. Edinburgh, 1773-1834.

> "Bound apprentice to William Downie, 16th March 1773. The Incorporation gave their consent to him to serve out his time with Normond Macpherson, present Deacon, 8th February 1777. Discharged of his indentures 6th May 1780. Presented a petition craving to be admitted freeman on 29th January 1785. On the application of George Skelton he was allowed one month more to give in his essay, 12th November 1785. Compeared on 27th December 1785, and presented his essay, being a plain watch movement begun, made, and

finished in his own shop in presence of Robert Aitchison, landlord, Laurence Dalgleish, Thomas Reid, and William White, essay masters, as they declared."—*E. H. Records.*

"WATCHMAKING.—George Skelton, watchmaker, a little below the Cross Well, north side of the High Street, Edinburgh, partner and successor to the late Mr Samuel Brown (q.v.), returns his grateful thanks to the company's employers in general, and his friends in particular; begs leave to acquaint them that he carries on the business in all its branches as formerly. G. Skelton had the entire management of the business during the last three years of Mr Brown's life, which he flatters himself has given general satisfaction, and he hopes by unremitting attention to merit a continuation of the public favour which he now solicits. Those who are indebted to the Company will please order payment as soon as possible to G. Skelton, who will grant proper discharges."—*Edinburgh Evening Courant*, 15th December 1787.

"George Skelton respectfully acquaints his friends and the public that, on account of the buildings being taken down, he has removed from his old shop near the Cross Well to the Parliament Close, south side, where he continues to carry on the business in all its branches, and solicits continuance of their favours."—*Edinburgh Advertiser*, 14th June 1793.

"SHOP REMOVED.—George Skelton, watchmaker, respectfully acquaints his friends and the public that he is now removed from No. 2 Hunter Square, to that shop formerly occupied by the late Mr Samuel Brown and him, below the Cross Well, north side of the High Street, now rebuilt, where he continues to carry on the business in all its branches, etc."—*Edinburgh Evening Courant*, 13th June 1796.

See Laurence Dalgleish, 18th June 1808, page 98.

"As a gentleman was going from the Old to the New town on Sunday evening last, he was jostled by two persons opposite to the Register Office, who picked his pocket of a silver hunting watch and two gold seals, maker's name Laurence Dalgleish, No. 504. Whoever will bring the watch and seals to George Skelton, watchmaker, opposite to the Cross Well, will be rewarded and no questions asked."—*Edinburgh Evening Courant*, 3rd February 1810.

"George Skelton, Clock and Watch Maker, No. 257 High Street, begs leave to inform his friends and the public, that having retired from business he has no more concern with the trade now carried on in his former premises. He would request the favour of those indebted to him to pay their accounts at his own house, 33 Richmond Place."—*Ibid.*, 20th February 1834.

His death occurring, as far as we can discover, about the end of 1834, closed a business career which was unique among the craftsmen of Edinburgh. When we consider that his business covered, through the partnership he entered into, a period of one hundred and fifty years, and had been in the possession of men, each of them intimately acquainted with one another, it will be seen that George Skelton has some claim to our admiration in having successfully preserved a connection which was a feature of the good old times.

SKEOCH, JAMES, sen. High Street, Stewarton, 1837.

SKIRVING, JOHN. Edinburgh, 1771-81.

We have been unable to find out where this maker was trained. His election as a freeman of the Edinburgh Hammermen was opposed by the whole of the clock-makers present at the meeting when his admission was proposed. The minutes which follow give full information regarding it, and will be found interesting as affording light on the jealousy prevailing among crafts-men in Edinburgh during the eighteenth century.

"At MAGDALEN CHAPEL, 23*rd March* 1771.—A letter was read from John Skirving, importing that he was desirous of becoming a member of the Incorporation as a clock and watch maker, and that he was willing to pay an adequate sum on account of his not having served for the freedom. Which letter was remitted to the locksmith's art, with power to them to meet and report their opinion against next quarter meeting."

5*th April* 1771.—"The locksmith's art met according to the remittance to them of the letter sent to the Incorporation by John Skirving, and after reading the same Deacon Lethem communicated to the art another letter from the said John Skirving addressed to him. After reasoning on both these letters a very great majority of the art agreed to reject his offer to procure the admission into the Incorporation, he having no legal title to be admitted a freeman of the Incorporation."

4th May 1771.—"A motion being made to approve of the report, after a good deal of reasoning thereanent, on the reading of the letter given in by Mr Lethem to the committee, wherein John Skirving offers Fifty Guineas for the freedom, a vote was proposed and agreed to whether or not the report should be approven of. But before voting William Nicoll protested against any such vote being put, and took instruments to whom William Turnbull, James Cowan, Robert Aitchison, Robert Clidsdale, Samuel Brown, John Gibson, John Murdoch, Normand Macpherson, William Downie, and James Duff adhered. Thereafter the vote being put, stood as follows :—

"Approve 24; not approve 45. The Incorporation accordingly disapproved of the said report of the locksmith's, whereupon James Cowan again protested and took instruments in respect the Incorporation had no power to admit Skirving without the consent of the watchmakers."

11th May 1771.—"A bill of suspension at the instance of Samuel Brown and other watchmakers int..nated to the Deacon being presented to the meeting, containing a demand to prohibit the Incorporation from entering John Skirving, which being read and reasoned upon, several members of the Incorporation being of opinion that the Incorporation had no concern to answer the bill, a note was proposed and seconded whether an answer should be given in name of the Incorporation or not. Before the vote was put James Cowan protested that however the vote should go, that no part of the expence should be paid out of the poor's fund. To whom William Nicoll (and names as in former minute) adhered. Thereafter the vote being put, it carried by a majority of Forty to Thirty that the bill of suspension should be answered and the clerk was ordered to do the same. William Turnbull protested that if the expences of the answer was to be paid out of the funds of the Incorporation the suspension should likewise be entitled to their expences out of the same funds, and thereupon took instruments."

15*th* *May* 1771.—"The occasion of the meeting being to consider a demand made by the watchmakers for giving their agent inspection of the Seals of Cause and Records belonging to the Incorporation, which demand the Committee thought reasonable and author-ised the clerk to give inspection required."

1*st* *June* 1771.—" A proposal from the watchmakers being made for admitting John Skirving for payment of Eighty pounds Sterling, and other members proposing to admit him for payment of Sixty pounds, it was motioned that as the watchmakers had intimated a "sist," obtained on a bill of suspension, prohibiting the Incorporation from entering Skirving. Which though an answer was made thereto was not yet advised. There would be a danger of incurring a contempt of authority; was the Incorporation to proceed in that matter before the suspension was refused by the Lords? Whereupon the watchmakers in presence of the whole house agreed to pass from the suspension and "sist," and consented that the Incorporation should immediately ascertain the sum for which they are willing to admit John Skirving a freeman. And the watchmakers at the same time declared that they would pay the expenses of any process with John Skirving, which should happen in consequence of the Incorporation ascertaining the entry money to be a greater sum than Skirving was willing to pay. And the whole watchmakers present granted an obligation for that purpose. John Spalding protested that no watchmaker should have a vote in any question relative to John Skirving as they were and ought to be considered as parties, and thereupon took instruments. To whom James Aberdour and James Milne adhered. Thereafter a vote was proposed and agreed unto whether John Skirving should be admitted for payment of Sixty or Eighty pounds, when it was carried fifty votes to nineteen that he was to pay Eighty pounds Sterling for being admitted a freeman, and the clerk was appointed to intimate the same to John Skirving. At the above vote there were ten watch-makers present who all voted Eighty pounds."

25th June 1771.—"A letter being read from John Skirving offering Seventy pounds Sterling for being admitted a freeman. Which being considered, the Incorporation, notwithstanding of the former resolution ascertaining the sum to be Eighty pounds, unanimously agree to admit him a freeman clock and watch maker for payment of Seventy pounds Sterling."

"Thereafter compeared the said John Skirving and presented a bill craving that an essay and essay master should be appointed upon payment of the said Seventy pounds. The prayer of which was granted. The essay to be presented between and Candlemas, and he paid to the Treasurer Thirty-five pounds sterling, and is to pay the like sum at his entry."

1st February 1772.—"Compeared and presented his essay, being a spring clock for repeating the quarters, begun, made, and finished in James Duff's shop in presence of James Duff, landlord, Robert Aitchison, William Downie, and Thomas Sibbald, essay masters as they declared, which was found to be a well-wrought essay and able to serve the lieges. He was thereafter admitted a freeman clock and watch maker. He paid the Treasurer Thirty-five pounds as the last half of his upset, and in token of his consent to the acts of the Incorporation conform to the oath of admission taken by him he signs these presents Jno. Skirving."—*E. H. Records.*

"By order of the trustees for the creditors of John Skirving, Watchmaker in Edinburgh. On Wednesday next, the 27th curt., will be sold by public roup at the shop of the said John Skirving in Luckenbooth's, Edinburgh, at 10 o'clock forenoon, his whole stock-in-trade, consisting of several watches and eight-day clocks, with a table and fine musical clock, and also his whole tools, benches, and other articles used by clock and watch makers; and on Thursday, the 28th, will be rouped and sold the whole household furniture that belonged to the said John Skirving at his house, Dons Close. All those standing indebted to the said John Skirving are desired immediately to pay their debts to Robert Tenant, at Mr Sprotts, writer, Morocco Close, Canongate. A person will attend from ten to two o'clock at the said shop to-morrow to show the goods.

"*N.B.*—The house and shop are to be let to Whitsunday next—for particulars apply as above."—*Caledonian Mercury*, 25th November 1776.

"LOST, the 30th of May last, 1779, in or about Edinburgh, an engraved Metal Watch, name H. N. James, Edinburgh, No. 135. Whoever has found the same will please acquaint John Skirving, watchmaker, Parliament Close, Edinburgh, and they will receive a handsome reward."—*Caledonian Mercury*, 4th June 1779.

27th January 1781.—"A letter was read from John Skirving craving a loan and offering caution. The Incorporation, in respect of the former regulations, refuse to lend any money to him or any other member of the house, at the same time authorise the Treasurer to lend ten guineas to the person proposed to be cautioner upon his single bill payable in twelve months, in case it shall appear to the treasurer and his committee that such person is apparently in good circumstances."

21st July 1781.—"John Skirving, upon condition of his going abroad (after reasoning upon his letter acquainting thereof), authorises Robert Clidsdale, Robert Aitchison, and Laurence Dalgleish to give to or pay on his account, as they shall think proper, fifteen guineas, and this sum the treasurer is authorised to pay to the above three members."—*E. H. Records.*

SLIMAN, ARCHIBALD. Cumnock, 1837-50.

SLIMEN, WILLIAM. 21 High Street, Ayr, 1836.

SMALL, THOMAS. Dundee, 1722.

SMALL, WILLIAM. Edinburgh, 1769-75.

Booked apprentice to John Murdoch, 28th January 1769. Discharged of his indentures 28th January 1775.

SMEITON, CHARLES. Dunbar, 1791.

"To be sold by private bargain, several eight-day clocks with and without cases, several silver watches, with a quantity of watch-glasses, chains, seals, and keys, being the whole stock-in-trade of the deceased Charles Smeiton, watchmaker in Dunbar. The whole are new and fashionable and will be disposed of considerably below prime cost for the encouragement of purchasers, who will be shown the same by applying to Mr John Tait, town-clerk of Dunbar.

"*N.B.*—William Drysdale, watch and clock maker from Edinburgh, is now carrying on that business at Dunbar, and has always on hand a large assortment of clocks and watches and a great assortment of Hardware and Jewellery articles which he sells on moderate terms."—*Edinburgh Evening Courant*, 24th February 1791.

SMITH, ALEXANDER. Dundee, 1718-42.

SMITH, ALEXANDER. Keithhall, Inverurie, 1846.

SMITH, ALEXANDER. Low Street, Banff, 1845.

SMITH, ALEXANDER. Tranent, 1837.

SMITH, ANDREW. Prestonpans, 1830.

Had a son named Robert in North Berwick and another named Alexander in Tranent, both clockmakers.

SMITH, A. P. Reform Street, Dundee, 1850.

SMITH, CHARLES. James Street, Aberdeen, 1846.

SMITH, DAVID. Pittenweem, 1827-34.

SMITH, DAVID. South Street, St Andrews, 1835-73.

Business continued by a son who died in 1904, and still carried on by a grandson of David.

"Helen Coupar or Smith, wife of D. Smith, watchmaker, St Andrews, served Co-Heir special to her father, David Coupar, merchant there, who died 6th January 1839, in shares of ground called the Nib in Fifeshire dated 15th March 1850. Recorded 27th March 1850."—*Services of Heirs.*

SMITH, GEORGE. Gordon Street, Huntly, 1837-46.

SMITH, GEORGE. High Street, Forres, 1837.

SMITH, GEORGE. Edinburgh, 1647.

It is not unlikely that there were other knokmakers in Edinburgh at this date, but this George Smith is the first name that appears in the *Hammermen's Records* as being admitted a qualified knokmaker and entered as a member of the locksmith craft. This last branch being made imperative on every aspirant for the freedom of the Incorporation, and a lock and key were invariably added as a test of their ability along with the essay peculiar to their art. When the Hammermen decided to allow knokmakers to become freemen is not known, as no "minute" is to be found recommending such an arrangement. Possibly there were so few of them in Edinburgh before this time that it was not worth while forcing them to join. Always suspicious about infringing their privileges, the fact of an outsider making the clock for their meeting-place drew their attention to a matter that they were shrewd enough to see would give rise to endless disputes. No doubt they were informed of what had been done in London in this same matter, as the clockmakers there had been in the custom of associating themselves under the blacksmith trade, but being more numerous in that city they broke away from this arrangement and formed a distinct Incorporation called the Clockmakers' Company of London in 1631.

As there was at least one clockmaker before 1647, James Smith,[1] who was the father of George and Robert Smith, it is just possible that he took advantage of the presence of James Alisone (q.v.) being in Edinburgh in 1640-1 to enlarge his own experience and so gain enough extra knowledge and practice as would enable him to instruct his two sons. Be that as it may, on the 6th September 1647 the records bear testimony that for the first time in the history of the Hammermen two aspirants presented themselves for admission as freemen knokmakers. As their admission is really the first authentic account of the beginning of an industry that,

---

[1] This James Smith died 31st May 1660; his name occurs in the volume published by the Scottish Record Society of the list of names of persons buried in the Greyfriars' Churchyard, Edinburgh.

as year after year rolled on, grew to great dimensions in Edinburgh, we give the minute dealing with the admission in full, as being of some interest:—

"Apud Magdalen Chapel, *6th September* 1647.—The qlk day Georg Smith, locksmith and knok maker, in presence of the Deacon, Masters, and haill house, presented his assay, to wit, ane lock with ane key, ane sprent band, and ane knok, ane mounter and dyell, qlk was found ane qualified and weill wrocht assay able to serve the king's liegis. Therefor the Deacon, Masters, and others above written, with consent of the locksmiths and knok makers, admitted and received him in amongst them as an freeman in the said arts, and that in respect he was lawfull son to James Smith, locksmith and knok maker, freeman and burgess of this burgh. His assay masters, Johne Tueidie, elder, and Patrick Nicolsone, locksmiths, gave their oath as use is, and he payed to the boxmaster for his banquet and upset thirty-three pounds, six shillings, eight pence, gave his oath, subscribed the covenant, produced his burgess ticket conform to the order, payed to the clerk and officer their dues, whereupon this act is made."

As his name does not appear again in the records, we conclude that he must have left Edinburgh and settled in some other town. It may have been Dundee, as a George Smith put in order a clock made by James Alisone, which had become faulty in 1648; and to follow this surmise further we have a William Smith, in 1660 in Dundee, who may have been his son, repairing a clock at the request of the Town Council.

SMITH, JAMES. Grantown, Inverness-shire, 1837.

SMITH, JAMES. Dundee, 1742.

SMITH, JAMES. Bridgegate, Irvine, 1837-50.

SMITH, JAMES. Edinburgh, 1790-1806.

"On the evening of Wednesday the 4th of August last, a gentleman was attacked on the Earthen Mound, betwixt the old and new town of Edinburgh, by four men who knocked him down and robbed him of a gold watch having a tortoise-shell outer case, maker's name Jas. Smith, Edinburgh, No. 103, with a silver seal."— *Edinburgh Evening Courant*, 21st August 1790.

"Whereas, on the evening of Thursday the 9th curt., a gold watch-chain and seal of which had been robbed on the evening of Wednesday the 4th of August last was found, wrapped in a grey paper, in a passage leading to a common stair of a tenement in Shakespeare Square. Whoever will give information to the Procurator-Fiscal of the County or city of Edinburgh, of the person or persons in whose possession the said watch-chain and seal have at any time been, from their being taken from the gentleman till found as above, shall receive a reward of ten guineas, and the name of the informer shall be concealed if required."—*Ibid.*, 11th September 1790.

"On Friday last there was lost in the old town a gold watch, maker's name John Lamb, London, No. 1994, with a gilt chain and gold seal. Whoever has found the same will please return them to Mr Smith, watch-maker, Leith Terrace, Edinburgh, and they shall receive a handsome reward."—*Ibid.*, 14th April 1796.

SMITH, JAMES. Edinburgh, 1641-48.

Although as far back as the year 1629 the name of James Smith appears in the *Hammermen Records*, it is not until 1641 that it is clear that he was a knok-maker. If the reader will turn to the notes on the clock and bell of the Magdalen Chapel (page 235), it will be seen that the committee who were appointed on the 23rd of February 1641 were requested to meet with James Smith or any other knokmaker, for estimates, etc. This states definitely that he followed that art, and although he did not get the contract (*see* James Alisone), he appears to have had sufficient business to warrant him making his two sons George and Robert (q.v.) clockmakers. They were the first two whose names appear as being properly qualified knokmakers in Edinburgh. As James Smith's name disappears from the list of freemen in the Incorporation of Hammermen after 1648, it is surmised that his death took place about that date. It is interesting to note that in the list given of names in 1640, his name occurs along with a brother craftsman named Adame Steill, who was, as a little note informs us, "kild and layd in ye bed of honour as a valient cavelier at Merstoun Muir near Zork (York)." This gives a sidelight on which side the Hammermen's sympathies were.

SMITH, JOHN. Canongate, Edinburgh, 1680.

Bracket Clock made by this man shown at Glasgow Exhibition 1911.

SMITH, JOHN. Trongate, Glasgow, 1783-1806.

"Lost, by a gentleman in High Street on Wednesday night last, a gold repeating watch, maker's name Collondon, Roux & Daffer, No. 80. Whoever will return it to John Smith, watchmaker, Glasgow, will receive two guineas reward."—*Glasgow Courier*, 7th April 1798.

SMITH, JOHN. Edinburgh, 1819-22.

SMITH, JOHN. Perth, 1791.

Admitted freeman into the Incorporation of Hammermen, Perth, in right of his father, 1791.

SMITH, JOHN. Pittenweem, 1770-1814.

This ingenious craftsman, owing to the peculiar side he took in the art of horology, has to be classed along with such makers as Matthew Parker and Thomas Reid, who were also his contemporaries, and belonged to the same county. While these last two men excelled in the production of movements requiring a vast amount of calculation, besides great skill in their execution, yet looking at the effects produced by John Smith, and the mechanical labour involved to produce such effects, credit must be allowed to him for the obstacles he surmounted in realising his ideas, owing to the secluded part of the country he resided in, and the want of proper facilities necessary for their construction. Living at a period when the production of clocks with more or less elaborate mechanical effects engaged the attention of quite a number of capable men all over Scotland, it was left to the then obscure fishing village of Pittenweem to produce a man who gave his brother craftsmen an object-lesson in this particular form of clockmaking.

Z

Unfortunately the place where he learned the art is not recorded, but in an advertisement issued by himself in the year 1775, he informs us that "he was bred in the trade and had never been out of the country," inferring that although he was a regularly bred clockmaker yet the mechanical parts of the clocks he so much delighted in making were entirely the work of his own hands, and that the effects were entirely original. Competent judges who have had occasion to examine some of those movements are astonished at the ingenuity displayed in their production, and the means taken to bring about the combinations he employed in working out such parts, the verdict always being that these were more than the labours of a craftsman—they were the creations of a genius. Of course this only applies to clocks having elaborate movements, as it is certain that he was assisted in the production of the ordinary class of timekeepers by skilled journeymen. But his fame as being more than an ordinary clockmaker was made by the clock described below; we feel certain that up to the date of its finish he must have toiled away unassisted to surmount the many experiments he undertook to arrive at the intricate movement which to-day remains as a lasting tribute to his patience and skill. Possibly the first he constructed, it yet remains one of the most elaborate, and an account of it is well worth recording.

" The case, which is of the finest mahogany, is seven feet high with fluted columns on each side of the body. Part of the flutes are filled with brass gilt with gold, and have brass Corinthian capitals and bases. The head has columns at the corners with similar capitals. The upper part of the head is ornamented with carving, fretwork, birds' eyes, and is gilded, having a golden bird with expanded wings standing in the middle of the head. This case contains a large eight-day musical clock with three dial plates, and a chime of sixteen bells. The work is divided into five different parts, each of which has its own particular weight. The first is the going part, the second drives a small musical barrel which plays a pleasant chime at the first, second, and third

ELABORATE MUSICAL CLOCK,
By John Smith, Pittenweem, 1770-1814. Valued by its maker at £900. View of
Principal Dial. The property of William B. Smith, Esq., Glasgow. (See p. 361.)

[To face page 354.

quarters, and plays once over a favourite tune before striking the hour. The third part strikes the hour, and the fourth drives a large musical barrel containing eight celebrated Scots tunes which are as follows :—

1. Highland Laddie; 2. Flowers of the Forest; 3. Tweedside; 4. Ettrick Banks; 5. Lass of Patie's Mill; 6. The Bonniest Lass in all the World; 7. Logan Water; 8. Roslin Castle.

One tune is played every three hours with great exactness. The last part changes the tune. The clock plays the eight in the twenty-four hours.

"The front dial plate measures about fifteen inches and has an arch; it shows the hour minute, and second; and also the day of the month, without variations, even on the 28th of February, throughout the whole year. In this plate likewise are two small hands, one of which discovers the day of the week. When Sunday comes these words, 'Remember Sunday,' is cast up. At twelve o'clock on Saturday night the clock stops playing till twelve strikes on Sunday night, when she begins her music and continues all the week till Saturday night again. The other hand stops the music, hours, and quarters, at pleasure.

"The dial plate on the right hand measures about eight inches. It contains a hand that points to the name of the tune the clock plays, and 't can be set to play any of them at pleasure. A small hand on the arch can be set to play common or triple time. The dial on the left hand is of the same dimensions as the one on the right. It represents the front of a house with the front door in the middle, and a stair with the King's Arms in the arch. At each side of the door stands an armed sentinel in the livery of the City Guard of Edinburgh, painted in lively colours on brass. Inside the doorway you see the macer of the Lords of Council and Session dressed in his robe with the mace in his right hand; and as soon as the clock begins to play he takes off his hat with his left hand and walks past the door. Then the fifteen Lords dressed in their robes, without hats, follow in procession. When the Lords are past, you see the macer come to his place with his hat in his hand and put it on again. The whole is well painted on thin brass, and several of the Lords are allowed to be striking likenesses."

In one of the contemporary Edinburgh newspapers a letter appears, signed by one who calls himself "A Lover of Genius," giving the above description, and this "feeler" is followed up shortly afterwards by the arrival of the clock in Edinburgh for the purpose of exhibition and disposal. This was in the year 1775, and it is quite plain from the announcements made about it that the movements had been finished long before the handsome case was got to contain them. We notice in that year, from the *Services of Heirs,* that John Smith was served heir to his aunt Helen Smith in Cupar, and this may have helped him to the possession of the means which enabled him to finish it and bring it to Edinburgh. Large numbers visited it at Balfour's Coffee House, each paying one shilling to see it, but as far as can be gleaned, although every endeavour was made, no purchaser was got. From this date up to 1804 no mention of it is to be found either as to location or owner. Probably no clock made by a Scotsman has been so often described or referred to. Accounts of it appeared in a large number of newspapers and magazines for many a year after, but, curiously enough, not the slightest hint was given into whose hands it had fallen. Some years ago a description of it was given in the pages of the *Weekly Scotsman* to see if its location would turn up, but no satisfactory reply was received, although one now in Dundee by the same maker was in some detail similar, but not the one described. An account of this same clock appeared in a local Fife newspaper of the date of 1891, where the information was given that "John Smith took it to London for the purpose of showing it to King George III., but unfortunately ere he reached the metropolis King George was blind and incapable of inspecting it. No offer, however, was made tempting enough to induce him to part with it. It was, therefore, brought back to Scotland

and eventually disposed of by Mr Smith to a landed proprietor in the West of Fife." The article closed thus: " The clock is now in the possession of a London firm who are offering it for sale. The price they put upon it is said to be £240."

This is how one writer disposes of this famous clock, but the story will not bear examination. King George III. did not turn blind until after 1800, at least twenty-five years after the clock was made. The writer of the article strangely mixes up another clock which John Smith took to London in 1808 and which is now in the possession of a gentleman near Alloa (this one will be referred to further on). In spite of the publicity of the description given in the *Weekly Scotsman*, along with other journals, nothing transpired to identify its location or owner. We had despaired of hearing anything about it, but a visit to Dalkeith in the summer of 1904 soon solved the mystery. Going into a local watchmaker's shop, a custom which we have been in the habit of doing, wherever we go, to have a chat about old time makers, the young man in charge of the shop informed me that John Smith's famous clock was at the present moment in Dalkeith Palace. Inquiring if he was sure that it was the long-looked-for clock, he replied that it agreed exactly with the description given in our book, a copy of which he had beside him, and further, that as he had the winding, etc., of all the clocks in the house to attend to, there was not the slightest doubt as to its being the self-same clock.

A request being forwarded to the proper quarter for permission to view it and establish its identity, it was graciously given effect to by his Grace the late Duke of Buccleuch, its owner, and on visiting the palace, to our delight, this masterpiece was seen in complete going order. Everything in the description was duly compared and found to be absolutely correct, and while we were there we not only saw the procession of the judges, but the musical chime played sweetly the first tune on the list, namely, " Highland Laddie." The whole clock was a revelation, everything being in perfect condition. Among the many fine clocks and timepieces to be found in this splendid mansion, a number of them being masterpieces of French and English makers, the clock by our old Scots craftsman easily held its own, both as regards appearance and performance.

To think that after a period of more than a century it performs its useful duty as time - keeper and its intricate and musical effects as complete as when first set agoing, points not only to the excellence of the materials and workmanship employed, but also to the care displayed in its preservation by its noble owners. How long it has been in the possession of the Buccleuch family has not transpired, but the late Duke of Buccleuch was, we understand, accustomed to its presence from childhood, now a period of over seventy years. This shows that its location in Dalkeith Palace is not a thing of yesterday, and the probability is that an ancestor of the duke purchased the clock when it was shown in Edinburgh in 1775.

Not much information is to be got about John Smith after the above date till the year 1808, when he again visited Edinburgh with two clocks, a description of which follows :—

One of them was what he terms a table clock, four feet ten inches high, moved by springs (*see* p. 354). The other was nine feet high, moved by weights, and having four dials. The first and largest showed the months and the number of days in each; the second, the days of the week, with "Remember the Sabbath" opposite Sunday; the third, having directions for arranging the striking of the clock; while the fourth told the seconds, minutes, and hours. It had an elaborate scene of a Royal Procession, and also had a chime of twenty-four bells, which played the following eight tunes :—

1. Mary Scott; 2. Duke of York's March; 3. Prince of Wales' March; 4. The Last Time I came ower the Muir; 5. God Save the King; 6. The Wauking of the Fauld; 7. Roslin Castle; 8. My Nannie.

Advised by his ardent friends, he resolved to carry

them to London. The journey itself in those days with such fragile wares was enough to daunt most men, but he evidently had the idea that London was the only goal where his labours would be recognised and recompensed. On his arrival there he had the honour of exhibiting these two clocks to the Royal Family and nobility and gentry. He also had them valued by three of the first makers in London whose appraisement for the table clock was fixed at the respectable figure of nine hundred pounds; the other at four hundred and seventy-two pounds. It was at this date, on his second visit to London, that he devoted his leisure time to mastering the intricacies of watchmaking. To what success he arrived at is not known, but the fact remains that watches bearing his name are exceeding rare (we have only heard of three), showing that his forte lay in clockmaking.

While no doubt he made a little by exhibiting his handiwork, no purchasers were to be found, so there was nothing else but to pack them up again and return to Scotland. Arriving in Edinburgh about the beginning of the year 1809, he proceeded to try his fortune with the citizens by the usual plan then of a lottery. Knowing that the prices put upon them were prohibitive, he set about in earnest to make his scheme as attractive as possible. As two prizes were not enough to draw subscriptions, he added six eight-day clocks[1] in mahogany cases, with moon's age and tide, value ten guineas each, one small gold watch with double cases, horizontal capped and jewelled, value £26, 5s., two silver watches at six guineas each, and three at three and a half guineas each. The £900 clock was reduced to the curious valuation of £892, 10s., making the fourteen prizes of the value of £1477, 7s. 6d. This was a big project, and as he fixed the price of each ticket at half a guinea, it meant the disposal of nearly 3000 tickets. He kept this subscription open for six months, and at the end of that period the drawing took place. The first prize was drawn by ticket No. 773, the second by No. 766,

[1] *See* illustration.

the third by 2768, and so on ; but into whose hands the prizes fell at this drawing has not transpired. The results, we are afraid, did not come up to the exposer's expectations, for it appears that after paying the necessary expenses incurred, he cleared £500, not one half the sum he valued the clocks at.

Towards the close of the year 1899 a short account of these two clocks was given in the pages of the *Weekly Scotsman* (a paper that circulates wherever Scotsmen are to be found), with the view of ascertaining if possible if they were in existence, and their location. To our surprise, on 10th December 1899 a communication was received from Colonel Harvey, Schaw Park, Clackmannan, informing us that having read the description given in the *Weekly Scotsman*, he begged to state that a clock corresponding to the description given, made by John Smith, Pittenweem, was in his possession. After describing more fully some details, he explained that unfortunately, "some years ago, when in the act of being removed it fell, and the workings of the procession were damaged. The clock itself, however, goes and keeps good time, and I don't doubt that this is the same clock, which was for many years in the possession of my grandfather, Mr Fernie of Kilmux."

In addition to the above there was also received from Mr J. D. Wallace, Watchmaker, Mill Street, Alloa, corroboration as to the identity of the clock. He wrote, " I have had the honour of cleaning the clock, which stands in the front hall of one of the large mansions in the neighbourhood, that of Colonel J. Bald Harvey, Schaw Park. I was glad to get the history of it, and whenever I read it I recognised it at once. Colonel Harvey is to be congratulated on having in his possession such a fine specimen of the clockmaker's art."

This is conclusive, and leaves no doubt as to the location of another fine specimen of this ingenious man's skill. On 15th January 1900, the late Rev. H. L. Nelthropp, M.A., Past Master of the Worshipful Company of Clockmakers, London, wrote to me that "a musical clock made by John Smith, Pittenweem, North

ELABORATE MUSICAL CLOCK.

Enlarged view of principal Dial, showing four subordinate dials controlling four
separate movements, also tide and moon phases in arch at top.   (See p. 361.)

[To face page 360.

Britain, having painted dial showing days of the week, and month and moon phases, painted at the sides with a view of the Horse Guards, and revolving procession of figures and other mechanical movements, fifty-eight inches high, standing on a square-shaped pedestal, was sold at Messrs Christie, Manson, & Woods, 8 King Street, St James Square, London." This is the table clock mentioned on page 359, which John Smith valued at £900.

In supplementing the foregoing information we are now enabled by the courtesy and kindness of its present owner, William B. Smith, Esq., 156 St Vincent Street, Glasgow, to present more fully additional particulars about this elaborate and unique musical clock. Standing, as it does, over four feet in height, it nowhere exhibits the least traces of being out of proportions. Every part has been carefully studied, and consequently its three dials, though differently treated, harmonise as a whole in a wonderful manner. These three dials, of course, show the particular movements they indicate, and the wonder is that, considering the limited space at the disposal of the ingenious craftsman, so much has been accomplished. In addition to the going part of the clock, it has musical barrels pricked for the large number of sixteen tunes. Then a procession which represents a number of figures portraying the then Royal Family fixed upon a revolving circle of brass, and also the moon and calendar parts, give a faint idea of the complexity of its construction. There is not the slightest doubt that John Smith brought all the powers of his life-long experience into its execution. The case, which is made of oak, is gilded, and that such a celebrated artist as Alexander Nasmyth is responsible for the various scenes and figures with which its dials are adorned, sufficiently accounts for the high value set upon it, when newly made. Although now over a century has passed since it was set agoing every part to-day is in complete working order, and it remains at the present time a marvel of patience and skill.

It may be explained that it chimes the first, second,

and third quarters, but at the fourth quarter or hour it plays one of the airs in the first list and then strikes the hour. The quarter chimes are not any of the conventional chimes, such as Westminster, Cambridge, or Whittingham chimes, but seem to have been specially composed for it as they vary as often as the airs do, that is, they have eight different changes for the quarters.

The following is the list of airs marked on the Music Dials—sixteen in all:—

Outer Circle.	*Inner Circle.*
1. Roslin Castle.	1. Free and Accepted Mason.
2. The Last Time I came o'er the Muir.	2. Bellisle March.
3. My Nannie O.	3. Yellow Hair'd Laddie.
4. God Save the King.	4. East Nook of Fife.
5. Prince of Wales' March.	5. 100 Psalm Tune.
6. Duke of York's March.	6. Nancy Dawson.
7. Katharine Ogie.	7. Lang Awa, Welcome Home, my Dearie.
8. Etterick Bank.	8. Up and Warthema Willie.

The airs named in the inner circle are at each hour instead of a chime before the hour is struck on the hour bell: each tune is played for three hours in succession, and then the barrel changes to the next one. The airs named in the outer circle are played every third hour, and form a march to the procession of the Royal Family on the opposite dial. After playing the march it changes on to the next air. On Sundays both airs and procession stopped.

Particulars of quite a number of ordinary eight-day clocks have been received, all more or less worthy of the maker, but as these are in no way distinguished from others made by less celebrated men, we now only note where five of his more elaborate clocks are at present located, namely, Dalkeith Palace, Clackmannan, Dundee, Glasgow, and Burntisland. This last was brought to Edinburgh to be sold by auction in Dowell's Room,

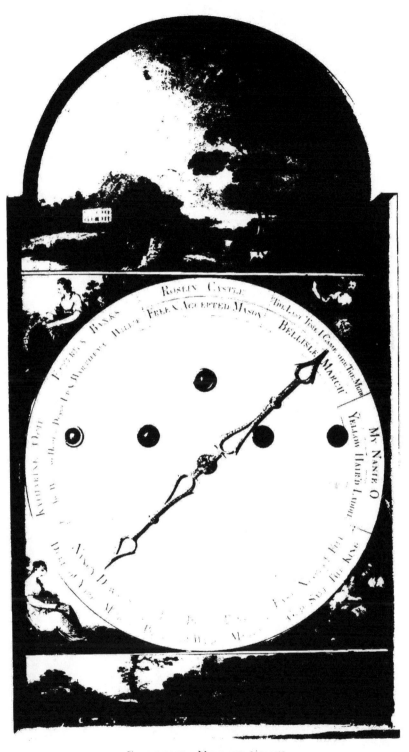

ELABORATE MUSICAL CLOCK.

Enlarged view of Music Dial, showing decorative treatment, top and bottom of dial, with names of all the airs it performs.

George Street, on Saturday the 12th of March 1904. It was marked lot 244 in the catalogue, and described as "Fine old grandfather chiming clock, by John Smith, Pittenweem; plays four old Scots tunes: 'Maggie Lauder,' 'The Lea Rig,' 'The Wauken o' the Fauld,' and 'The Flowers of Edinburgh'; omits playing on Sunday—see dial plate 'Rem'ber Sabbath,' in mahogany case."

It passed into the possession of J. Johnstone Kirke, Esq., of Rosend, Guildford, Surrey, a son of the late owner, at the price of 90 guineas. The following particulars regarding its former history were kindly forwarded to us:—"It was bought by Mr Kirke, my grandfather, on the 28th of July 1858, at the second of the three days' sale of the effects of Mr Thomas Shaw, Keeper of the Register of Sasines for the County of Fife. The price paid for it I do not know. The clock 'Maggie Lauder' has been in our family for nearly 50 years, and, as can be seen above, will still remain in the family." The present owner was kind enough to forward three capital photographs of this clock along with the information "that it has suffered very little in transit and is going steadily."

From 1809 up to his death on the 11th April 1814 we have been unable to unearth any further information about this ingenious man; but it is highly probable that with the sum realised by the venture of the lottery and the profits of a good-going business he was enabled to spend the remainder of his days in that leisure which he richly deserved.

A pilgrimage on our part to the quaint little town of Pittenweem for the purpose of gleaning any new facts about him brought to light the interest taken regarding his memory and work by the dwellers in Pittenweem. It appeared to us that his fame will long be preserved, owing to the appreciation of his talents by all classes in that old-world fishing town, and an interview with one of their oldest and most highly respected townsmen, a watchmaker of the ripe old age of eighty years, showed how deeply he felt being a native of the place that produced such a clockmaker as John Smith. Naturally he was interested in our inquiries, and the fact that his own grandfather had been an apprentice of Smith's drew out, among other traditions, that John Smith was credited as being able to do anything—nothing was too difficult for him to turn his attention to. One incident he related as showing the versatility of his genius, was that one of the Bailies of Pittenweem had the misfortune to get a sixpence broken into two pieces. Unwilling to loose such a sum he took it to John Smith and inquired if he could mend it. This he was not long in doing, and the Bailie, greatly pleased, asked the charge for so small a job. The answer was sixpence, which was paid, but with a grudge.

The site was pointed out where the old craftsman had his shop, it being nearly opposite the Water Wynd, a steep descent that leads down to the harbour. All traces of this workshop have passed away, a modern erection now taking its place. Along with this has also disappeared the old town clock, which was the work of his hands. It had done duty for nearly ninety years, and partly from old age and also having been constructed to go only forty-eight hours without fresh winding, was supplanted by a new one near the close of last century.

Our wanderings included a visit to the old church-yard, which is situated under the shade of the tower in which this old public clock was placed, to see if there were any memorial stone marking his last resting-place. This "God's acre" does not cover a great extent, but it took some time to discover the stone which marks his burial ground. Owing to its modest appearance and from the illegibility of the lettering it could easily be missed, and we regret to say that unless some steps are taken to recut the inscriptions it will only be a matter of a few years until the whole will have disappeared. This monument consists of an oblong, upright stone standing about three feet above the ground and divided into three spaces, a centre panel and two pilasters. It bears on the centre space the following inscription: "John Smith erected this stone in memory of Helen Brown,

ELABORATE MUSICAL CLOCK.

View of Procession, Dial, and its Decorative Treatment. Figures of the then Royal Family, fifteen in number, are shown here, passing opening between the two lower niches. Note the heraldic quartering of the Royal Arms in arch, which show the inclusion of that of France.

To face page 364

his beloved spouse"—(rest undecipherable). On left pilaster, "Be ye not slothful, but followers of them "[1] —(rest undecipherable). On right pilaster, "How happy the husband in such a sharer of my bed "—(rest undecipherable). There is nothing left recording his own memory, if buried here, but as two-thirds of the stone is entirely wasted the preservation of what is left is due to the fact that these are the parts farthest from the ground. The probability is that his own name filled up the lower part and has now entirely vanished.

What is noted here was only deciphered after a good deal of patience and trouble, but enough has been quoted to show that this stone undoubtedly marks the site of his last resting-place. The uncommon inscription on the right pilaster reveals the tender, loving husband. We were informed that during an alteration in the interior of the church, which is close to his tomb, an old timepiece, which was affixed to the front of the gallery was removed, and a brass plate was discovered bearing the following inscription: "Presented by John Smith in loving memory of my spouse." One Sabbath evening a visit was paid to Smith's grave just as the congregation in the church were singing the concluding hymn, "The sands of time are sinking." This well-known hymn created a great impression on our mind, for there, at our feet, lay one who had made good use of his time, and now waits "Till dawn of Heaven breaks."

SMITH, ROBERT. Edinburgh, 1647-60.

"Son of James Smith (q.v.), knokmaker, Edinburgh, and brother of George Smith (q.v.); admitted freeman knokmaker on the same day as his brother and under the same conditions, but with the exception that the two 'essay masters' were different, one being named Andro Bronne, the other James Pattone."

The admission of these two brothers as members of this close incorporation does not seem to have been

[1] The following may be the full reading, which is noted on a tombstone at Anstruther and quite near to Pittenweem: "Be ye not slothful, but followers of them who through faith and patience inherit the promises" (Heb. vi. 12).

unanimous. The jealousy of kindred trades appear to
have been aroused, as the following minute bears out :—

"Apud MAGDALEN CHAPEL.

"*6th September* 1647.—The qlk day Johne Sharpe,
Brasier, in name of the rest of his airt, askit in termis
that the above namit George & Robert Smith should
not work ony copper or brass, but that allenerlie
appertene to their essay. This was betwixt and 8
hours in the morning in the place foresaid, in presence
of the Deacon and others, etc."

This protest did no harm, but the brazier craft
wanted to make it clear that clockmakers were not
to take in hand work outside of their own trade, a
condition which was rigorously adhered to by that body.

As Robert Smith's name only turns up in the records
once again, namely, in connection with the dispute over
his apprentice James Kirk (q.v.) in 1648, we conclude
that the evidence of the treatment of the lad was so
conclusive that it is just possible he would have some
difficulty in getting new apprentices, consequently his
name would be left out in their transactions. He
married Elspeth Alexander on 17th August 1660.

SMITH, ROBERT. High Street, North Berwick, 1835.

SMITH, ROBERT. 17 Church Street, Inverness, 1840.
See note on William Smith, Church Street, Inverness.

SMITH, ROBERT. Irvine, 1820.

SMITH, WALTER. Aberdeen, 1799.

SMITH, WILLIAM. Church Street, Inverness, 1805-53.

"Mr William Smith, who died in 1853, started
business, it is believed, about the year 1805 in the shop
which, 30 years ago, was known as No. 77 Church Street,
and which stood on the site of the western entrance to
Queensgate. He was succeeded by his son Robert
Smith, by whom, over forty years ago, our esteemed
townsman Mr Alexander Dallas was initiated into the
mysteries of the profession. Mr Dallas occupied the
same shop as apprentice and master till 1874, when he
removed a few yards nearer the south end of the street,
next door to the Episcopal Church, and for twenty-seven

years conducted a steady and prosperous business at No. 30. Now, with the completion of the south side of Queensgate, which also includes a portion of the block in Church Street, Mr Dallas is back to No. 44 and very close to the scene of his early labours, of which he has many happy reminiscences. The new shop is a decided improvement."—*Highland News*, 29th June 1901.

SMITH, WILLIAM. Foot of Leith Walk, Leith, 1825.

SMITH, WILLIAM. Bridgegate, Irvine, 1821-50.

SMITH, WILLIAM. Loanhead, 1836.

SMITH, WILLIAM. Perth, 1772.

Apprenticed to James Greig, 1772.

SMITH, WILLIAM. Musselburgh, 1847-1903.

" Description and drawing of a time-piece moved by a spring of Vulcanized Caoutchouc, read at a meeting of the Society of Arts held at Edinburgh, 30th April 1849, by William Smith, Musselburgh, for which the Society's Silver Medal, value five sovereigns, was awarded. The author stated that he conceives the superiority of this spring to consist in its perfect invariability from the absence of friction, and the simplicity of its application, being in the form of a ring, one end of which is passed through a piece of steel with an eye, to which is attached a hook connecting it with the pulley, both ends being fixed at the bottom of the column by a steel pin passed over them."

SMITH, WILLIAM. Edinburgh, 1815.

Apprenticed to Robert Bryson, 4th November 1815.

SMITH, WILLIAM. Fort William, 1837.

SMITH, WILLIAM. Dundee, 1668.

SMYTH, GEORGE. Glasgow, 1610. *See* page 161.

SMYTHE, PHILEMON. Edinburgh, 1800.

SOMERVILLE [SOMERVEIL], DAVID. St Ninians, 1805-20.

The following letter (no date) refers in a whimsical manner to the above clockmaker. It also affords a sidelight on the temperament of the writer, the late Hugh Scott Riddell, 1796-1870 (one of our minor

Scottish poets), who evidently was residing at Bridge of Allan at the time it was penned :—

"Confined by rain to the house. Tormented by a clock, the most solemn, precise, pedantic horologe that ever proclaimed the flight of time. It has just struck eleven, and in the same space of time might with moderate rapidity have struck thirty. How it will manage to get through its meridian task, I wot not. It is animated, I verily believe, by the ghost of a dominie.

"There is a certain nasal twang of most insufferable conceit in every stroke. Twang—(long pause)—Twang—Twang—a most villainous highland tone, and yet, on inspection, I find the clock was made by D. Somerveil of St Ninians. (Sketch of the clock head comes in here.) It rains profusely, but tho' it should pour like the Forth, I will fly from this house when warning is given of St Ninians' noonday operations. I could not endure to hear the snivelling, drawling blockhead twanging one dozen mortal blows on the empty skull of the patient bell. I wish I could commit to paper the image in my mind's eye of the old snuffy dominie with his scratch wig of penurious locks, and long-backed, broad-skirted blue coat, but I am not a Harvey—or a Macduff or a Wilkie—else I should exorcise that clock and make its professor the pedagogue stand forth in black and white. After 12 I shall have peace for 4 or 5 hours, but then my trials will begin again anew.

"How the evening is to be got thus I cannot tell.—Hark—is that the warning of Ringan—let me fly."

SOMERVILLE, ROBERT. Glasgow, 1798-1804.

SPARK, WILLIAM. Marischal Street, Aberdeen, 1820.

SPEED, GEORGE. Dundee, 1749.

SPINK, ——. Elgin subsequent to 1820.

SPENCE, HUGH. Gordon Street, Huntly, 1837.

SPENCE, JOHN. South End, Stromness, Orkney, 1836.

SPENCE, ROBERT. Dysart, Fife, 1780.

SPENCE, THOMAS. Dysart, Fife, 1780.

SPENS, JAMES. Edinburgh, 1808.

Apprenticed to John Picken, 30th April 1808.

SPITTAL, JAMES. Glasgow, 1793.

SPRUNT, DAVID. 41 George Street, Perth, 1848.

STEEL, JOHN. Edinburgh, 1810.

Apprenticed to Robert Green, 3rd November 1810.

STEEL, PETER. Perth, 1792.

Apprenticed to James Young, 1792.

STEEL, THOMAS. Edinburgh, 1784.

Apprenticed to John Macpherson, 20th July 1784.

STEEL, THOMAS. High Street, Kirkintilloch, 1837.

STEEL, WILLIAM. Glasgow, 1818.

STEELE, ALEXANDER. 6 South St Andrew Street, Edinburgh, 1799.

"A. Steele, late partner of the company of Scott & Steele, Clock and Watch Makers, Princes Street, Edinburgh, begs leave to inform the public that he carries on the Clock and Watch Making trade in all its branches, for his own behoof, at his shop No. 6 St Andrew Street. A. Steele, from his long and constant employment in the repairing of watches of every description, both while he managed as partner and while he acted under the late Mr Scott as journeyman, has acquired such proficiency in the trade that he trusts he will give full satisfaction to those who shall be pleased to favour him with their employment."—*Edinburgh Evening Courant*, 8th August 1799.

STEELE, ALEXANDER. 13 Princes Street, Edinburgh, 1800.

STEELE, JOHN. Edinburgh, 1802.

Apprenticed to Robert Hinmers, 2nd November 1802.

STEELL, ALEXANDER. Edinburgh, 1795.

STEINSONE, ROBERT. Glasgow, 1690.

STEPHEN, JAMES. Old Meldrum, Aberdeenshire, 1837.

STEVENSON, ADAM. Dunfermline, 1723-52. *See* notes on Dunfermline Town Clocks, page 128.

STEVENSON, ALEXANDER. Edinburgh, 1779-86.

"Bound apprentice to James Cowan, 2nd April 1779. The Incorporation directs him to finish his indentures with Thomas Reid, 17th September 1785. Discharged of his indentures, 6th May 1786."— *E. H. Records.*

STEVENSON, DAVID. Kilmarnock; died 13th January 1786.

STEVENSON, WILLIAM HART. Edinburgh, 1766-81.

"Booked apprentice to Normond Macpherson, 30th May 1766. Discharged of his indentures 23rd September 1773. Petitioned that the Incorporation authorise the treasurer to repay him nine pounds sterling, which he had paid as the first half of his entry money, having now laid aside all thoughts of becoming a freeman upon a proper discharge."— *E. H. Records.*

STEWART, ALEXANDER. Edinburgh, 1722.

"Son to ye deceasit Mr James Stewart of Tugrey ; booked apprentice to Patrick Gordon, 3rd February 1722."

STEWART, ALEXANDER BAIKIE. Kirkwall, Orkney, 1835.

STEWART, ALLAN & ROBERT. 162 Trongate, Glasgow, 1835.

STEWART, CHARLES. Brown Street, Blairgowrie, 1836.

STEWART, CHARLES. Edinburgh, 1766.
Apprenticed to William Downie, 11th July 1766.

STEWART, FRANCIS. High Street, Brechin, 1837.

STEWART, GEORGE. Perth, 1765.
Apprenticed to William Young, 26th February 1765.

STEWART, JAMES. Trongate, Glasgow, 1778-99.

"Lost last week in Glasgow, a silver watch, maker's name E. Steel, Whitehaven, without any number, with a gold seal and Saracen's Head as crest. Whoever will return it to James Stewart, Trongate, Glasgow, shall be handsomely rewarded."—*Glasgow Courier*, 16th February 1797.

STEWART, JOHN. Auchterarder, 1837.

STEWART, JOHN. Edinburgh, 1772.

Apprenticed to John Skirving, 11th November 1772.

STEWART, JOHN. Edinburgh, 1771.

Booked apprentice to William Downie, 9th April 1771.

STEWART, JOHN. Dunbar, 1792.

STEWART, ROBERT. Allan Street, Blairgowrie, 1836.

STEWART, ROBERT. Trongate, Glasgow, 1841.

STEWART, THOMAS. Auchterarder, 1798.

STIEL or STEILL, JOHN. Edinburgh, 1741-55.

"Lawful son to Archibald Stiel, late schoolmaster at Kilbirnie; booked apprentice to John Brown, watchmaker, 2nd May 1741. Presented a bill for being admitted a watchmaker in right of his service, 5th November 1748. Compeared on 6th May 1749 and presented his essay, being a plain eight-day clock. His essay masters were George Aitken, Archibald Straiton, and William Nicoll. His essay was made in his own shop, John Brown, landlord."—*E. H. Records.*

"Lost between Bonnington Mills and the city a small sized silver watch with a green silk string, the maker's name Lemoyne, London, number forgot. Whoever has found it or knows anything of it will be so good as to acquaint John Stiel, watchmaker in Edinburgh, who will handsomely reward you."—*Edinburgh Evening Courant*, 22nd March 1750.

"Lost between Leith and Edinburgh a silver watch, maker's name Tobe Garrison, Ipswich. The watch had a silver seal with a red ribbon. Whoever has found the same by delivering it to John Stiel, watchmaker, opposite to the Cross, Edinburgh, shall be handsomely rewarded."—*Caledonian Mercury*, 10th October 1752.

"Margaret Boswell or Steill, wife of John Steill, watchmaker, married 3rd June 1750, in Edinburgh, served Heir of Provision General to her father, Alexander Boswell, painter there, dated 16th July 1752. Recorded 14th November 1752."—*Services of Heirs.*

STILL, WILLIAM. 44 Gelleymill Street, Aberdeen, 1846.

STIRLING, ROBERT. 9 Baker Street, Stirling, 1820-60.

STIRLING—Notices regarding the Common Clock of the
Burgh of, from 1519 to 1548.

13*th February* 1519.—Johne Bully, presented in
presence of the provost and baillies an instrument of
Sir Alexander Fressall hand (writing), the quilk
proportit and bare in the selfe the donation and
gift of the parocht (parish) clerkship and the keeping
of the Knok for all the days of his lifetime as he
allegit."

17*th January* 1520.—"Johne Bully protested that
the provost, baillies nor council of this said burgh should
not be displeased at him quhowbeit he called them
and pursued them before another judge for the wrong-
ful holding of his fee for keeping of the Knok as he
allegit, nor that it should hurt him or his freedom
by any ways. The saidis Provest, baillies, and council
being present for the time required the said Johne
Bully to show an attested document of the gift of
the keeping of their Knok and what he should have
therefore and he should be answerit."

6*th May* 1521.—" David Crag, treasurer of the said
burgh for the time, required at the provost, baillies,
council, and community being present for the
time if they thought it expedient to sustain the pleas
of their rights, touching the summons made upon them
by Master William Hamiltoun, vicar of the said burgh,
and Johne Bully, parish clerk, anent four acres of
land of the burgh meadows of the common of the
said burgh claimed by the said vicar to pertain to
him and his successors, and anent a certain money
claim by the said Johne to be uplane yearly of the
common good for the keep of the Knok, as he
allegit, which is depandand the law before the
official of Loudean ; and the said provost, baillies, and
council being advised all in a voice concluded that they
would sustain the plea and defend the said actions,
because they understood that these actions pursued

by the said vicar and clerk was unjust and that they had no title to the said acres or money."

9th August 1521.—" Johne Bully of his own free-will, in presence of the said provost and baillies in the said fenced court, has renounced freely and given over the keeping of the Knok of the Reid Kirk, and never to claim any right to the same and the guid toun to dispose of the same as they think most expedient."

8th January 1546.—" David Forester of Garden, provost of the burgh of Striveling, with advice of the baillies and council thereof, has condusit and feit William Purves, Knokmakair, to renew and repair the auld Knok of the said burgh, making all manner of graith thereof new forged, that is necessary to be made new, and the remnant that is sufficient to be repaired as efferis so that the said knok be also substantial, also just, keeping also good course, also permanent in rule and course, as any knok of her quantitie within this realm does, and, in like manner, shall make and repair of new graith ane orlege and moon with all necessaries thereof, keeping just course from xij hours to xij hours, as well night as day, and just change of the moon yearly throughout as efferis with one board of eistland burde painted with gold and oil colours of v quarters broad and a half and vj quarters l ng, with all circumstances and reparations necessary, to be completed betwixt the date hereof and the feast of Whitsunday next to come, for the quilk the said provost shall content and pay to the said William the sum of xxxv lib. money of this realm, thereof x lib. at his first entering to his labours, and other x lib. at the perfection of the said Knok, set up at all point and repaired, and the remanent xv lib. at the completing of the hale wark in manner above expremit."

24th April 1548.—" William Purves, Knokmakair, granted him to have received by the hands of Alexander Watson, one of the baillies of the burgh of Striveling the sum of ten pounds in hale and complete payment of all sums that he may ask or crave for his labours

of knok and moon making and all other labours to this
hour, and quit claims and discharges the town and all
others whom it efferis for ever, and shall warrant his
work sufficient conform to his contract before contained
in this book."

3rd December 1548.—"The provost and baillies
ordain xls. to be given to Wilyem Kerslaw for keeping
of the Knok in the year of the common good."—*Records
of the Burgh of Stirling.*

STODDART, GEORGE. Goosedub, Edinburgh, 1793; 11
Buccleuch Street, 1822.

STODDART, JAMES. Edinburgh, 1750.

"Bound apprentice to James Geddes, 11th May 1750.
Impowered the Deacon to commune with the widow
of James Geddes, watchmaker, and with her consent to
transfer James Stoddart, his late apprentice, to Robert
Clidsdale, watch and clock maker, for the space yet to
run of the indentures."—*E. H. Records.*

STODDART, JOHN. Canongate, Edinburgh, 1761.
Apprenticed to George Monro.

STODDART, ROBERT. Edinburgh, 1787.
Bound apprentice to Alexander Dickie.

STRACHAN, ANDREW. A Scotsman practising in London,
1691.

STRAUCHAN, THOMAS. Canongate, Edinburgh, about
1701.

STRAITON, ARCHIBALD. Edinburgh, 1726-59.

"Son to Charles Straiton, residenter at Claret-Hall;
booked apprentice to Alexander Brownlee, clockmaker,
11th February 1726.

"Presented his bill craving to be admitted a freeman
watchmaker, which was received accordingly. He paid
the treasurer five pounds sterling as the half of his upset
and the Maiden Hospital dues 31st March 1739. Married
Isobel Gifford, 19th December 1739.

"Compeared on 13th September 1739 and presented

his essay, viz., ane eight-day clock, which was found a well-wrought essay, etc., and therefore they admit him to be a freeman watchmaker among them. His essay masters were William Richardson, Patrick Gordon, and Andrew Dickie. His essay was made in Hugh Barclay's shop."—*E. H. Records.*

"There was found on Thursday last a piece of gold and a pair of steel buckles. Any person who can instruct the property may have them returned on paying the charges and satisfying the finder. Enquire for Archibald Straiton, watchmaker in Edinburgh."— *Caledonian Mercury,* 16th December 1745.

See also note on Robert Foot.

STRAITON, DAVID. Montrose, 1820-37.

STRANG, JAMES. Glasgow, 1834.

STUART, ALEXANDER. High Street, Kirkwall, 1836.

STURROCK, WILLIAM. 12 St Andrew Square, Edinburgh, 1855. *See* pages 25-26.

STRANG, ROBERT. Alloa, 1842-89.

"Robert Strang, Watch and Clock Maker, begs leave respectfully to inform the inhabitants of Alloa and its vicinity that he is about to open that shop in Mar Street, lately possessed by Mr Gibson, Bookseller, with a new and well selected stock of every article in the above line, when with extreme lowness of charges and the strictest attention to business he hopes to obtain a liberal share of public patronage."—*Alloa Monthly Advertiser,* 5th November 1842.

SUTHERLAND, DAVID. Leith, 1775.

SUTHERLAND, DAVID. Keith, 1805.

SUTHERLAND, GEORGE. Stonehaven, 1830.

SUTHERLAND, GEORGE. Elgin; admitted freeman, 1803-37.

SUTHERLAND, GEORGE. Elgin.

Son of the above; 1820.

SUTHERLAND, JAMES. Shambles Wynd, Forres, 1837.

SUTHERLAND, JOHN. 27 Marischal Street, Aberdeen, 1836.

SUTHERLAND, WILLIAM. Bank Street, Pulteney, Wick, 1837.

SUTOR, WILLIAM. Edinburgh, 1704-18.

"At MAGDALEN CHAPEL, 21st *November* 1704.—The whilk day, in presence of the haill incorporation, William Sutor, son to ye deceast George Sutor, gardener in Mountain-hall (probably Monkton Hall near Mussel-burgh), is booked apprentice to Richard Alcorn, clock-maker, who paid the boxmaster forty shillings of booking money, forty shillings to the Maiden Hospital, and one pound ten shillings for being five times absent, and other dues."

24th *May* 1712.—"The which day, in presence of the incorporation, after William Sutor's bill for being a freeman clockmaker was read and received the said William Sutor publicly declared that out of kindness to the incorporation he would give 100 merks for the poor of the incorporation, and desires his wife's name might be set up in gold letters yairfor. To which the incorporation ordained to be done and give the said William Sutor thanks for his kindness."

"Compeared on 14th February 1713 and presented his essay, an eight-day pendulum clock and a lock to the door with a key, which was found a well wrought essay, etc. His essay masters were Richard Alcorn and Thomas Drysdale; his essay was made in Thomas Gordon's shop. The boxmaster acknowledges that he had received from William Sutor the 100 merks which he promised to give to the poor of the Incorporation. Appoints his name to be put up in gold letters[1] in the way and manner he desires the same."—*E. H. Records.*

SWAN, GEORGE. Edinburgh, 1789-1822.

Watch-case maker; bound apprentice to Andrew Milligan, 2nd April 1789.

SYM, ——. Edinburgh, 1773.

Bound apprentice to Samuel Brown, 4th March 1773.

[1] This memorial tablet remains to this day in the Magdalen Chapel, Cowgate, Edinburgh.

SYMINGTON, ANDREW. Kettle, Fife, 1834-45.

A man of considerable ability, as the following scant notices show :—

"KETTLE.—A curious piece of machinery to measure time has been invented by Mr Andrew Symington, watchmaker here. This time-piece is more simple in its construction than the common eight-day clock—requires only to be winded up once in twelve months—and being quite silent in its movements will be admirably adapted for bedrooms. In this timepiece the pendulum and scapement are done away with, and a simple but efficient substitute is applied to the crown wheel as a detent, which only allows it to revolve once in an hour, and has quite a uniform motion without producing the smallest vibration on the machinery. Another important part of the discovery is a particular material for the pivots to move in, which is quite free from any cohesive quality and requires no oil, therefore avoiding the irregular motion produced by the evaporation of the oil and other causes. These are some of the advantages of this ingenious piece of mechanism, but we are not at present permitted to give a more particular description of it as the inventor intends to secure it by patent. Mr Symington is about to construct one to be sent to London for the purpose of being exhibited there."— *Edinburgh Evening Courant*, 2nd June 1834.

"KETTLE.—New Invention.—Our ingenious towns-man, A. Symington, has constructed a machine to make reeds for the manufacture of cloth upon an entire new principle invented by himself. The machine is in operation at the house of James How, reedmaker here. The accuracy with which it does the work renders it far superior to any of the machines in use at present, and the simplicity of the mechanism will admit of a consider-able reduction in the price. Mr Symington intends to send a drawing and description to the *Society of Arts* that the trade in general may have the benefits of the invention."—*Fifeshire Advertiser*, 1835.

"Drawing and description of a Pendulum Escapement by Mr Andrew Symington, watchmaker, Kettle, Fife."— See *Transactions of the Royal Scottish Society of Arts*, vol. i., 11th January 1837.

Maker of new clock in Markinch Town Hall, 1840.

"HYDRAULIC CLOCK BY MESSRS SYMINGTON & TEMPLE.—This important invention, being now registered, according to the Act of Parliament, we are at liberty to explain the principles on which the Hydraulic Clock is constructed. Attached to the axis of the crown wheel is a small bucket wheel on which the propelling power, a single drop of water in a second, acts. The action of a pendulum keeps the motion in perfect regularity and the other machinery is of the most simple description. It requires no winding up, and from its great durability in the absence of friction it will be attended with very little expense in keeping it in repair. It exhibits time with the most perfect accuracy, and from its elegant appearance it is beautifully adapted for gentlemen's houses and public buildings.

"A clock fitted up in Falkland House, the residence of O. T. Bruce, Esquire, by the inventors, Messrs Symington and Temple, has kept time with the greatest possible precision for the last nine months, and so highly pleased has that gentleman been with it that he has now got another fitted up in the hall of that princely edifice."—*Edinburgh Evening Courant*, 20th December 1845.

SYMSONE, JAMES. Dunfermline, 1773. *See* page 131.
　　See Turnbull & Symsone.

TAINSH, DAVID. Crieff, 1816.

TAIT, ARCHIBALD. Edinburgh, 1821.
　　Apprenticed to Robert Bryson, 6th November 1821.

TAIT, CHARLES. Peebles, 1836.

TAIT, DAVID. Canongate, Edinburgh, 1798.

TAIT, WILLIAM. Main Street, Wigtown, 1820-37.

TAYLOR, CHARLES. Kinross, 1836.

TAYLOR, JAMES. Strichen, 1799-1846.
　　"James Taylor, who died 12th November 1846, aged 90, was watchmaker in Strichen nearly 47 years; born in London but his ancestors belonged to the city of Perth, where they were Hammermen and burgesses time immemorial. Tradition says that Taylor's real name was Douglas and that he had to leave London during the political disturbances which took place there towards the beginning of the present century. A

memorial stone was erected by his son Joseph Douglas, Strichen, who died in 1851, aged 57 years."—JERVISE'S *Epitaphs and Inscriptions.*

TAYLOR, JAMES. Mormond, 1847.

"Charles Taylor, weaver, Kinross, served Heir of Conquest General to his uncle, James Taylor, watchmaker, Mormond, dated 28th July 1847. Recorded 6th Augt. 1847."—*Services of Heirs.*

TAYLOR, JAMES. Tillicoultry, 1837.

TAYLOR, JAMES. East Street, Doune, 1837.

TAYLOR, JOSEPH. Strichen, 1837.

TAYLOR, JOSEPH. Perth, 1774-90.

"Joseph Taylor, watchmaker in Perth, served Heir General to his grandfather Joseph Taylor, Hammerman there, dated 24 Decr. 1774."—*Services of Heirs.*

TAYLOR, THOMAS. Kinross, 1836.

TAYLOR, WILLIAM. 96 High Street, Dumfries, 1817-23.

His wife, Mrs Janet Paul, only surviving sister of the celebrated Paul Jones, died in 1817, aged 80 years.

TELFER, ALEXANDER. Aberdeen ; died in Antigua, 1805.

TELFER, ALEXANDER. Glasgow, 1770.

"Alexander Telfer, watchmaker in Glasgow, served Heir General to his mother, Janet Morton or Telfer, 4 Septr. 1770."—*Services of Heirs.*

TELFER, JOHN. Glasgow, 1752.

"George Stirling, served Heir of Provision General to Margaret Telfer, daughter of John Telfer, watchmaker in Glasgow, dated 2nd June 1815. Recorded 20th June 1815."—*Services of Heirs.*

TELFER, SAMUEL. Glasgow, 1720.

TEMPLETON, DAVID. Maybole, 1850.

TEMPLETON, JAMES. Gorbals, Glasgow, 1818.

TEMPLETON, JOHN. 145 High Street, Ayr, 1836-50.

TEMPLETON, M. Strand Street, Beith, 1850.

TEMPLETON, ROBERT. 120 High Street, Ayr, 1850.

TEMPLETON, THOMAS. Dalmellington, 1837-50.

THEMAN, DAVID. Aberdeen, 1493. *See* note on Aberdeen Town Clocks.

THIBOU, JACQUES. Edinburgh, 1695.

Booked journeyman to Paul Roumieu, 7th April 1695.

THOMPSON, ANDREW. Back Street, Campbeltown, 1836.

THOMSON, ALEXANDER. High Street, Kirkwall, 1836.

THOMSON, ALEXANDER. Canongate, Edinburgh, 1736.
Apprenticed to Thomas Hall, 1736.

THOMSON, ALEXANDER. Keith, Banffshire, 1807.

THOMSON, ANDREW. Brunswick Street, Glasgow, 1827-41.

THOMSON, ARCHIBALD. Hastie's Close, Edinburgh, 1794.

THOMSON, ARCHIBALD. Edinburgh, 1800-36. 15 North Bridge and 64 Princes Street.

THOMSON, DAVID. Perth, 1733-44.

Apprenticed to John Thomson 1733; admitted freeman into the Incorporation of Hammermen, Perth, 1737.

THOMSON, GEORGE. Edinburgh, 1734.

Apprenticed to James Nicoll, 1734.

THOMSON, GEORGE. Argyll Street, Glasgow, 1833.

THOMSON, GEORGE. Portland Street, Kilmarnock, 1820-37.

THOMSON, JAMES. Edinburgh, 1696.

Son to John Thomson, fermorar in Ogilvie, in the parish of Blackford; booked apprentice to Richard Mills, 2nd May 1696.

THOMSON, JAMES. Leslie, Fife, 1825,

THOMSON, JOHN. Leslie, Fife, 1789.

"John Thomson, watchmaker in Leslie; served Heir General to his father James Thomson, smith in Kettle, dated 17 Augt. 1789. Recorded 16 Septr. 1789."— *Services of Heirs.*

THOMSON, JOHN. Broad Street, Stirling, 1836.

THOMSON, JOHN, sen. Leith, 1768.

THOMSON, JOHN. Nicolson Street, Edinburgh, 1794-1814.

THOMSON, JOHN. Edinburgh, 1811.

Apprenticed to James Clark, 1811.

THOMSON, JOHN. Perth, 1706-37.

"PERTH COUNCIL HOUSE, 30 *Septr.* 1706. — Whilk day the Deacon and haill brethren of the Hammermen calling of the said burgh being solemnly convened anent the trade affairs, it was reported to them by John Thomson, Clock and Watch Maker, that although ye calling had formerly entered him to the said airt gratis, in respect there was no other of that profession in ye place, yet to avoid all doubt that may hereafter arise betwixt any of the brethren and him by upcasting of his gratis freedom or other ways, he was content to give ye calling twenty-five pounds of compliment and desired to be booked accordingly. Of the whilk compliment ye calling accepted and ordained him in their presence to be booked freeman to the said Clock and Watch Maker airt, and haill liberties and priviledges thereto belonging. Declaring ye said John Thomson to be also free and brother in the said incorporation, and to have also good right yairin and to what belongs thereto as any of the other brethren whatsover had, have, or heirtofore may enjoy."—*Perth Hammermen Records* (MSS.).

THOMSON, PETER NEILUS. Canongate, Edinburgh, 1756.

Apprenticed to George Monro.

THOMSON, ROBERT. Glasgow, 1788-1801.

"Lost on Friday night last, a silver watch with gold hands, a steel chain and small silver seal, maker's name John Milton, London, No. 7405. Any person having found the same, by returning it to Robert Thomson, watchmaker, High Street, Glasgow, shall be handsomely rewarded."—*Glasgow Courier*, 26th March 1799.

THOMSON, ROBERT. Borrowstounness or Bo'ness, 1760-88.

See also note on Linlithgow Town Clock.

"Stolen out of the Nether Hillhouse in the parish of Torphichen and county of Linlithgow on the night between the eleventh and twelfth of April, a watch, maker's name Robert Thomson, Borrowstounness, No. 674. Whoever can give an account of the said watch to the maker at Borrowstounness shall be handsomely rewarded."—*Caledonian Mercury*, 17th April 1762.

"Elizabeth Davidson or Thomson, wife of Thos. Davidson, weaver, London, served Heir General to her father Robert Thomson, watchmaker, Bo'ness, dated 22nd March 1788. Recorded 4 April 1788."—*Services of Heirs*.

THOMSON, WILLIAM. Perth, 1772.

THOMSON, WILLIAM. Edinburgh, 1766-82.

"Bound apprentice to Robert Clidsdale 13 June 1766. Discharged of his indentures 18 June 1773. Compeared on 4th Novr. 1780, and presented his essay, being a watch movement, made and finished in his own shop, in presence of Robert Clidsdale, landlord, Samuel Brown and Thomas Sibbald, essay masters (the other absent), as they declared."—*E. H. Records*.

THOMSON, WILLIAM. Clerk Street, Edinburgh, 1849.

THOMSON, WILLIAM. South Street, Dalkeith, 1840.

THORKEIN, WILLIAM. Edinburgh, 1695.

Booked journeyman to Paul Roumieu, 1695.

TODD, DANIEL. Glasgow, 1848.

"Daniel Todd, watchmaker in Glasgow; served Heir General to his father, William Todd, watchmaker there, dated 8th Augt. 1848. Recorded 18th Augt. 1848."—*Services of Heirs*.

TODD, JOHN. Trongate, Glasgow, 1823-37.

TODD, JOHN. 5 St Andrew Street, Dumfries, 1837.

TODD, WILLIAM. Glasgow, 1838-48.

TORCHER, ALEXANDER. Greenlaw, Berwickshire, 1837.

TORRY, ALEXANDER. Banchory Ternan, Aberdeenshire,

TOSHACH, PATRICK. Perth, 1778-85.

"Refused to enter into the Incorporation of Hammermen's Society, Perth, 1778. Next year he agreed to pay, after decreet had been obtained against him, the sum of £16 Sterling with the other dues."—*Perth Hammermen Records* (MSS.).

"TO CLOCK AND WATCH MAKERS.—Upon Tuesday the 2nd of August next at one o'clock forenoon will be exposed for sale by public roup, within the shop of the late Patrick Toshach, watchmaker in Perth, a complete set of watchmaker's tools, including two cutting engines made on the best principles. At same time there will be exposed separately, as purchasers may incline, four musical clocks, with a very fine chamber organ all neatly finished; a Regulator and some common clocks complete. The different articles will be shown any time betwixt and the day of sale by applying to Mr James Paton, writer, Perth."—*Edinburgh Evening Courant*, 27th July 1785.

A handsome musical clock made by him is now the property of Mrs Gillon, 13 Pilrig Street, Edinburgh, which may possibly be one of the four referred to above. Enclosed in a mahogany case of perfect proportions, the list of tunes it plays as marked on the dial are as follows :—"College Hornpipe," "Flowers of Edinburgh," "Kist Yestreen," "Dainty Davie," "Dusky Night," "Sham M'Garry," "Soldier's Joy." Although the musical bells are out of order, in spite of this defect it is a splendid specimen of this craftsman's skill.

TOUGH, REV. GEORGE. Ayton, Berwickshire, 1837.

"We have just seen an instrument in illustration of the principles of astronomy. This instrument consists essentially of but one wheel and pinion, illustrates with beautiful distinctiveness the annual revolution of the earth through the various signs of the ecliptic, the simultaneous revolution and phases of the moon, and, above all, for elegance and original simplicity the parallelism of the earth's axis and the consequent variety of the seasons. There is also adapted to the instrument a long ellipse having the sun in one of the foci as a representation of the orbit of a comet. The plane of the ellipse can be made to incline at any angle to the plane of the ecliptic, its longer axis to point in any direction, thus showing with the utmost clearness what really obtains in the heavens in reference to the orbits of these bodies."—*Edinburgh Evening Courant*, 21st April 1837.

TOWNSEND, ROBERT. Greenock, 1777.

"Whereas on the night betwixt the 23rd and 24th the shop of Robert Townsend, watchmaker in Greenock, was broke into and the following articles stolen, viz., one plain Gold watch, jewelled, maker's name Robert Townsend, Greenock, No. 296; one small Gold watch with gilt hands and shagreen outer case, with the inside case and box in one, name Da Cheshe, London, No. 6442; one Silver watch, name Robert Townsend, number uncertain—this last is a new one; one do. do., new cap'd, name Daniell Marshall Wakefield, a high number but uncertain what it is; one old silver watch with seconds in the centre, the verge pivot broke, name Robert Townsend, Greenock, No. 132; one old watch, shagreen case, gilt box, name Rt. Johnston, London, No. 7704; one old silver watch, name Howard, London, number uncertain, had a new outer case unlined; one old silver watch, name Thomas Moore, London, No. 6571; three pair new silver watch cases of the best kind without pendants; one old silver watch box and an old agate watch case; two tortoise-shell watches with Gilt boxes, Nos. 9026 and 110.

"These are therefore offering a reward of Ten Guineas to any person or persons who will discover or apprehend the persons concerned in the said theft, to be paid by the said Robert Townsend, upon conviction of the offenders. And it is hereby requested that all watchmakers and others will stop any of the above articles that may come into their hands and send the said Robert Townsend timely notice thereof."— *Caledonian Mercury*, 26th November 1777.

TOWNSEND, WILLIAM. Greenock, 1791.

TROTTER, ALEXANDER. Jedburgh, 1788-1815.

TROTTER, ROBERT. Leith, 23 Couper Street, 1822; Kirkgate, 1836.

TULLOH, JOHN. Shore Street, Nairn, 1836.

TURNBULL, JOHN. Edinburgh, 1765-72.

Apprenticed to Alexander Farquharson on 7th May 1765. Discharged of his indentures by Turnbull & Aitchison, 25th July 1772.

TURNBULL, JOHN. Hawick, 1827.

"Anna Maria Brown or Turnbull, wife of C. Brown, Traveller, London ; served Heir Portion General to her uncle, John Turnbull, watchmaker, Hawick, dated 3rd Augt. 1827. Recorded 13 Augt. 1827."—*Services of Heirs.*

TURNBULL, JOHN. Dunfermline, 1780.

"Lost in the town of Dunfermline, the 14th of May current, a gold watch with an old shagreen case, maker's name John Berry, London. Any person that has found said watch and will return her to Messrs Turnbull and Aitchison (q.v.), watchmakers, Edinburgh, or to John Turnbull, watchmaker, Dunfermline, shall receive a handsome reward. If offered for sale it is hoped she will be stopt and information given as above."— *Edinburgh Evening Courant,* 31st May 1780.

See Turnbull & Symson, Dunfermline.

TURNBULL, PETER. Glasgow, 1812.

"Peter Turnbull, successor to the late William Hannington, begs leave to inform his friends that he has removed from Argyll Street to No. 90 East Side, Glassford Street. P. T. having been several years with Mr Hannington, he hopes from a strict attention to business to render satisfaction to his employers."— *Glasgow Chronicle,* 20th May 1812.

TURNBULL, ROBERT. New Street, Greenock, 1790-1832.

"Andrew Turnbull, merchant, Dunfermline, served Heir of Conquest General to his brother, Robert Turnbull, watchmaker, Greenock, dated 1st Feby. 1833. Recorded 5th Feby. 1833."—*Services of Heirs.*

TURNBULL, WILLIAM. Edinburgh, 1758-82.

"Son of David Turnbull, dyster, in Torryburn; booked apprentice to Deacon John Dalgleish, 4th February 1758. Discharged of his indentures, 8th January 1766. Presented a bill craving an essay and essay masters to be appointed in order to his being

2 B

admitted a freeman, 7th May 1768. Compeared on 12th November 1768 and presented his essay, being an horizontal watch movement, begun, made, and finished in his own shop in presence of John Murdoch, John Gibson, and William Richardson, and John Dalgleish, landlord."—*E. H. Records.*

Entered into partnership with Robert Aitchison, who was admitted a freeman the same day as himself. *See* Turnbull & Aitchison.

"To be sold by public roup on Wednesday, the 30th Jany., betwixt the hours of five and six afternoon, the dwelling-house and foreshop being the first story of a tenement at the head of Bell's Wynd, as now possessed by Mr Turnbull, Watchmaker, per tack for 19 years from Whitsunday 1773 at £14, 14s. per annum, upset £147, 14s. 8d."—*Caledonian Mercury*, 12th January 1782.

TURNBULL, WILLIAM. Inverkeithing, 1795.

TURNBULL & AITCHISON. Back of the City Guard, High Street, Edinburgh, 1768-77.

"Within these eight days past, there was lost in the near neighbourhood of Edinburgh, a plain silver watch, maker's name Allan Fowlds, Kilmarnock, No. 3429, with a steel chain and silver cornelian seal, impression a rose. Any person who is possessed of said watch is requested to deliver the same to Messrs Turnbull and Aitchison, watchmakers in Edinburgh, and a handsome reward will be given therefor. If on this notice it is not returned and she is offered for sale, it is entreated that the watch and person may be detained and notice thereof given to the said Messrs Turnbull & Aitchison, who will, beside paying all charges, give a reward of five guineas upon the watch being secured and the person detained until examined by a judge." — *Caledonian Mercury*, 3rd March 1777.

TURNBULL & SYMSON. Dunfermline, 1776.

"Turnbull & Symson, Watch and Clock Makers in Dunfermline.—John Turnbull begs leave to inform his friends and the public that although it has been said that he had given up business, he still continues to carry on the business in his shop with more spirit than ever, and as he has entered into company with one who understands watch and clock making in all its branches,

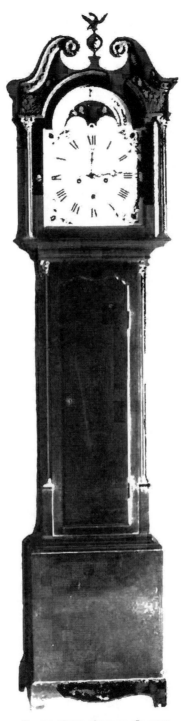

EIGHT-DAY CHIME CLOCK,

In mahogany case, with moon's age and tide dial. By John Smith, Pittenweem, 1770-1814. The property of Alexander Hay, Esq., Cluny Gardens, Edinburgh. (See p. 362.)

[To face page 338.

he hopes for a continuance of the favours of his customers, as they may depend upon being punctually answered.

"*N.B.* — Letters and commissions addressed to Turnbull & Symson, watch and clock makers, Dunfermline, will be duly attended to."—*Caledonian Mercury*, 17th July 1776.

TURNER, JAMES. Luckenbooths, Edinburgh, 1811.

URE, WILLIAM. Cumbernauld, 1836.

URQUART, ——. Elgin, subsequent to 1820.

URQUHART, JOHN. George Street, Perth, 1805-37.

VEITCH, ROBERT. Edinburgh, 1774-82.

Apprenticed to Normond Macpherson 1st December 1774. Discharged of his indentures 18th February 1782.

VEITCH, WILLIAM. Edinburgh, 1778.

Apprenticed to Normond Macpherson 15th July 1778.

VEITCH, WILLIAM. Haddington, 1758-81.

The first clockmaker to be admitted as a freeman in the Incorporation of Hammermen of Haddington, 30th August 1758.

"Lost on Tuesday last betwixt Edinburgh and Tranent, a silver watch with three seals, No. 241, maker's name William Veitch, Haddington. The seals were as follows: One of them with a cairngorm stone with A and S engraved, sunk, and flourished; the other with the figure of Hope leaning upon an anchor; both same stone, only one of them gold and the other pinchbeck; the third a gold one and a compound stone with a head. Whoever will return the same to the publisher of this paper or to Mr Veitch at Haddington will be handsomely rewarded."—*Edinburgh Evening Courant*, 1st August 1781.

Admitted a member of Lodge St David, Edinburgh, 10th April 1754.

WADDELL, JOHN. Gallowgate, Glasgow, 1826.

WALDIE, WILLIAM. Dunse, 1831.

WALKER, JAMES. Penicuik, 1836-50.

WALKER, JAMES. High Street, Montrose, 1820-37.

"James Walker, watchmaker, Montrose; served Heir General to his sister Isabella, daughter of James Walker, there at Strathbrae, dated 9th Augt. 1827; recorded 3rd Sept. 1827."—*Services of Heirs.*

WALKER, GEORGE. Canongate, Edinburgh, 1789-92.

Married Christian Grahame, 11th October 1792.

WALKER, ROBERT. 14 London Street, Glasgow, 1836.

WALLACE, ANDREW. Ayr, 1816.

WALLACE, GEORGE. Prestonpans, 1646.

WALLACE, JOHN. Leven, Fife, 1790-1835.

Died 15th September 1835, aged 69 years.

WALLACE, JOHN. Dambrae, Musselburgh, 1836.

WALLACE, JOHN. Paisley, 1603. *See* page 289.

WALLACE, ROBERT. Forfar, 1798.

WALLACE, WILLIAM. Aberdeen, 1533. *See* page 1.

WANHAGAN, PATRICK. Aberdeen, 1651. *See* page 6.

WARDLAW, JAMES. Perth, 1768.

Granted liberty to exercise his trade in Perth by the Hammermen's Incorporation, 8th August 1768.

WARREN, GEORGE W. London, 1880. *See* page 25.

WATERS, WILLIAM C. Milnathort, 1834.

WATSON, ALEXANDER. Glasgow, 1835.

WATSON, DAVID. Dundee, 1748.

WATSON, GEORGE. Edinburgh, 1814.

"Compeared 31st Augt. 1814, and presented a petition craving to be admitted a freeman in right of his wife Helen, lawful daughter of the late John Clelland, watchmaker, and member of this Incorporation. The prayer of which petition was granted and he paid six pounds sterling, being the first moiety of his entry money. Compeared 13th May 1815, and produced his essay, a watch movement, begun, made and finished in his own shop, in presence of William Drysdale, landlord, and James Clark and James Innes, essay masters, as they declared, and was accordingly admitted and paid six pounds stg., being the second moiety of his entry money."—*E. H. Records.*

WATSON, JAMES. Edinburgh, 1758.

Son of James Watson, one of the town officers of Edinburgh; bound apprentice to Samuel Brown, 29th December 1758.

WATSON, JAMES. Aberdeen, 1840-50.

WATSON, JOHN. Pier Head, Kirriemuir, 1837.

WATSON, ROBERT. High Street, Alyth, 1836.

WATSON & MARSHALL. High Street, Edinburgh, 1810.

"Have the honour to intimate that their stock of duplex, horizontal, and vertical watches in gold, silver and metal cases are extensive as any out of London, and from the experimental knowledge of one of the partners, many years a maker of watches in London, they are enabled with confidence to warrant their performance."—*Edinburgh Evening Courant,* 24th March 1810.

WATT, JAMES. Edinburgh, 1787.

9th May 1789.—" James Watt, apprentice to Laurence Dalgleish, petitioned that in respect the consent of his master, Laurence Dalgleish, agreed that the said James Watt be allowed to serve the remainder of his time with any other master he can find, but on condition that he serve one year more than specified in his indenture, by reason of his having been absent from his late master about 12 months."—*E. H. Records.*

WATT, JOHN. High Street, Irvine, 1827-50.

WATT, THOMAS & CO. 73 Princes Street, Edinburgh, 1823.

"Take the liberty of intimating to their friends and the public, that they have commenced in the above line on their own account, and from long experience and a strict attention to business, they hope to merit a share of the public favour so long and largely conferred on the company of Reid & Auld.

"T. Watt, nephew to Mr Reid, and who has been in the employment of Messrs Reid & Auld upwards of twenty years, looks with some confidence for the support of those who favoured the late company with their patronage. T. W. & Co. make every kind of watches and clocks to order, also repairing any article in the line. Orders attended to with punctuality and despatch." —*Edinburgh Evening Courant*, 1823.

WATT & M'ALPINE. 45 Princes Street, Edinburgh, 1825-37.

WATTERS, WILLIAM. 29 Church Street, Inverness, 1837.

WAUGH, JOHN. Main Street, Wigton, 1820-41.

"John Waugh, watchmaker, Wigton, served Heir General to his grandmother, Agnes Shank there, dated 18th Augt. 1841. Recorded 26th Augt. 1841."—*Services of Heirs.*

WEATHERBURN, ROBERT. Tweedmouth, Berwick-on-Tweed, 1820.

WEBSTER, JAMES. 107 West Port, Edinburgh, 1840-68. Son of below.

WEBSTER, JOHN. 107 West Port, Edinburgh, 1826-69.

Came from Peterhead, and entering the employment of James Whitelaw, Register Street, Edinburgh, rose to the position of foreman with him. He commenced for himself by acquiring the business carried on by Alexander Breakenrig at the above address about 1826, which he carried on till 1869. His grandson, John R. Webster, is in business in Dalkeith. It is interesting to note that in the watch made by Paul Roumieu referred to on page 321, this man's watch paper is to be found inside case as having repaired or cleaned it at some period now unknown.

WEBSTER, THOMAS. Dundee, 1689.

WEDDERBURN ———. Tweedmouth, 1823.

WEIR, DAVID. Glasgow, 1690.

WEIR, ROBERT. Lanark, 1798.

WELSH, GEORGE. High Street, Dalkeith, 1820.

WELSH, JOHN. George Street, Glasgow, 1825.

WELSH, ROBERT. Dalkeith, 1777.

"Lost on Monday last, the 8th of Septr., between Cameron Bridge and the Pleasance of Edinburgh, a fashionable silver watch, maker's name Millington and Co., Salop, No. 603. Whoever shall bring the said watch to Robert Welsh, watchmaker in Dalkeith, or give such information to him as said watch may be recovered, shall be handsomely rewarded.

"*N.B.*—It is entreated that watchmakers will stop her if presented for sale or repair, and give information as above."—*Caledonian Mercury*, 13th September 1777.

WEST, JOHN. Riccarton, Linlithgow, 1850.

John West was a millwright at Riccarton, three miles west of Linlithgow. He emigrated to Canada about 1850, and moved to Oregon, U.S.A., about 1860. He settled on the Columbia River 40 miles from its mouth, started a sawmill, and named the place West Port. A clock bearing the above name is now located in Portland, Oregon (whether John West was the maker has not transpired). The above particulars were forwarded by Mr Alexander Muirhead, 728 Lovejoy Street, Portland, Oregon, U.S.A.

WETHERSPON, ALEXANDER. Haddington, 1796-1803.

WHELAR, SAMUEL. Glasgow, 1810.

WHITE, ANDREW. High Street, Forres, 1837.

WHITE, GEORGE. Trongate, Glasgow, 1824-49.

WHITE, JAMES. Paisley, 1809.

WHITE, ROBERT. High Street, Edinburgh, 1791-1804.

Apprenticed to Laurence Dalgleish 29th July 1791. Discharged of his indentures 16th September 1798.

WHITEHEAD, ROBERT. Edinburgh, 1770.

Apprenticed to John Murdoch, 17th October 1770.

WHITELAW, ALEXANDER. 75 Princes Street, Edinburgh, 1824.

WHITELAW, DAVID. 16 Princes Street, Edinburgh, 1815-35.

"Silver watch lost between North Bridge and Greenside, with a gold chain and pebble seal, mounted with gold and initials, maker's name J. Hall, Edinburgh, No. 26. Whoever has found the same and will return it to Mr Whitelaw, watchmaker, No. 16 Princes Street, shall receive one guinea of reward."—*Edinburgh Evening Courant*, 6th November 1815.

"At a meeting of the Society of Arts for Scotland held on 17th June 1829, Prize awarded to Mr David Whitelaw, watchmaker, Princes Street, Edinburgh, of the Society's Silver Medal, value £5, 5s., for his description and drawings of a clock pendulum without the crutch, and in which the pendulum receives the impulse directly from the swing wheel. This communication, although only read in the beginning of the current year, was notified to the Society in 1828 and is so intimately connected with the one by Mr Alexander Doig, Musselburgh, that in justice to neither of these individuals can they be separated, and the committee recommend to the Society the donation of a prize to each without entering into any inquiry as to the priority of invention."

Paper read at a meeting of the Society of Arts for Scotland 5th June 1830.—"Description of a pendulum chronometer in which the arbors of the wheels move on friction rollers, and the pinion leaves are made so as to revolve by the impulse of the wheel teeth, which are of a peculiar form made by Mr David Whitelaw, watch and clock maker, No. 16 Princes Street, Edinburgh, for the late Andrew Waddell, Esq., Hermitage Hill, Leith."

Paper read by John Robinson, Esq., Secretary of the Royal Society, Edinburgh, 7th February 1831, regarding a time-keeper in the hall of the Royal Society of Edinburgh.[1]—"The principal circumstances in which this time-keeper differs from the usual construction are these :—

"1st. In having an escapement which requires no oil.

"2nd. In having the pendulum and ball formed of a material not hitherto used for this purpose.

"3rd. In having the mechanism entirely secured against the effects of dust, and in a great degree against those of hygrometric changes in the atmosphere.

[1] If this is the same clock which is at present in the hall, George Street, the following is the inscription on dial :—" Presented to the Royal Scottish Society of Arts by Reid & Auld, late Clock and Watch Makers, Edin., by whom a bequest has been made to the Society for the benefit of the journeymen clock and watch makers, 1846. Reid & Auld, 1791, Edin."

"The escapement is the invention of Mr Whitelaw, a very ingenious artist in this city, who has been employed to make the clock. The next peculiarity in this clock is the material of which the pendulum rod and ball have been made. Marble has been adopted for this purpose in consequence of a suggestion made to me by Dr Brewster. Case was made air-tight, excepting in one place where a short tube is fixed in an opening from which projects externally about two inches, on which a half-distended air-bag is made fast."

David Whitelaw died at 6 So. St Andrew Street, Edinburgh, 9th April 1846, aged 70 years.

WHITELAW, JAMES. Edinburgh, 1820-46; 15 Register Street, 1820-28; West Register Street, 1846; died at 6 So. St Andrew Street, 9th April 1846, aged 70.

WHITELAW & FLETCHER. 75 Princes Street, Edinburgh, 1824.

"Whitelaw and Fletcher, watch and clock makers, long in the employment of Mr Bryson, beg leave to intimate that they have commenced business at 75 Princes Street, opposite to the Mound. From the long experience they have had in all the branches of their business they beg to assure those who may honour them with their employment that no pains will be spared to give satisfaction. Both the partners have been much in the practice of repairing musical clocks, watches, and boxes, and their friends may rely that any entrusted to their care will be attended to in the best manner."
Edinburgh Evening Courant, 10th June 1824.

WHYTE, DUNCAN. George Street, Oban, 1837.

WHYTOCK, PETER. Overgate, Dundee, 1844.

WIGHT, ANDREW. Ayr, 1848.

WIGHTMAN, ALEXANDER. Moffat, 1837.

WILD. F. J. Murraygate, Dundee, 1844.

WILKIE, JOHN. Cupar-Fife, 1830-54.

Son of below.

WILKIE, ROBERT. Cupar-Fife, 1792-1830.

"Stolen in Cupar Market on the 18th April 1792, a silver watch, marked No. 8698, maker's name P. Parker, London. Whoever will deliver the above watch to

Robert Wilkie, watchmaker, Cupar-Fife, will be suitably rewarded, and it is expected that watchmakers and others will stop the same if offered for sale."—*Edinburgh Evening Courant*, 26th April 1792.

WILKIE, ROBERT. Leven, Fife, 1825-75.

Born 25th February 1805 ; died 24th March 1875.

WILKINSON, JOSEPH. Carlisle and Annan, 1843.

WILL, ALEXANDER. Huntly, 1822.

"Catherine Will in Hexham served Heir Portioner of Conquest General to her uncle, Alexander Will, Clockmaker, Huntly, dated 12th Octr. 1822. Recorded 18th Octr. 1822."—*Services of Heirs*.

WILLIAMS, PETER. Dunfermline, 1760-8.

The following is copied from the tombstone marking his last resting-place in the churchyard of Dunfermline Abbey.

"Here lies the corpse of Peter Williams, Watch and Clock Maker in Dunfermline, who died Februarie 1768, aged 23 years, and Christian Williams, wife of James Murrie, who died 28th of February 1800.

"In memory of two most affectionate and dutiful parents, Thomas Williams, who departed this life 22nd January 1784, in 69th year of his age, and Elish. Haig, his wife, who departed this life 10th July 1785, in 68th year of hir age.

"Of worldly cares we had our share
When in this world as you now are
But now our Bodies rest in dust
Waiting the rising of the just."

WILLIAMSON, GEORGE. 11 Kirkgate, Leith, 1819.

WILLIAMSON, JAMES. Dundee, 1824.

WILLIAMSON, JOHN. Canongate, Edinburgh, 1750.
Apprenticed to Thomas Hall, 1750.

WILLIAMSON, JOHN. Edinburgh, 1778-1825.

Apprenticed to Turnbull & Aitchison, 28th May 1778. In business, Blackfriars Wynd, 1800 ; 279 Cowgate, 1825.

WILLIAMSON, ROBERT. Falkirk, 1825-37.

WILLIAMSON, WILLIAM. Banff, 1626. *See* p. 37.

WILLOX, ALEXANDER. Aberdeen, 1632. *See* p. 5.

WILSON, DAVID. Whang Street, Beith, 1837-50.

WILSON, GEORGE. Edinburgh, 1760.

Apprenticed to Robert Cliedsdale, 12th April 1760.

WILSON, HUGH. Edinburgh, 1772-80.

Apprenticed to Laurence Dalgleish, 2nd June 1772. Discharged of his indentures 6th May 1780.

WILSON, JAMES. Ettrick. Born 1748; died 1821.

WILSON, JAMES. Kelso, 1809.

Died on the 11th November 1809 at his lodgings in Goodge Street, Tottenham Court Road, Mr James Wilson, watchmaker, late of Lombard Street, London.

"This lamented gentleman was a native of Kelso and when living was honoured by the intimacy of many of the learned and wise of all nations who might reside in the Empire. His force of intellect was far superior to the station in which fortune had placed him, as when encircled with the *beaux esprits* of the age he suffered no diminution in the character of his mind by comparative brilliancy, but issued his attic flashes with equal point and poignancy. Wherever he associated good sense stood at his right hand and good manners at his left, and he was in his own liberal department a luminous illustration of what a gentleman should be, intelligent without peaantry, graceful without affectation, affectionate to the objects of his friendship, but kind to every being who came within the circle of his action. He loved all mankind as his natural brethren but he loved Great Britain better than any other, yet the influence of the *natale solum* could never make him unjust or ungenerous. This brief and frail testimony comes from no venal pen; it is the spontaneous tribute of an honest heart towards departed worthiness. It is not a purchased eulogy which declares on the lying monument everything but what is true, but the sorrowing result of meditation over the ashes of a rare and good man, who when living made society happier by his discourse and more refined by his example."—*Edinburgh Evening Courant*, 30th November 1809.

WILSON, JAMES. Loop, Turriff, about 1800.

WILSON, John. George Street, Oban, 1837.

WILSON, John. Edinburgh, 1708-14.

    Apprenticed to Richard Mills, 5th July 1708.

    22nd March 1711.—"The which day in presence of the incorporation, there being a petition given in by John Wilson, late apprentice to the deceast Richard Mills, clockmaker, publickly read, craving that he may serve the time of his indentures yet to run with any of the freeman clockmakers, or to take liberty to work where he finds it convenient until the time of his indentures be expired, that he may get a discharge from the incorporation in order to get his freedom. The meeting unanimously do remit the petitioner to endeavour to settle with any of the freemen clockmakers betwixt and the next quarter day to teach him his trade, and declares that if none of them accept of and have work for him, that they allow him to work where he finds it without the privileges of the town until his indentures be expired. And then the house will grant him a discharge of his indentures that he may get his freedom thereby in due time."

    5th August 1714.—"The house grants warrand to the present Deacon and Boxmaster to discharge John Wilson, late apprentice to John Mellns, clockmaker, in respect the time continued 'yairin' is expired in regard the Incorporation by their act dated first day of May 1713 did allow him to work where he pleased until the time of his indentures were done, and there they declared they would grant him a discharge that he might get his freedom yairby."—*E. II. Records.*

WILSON, P. Keith, 1846.

WILSON, T. H. 11 Leith Street, Edinburgh, 1850.

WILSON, Thomas. High Street, Stewarton, 1837.

WILSON, Thomas. Edinburgh, 1742.

    Son to Mr John Wilson, schoolmaster at Fourdoun ; booked apprentice to Patrick Gordon 7th August 1742.

WILSON, William. Loup, Auchterless, about 1830.

WINTER, ROBERT. 12 North Bridge Street, Edinburgh, 1837.

WISEMAN, JAMES. Hamilton, 1849.

WITHERSPOON, ALEXANDER. Edinburgh, 1831-34.

"Prepare for dark Winter ere it comes upon you. Alexander Witherspoon, Watchmaker, 3 Greenside Place, Edinburgh, takes the liberty thus to draw the notice of the public to those points in which he considers himself able to render them a service. Happy is it for the individual and the public when their interest is in such harmony, that the more the individual pursues his own he equally promotes the public advantage. A. W. flatters himself he is so placed in the service he offers. He announces among a variety of inventions in Chronometry that of converting any watch having a brass edge into a substitute for a repeating watch by which the hour will be most readily known throughout the dark nights of winter. Repeaters would be generally used were it not for the great expense of keeping them in repair; they are a luxury. To give a well appropriate substitute for such a desirable thing at little original and no current expense must be hailed by many as a good contribution to the comforts of society. Good old family watches will answer well for such conversion. This is not selected as the greatest of the inventions noticed, and to which the attention of the public will in turn be claimed, but for being of such evident usefulness that orders may be given instanter. Specimens of watches so rendered and of the other inventions will at any time be seen at the shop. Watches forwarded from the country either for repair or for being so rendered will be most pointedly attended to. Clocks and watches repaired with every attention to their improvement. He particularly invites to send him their most faulty ones accompanied with a statement of what they complain.

"A. W. having just commenced business here will be glad to serve his friends and the public with new clocks and watches on very moderate terms."—*Edinburgh Evening Courant*, 20th August 1831.

"Mr C. B. Tait begs to inform that on Friday, May 9th, he will sell by auction in his great room, No. 11 Hanover Street, the stock of Mr Witherspoon, watchmaker, Greenside Place, leaving this country for America, consisting of timepieces of a novel and extraordinary construction recently exhibited in the Caledonian Bazaar. Several of the timepieces have the new detached pendulum escapement, for which Mr Witherspoon was awarded the highest prize by the Society of Arts for Scotland, and others having escapements equally novel and ingenious."—*The Scotsman*, 28th April 1834.

WITHERSPOON, ALEXANDER. Tranent, 1841.

In the *Transactions of the Royal Scottish Society of Arts* for the year 1841, vol. i., page 95, is given a description of a new detached pendulum escapement invented by Alexander Witherspoon, watchmaker, Tranent. As the account given in the above volume runs into a paper of six octavo pages, readers interested are invited to a perusal of the account given for fuller details, but it seems certain that this is the same individual who was in Edinburgh, and who may or may not have been in America as the notice of the sale of his stock hints at.

WOOD, ALEXANDER. Stirling, 1834.

WOOD, ALEXANDER. 22 Argyle Street, Glasgow, 1836.

WOTHERSPOON, JOHN. Glasgow, 1830.

WRIGHT, WALTER. Ecclefechan, 1837.

WRIGHT, WILLIAM. High Street, Dunbar, 1820-37.

WYLIE, DAVID. Laigh Street, Greenock, 1783.

WYLIE, GEORGE. Dumfries, 1796.

WYLIE, WILLIAM. Edinburgh, 1756.

Son of John Wylie, teacher of English in Edinburgh; booked apprentice to Robert Clidsdale, 7th February 1756.

WYLIE, WILLIAM. Stromness, Orkney, 1836.

WYLLIE, ALEXANDER. Canongate, Edinburgh, 1721.
Apprenticed to George Scott.

WYLLIE, ALFRED. Dumfries, 1753.
"Janet Bishop or Wyllie, wife of Alfred Wyllie, watchmaker, Dumfries, served Heir Portioner General to her God Father David Bishop, dated 7th July 1753."
—*Services of Heirs.*

YEAMAN, JAMES. Edinburgh, 1791.
Apprenticed to George Skelton, 14th May 1791.

YEAMAN, JOHN. Canongate, Edinburgh, 1734-49.

YOUL, GEORGE. Edinburgh, 1773.
"Apprenticed to John Skirving, 14th December 1773. The incorporation with the approbation of John Skirving, the master, gave their consent that George Youl should serve the reminder of his time with Robert Clidsdale, 30th Octr. 1779."—*E. H. Records.*

YOUNG, ARCHIBALD. Murraygate, Dundee, 1828.

YOUNG, CHARLES. Perth, 1795.

YOUNG, JAMES. Canongate, Edinburgh, 1757.
Apprenticed to George Monro, 23rd March 1757.

YOUNG, JAMES. Edinburgh, 1752.
Son to William Young, indweller in the "Abbay" of Holyrood House; booked apprentice to Archibald Straiton 9th September 1752.

YOUNG, JAMES. Wellgate, Dundee, 1828.

YOUNG, JAMES. Perth, 1764-92.
Admitted freeman of the Incorporation of Hammermen, Perth, 1764. Elected boxmaster 1765.
"Lost or carried off on the 30th November 1769, a silver watch, name J. Greenwood, London, No. 10043, with a whitned cock. Whoever can stop the said watch let them acquaint James Young, watchmaker in Perth, who will reward them for their trouble."—*Edinburgh Advertiser*, 12th December 1769.

YOUNG, JOHN. Factory Street, Pollokshaws, Glasgow, 1836.

YOUNG, JOHN G. Murraygate, Dundee, 1850.

YOUNG, MALCOLM. Edinburgh, 1772.

>Apprenticed to Laurence Dalgleish, 28th February 1772.

YOUNG, MALCOLM. Perth, 1781.

YOUNG, PATRICK. Forfar; died 18th January 1811.

YOUNG, SAMUEL. Perth, 1781.

YOUNG, THOMAS. Edinburgh, 1713.

>Son to John Young, brewer, burgess of Edinburgh; booked apprentice to William Sutor, 5th May 1713.

YOUNG, THOMAS. Perth, 1789. Murray Street up to 1848.

>Apprenticed to Alexander Macfarlane.

YOUNG, THOMAS. Edinburgh, 1823-50, 22 Carnegie Street and 4 East Adam Street.

YOUNG, THOMAS. Wellgate, Dundee, 1850.

YOUNG, THOMAS. Watch glass maker, 5 North Bridge Street, Edinburgh. 1837.

YOUNG, WILLIAM. Auchtergaven, Perthshire, 1836.

YOUNG, WILLIAM. Perth, 1763.

>Admitted freeman of the Incorporation of Hammermen, Perth, 28th November 1763. Elected Deacon 1765.

YOUNG, WILLIAM. High Street, Dundee, 1805-43.

YOUNG, WILLIAM. Stirling, 1824.

>"SALE OF WATCHES, WATCH TOOLS, ETC.—There will be sold by public roup on Wednesday first, the 11th day of July curt., within the sale-room of Mr Birch, auctioneer, Stirling, the stock-in-trade of the deceased Mr William Young, watchmaker in Stirling, consisting of a few watches, an assortment of watch-chains and seals, watch-glasses and hands, clock dials, watch tools, etc., all for ready money."—*Stirling Journal*, 8th July 1824.

YUIL, THOMAS. Queen Street, Castle Douglas, 1836.

YUILL, ROBERT. Gorbals, Glasgow, 1840-49.

YULE, JAMES. King Street, Castle Douglas, 1836.

APPENDIX

List of Names of Clock and Watch Makers in various English, Irish, and Isle of Man towns, all in business at the dates given.

OLD ENGLISH CLOCKMAKERS

ALNWICK

Collingwood, Matthew, Bondgate Street (1820)
Gibson, John (1820)
Tate, Thomas, Fenkle Street (1820)
Odgen, J. (1720)

BELLINGHAM (1785)

Graham, William
Graham, Thomas

BRENTFORD (1712)

Atfield, James

CARLISLE

Baird, George Street (1820)
Blaylock, J. & W., Rickergate (1820)
Gardner, John, Annetwell Street (1820)
Ivison, John, St Alban's Row (1820)
Moss, George, English Street (1820)
Rennie, James, Scotch Street (1820)
Routledge, Adam, English Street (1820)
Monkhouse, John (1790)

Blaylock, John, 53 Scotch Street (1836)
Carruthers, James, 17 Scotch Street (1836)
M'Duff, James, Irish Gate Brow (1836)
Ivison, Thomas, 3 Green Market (1836)
Rennie, James, 15 Scotch Street (1836)
Robinson, Enoch, 58 English Street (1836)
Routledge, Adam, 32 English Street (1836)
Wheatley, Thomas, 31 English Street (1836)

BLANFORD, DORSETSHIRE

Ward, Henry (1808)

COCKERMOUTH (1820)

Graham, George
Mitchell, Barwise
Simpson, Mary

COVENTRY, WARWICKSHIRE

Smith, Samuel (1812)

DARLINGTON (1820)

Monkhouse, John, High Row

DURHAM (1820)

Bolton, John, New Elvet
Charlton, John, Elvet Bridge
Denham, Charles, Clay Path
Hodgson, Thomas, Silver Street
Loughborough, John, Cross Gate
Oswald, Robert, Market Place
Raine, Joseph, Silver Street

HANLEY, STAFFORDSHIRE

Massey, Edward (1804)

HEXHAM

Morpeth, Thomas (1725)
Richardson, J. (1710)
Weatherall, Thomas (1796)

KENDAL (1820)

Burton, Emanuel, Finkle Street
Muncaster, John, Stricklandgate
Parkinson, Nathaniel, Finkle
Street
Pennington, Christopher, Market
Place
Scales, William, Stramongate
Squire, James, Stricklandgate
Wilkieson, John (1771)

MARYPORT (1820)

Creig, Joseph, Senhouse Street
Thompson, John, Senhouse Street

MORPETH

Bowman, Daniel, Newgate Street
(1820)
Clark, Michael, Newgate Street
(1820)
Hardie, John, Capper-Chare (1820)
Rawson, John, Newgate Street
(1820)
Liddle, John (1780)

NESSFIELD, YORKSHIRE (1805)

Prior, John

NEWCASTLE-UPON-TYNE

Craig, John, Pilgrim Street (1820)
Fallow & Kromer, 34 Mosley
Street (1820)
Fletcher, Thomas, Ballast Hill
(1820)
Frames, George, New Street,
Gateshead (1820)
Greaves, Thomas, Quay Side
(1820)
Laidlow, Thomas, High Bridge
(1820)
Lamb, Thomas, High Friar Street
(1820)
Lister, William, 33 Mosley Street
(1820)
Loraine, James, Side (1820)
Marshall, John, High Bridge
(1820)
Sessford, Joseph, Groat Market
(1820)
Smith, John, Head of the Side
(1820)
Smith, Thomas, Quayside (1820)
Stuart, George, 13 Groat Market
(1820)
Tinkler, Strachan, Sandgate
(1820)
Trotter, Joseph, Broad Chare (1820)
Watson, Michael, Old Butcher
Market (1820)
Tickle, William (1740)
Travis, T. (1710)
Barr, Fedel, 21 Groat Market
(1836)
Broadbelt, George, 27 Church
Street (1836)
Donald, James, 34 Mosley Street
(1836)
Fallow, Jos., 4 Northumberland
Street (1836)
Fallow, Martin, 73 Pilgrim Street
(1836)
Forster, John, 20 High Bridge
(1836)
Frame, George, Church Street,
Gateshead (1836)

Kirton, William, 14 Colingwood Street (1836)

Lewis, George Samuel, 6 Mosley Street (1836)

Lister, William, 16 Mosley Street (1836)

Long, Theodore, 3 Bridge, Gateshead (1836)

Loraine, James, Felling Shore (1836)

Maughan, Joseph Heppell, Bottle Bank, Gateshead (1836)

Reid & Sons, 12 Dean Street (1836)

Rennison, William, St Ann's Street (1836)

Robeson, William, 52 Quayside (1836)

Robson, James, Fenkle Street (1836)

Sessford, Joseph, 10 Groat Market (1836)

Sharp, John, Byker Hill (1836)

Smith, Edward, Pilgrim Street (1836)

Smith, John, 44 Head of the Side (1836)

Stuart, George, 82 Westgate Street (1836)

Tinkler, Nicholas, St Ann's Street (1836)

Trotter, Joseph, 16 Broad Chare (1836)

Tweedy, William, 67 Head of the Side (1836)

Watson, Robert, Cloth Market (1836)

Watson, Thomas, 106 Side (1836)

Whitnall, James, 28 Close (1836)

Willer, Henry, Castle Garth (1836)

Young, Mark, 13 Bigg Market (1836)

NORTH SHIELDS (1820)

Blackwood, William, Union Street

Brown, William, Low Street

Coulson, William, Low Street

Gibson, George, Union Street

Howgarth, John, Stevenson Street

Robson, William, Low Street

PENRITH (1820)

Peacock, John, Little Docray

Posthouse, William, Docray

Rawson, John, Market Place

Roper, Martin, Little Docray

Wilkinson, Joseph, Castlegate

SOUTH SHIELDS (1820)

Burton, William, Fairles Street

Fenwick, John, Long Row

Gallon, William, East Holborn

Stockton, George, Long Row

SUNDERLAND (1820)

Airey, Smith, High Street

Arlot, William, Bodlewell-la

Atkin, John, High Street

Cockburn, William, High Street

Dodds, Moses, Mark Quay

Grawland, Clement, High Street

Hills, Ralph, High Street

Nesbitt, George, High Street

Parton, William, Mark Quay

Taylor, G. R., High Street

WHITEHAVEN (1820)

Crabb, James, 44 Strand Street

Dawes, John, 8 Roper Street

Jackson, William, 50 King Street

Muncaster, William, 11 Hamilton Lane

Pearson, John, 20 Church Street

Thompson, Joseph, 8 Duke Street

WIGTON 1820

Howe, John, High Street

Musgrave, Richard, Coupland Square

Simpson, John, Allonby Road

Telford, John, High Street

WORKINGTON (1820)

Simpson, Daniel, Finkle Street
Walker, Joseph, Wilson Street
Wood, Robert, Market Place

YORK (1715)

Hindley, I.

BIRMINGHAM (1836)

Allport, Samuel, 83 Bull Street
Betteridge, Richard Ezekiel, 18 Church Street
Biddle, George, 56 Coleshill Street
Birley, Samuel, 76 High Street
Boddington, William, 22 Jamica Row, Smithfield
Brunner, Ignatius (and Musical Box), 66 Edgbaston Street
Carr, Samuel, 113 Lancaster Street
Dowling, James, 178 Bromsgrove Street
Eaves, Charles, Prospect Row
Ford, James, 22 Carr's Lane
Greatbatch, Richard, 2 Lower Temple Street
Greatbatch, William, 52 Summer Lane
Griffiths, William, 4 Church Street
Hadley, Thomas, 9 Smallbrook Street
Hognet, Augustus, 112 Great Charles Street
Holt, Robert, 20 Bromsgrove Street
Louis, Abraham, 30 Dean Street
Moore, John Hassell, 33 Moor Street
Nicholas, Caleb, 26 Digbeth
Pritchard, William, 135 New Street
Summons, Josiah H., 4 Ashton Road
Starkey, Richard, 220 High Street, Deritend
Tansley, Thomas, Ashted Row
Tansley, Sarah, 44 Constitution Hill
Taylor, Sarah, 11 Ashton Street
Turner, Isaac, 12 Upper Temple Street
Waight, John, 33 Snowhill
Waight, William, 72 Coleshill Street
Warwick, Thomas, 32 Colmore Row
Watkins, John Stickley, 105 Bromsgrove Street
Watkins, Thomas Henry, 2 Cheapside
Wilson, Thomas, 118 Lancaster Street
Woller, Charles (and Musical Box), 63 Edgbaston Street

HULL (1836)

Alexander, George, 33 Silver Street
Armstrong, George, 9 Myton Street
Arthur, James, 1 Dock Office Row
Barnaby, Bishop, 13 Market Place
Barnett, Joseph, 53 Market Place
Bedell, Peter, North Bridge, Witham
Blanchard, William & Son, 11 Silver Street
Brunner, Engelbert, 62 Myton Gate
Cooper, Matthew, 2 Witham
Crackles, Samuel, 13 Blanket Row
Drescher, S. M., 21 Myton Gate
Dunn, John, 33 Finkle Street
Ferrier, William Thornton, Queen Street
Forrester, C. A., 67 Whitefriar Gate
Forrester, Patrick, 17 Market Place
Gardner, William, 19 Scale Lane
Harrison, James (Church Clock) Hessle Road
Jacobs, Bethel, 7 Whitefriar Gate

Jacobs, Emanuel, Beverley Road

Larard, Thomas, 32 Market Place

Lupie & Solcha, 17 Humber Dock Walls

Maspoli, Augustino, 79 Lowergate

Northen, Richard, 50 Lowgate

Payne, Robert, Trippett

Ross, John, Waterworks Street

Shipham, John, 21 Market Place

Symons, Julia, Queen Street

Terry, William, 66 Lowgate

Thornham, George, Todd's Entry, Silver Street

LEEDS (1836)

Abrahams, Phineas, 15 Briggate

Brownhill, Thomas, 20 Briggate

Fowler, Robert, 3 Hunslet Lane

Fryer, William, 5 Lydgate

Galloway, James, St Peters Street

Galloway, Matthew, Kirkgate

Galloway, Thos. & John, Kirkgate

Galloway, William, 125 West Street

Groves, William, 32 Kirkgate

Helliwell, William, 54 Duke Street

Hermann, Joseph, Kirkgate

Hirst, George K., 97 Briggate

Hunter, Richard, Hunslet Lane

Kettlewell, John, & Kaberry, 157 Briggate

Prior, George, 1817-1836, 4 Woodhouse Lane

Scott, Joseph, 221 Lowerhead Row

Stephenson, John, 18 Little Templar Street

Stonehouse, Robert, East Street

Swaine, John, 5 Boar Lane

Terry, Henry, 29 Briggate

Waithman, Mary Ann, 165 Briggate

Westerman, Richard, 1 Kirkgate

Wilkinson, John, 54 Briggate

LIVERPOOL (1836)

Armstrong, Thomas, 31 South John Street

Barrington, Isaac, 118 London Road

Barton, Joseph, Derby Street, Edge Hill

Beesley, George & Robert, Boundary Street

Bennet, Thomas, 11 Newsham Street

Bibby, Thomas, 3 Renshaw Street

Birch, James, 12 Standish Street

Blundell, Thomas, 54 Upper Pitt Street

Bold, Caleb, Great Richmond Street

Bradley, James Gibson, 99 Richmond Row

Bradshaw, William, 9 Tarleton Street

Brindle, Ralph, Derby Street, Edge Hill

Brownhill, James, 62 Whitechapel

Brownhill, James, 10 Richmond Row

Brownhill, John, 48 Prussia Street

Caddick, Richard, 10 Birkett Street

Cawson, Eleanor, 110 Park Lane

Chadwick, Benjamin, 34 Old Haymarket

Chapman, James, 23 Peter Street

Chapman, Moses, 45 Castle Street

Christian, John, 20 Plumbe Street

Clitherow, Thomas, 10 Warren Street

Cohan, Asher, & Sons, 26 South Castle Street

Cohan, John, 82 Paradise Street

Cohen, Priscilla, 8 Byrom Street

Cohen, Simon, 34 Sir Thomas's Buildings

Condliff, James, Fraser Street

Cooke, William, 56 Great George Street

Cranage, Thomas Stokes, 129 Islington

Culverwell, Richard Major, 21½ Tithebarn Street

Daniel, Henry & John, 32 Lord Street

Deutch, A., 6 Great Charlotte Street

Doke, Richard, 33 Lord Street

Donking, James, 46 Dale Street

Dowling, William, 29 Circus Street

Drielsma, Isaac Jones, 36 Hanover Street

Drury, Francis, 45 School Lane

Dumbell, John, 106 Scotland Road

Dutch, Lesser, 99 Whitechapel

Fairhurst, John, 19 Copperas Hill

Finney, Richard, Claremont Place, Kirkdale

Fisher, Richard, 13 Tarleton Street

Forber, Edward, 75 Gerard Street

Forber, Joshua, 99 Park Lane

Ford, Thomas, 68 Circus Street

Foster, John, 5 Williamson Square

Frodsham, Henry, 38 Castle Street

Gleave, John, 1 Hill Street, Brownlow Hill

Gore, John, Gerard Street

Grimshaw, John, 42 Sir Thomas's Buildings

Harrison, John, 14 Castle Street

Hart, Nathan, 13 North John Street

Haworth, Richard, 38 Pitt Street

Heineky, Robert, 19 Gerard Street

Helsby, James Gooden, 7 Elliott Street

Helsby, John, Bevington Hill

Hoffmayer, Martin, 90 Dale Street

Holmes, Peter, 50 Greenland Street

Hornby, James, 34 St Paul's Square

Hornby, John, 49 Prussia Street

Hornby, Richard, South Castle Street

Huges, Lewis, 94 Sparling Street

Hulme, Richard, 5 Leigh Street

Isaac & Co., 19 South Castle Street

Jackson, Abraham, 42 Castle Street

James, John, 7 Birket Street, Soho

Johnson, Mary, 28 Church Street

Jones, Charles, & Charles Vaughan, South Castle Street

Jones, John, 3 Parliament Street

Jones, John, 37 Gerard Street

Jones, John, 4 Parliament Street

Jones, Peter, 68 Rose Place

Kelly, John, 33 Richmond Row

Latham, Thomas, 47 Hanover Street

Leders, John, London Road

Lee, Isaac, 68 Scel Street

Leigh, Joshua, 48 Gerard Street

Leve, Barnet, 6 Lime Street

Levien, Lewis Woolf, 64 Paradise Street

Linaker, Henry, 21 Torbock Street

Litherland, Davis, & Co., 19 Bold Street

Longsworth, Peter, 5 St John's Lane

Moorhouse, William, 33 Ranelagh Street

Moncas, Thomas, Richmond Row

Moss, James Dennet, 100 Brownlow Hill

Nathan, Phillip, 25 Castle Street

Nelson, Thomas, 3 Bevington Bush

Newton, Joseph, 11 Bath Street

Norris, Francis, 108 Mount Pleasant

Parr, Mary, 121 Whitechapel

Penlington, Joseph, 36 Church Street

Pickford, John, 20 Mersey Street

Pinnington, Thomas, 66 Great Crosshall Street

Poole, James, 4 Tenterden Street

Priest, John, Stanley Street

Priest, Jonas, 2 St Anne's Street

Radcliffe, Charles, 21 Duke Street

Rigby, James, 30 Richmond Row

Rigby, William, 38 Tenterden Street

Roskell, Robert & Son, 13 and 14 Church Street
Rowley, Henry, 71 Rose Place
Russell, William, 59 Pitt Street
Samuel, F. & Co., 3 Clarence Buildings
Samuel, L. H. & Co., 38 South Castle Street
Samuel, Lewis, 7 Lord Street
Samuel, Louis, 72 Paradise Street
Samuel, Samuel J., 23 Basnett Street
Samuel, Simpson, Temple Court
Scramble, Peter, 7 Exchange Street, East
Seager, John, 20 Simpson Street
Sewill, Joseph, 35 South Castle Street
Spears, Frederick, Tenterden Street
Spencer, John, 28 Russell Street
Speth and Brothers, 87 Dale Street
Stuart, Henry, 75 Park Lane
Stubley, Benjamin, 180 Vauxhall Road
Stubley, John, 66 Vauxhall Road
Taylor, John & Co., 88 Whitechapel
Taylor, John Daniel, 47 Whitechapel
Taylor, William, 16 Basnett Street
Tobias, Miah, Isaac & Co., Dorans Lane
Townley & Quilliam, 60 Renshaw Street
Townley, John, 16 Harford Street
Verley, Daniel, 10 Parker Street
Walker, James, 15 Collingwood Street
Wardlow, Henry, 64 Lime Street
Weatherilt, Samuel, 23 Great Crosshall Street
Weatherilt, William, 25 Lawrence Street
Wignall, Charles, 18 Soho Street
Wilcockson, Henry, 111 Copperas Hill
Winter, Thomas, 51 Gerard Street

Wood, William, 31 Seymour Street
Woods, Peter, 20 Scotland Place
Woolf, Lewis, Church Street
Wright, R. & J., 58 Lime Street
Yates & Hess, 16 Lord Street

MANCHESTER (1836)

Abbott, Francis, 50 Market Street
Abrahams, Isaac (Dealer), 69 Hanover Street
Armstrong, Joseph, 88 Deansgate
Armstrong, Robert, 15 Old Millgate
Barnett, Peter, 15 Greengate, Salford
Brown, Thomas, 20 Bridge Street
Bunyan, Thomas, 120 Greengate, Salford
Clare, Peter, 16 Quay Street
Clegg, James, 17 Bradford Street
Clement, J., 6 St Mary's Gate
Cooke, Henry, 6 Esdailes Buildings, Oxford Street
Davies, Emanuel, 68 Chapel Street, Salford
Drescher, Simon, 44 Shudehill
Fallows, John Baptist, 5 Old Bridge Street
Franklin, Abraham, 1 St Ann's Place
Glatz, Joseph, 4 Old Bridge Street
Gledhill, Richard, 258 Oldham Road
Greenhalgh, John, 125 and 127 London Road
Harris, Henry James, 6 New Richmond
Hatfield & Hall, 56 King Street
Hemingway, John, 111 Piccadilly
Jacob, Henry, 6 Bank Buildings
Jones, John, 32 Long Millgate
Jordan, John, 8 Hanging Ditch
Kemshead, Widow, 26 Market Street
Kent, William Worsley, 63 Deansgate
Knight, Thomas, 55 Oldham Street

Lacker, Michael, 141 Deansgate

Mayo, William & Son, 13 Market Street

Mendelson, Henry, 38 King Street

Moss, William Selby, 71 Oldham Street

Nathan, Asher, 8 King Street

Ollivant, Thomas and John, 2 Exchange Street

Plant, William, 39 Portland Street

Rennie, William & Co., 61 Lever Street

Rhind, James, 33 Woburn Place

Richardson, John, 5 St George's Road

Richardson, Thomas, 20 Swan Street, Shudehill

Robertshaw, John, 41 Great Bridgewater Street

Robertson, Joseph, 17 Brook Street

Robinson, Benjamin, 56 Chapel Street, Salford

Sneddon, William, 4 Chester Road, Hulme

Sermin & Kaltinbach, 18 Chapel Street, Salford

Simmons, Isaac, 9 St Ann's Square

Smith, John, 59 Water Street, Bridge Street

Taylor, Thomas, 3 Mason Street, Swan Street

Terry, Thomas, 12 Bridge Street

Thelwell, Richard, 3 St Ann's Square

Warmisham, William, 5 Half Street

Whitehead, William, 16 St Mary's Gate

Wyatt, Lewis, 11 Portland Street

SHEFFIELD (1836)

Beal, Samuel, 2 Cumberland Street

Bright & Sons, 19 Market Place

Brookhouse, John, 81 Fargate

Brown, William, Hawksworth Court, High Street

Chumbley, William, 2 Castle Fold

Donking, James Gerard, 38 Fargate

Evatt, Henry R., 15 Queen Street

Flather, William, 18 Church Street

Heaton, Thomas, 33 King Street

Heseldin, George, 10 Shales Moor

Holden, George, 21 Fargate

Johnson, David, 49 Campo Lane

Lomas, Joseph, Broad Street, Park

Raven, William, 13 Waingate

Robinson, Thomas, 28 High Street

Russell, John, 9 Coulston Street

Smith, Samuel, 6 Allen Street

Snidall, Samuel, 16 High Street

Swearer, Lawrence, 4 Watson Walk

Symmons, Samuel, 57 Campo Lane

Wilson, Edmund, 47 King Street

Wilson, John, South Street

SCARBOROUGH (1808)

King, R.

SOME ISLE OF MAN CLOCKMAKERS, 1837.

Clucas, William, North Quay, Douglas

Clurphey, William, Duke Street, Douglas

Craystile, John, Market Place, Ramsey

Cotrier, John, Market Street, Peel

Graves, William, Market Place, Ramsey

Higgin, John, Big Street, Peel

Kneale, John, Malew Street, Castletown

Lemon, Abraham, & Morris, Duke Street, Douglas

Moughtin, Thomas, Ballaugh

Muncaster & Son, Arbory Street, Castletown

Muncaster, William & Son, Factory Lane, Douglas

White, Dominic, Barometer Maker, North Quay, Douglas

SOME OLD IRISH CLOCKMAKERS, 1820-1.

A few in Dublin earlier specially dated.

ATHLONE

Byrne, James, Barrack Square

Good, John, Bridge Street

Harvey, Theophilus, Dublin Street

Hill, John, Dublin Street

Prosser, Simon, Dublin Street

BANDON

Coppinger, Francis, Gallows-Hill

Jenkins, William, North Main Street

BELFAST

Bell, James, 95 North Street

Cochran & Shaw, 4 Bridge Street

Coleman, James, 88 North Street

Johnston, Thomas, 41 Anne Street

Lawler, J., Bridge-end

Moore, James, 68 High Street

Neil, Robert, 25 High Street

CARLOW

Dyer, Henry, Tullow Street

Foster, Joseph, Tullow Street

CLONMEL

Brodrick, William, Dublin Street

Doherty, James, Dublin Street

COLERAIN

Caldwell, James, Waterside

Huston, Samuel, Bridge Street

Mathers, Adam, Church Street

M'Kown, J., New Row

CORK

Bagley, Richard, 13 Grand Parade

Bagley, Richard, junr., 12 Grand Parade

Bagley, William, Nile Street

Byrom, William, 2 Patrick Street

Fuller, Richard, 21 Patrick Street

Hawkesworth, Edward, Grand Parade

Haynes, Samuel, Grand Parade

Mangan, James, Patrick Street

Montjoy, John, Bridge Street

Montjoy, Thomas, 1 Batchelor's Quay

Murphy, John, 8 Patrick Street

O'Shaughnessy, Mark Stephen, Grand Parade
Ross, Charles, Warren's Quay
Ross, William, South Mall
Statesbury, George, North Main Street
Thornhill, Walter, Broad Lane

DROGHEDA

Adams, Charles, 111 West Street
Atkinson, Samuel, 2 West Street
Glover, Thomas, Peter Street
North, Thomas, 1 Lawrence Street

DUBLIN

Bigger, Gilbert (1783)
Bull, Isaac (1767)
Martin, Samuel (1790)
Meakin, William (1697)
Read, Thomas (1765)
Simerell, Thomas (1683)
Teare, John (1699)
Wesoncraft, Joseph (1692)
Wittam, John (1685)
Verney, Moses (1743)

Allen, Richard, 40 Capel Street
Barrington, Isaac, 20 Westmoreland Street
Beith, Robert, 16 George's Quay
Blundell, Thomas, 142 Abbey Street
Bradshaw, Robert, 19 Henry Street
Buchonnon, Thomas, 31 College Green
Bulloch, William, 8 Capel Street
Burke, James, 37 Stephen Street
Carty, William, 33 Great George Street
Chancelor, John, 35 Lower Sackville Street
Clarke, William, 1 Ellis Quay
Connor, John, 153 Capel Street
Craig, Richard, 48 Thomas Street
Crosthwaite, John, 1795

Dalrymple, John, 42 Aungier Street
Farley, Thomas, 82 Grafton Street
Fry, Samuel, 8 Trinity Place
Garty, George, 30 William Street
Gaskin, John, 22 College Green
Gordon & Fletcher, 77 Dame Street
Hanlon, W., 93 Dame Street
Hartstone, Henry, 10 Mercer Street
Heney, Pat, 65 Capel Street
Hodges, Frederick, 27 Grafton Street
Holmes, Christopher, 18 Ormond Quay
Hughes, Patrick, 75 North King Street
Johnson, J. F., 19 Parliament Street
Johnson, F. T., 8 Parliament Street
Kennedy, Patrick, 22 Arran Quay
Kennedy, Roger, 54 Mary Street
Kisler, Anthony, 34 Great George Street
L'Estrange, Anthony, 81 Dame Street
M'Master, Maxwell, 97 Grafton Street
May, John, 29 Grafton Street
Morgan, William, 105 Grafton Street
Osborne & Molyneux, 2 Grafton Street
Peter & Co., 109 Grafton Street
Pilkington, Thomas, 30 Upper Sackville Street
Rorke, Walter, 20 Lower Sackville Street
Scott & Son, 41 Grafton Street
Seed, Richard, 20 Bride Street
Sharpe, Christopher, 57 Exchequer Street
Sinclair, William, 164 Capel Street
Smith, Edward, 54 Jervis Street
Vizer, Barnaby, 26 Upper Exchange Street

Walsh, James, 33 Capel Street
Warner & Hinds, 9 College Green
Waugh, James & Son, 24 Lower
James Street

DUNDALK

M'Cormack, Andrew, Middle-Ward
Townley, Edward, Middle-Ward

GALWAY

Burdge, Nicholas, Shop Street
Clinch, James, High Street
Robinson, Andrew, High Street
Verdon, Charles, High Street

KILKENNY

Colles, Nicholas, High Street
Doyle, Edmund, King Street
Reily, Frederick, High Street

KINSALE

Browne, John, Lower Fisher Street

LIMERICK

Baynham, ——, 22 Patrick Street
Glover, William, 11 Rutland Street
Goggin, Richard, 28 Patrick Street
O'Hogan, Lawrence, 10 Francis Street
O'Shaughnessy, Robert, 17 George Street
Purcell, John, 21 Patrick Street

LISBURN

Dixon, Charles, Bow Lane
Parsons, Robert, Bridge Street
Wiley, Alexander, Bow Lane

LONDONDERRY

Colhoun, James & Son, Ship Quay Street
Colhoun, James, junr., Ferry Quay Street

Hamilton, William, Ferry Quay Street
Hutchinson, George, Water Side
Kirwan, Matthew, Artillery Lane
M'Colgan, John, Ferry Quay Street
Macky, George, Bishop Street

NEW ROSS

Lynch, Timothy, South Street
Whitney, Andrew, South Street

NEWRY

Aickin, Greaves, Water Street
Blackham, George, Hill Street

SLIGO

Lattimer, Joshua, Thomas Street
M'Dowall, James, Castle Street
Molyneaux, William, Market Street

STRABANE

Bell, Dawson, Main Street
Cook, John, Castle Street
M'Cardle, James, Main Street

WATERFORD

Dillon, Jonathan, Mall
Glanville, David, Quay
Maddock, Patrick, Barren Strand Street
Murphy, Patrick, Quay
Shallow, Philip, Patrick Quay

WEXFORD

Hatchells, Nicholas, Main Street
Higginbotham, Joseph, Main Street

YOUGHAL

Dease, John, South Main Street
Sangster, James, North Main Street

INDEX

Coleman, Thomas, Leith, 86
Collison, Alexander, Stonehaven, 86
Common, James, sen., Coldstream, 86
 James, jun., Coldstream, 86
Conquer, Patrick, Perth, 86
Conqueror, Peter, Berwick-on-Tweed, 86
Constable, Alexander, Dundee, 86
 George, Cupar-Fife, 86
 William, Dundee, 86
 William, Dundee, 86
Cook, James, Strichen, 86
 James, Dumfries, 86
 William, Aberdeen, 6, 86
Cooper, William, Hamilton, 87
 Thomas, Hamilton, 87
Corbet, Robert, Glasgow, 87
Cordingley, Thomas, Wick, 87
Corrie, Philip, Langholm, 87
Coulter, William, Saltcoats, 87
Couper, Andrew, Edinburgh, 87
Cousteill, John, Edinburgh, 87, 88, 327
Coutts, James, Perth, 88
Cowan, Hugh, Thurso, 88
 James, Edinburgh, 9, 10, 12, 22, 28,
  60, 63, 66, 88, 89, 94, 99, 143 147,
  194, 203, 283, 310, 311, 315, 345,
  370
 William, Glasgow, 89
 William, Lennoxtown, 90
Craig, David, Pathhead, 90, 226
 James, Glasgow, 90
 Peter, Glasgow, 90
 Robert, Kilmarnock, 90
 Robert, Kilmaurs, 90
Craw, James, Forfar, 90
Crawford, Archibald, Largs, 91
 George, Falkirk, 91
 James, Johnstone, 91
 Robert, Dunse, 91
 William, Glasgow, 91
 William, Markinch, 91
Cree, John, Glasgow, 91
Creighton, David, Greenock, 91
Creith, Robert, Leith, 91, 134, 135
Creych, Robert, Edinburgh, 91, 134,
 135
Crichton, David, Glasgow, 91
 George, Mid-Calder, 91
 John, Leith, 91
Crighton, John, Dundee, 91

Crighton, Walter, Haddington, 91
Croll, Colin, Edinburgh, 91, 92
 Colin, Perth, 92
 William, Dundee, 92
Crone, William, Aberdeen, 92
Crooks & Burn, Edinburgh, 92, 93
Cross and Carruthers, Edinburgh, 93
Cross or Corse, James, Perth, 93
Crouch, William, Edinburgh, 93
Cruickshanks, George, Elgin, 93
Crukshanks, Johne, Aberdeen, 1, 93
Cumming, Alexander, Edinburgh and
 London, 93
 Alexander, Inveraray, 93
 Charles, Edinburgh, 94
 James, Edinburgh, 94
 John, Edinburgh, 94
Cunningham, James, Haddington, 94
 William, Sanquhar, 94
 W. and A., Edinburgh, 94
Currer, John, Peebles, 94
 Robert, Peebles, 94
Currie, Thomas, Edinburgh, 94
Cuthbert, James, Perth, 94
Cuthbert, John, Perth, 95

DALGARNO, Alexander, Aberdeen, 95
Dalgleish, John, Edinburgh, 66, 84, 85,
 95, 96, 97, 98, 121, 142, 165, 208,
 254, 258, 385, 386
 Laurence, Edinburgh, 98, 99, 111,
  169, 274, 280, 292, 343, 348, 389,
  391, 395, 400
 Robert, Falkirk, 99
 and Dickie, Edinburgh, 99
Dall, Thomas, Dundee, 100
Dallas, Joseph, Perth, 100
 Alexander, Inverness, 100
Dallaway & Son, Edinburgh, 100, 101,
 102, 103, 104, 105, 106
Dalrymple, William, Edinburgh, 106
Dalzeil, James, Fraserburgh, 106
Danks, ——, Edinburgh, 106
Darling, Robert, Edinburgh, 106
 Robert, Haddington, 106
 Robert, Lauder, 106
Davidson, Andrew, Stranraer, 106
 ——, Dunse, 106
 Charles, Forfar, 107
 James, Dunbar, 107
 James, Old Deer, 107

2 D

434 **INDEX**

NAMES OF MAKERS FURTH OF SCOTLAND OCCURRING IN TEXT.

OLIVER AND BOYD, PRINTERS, EDINBURGH, SCOTLAND

3191687

Made in the USA